Uncovering Anna Perenna

Also published by Bloomsbury

Ancient Magic and the Supernatural in the Modern Visual and Performing Arts,
Filippo Carlà-Uhink and Irene Berti
Canidia, Rome's First Witch, Maxwell Teitel Paule
Rome: A Sourcebook on the Ancient City, Fanny Dolansky and Stacie Raucci
Women in Ancient Rome, Bonnie MacLachan

Uncovering Anna Perenna

A Focused Study of Roman Myth and Culture

Edited by
Gwynaeth McIntyre and Sarah McCallum

BLOOMSBURY ACADEMIC
LONDON • NEW YORK • OXFORD • NEW DELHI • SYDNEY

BLOOMSBURY ACADEMIC
Bloomsbury Publishing Plc
50 Bedford Square, London, WC1B 3DP, UK
1385 Broadway, New York, NY 10018, USA

BLOOMSBURY, BLOOMSBURY ACADEMIC and the Diana logo are trademarks of
Bloomsbury Publishing Plc

First published in Great Britain 2019

Copyright © Gwynaeth McIntyre, Sarah McCallum and Contributors, 2019

Gwynaeth McIntyre and Sarah McCallum have asserted their right under the Copyright,
Designs and Patents Act, 1988, to be identified as Author of this work.

For legal purposes the Acknowledgements on p. x constitute an extension of
this copyright page.

Cover image: Vasily Ivanovich Denisov, *Sea Bottom*, late 19th or early 20th century.
Heritage Image Partnership Ltd / Alamy Stock Photo

All rights reserved. No part of this publication may be reproduced or transmitted
in any form or by any means, electronic or mechanical, including photocopying,
recording, or any information storage or retrieval system, without prior permission
in writing from the publishers.

Bloomsbury Publishing Plc does not have any control over, or responsibility for, any
third-party websites referred to or in this book. All internet addresses given in this
book were correct at the time of going to press. The author and publisher regret
any inconvenience caused if addresses have changed or sites have ceased to exist,
but can accept no responsibility for any such changes.

A catalogue record for this book is available from the British Library.

Library of Congress Cataloging-in-Publication Data
Names: McIntyre, Gwynaeth, editor. | McCallum, Sarah, editor.
Title: Uncovering Anna Perenna : a focused study of Roman myth and culture /
edited by Gwynaeth McIntyre and Sarah McCallum.
Description: London : Bloomsbury Academic, 2018. |
Includes bibliographical references and index.
Identifiers: LCCN 2018024984| ISBN 9781350048430 (hb) | ISBN 9781350048454 (epub)
Subjects: LCSH: Anna Perenna (Mythological character) | Anna Perenna
(Mythological character—In literature. | Mythology, Roman. | Rome—Religion.
Classification: LCC BL805 .U536 2018 | DDC 292.2/114–dc23
LC record available at https://lccn.loc.gov/2018024984

ISBN: HB: 978-1-3500-4843-0
ePDF: 978-1-3500-4844-7
eBook: 978-1-3500-4845-4

Typeset by RefineCatch Limited, Bungay, Suffolk

To find out more about our authors and books visit www.bloomsbury.com
and sign up for our newsletters.

Contents

List of Illustrations — vii
Preface — viii
Acknowledgements — x
List of Abbreviations — xi
Notes on Contributors — xiii

Introduction: Anna and the *Plebs*: A Synthesis of Primary Evidence
    T.P. Wiseman — 1

From Carthage to Rome

1. Rivalry and Revelation: Ovid's Elegiac Revision of Virgilian Allusion
   Sarah McCallum — 19

2. Calendar Girl: Anna Perenna Between the *Fasti* and the *Punica*
   James S. McIntyre — 37

3. Not Just Another Fertility Goddess: Searching for Anna in Art
   Gwynaeth McIntyre — 54

Anna and Her Nymphs

4. Anna, Water and Her Imminent Deification in *Aeneid* 4
   David J. Wright — 71

5. How to Become a Hero: Gendering the Apotheosis of Ovid's Anna Perenna
   A. Everett Beek — 83

6. Instability and Permanence in Ceremonial Epigraphy: The Example of Anna Perenna
   Anna Blennow — 94

Champion of the Plebs

7   Ovid's Anna Perenna and the Coin of Gaius Annius
    Teresa Ramsby ... 113

8   Infiltrating Julian History: Anna Perenna at Lavinium and Bovillae
    Carole Newlands ... 125

The Afterlife of Anna Perenna

9   Riverrun: Channelling Anna Perenna in *Finnegans Wake*
    Justin Hudak ... 149

Notes ... 163
Bibliography ... 216
Index Locorum ... 231
General Index ... 235

Illustrations

3.1 South-Eastern Panel of the Ara Pacis. Photograph: Scala / Art Resource, NY. — 55
3.2 Silver didrachm minted in Camarina. Kamarina on a swan on reverse. British Museum: 1952,0409.2 © Trustees of the British Museum. — 56
3.3 Terracotta relief of a Nereid on a hippocamp, 50 BCE–100 CE. British Museum: 1805,0703.302 © Trustees of the British Museum. — 57
3.4 Relief from Carthage. Altar © RMN-Grand Palais / Art Resource, NY. — 64
6.1 Inscription of Eutychides libertus. Drawing: Lisa Trentin. — 96
6.2 Inscription of Suetonius Germanus and Licinia. Drawing: Lisa Trentin. — 98
6.3 Inscription of Suetonius Germanus. Drawing: Lisa Trentin. — 99
7.1 Denarius of Gaius Annius depicting Anna Perenna on obverse, 82–81 BCE (RRC 366.1.1). © Trustees of the British Museum. — 114
7.2 Denarius of Lucius Thorius Balbus depicting Juno Sospita on obverse, 105 BCE (RRC 316.1.1). © Trustees of the British Museum. — 117
7.3 Denarius of Quintus Caecilius Metellus Pius depicting Pietas on obverse, 81 BCE (RRC 374.1.1). © Trustees of the British Museum. — 118
7.4 Denarius of Decimus Iunius Silanus depicting Silenus on obverse, 91 BCE (RRC 337.1.1). © Trustees of the British Museum. — 119
7.5 Aureus of C. Clodius Vestalis depicting the vestal Claudia on reverse, 41 BCE (RRC 512.1.1). © Trustees of the British Museum. — 119

Preface

This volume originated from a shared interest in pursuing the figure of Anna Perenna, who embodies the complexity and richness of Roman myth and culture. Her appearances in central works of literature, together with evidence from archaeological and epigraphic sources, confirm her importance to Roman thought and practices. Ovid's collection of competing origin narratives for Anna Perenna in the *Fasti* underscores her prominence in the Roman imagination and the multiplicity of her identity. Other literary treatments of Anna in the *Aeneid* and the *Punica* connect her to the foundational legends and military history of Rome. Fragments of Decimus Laberius's *mimus* about Anna situate her within the context of Roman performance and spectacle, while recent archaeological and epigraphic discoveries establish her association with cult rituals and ancient magic. The commemorative depiction of the goddess on a coin minted by Gaius Annius exemplifies the social trends of the first century BCE, when elite Roman families solidified power and prestige by claiming ancestry from mythic and divine sources. Her presence in post-classical reinterpretations of ancient sources offer further confirmation of her perennial significance as part of the Roman tradition.

Our vision for *Uncovering Anna Perenna* was to invite a range of scholars to contribute to a focused study that represents the intersection between Roman literature, history, and culture. The chapters collectively seek to highlight the importance of Anna Perenna, the fluidity of her identity, and the intricacies of her various manifestations in text and material culture. In exploring Anna Perenna, the contributors apply different perspectives and critical methods to an array of compelling evidence drawn from central texts, monuments, coins, and inscriptions that encapsulate Rome's shifting artistic and political landscape. We thus hope that this volume will be of interest to literary scholars, cultural historians, material culture specialists, and synthetic enthusiasts of the Roman world and its enduring impact.

The four sections of this volume present a framework for categorizing and contemplating Anna's different identities and associations through time, space, and medium. In Part I, 'From Carthage to Rome', contributors explore the liminal and transitional nature of Anna as a Carthaginian princess coopted into Rome's literary, mythological, and artistic heritage. Sarah McCallum discusses the significance of the Carthaginian Anna within Virgil's *Aeneid* and Ovid's *Fasti*, two poetic works designed to celebrate and commemorate Roman foundation and tradition. Turning to the *Punica* of Silius Italicus, James McIntyre demonstrates the problematic ambiguity and tension that results from Anna's Carthaginian origins and subsequent role as a Roman goddess. Gwynaeth McIntyre highlights the challenges of identifying Anna Perenna in artistic depictions and suggests that her uncertain identity may provide new insights into our interpretation of Rome's *Ara Pacis* and a compellingly similar relief from Carthage.

The three contributions in Part II, 'Anna and her Nymphs', focus on Anna in her divine capacity as a Roman nymph and goddess. David Wright pinpoints specific allusions in the *Aeneid* to Anna's divine status as a nymph and shows how Virgil's wordplay and hymnic language serves to connect her to Juturna. A. Everett Beek interprets Ovid's narrative in the *Fasti* from the perspective of gender and sexuality to argue that Anna's journey to Italy and apotheosis in the Numicius reflect a conventionally masculine, rather than feminine, experience. Anna Blennow, by comparing evidence from three votive inscriptions and *tabellae defixiones* found within the sanctuary of the goddess Anna Perenna, examines the conceptual importance of change and transition to Roman epigraphic expression.

Yet another notable identity of Anna forms the underpinning of Part III, 'Champion of the Plebs', in which two contributors explore the ways in which her depiction as the old woman from Bovillae reflects Roman cultural and political sensibilities. Teresa Ramsby analyses the portrayal of Anna Perenna, a goddess beloved by the plebeian class, on a coin minted by Gaius Annius as a strategic manipulation designed to secure the loyalty of his troops at a pivotal and perilous moment in his military career. Carole Newlands demonstrates how Ovid's treatment of the Ides of March in the *Fasti* privileges narratives about Anna that emphasize the centrality of festive, populist traditions and liberty of speech, including women's speech, to Roman tradition.

By way of conclusion, Part IV, 'The Afterlife of Anna Perenna', presents Justin Hudak's intriguing meditation upon influence, in which he demonstrates that an important but overlooked source for *Finnegans Wake*'s Anna Livia Plurabelle (ALP) is the *Fasti*'s Anna Perenna, a luminal figure whose exilic status and Phoenician associations, together with her fluctuating and unstable identity, merit her incorporation into Joyce's magnum opus. This final contribution reveals the potential of reception studies for further investigation and contemplation of Anna Perenna. Indeed, a vast wealth of evidence from post-classical literature, opera, and art holds the promise of additional incarnations of Anna Perenna waiting to be uncovered.

Acknowledgements

This volume could not have come together without the generous encouragement, support, and dedication of a great many people. First, we would like to express our gratitude to the organizers of the 2015 Annual Meeting of the Classical Association in Bristol for including our panel on Anna Perenna in the conference program. The enthusiastic and insightful discussion of our audience members there was an inspirational point of departure for developing this collection of essays. We would like to express our gratitude to all of our contributors, whose collaborative spirit and commitment have made this project possible. A special thanks to Peter Wiseman, who reviewed preliminary drafts of each contribution and offered substantive feedback to help shape and revise the manuscript. The comments of the referees from Bloomsbury Publishing were extremely helpful, and we appreciate their thoughtful input. We are pleased to acknowledge the financial support of the University of Otago Humanities Research Grant, which allowed us to enlist the assistance of Bill Richardson, whose tireless efforts were instrumental in preparing the volume for publication. We are especially thankful to Alice Wright, Lucy Carroll, Clara Herberg, Emma Payne, and the rest of the Bloomsbury Publishing team for their support and guidance throughout the entire publication process.

Sarah McCallum
Gwynaeth McIntyre
April 2018

Abbreviations

Abbreviations of Greek and Latin authors and their works follow those of the Oxford Latin Dictionary, Liddell-Scott-Jones Greek English Lexicon, or Oxford Classical Dictionary, as appropriate. Other abbreviations are as follows:

ACD	*Acta Classica Universitatis Scientiarum Debrecensis*
AE	*L'Année épigraphique* (Paris 1888–)
AJA	*American Journal of Archaeology*
AJP	*American Journal of Philology*
BICS	*Bulletin of the Institute of Classical Studies*
CIL	*Corpus Inscriptionum Latinarum* (Berlin 1863–)
CJ	*Classical Journal*
CP	*Classical Philology*
CQ	*Classical Quarterly*
CW	*Classical World*
HSCPh	*Harvard Studies in Classical Philology*
ILLRP	A. Degrassi (ed.), *Inscriptiones Latinae Liberae Rei Publicae*, 2 vols. (Florence 1965)
ILS	H. Dessau (ed.), *Inscriptiones Latinae Selectae* (Berlin 1892–1916)
JHS	*Journal of Hellenic Studies*
JRA	*Journal of Roman Archaeology*
JRS	*Journal of Roman Studies*
LIMC	P. Müller, C. Auge, and J.-R. Gisler (eds), *Lexicon Iconographicum Mythologiae Classicae* (Zürich-Munich-Dusseldorf 1981–1997)
MD	*Materiali e discussioni per l'analisi dei testi classici*
MHNH	*Mene: revista internacional de investigación sobre magia y astrología antiguas*
Neue-Pauly	H. Cancik, H. Schneider, and M. Landfester (eds), *Der Neue Pauly* (Leiden 2003)
OLD	P.G.W. Glare (ed.), *Oxford Latin Dictionary* (Oxford 1968–1982)
PBSR	*Papers of the British School at Rome*
PCPhS	*Proceedings of the Cambridge Philological Society*
Pichon	R. Pichon, *Index Verborum Amatorium* (Hildesheim 1966)

RE	A. Pauly, G. Wissowa, and W. Krolls (eds), *Realencyclopädie der classischen Altertumwissenschaft,* 86 vols. (Stuttgart 1893–2000)
RIC	H. Mattingly (ed.), *Roman Imperial Coinage* (London 1913–1956)
RPh	*Revue de Philologie*
RRC	M. Crawford, *Roman Republican Coinage* (Cambridge 1974)
SEG	*Supplementum Epigraphicum Graecum* (Leiden 1923–)
TAPA	*Transactions of the American Philological Association*
TLL	*Thesaurus Linguae Latinae* (Leipzig 1900–)
YCIS	*Yale Classical Studies*
ZPE	*Zeitschrift für Papyrologie und Epigraphik*

The translations of Latin and Greek passages are each contributor's own unless otherwise noted.

Contributors

A. Everett Beek (University of Memphis): A. Everett Beek primarily studies Augustan Latin poetry, particularly depictions of apotheosis, the afterlife, and catabasis; she also studies women and the construction of gender. She is currently examining literary depictions of the dead, e.g. as ghosts or shades, focusing on how literary depictions diverge from folk and religious beliefs.

Anna Blennow (University of Gothenburg): Anna's research interests include classical and medieval Latin epigraphy and epigraphic theory. A recent publication of importance is the first scientific edition of the medieval Latin inscriptions in Sweden, published by the Swedish National Museum in 2016. She is also the leader of an interdisciplinary project on the history of guidebooks to Rome, based at the Swedish Institute of Classical Studies in Rome.

Justin Hudak (University of California, Berkeley): Justin studies Augustan poetry and its reception in twentieth-century literature. His current projects, which revolve around questions of literary influence and poetic faith, examine Ovid alongside James Joyce and Horace alongside Wallace Stevens.

Sarah McCallum (University of Arizona): Sarah McCallum is an Assistant Professor of Classics at the University of Arizona. Her research focuses on Greek and Roman language and literature, particularly epic, elegiac, and pastoral poetry. She is especially interested in the complex negotiation between tradition and innovation that characterizes the development of Roman poetry in the first century BCE.

Gwynaeth McIntyre (University of Otago): Gwynaeth McIntyre is a Lecturer of Classics at the University of Otago. Her research focuses on political, social, and religious history of Rome and the ways in which mythology and religion define particular communities. She is the author of *A Family of Gods: The worship of the imperial family in the Latin West* (2016).

James S. McIntyre (Cambridge University Press): James S. McIntyre is the Commissioning Editor with responsibility for classics and archaeology journals at Cambridge University Press. His main scholarly interests are Roman epic (particularly Lucan and Silius Italicus) and the reception of classical literature and history in Scotland. He is currently working on a monograph dealing with representations of the *locus amoenus* in the poems of Lucan, Valerius Flaccus, Statius and Silius Italicus.

Carole Newlands (University of Colorado, Boulder): Carole Newlands is Professor of Classics at the University of Colorado, Boulder. She has published widely on Ovid, on Flavian literature, and on medieval poetry. Her research interests include Roman religion, gender, landscape, and reception. She is currently working on the reception of Catullus by Flavian poets, and on the changing role of translation of the Classics in Scotland.

Teresa Ramsby (University of Massachusetts Amherst): Teresa's research explores aspects of social and literary interaction, including a study on literary inscriptions in Augustan poetry within the context of epigraphic habits at Rome and social change, and a co-edited study on the contributions of freedmen to the Roman Empire.

T.P. Wiseman (University of Exeter): T.P. Wiseman is Emeritus Professor of Classics and Ancient History at the University of Exeter. His books include *Catullus and his World* (1985), *The Myths of Rome* (2004), which won the American Philological Association's Goodwin Award of Merit, *Remembering the Roman People* (2009), and *The Roman Audience* (2015). He and Anne Wiseman have translated Ovid's *Fasti* (Oxford World's Classics, 2013).

David J. Wright (Rutgers University): David's research interests include Latin poetry of the Augustan era and Roman history. He is currently writing a dissertation on Titanomachy and Gigantomachy and its connection to civil strife in Greco-Roman literature.

INTRODUCTION

Anna and the *Plebs*: A Synthesis of Primary Evidence

T.P. Wiseman

What makes 'interdisciplinary approaches' hard to achieve is the sheer volume of scholarship accumulated by the separate intellectual traditions – literary, historical, archaeological – that claim to offer an understanding of the ancient world. Literary scholars concentrate on the great classic texts, archaeologists on the material remains revealed by excavation; when they try to access each other's insights, neither group can possibly master all the scholarly literature in the other's field, or even judge what counts as a good or bad argument in an unfamiliar intellectual environment.

The problem can be avoided by concentrating our attention on the primary evidence – the texts and artefacts that happen to have survived to our own time – on which all the traditions, in their different ways, ultimately depend. 'Above all', said Erasmus,[1] 'we must hasten to the sources' – and his phrase *ad fontes* is particularly appropriate in the case of Anna Perenna, at whose sacred spring altars were dedicated *gratis fontibus*.[2]

I

Our best source for the annual festivals of the Roman republic is the calendar, discovered in 1915, that was painted on the walls of a room in a Roman villa at Antium (modern Anzio) at some time between 84 and 46 BCE.[3] Known nowadays as the *fasti Antiates maiores*, the calendar includes annotations for 51 of the days of the year, almost all of them naming the deity or deities to whom cult was due on that day. For the Ides of March the annotation reads *ANN(ae)* | *PERENNAE*, on two separate lines. Since the calendar lists multiple cult recipients in asyndeton (see for instance the annotation for 8 December, *TIBERINO* |

GAIAE),[4] it is not clear whether the day was the festival of a single deity, Anna Perenna, or of two, Anna and Perenna.

The question matters because a contemporary source names Anna and Peranna (*sic*) as separate entities:

> te Anna ac Peranna, Panda, te calo, Pales,
> Nerienes <et> Minerva, Fortuna ac Ceres
>
> I call on you, Anna and Peranna, and you, Panda, Pales, Nerienes and Minerva, Fortuna and Ceres.
>
> Var. *Men*. fr. 506 Astbury[5]

The quotation is from *Fighting Shadows: On Nonsense*, one of the 150 'Menippean satires' composed by Varro probably in the seventies and sixties BCE. Why the speaker should invoke such a strange collection of major and minor deities is, alas, unknown, but we do at least know something about the first two names:

> eodem quoque mense et publice et privatim ad Annam Perennam sacrificatum itur, ut annare perannareque commode liceat.
>
> In the same month [March] people go to Anna Perenna to sacrifice both publicly and privately, that they may prosperously *annare* and *perannare*.
>
> Macr. 1.12.6[6]

The first of the two verbs is unparalleled, but must mean something like 'pass the year'; the second is glossed by the *Oxford Latin Dictionary* as 'to continue for a long time, endure'. They were evidently not synonyms, and therefore Anna and Peranna could have been two separate deities in charge of two separate functions. For Macrobius, of course, writing long after Ovid and Silius Italicus, Anna Perenna was a single entity. But that was not necessarily the case in the late republic.

The naming of specialist divinities with very particular functions was the responsibility of the Roman *pontifices*. Servius's commentary on Virgil explains:

> quod autem dicit 'studium quibus arva tueri', nomina haec numinum in indigitamentis inveniuntur, id est in libris pontificalibus, qui et nomina deorum et rationes ipsorum nominum continent, quae etiam Varro dicit. nam, ut supra diximus, nomina numinibus ex officiis constat inposita, verbi causa ut ab occatione deus Occator dicatur, a sarritione Sarritor, a stercoratione Sterculinius, a satione Sator.
>
> As for [Virgil] saying 'those [gods] whose work it is to protect the fields', these names of divine powers are found in the *indigitamenta* – that is, in the books of

the *pontifices* that contain the names of the gods and the reasons for their names. Varro also states them. For as we said earlier, it is well known that divine powers are named after their functions, as for example the god Occator from *occatio* (harrowing), Sarritor from *sarritio* (hoeing), Sterculinius from *stercoratio* (manuring), Sator from *satio* (sowing).

Serv. on Virg. G. 1.21

The reference to Varro is evidently to his *Divine Antiquities*, which were written precisely to help his fellow citizens understand which deities to worship, and why:

> dicens non modo bene vivere sed vivere omnino neminem posse, si ignoret quisnam sit faber, quis pistor, quis tector, a quo quid utensile petere possit, quem adiutorem adsumere, quem ducem, quem doctorem; eo modo nulli dubium esse asserens ita esse utilem cognitionem deorum, si sciatur quam quisque deus vim et facultatem ac potestatem cuiusque rei habeat.

> Not merely can a man not live well, [Varro] says, but he cannot live at all if he is unaware of who is a craftsman, or a baker, or a plasterer, or whom to go to to obtain something he needs, or whom to call on to assist or guide or teach you. He maintains that similarly no one doubts that knowledge of the gods is useful only if you know the power, skill, and competence which individual gods possess in their particular spheres.

Var. *Antiquitates divinae* fr. 3 Cardauns[7]

In Book 14 of the *Divinae Antiquities* Varro discussed a long sequence of such specialist deities under the heading *di certi* – presumably gods who were 'certain' because their names and functions were guaranteed by inclusion in the pontifical books.[8] We don't know whether Anna and Peranna were on his list, but Mena (from *mensis*) certainly was, as the month-goddess who looked after menstruation.[9]

These one-purpose deities were seized on by Christian polemicists eager to ridicule pagan beliefs, above all by Augustine in the *City of God*, who had a great admiration for Varro and a detailed knowledge of his works.[10] It was probably from Varro that he took his metaphor of 'plebeian gods' to distinguish the countless specialist deities from the great Olympians; the latter were dealt with in Book 16 of the *Divine Antiquities* under the heading of *di praecipui atque selecti*.[11] Certainly the divine hierarchy reflected the social structure of Varro's own time:

> in his minutis operibus, quae minutatim diis pluribus distributa sunt, etiam ipsos selectos videamus tamquam senatum cum plebe pariter operari ...

> We can see that the *di selecti* themselves are equally involved in these minute functions that are minutely allotted to the multiple gods, just like the Senate with the *plebs*.
>
> August. *C.D.* 7.3.7

Since Varro used the term *ignobilis* to describe the humbler deities,[12] we may reasonably infer that he thought of the Olympian gods as the divine *nobilitas*.

Varro's *Divine Antiquities* were dedicated to Julius Caesar as *pontifex maximus*.[13] So too was Granius Flaccus's *De indigitamentis*, which also dealt with the deities named in the books of the *pontifices*.[14] At about the same time, a work in at least three volumes *On the Names of the Gods* was written by a Cornificius who may have served under Caesar as quaestor in 48 BCE.[15] It is worth asking why the subject should have been so popular at just this time.

II

At the beginning of the republic, oppressed by the domination of the rich and powerful,[16] the plebeians left Rome *en masse* and occupied the Mons Sacer; this 'secession' was only ended with the creation of plebeian tribunes to protect the ordinary citizen against exploitation and the abuse of power. For centuries thereafter the republic managed its political differences without violence, but in 133 BCE the tribune Tiberius Gracchus was murdered at a public assembly by a group of senators and their attendants, and no one was ever prosecuted for the crime. From that moment on the republic was again 'split into two parts', as Cicero put it,[17] and the use of violence became commonplace.[18] When the inevitable civil war came, the 'cause of the *nobilitas*' prevailed;[19] Sulla drastically reduced the tribunes' powers, effectively reversing the outcome of the secession.

The rich and powerful now called themselves 'aristocrats' (*optimates*, translating the Greek *aristoi*), and their opponents on behalf of the Roman People (*populares*) were patronizingly described as 'those who wanted their words and deeds to be welcome to the multitude'.[20] The historian Sallust, in his powerful contemporary analysis of the corruption of the republic, used different terms to describe the two sides: the conflict was between an oligarchy ('the powerful few'), sometimes called the *nobilitas*, and the *plebs* or *populus* itself.[21] Our best evidence for the views of the *populares*, a necessary counterweight to Cicero's optimate sympathies, comes from the speeches Sallust gives to their spokesmen: the tribune C. Memmius in 111 BCE, the consul M. Lepidus in 78, the tribune Licinius Macer in 73, and the centurion C. Manlius in 63. All four of them refer back to the ancient secession of the *plebs* as an admirable precedent.[22]

As a young man, Caesar had taken part in the agitation for the restoration of the tribunes' powers,[23] which eventually happened in 70 BCE. Seven years later, at the time of his election as *pontifex maximus*, the consul at a Senate meeting described him as 'one who has taken what is called the *popularis* line in public life', and the election itself was a demonstration of the People's will.[24] Why it mattered to them becomes clear in our sources for Numa's original creation of the pontificate:

> ὁ δὲ μέγιστος τῶν ποντιφίκων οἷον ἐξηγητοῦ καὶ προφήτου, μᾶλλον δὲ ἱεροφάντου τάξιν εἴληχεν . . . καὶ διδάσκων ὅτου τις δέοιτο πρὸς θεῶν τιμὴν ἢ παραίτησιν.
>
> The *pontifex maximus* had the duty of expounding and interpreting the divine will, or rather of directing sacred rites . . . as well as teaching whatever was requisite for the worship or propitiation of the gods.
>
> Plu. *Num.* 9.4[25]

> eique sacra omnia exscripta exsignataque attribuit, quibus hostiis, quibus diebus, ad quae templa sacra fierent, atque unde in eos sumptus pecunia erogaretur. cetera quoque omnia publica privataque sacra pontificis scitis subiecit, ut esset quo consultum plebes veniret . . .
>
> [Numa] entrusted to his keeping all sacral lore which, written out and authenticated, specified with what victims, on what days, and at what temples sacrifices were to be made, and with what moneys expenses were to be paid. He then subjected all other public and private religious matters to the decrees of the pontiff; it was to him that the *plebs* should come for advice.
>
> Liv. 1.20.5–6[26]

In the politically polarized late republic, the selection of *pontifices* became a *popularis* issue.[27] A tribune's law in 104 BCE replaced the old co-optation system with popular election, but that was repealed by Sulla.[28]

The *pontifex maximus* appointed in Sulla's time was his close ally Q. Metellus Pius, the loyal son of a notoriously arrogant optimate.[29] We may doubt whether many craftsmen, bakers or plasterers would consult *him* about the forms of worship appropriate to their needs. Caesar, on the other hand, lived among them in the noisy, crowded Subura.[30] When Metellus Pius died, it was time to change the system back:

τὰς αἱρέσεις τῶν ἱερέων, γράψαντος μὲν τοῦ Λαβιήνου σπουδάσαντος δὲ τοῦ Καίσαρος, ἐς τὸν δῆμον αὖθις ὁ ὅμιλος παρὰ τὸν τοῦ Σύλλου νόμον ἐπανήγαγεν, ἀνανεωσάμενος τὸν τοῦ Δομιτίου.

The popular assembly, on the proposal of [the tribune] Labienus with Caesar's support, returned the election of priests to the People, renewing Domitius's law [of 104 BCE] against that of Sulla.

D.C. 37.37.1[31]

Once Caesar was elected, no doubt the manner of the pontiff's exercise of his duties changed too. It can only be guesswork, but the new 'people-friendly' circumstances of Caesar's pontificate may explain why so many Roman authors at just this time were offering their own learned interpretations of the names and personalities of the 'plebeian' deities.

III

One (or two) of those deities was Anna Perenna, who had a story of her own at least by the fifties or forties BCE, when the playwright Decimus Laberius was active.[32] It would be good to know what the plot of Laberius's *Anna Peranna* was,[33] and whether he invented it himself or found it in Varro or Cornificius or some other learned author. Four of the six versions listed by Ovid look like conjectures from that sort of literature:

> sunt quibus haec Luna est, quia mensibus impleat annum,
>   pars Themin, Inachiam pars putat esse bovem.
> invenies, qui te nymphen Azanida dicant
>   teque Iovi primos, Anna, dedisse cibos.

> There are those for whom this goddess is Luna, because she fills up the year with months. Some think she is Themis, some the Inachian cow [Io]. You will find people, Anna, who say you're a nymph, daughter of Azan, and that you gave Jupiter his first food.

Ov. *Fast.* 3.657–60[34]

Why Themis or Io, nobody knows;[35] but Azan was an Arcadian hero, and Jupiter – to whom the Ides of every month were sacred – was born in Arcadia in one version of the myth.[36]

Ovid's other two stories are of Anna the Phoenician princess and Anna the old baker-woman of Bovillae. Phoenician Anna was mentioned in Naevius's epic on the Punic War: commenting on Virgil's first reference to *Anna soror*, Servius observes laconically, 'Whose daughters Anna and Dido were, Naevius tells us', but does not give a name.[37] By Varro's time, at least, she had a story:

> Varro ait non Didonem sed Annam amore Aeneae impulsam se super rogum interemisse ... sane sciendum est Varronem dicere Aenean ab Anna amatam.
>
> Varro says that Anna, not Dido, was driven by love for Aeneas to kill herself on the funeral pyre.... It is certainly worth knowing that Varro says Aeneas was loved by Anna.
>
> Serv. Dan. *ad* Virg. *A.* 4.682; Serv. *ad* Virg. *A.* 5.4[38]

Varro was interested in the Trojans' voyage to Italy, and had visited some of their landfalls already in 67 BCE, when he commanded a fleet in the Adriatic in the war against the pirates.[39] But would he have invented this story himself? How Naevius's view of Carthage and Rome evolved into Virgil's,[40] and what other lost versions may once have existed, are matters beyond our knowledge. In particular, it is impossible to say what authors, if any, identified Dido's sister as Anna Perenna before Ovid did.

With Anna of Bovillae, we are much better placed. As we have noticed already,[41] the secession of the *plebs* was a story with topical relevance in the ideological struggles of the late republic. Not only that, but Bovillae, supposedly a colony of Alba Longa,[42] was the family cult centre of the *gens Iulia*.[43] Help coming from there to needy plebeians is an idea that might have appealed to Laberius, who liked to use current affairs for his comic plots.[44]

The second half of Ovid's story about Anna of Bovillae,[45] the farcical tale of Anna, Minerva and Mars, is a perfect example of what Varro deplored about the dramatic literature of the time:

> tria genera theologiae dicit esse, id est rationis quae de diis explicatur, eorumque unum mythicon appellari, alterum physicon, tertium civile ... prima, inquit, theologia maxime accommodata est ad theatrum, secunda ad mundum, tertia ad urbem ... primum, inquit, quod dixi, in eo sunt multa contra dignitatem et naturam immortalium facta.
>
> There are three kinds of theology or ways of explaining the gods, the first of them being termed the mythical, the second the physical, and the third the civic.... The first theology is associated chiefly with the theatre, the second with the universe, and the third with the city.... The first type which I mentioned contains much fiction prejudicial to the dignity and the nature of the immortals.
>
> Var. *Antiquitates divinae* frr. 7 and 10 Cardauns[46]

It is clear from Augustine's use of the *Divine Antiquities* that what Varro objected to were plays with burlesque mythological plots put on at the *ludi scaenici*;[47] in particular, he disliked stories in which gods were portrayed as thieves (like Mercury) or adulterers (like Jupiter) or slaves to a mortal (like Hercules).[48] The deception of amorous Mars would certainly count as such a plot.

It is important not to overlook this authoritative body of evidence for a late-republican dramatic genre that is otherwise practically unattested. The nearest thing we have to confirmation of it is another fragment from one of Varro's own Menippean satires, where the speaker is commenting on the ruinous expense of keeping slaves and hunting dogs:

> crede mihi, plures dominos servi comederunt quam canes. quod si Actaeon occupasset et ipse prius suos canes comedisset, non nugas saltatoribus in theatro fieret.
>
> Believe me, more masters have been eaten up by their slaves than by their dogs. If Actaeon had got in first and eaten his dogs before they ate him, he wouldn't be rubbish for dancers in the theatre.
>
> Var. *Men.* 513 Astbury[49]

Actaeon was a subject for tragedy, with even a special mask equiped with antlers for the protagonist,[50] but the comic exploitation of tragic plots had been familiar in Italy since the third century BCE, when Rhinthon pioneered the dramatic form called 'cheerful tragedy'.[51] Since *Rhinthonica* are listed by the grammarians as a recognized type of Roman comedy,[52] it would be an economical hypothesis to identify them with the performances Varro complained about.

Note too that the role of Actaeon was *danced*. Cicero mentions in one of his speeches a dancer called Dionysia who charged 200,000 sesterces for a single performance.[53] She too must be part of this ill-attested dramatic culture, a style of performance preceding – and perhaps developing into – the hugely popular *pantomimus* dance-drama associated with Bathyllus and Pylades in the twenties BCE.[54] Pylades specialized in tragic roles, but Bathyllus's style was 'more cheerful' (the word used of Rhinthon's burlesques), exemplified by 'the nymph Echo or some Pan or satyr revelling with Eros'.[55]

Paying proper attention to this scattered and neglected evidence, and bearing in mind Varro's strictures on material 'unworthy of the divine majesty',[56] we should remember Propertius 4.9, where thirsty Hercules utters 'words unworthy of a god', or Ovid's account of the 'silent goddess' in *Fasti* 2, where Jupiter, lusting after Juturna, 'put up with many things so great a god shouldn't have to endure'.[57]

If we ask, as we should, where the poets found such stories, the answer may be that they were 'attested by the stage'.[58]

Erotic plots like Jupiter's amorous pursuits were evidently typical of this theatrical tradition,[59] and in Varro's time erotic entertainment was particularly associated with the *ludi Florales*. It was a popular spectacle in both senses of the word: when Marcus Cato, the most outspoken of the *optimates* and Caesar's lifelong enemy, was present at the *ludi Florales* in 55 BCE (he was standing for election as praetor at the time), the audience would not allow the show to begin until he got up and left.[60] The three authors who refer to this event use the term *iocus* to describe Flora's games; so too does Ovid in the *Fasti*, and he calls Flora's naked showgirls a 'plebeian chorus'.[61]

Ovid also uses the word *iocus* of the stories of Priapus's attempt on the nymph Lotis, of Faunus's pursuit of Omphale, of Priapus's attempt on Vesta, and negatively (no *ioci* here) of a non-erotic tale involving satyrs.[62] Since Faunus was identified as Pan, and the two Priapus stories are set at divine festivals attended by satyrs, Pans and nymphs,[63] this is all reminiscent of Bathyllus's dance world of nymphs, Pans and satyrs revelling. The notion of *iocus* occurs twice more in the *Fasti*: to describe the old songs sung by the pipers on the Ides of June (the first of all pipers was a satyr, Marsyas),[64] and the indecent songs sung by the girls at the festival of Anna Perenna (who was a nymph in two of the stories Ovid knew).[65]

The girls on the Ides of March sang 'specific obscenities' (*certa probra*), a puzzling adjective that seems to suggest a fixed form of words. If Varro's *di certi* were so-called because they featured in the books of the *pontifices*, perhaps set formulae for the cult of Anna Perenna were listed there too. We cannot know; but if we are right to infer a change of pontifical style after Caesar's election in 63 BCE, it is conceivable that new liturgies as well as new stories were being created for the 'plebeian' deities.

What we do know is that Ovid was very familiar with the idea of a divine *plebs*. In Book 5 of the *Fasti*, Polyhymnia – the Muse who looked after the *pantomimus* dance genre – reports an early divine world in which all rank was equal and a 'plebeian god' might sit on the throne of Saturn.[66] The *locus classicus* for the idea of plebeian divinities comes in Ovid's curse-poem from exile:

> vos quoque, plebs superum, Fauni satyrique Laresque
>   fluminaque et nymphae semideumque genus.
>
> You too, the *plebs* of the heavenly ones, Fauns and satyrs and Lares and rivers and nymphs and the race of half-gods.
>
> Ov. *Ib*. 81–2[67]

Already, in the great opening sequence of his epic, Ovid had presented Jupiter convening the Olympian Senate to the 'heavenly Palatine', where the *atria* of the *nobiles* are crowded like those of their mortal counterparts.[68] 'The dwellings of the *plebs* are elsewhere',[69] and in his speech Jupiter tells us where:

> sunt mihi semidei, sunt rustica numina nymphae
> Faunique satyrique et monticolae Silvani;
> quos, quoniam caeli nondum dignamur honore,
> quas dedimus certe terras habitare sinamus.
>
> I have [to think about] the half-gods, the countryside divinities, nymphs and Fauns and satyrs and mountain-dwelling Silvani; since we do not yet deem them worthy of heaven, let us at least allow them to inhabit the earth that we have granted them.
>
> Ov. *Met.* 1.192–195

'Not *yet* worthy of heaven', but there was always the chance of promotion, for instance from nymph to goddess, like Flora or Juturna.[70]

Promotion came also to the mortal Anna of Bovillae, and it was the Roman plebeians who brought it about by setting up a cult statue.[71] We might express it in a different idiom, and suggest that under the *popularis* pontificate of Julius Caesar the merely functional concept of Anna Perenna (or Anna and Peranna) evolved into an anthropomorphic divinity, accumulating a collection of stories to explain her name and her plebeian status.

IV

The plebeians who honoured Anna of Bovillae were 'still unprotected by any tribunes':[72] the secession itself enforced the creation of the tribunate of the *plebs*, to protect the Roman People from the abuse of power. Four and a half centuries later, in January 49 BCE, the *optimates* drove two tribunes out of Rome, to prevent them from exercising their legal right of veto.[73] The tribunes fled to Caesar, now proconsul of Gaul. Caesar marched his army into Italy, making it clear in a public statement what was at stake:

> se non malefici causa ex provincia egressum sed uti se a contumeliis inimicorum defenderet, ut tribunos plebis in ea re ex civitate expulsos in suam dignitatem restitueret, ut se et populum Romanum factione paucorum oppressum in libertatem vindicaret.

> [He said] he had left his province not for any criminal purpose, but to defend himself against the slanders of his enemies, to restore to their proper place the tribunes of the *plebs* who had been expelled from the city for that reason, and to bring about the freedom of himself and the Roman People from oppression by a faction of a few men.
>
> Caes. *Civ.* 1.22.5

Caesar had enthusiastic popular support,[74] expressed after the war was over by the honorific title 'Father of the nation' (*parens patriae*).[75]

The Roman People were outraged by the murder of Caesar, and demanded vengeance.[76] It was provided by Caesar's heir and adopted son, whom they elected as consul at the age of nineteen, and as '*triumvir* for the establishment of the republic' (*rei publicae constituendae*) at the age of twenty.[77] One of the first acts of the Triumvirs was the establishment of a cult for *Divus Iulius*, the deified Caesar, with a temple to be built in the Forum at the place where the People had insisted on burning his body.[78] Celebrations would be held on Caesar's birthday,[79] in the month now called 'July' (material for Ovid's seventh book, if the *Fasti* had ever been finished).

For the Ides of March a quite different sort of annual remembrance was proposed:

> curiam in qua occisus est obstrui placuit Idusque Martias Parricidium nominari, ac ne umquam eo die senatus ageretur.
>
> It was voted that the hall in which he was slain be walled up, that the Ides of March be called the Day of Parricide, and that a meeting of the Senate should never be called on that day.
>
> Suet. *Jul.* 88[80]

But though 'parricide' long remained the accepted phrase for the assassination,[81] *Parricidium* never appears on the surviving Augustan calendars; the Ides are marked only as Anna Perenna's cult day.[82]

Perhaps it was thought that giving the day *any* special name would be an inappropriate glorification. That may be the reason for Ovid's intention to say nothing about the murder, and certainly his change of mind, encouraged by Vesta, deals with the event in a way his audience would approve, emphasizing the elder Caesar's divinity and the younger Caesar's dutiful exaction of vengeance.[83] The audience would not need reminding that the younger Caesar, now Caesar Augustus, had been granted the powers of that very tribunate of the *plebs* that the secession of the plebeians had first won and the elder Caesar had gone to war to defend.[84]

V

The festival of Anna Perenna took place close to the Tiber on the north side of Rome, at the first milestone on the Via Flaminia.[85] That information allows us to place Ovid's scene quite precisely. In modern terms, it is the neighbourhood of Via di Ripetta from Piazza del Popolo south to the Mausoleum of Augustus, bounded by the river to the west and the Corso (Via Flaminia) to the east.

The sacred-spring site found in 1999 at Piazza Euclide, identified epigraphically as a cult centre for Anna Perenna and the 'consecrated nymphs',[86] is two kilometres north of Piazza del Popolo as the crow flies; it is not on the Via Flaminia and it is nowhere near the Tiber bank. It is therefore not the scene of Anna Perenna's festival as described by Ovid. The earliest of the many coins found in the basin are of Augustan date, but we cannot know how long they had been in circulation when the site first came into use.

A change in the circumstances of Anna's cult is also suggested by Martial's poem about the villa of Julius Martialis. He describes the villa as 'on the long ridge of the Janiculum', but in fact the view it commanded is the view from Monte Mario:

>   hinc septem dominos videre montis
>   et totam licet aestimare Romam,
>   Albanos quoque Tusculosque colles
>   et quodcumque iacet sub urbe frigus,
>   Fidenas veteres brevesque Rubras,   15
>   et quod virgineo cruore gaudet
>   Annae pomiferum nemus Perennae.
>   illinc Flaminiae Salariaeque
>   gestator patet essedo tacente,
>   ne blando rota sit molesta somno,   20
>   quem nec rumpere nauticum celeuma
>   nec clamor valet helciariorum,
>   cum sit tam prope Mulvius sacrumque
>   lapsae per Tiberim volent carinae.

On one side you may see the seven imperial mounts and appraise all Rome; likewise the hills of Alba and Tusculum and whatever cool spot lies near the city, ancient Fidenae and little Rubrae and the fruitful grove of Anna Perenna that rejoices in the blood of virgins. On the other side the traveller on the Flaminian and Salarian way is on view; but his carriage makes no sound, lest the wheel disturb soothing slumbers that neither boatswain's call nor bargee's shout can interrupt, even though Mulvius [the Milvian bridge] be so near and keels glide rapidly down sacred Tiber.

Mart. 4.64.11–24[87]

There was no grove in Ovid's account of Anna Perenna, and the girls who sang and danced on that easy-going occasion were clearly not virgins.

What Anna's grove 'rejoiced in' at line 16 must be either human sacrifice, obviously impossible in Martial's time, or the sort of pre-marriage 'initiation' of brides that was associated with Mutunus Tutunus, another 'functional' deity with a double name:

> ipse sit Mutunus vel Tutunus, qui est apud Graecos Priapus ... Priapus nimis masculus, super cuius immanissimum et turpissimum fascinum sedere nova nupta iubebatur, more honestissimo religiosissimo matronarum.

> Let him [the 'one god' of the pagans] be Mutunus or Tutunus, whom the Greeks call Priapus ... Priapus who is all too masculine, on whose most enormous and foul member the new bride used to be ordered to sit, in the most honourable and pious custom of married women.

Var. *Antiquitates divinae* fr. 151 Cardauns[88]

We happen to know that Mutunus Tutunus had a shrine on the Velia, which was converted into baths for the house of Cn. Domitius Calvinus (consul in 53 and 40 BCE);[89] but what happened to his cult after that?

Another Martial passage may be relevant, warning his female readers of obscene poems in the rest of his volume:

> hinc iam deposito post vina rosasque pudore,
>   quid dicat nescit saucia Terpsichore,
> schemate nec dubio, sed aperte nominat illam
>   quam recipit sexto mense superba Venus,
> custodem medio statuit cum vilicus horto,
>   opposita spectat quam proba virgo manu.

> Henceforth tipsy Terpsichore, laying modesty aside after the wine and roses, knows not what she is saying, naming openly and with no ambiguous turn of phrase that object which Venus proudly welcomes in the sixth month, which the bailiff sets for guard in the middle of the garden, which a good girl eyes behind her hand.

Mart. 3.68.5–10[90]

The object is of course Priapus's erect member, and the sixth month, after the Ides of June, was the well-omened time for weddings.[91] At some point Anna's festival

(*Annae sacrum*) was moved from 15 March to 18 June.[92] The *terminus ante quem* for the change is 354 CE, but Martial's allusion seems already to presuppose it.

Priapus and the nymphs were fellow-revellers,[93] and a hymn to the phallic god set up some time in the first century CE suggests what his relationship may have been with the *nymphae sacratae* of Anna Perenna's grove and spring:

> convenite simul quot es[tis om]nes,
> quae sacrum colitis [ne]mus [pu]ellae,
> quae sacras colitis a[q]uas puellae,
> convenite quot estis atque [be]llo
> voce dicite blandula Priapo
> 'salve, sancte pater Priape rerum'.
> [i]nguini oscula figite inde mille,
> [fasci]num bene olentibus [cor]onis
> [cing]ite illi iterumque dicite omnis
> ['salve, san]cte pater Priape rerum'.

> Come together all of you, you girls who dwell in the sacred grove, you girls who dwell in the sacred waters, come together all of you and sing with seductive voice to handsome Priapus: 'Greetings, holy Priapus, father of all things'. Then plant countless kisses on his groin, put sweet-smelling garlands round his member, and sing again: 'Greetings, holy Priapus, father of all things'.
>
> CIL 14.3565.13–22[94]

The 'girls' are of course nymphs, addressed a few lines further on as *deae puellae*.

The evidence therefore suggests that during the first century the cult of Anna Perenna acquired a new site, a new date and a new purpose. That need not surprise us: we have already seen the eighty years from Varro's Menippean satires to Ovid's *Fasti* transform her from two verbal personifications (*Anna ac Peranna*...) into a nymph or goddess with many different meanings, and there is no reason to think that the nature of her cult was any more static during the next eighty years, from Ovid's *Fasti* to Martial. For us, the challenge is to pay proper attention to the sources in their chronological order.

The ex-consul Silius Italicus was composing his huge epic poem *Punica* in the eighties and nineties CE.[95] The excursus in the eighth book, on Anna Perenna as Punic princess and Roman goddess, obviously draws on the first of Ovid's Anna stories, though one or two of the details – the glassy caves, the sisterhood of nymphs – may perhaps reflect conditions new since Ovid wrote.[96] But Carthaginian Anna was part of an epic tradition going back to Virgil and Naevius; Ovid's plebeian Anna would have been less easy for Silius to assimilate.

The *popularis* ideology of Julius Caesar and Caesar Augustus was still a living force in 25 CE, when praise of the assassins was a crime of high treason, and in 41 CE, when the Senate hoped to re-establish an optimate republic and the Roman People wanted a Caesar to prevent them from doing so.[97] But that soon changed, in part thanks to the brilliant success of Lucan's *Pharsalia* in mythologizing the *optimates*: his Caesar was the tyrannical enemy of freedom, his Cato and Brutus the heroes of a doomed but noble cause. By the time Tacitus wrote his *Annals* in the early second century, the assassination was simply a historical event about which opposite opinions were equally legitimate: 'to some the worst of acts, to others the finest'.[98] Moreover, it is likely that by then Anna's cult no longer had anything to do with the Ides of March.

About two generations after Silius and Tacitus, the cult site of Anna Perenna received two new altars, each inscribed with a short poem in iambic *senarii*. The first is headed 'to the consecrated nymphs' and dated at the end to 5 April 156 CE:

> Suetonius Germanus cum Licinia coniuge,
> Annae Perennae votum quod susceperant
> si se victores statuerent
> aram marmoream se posituros, denuo
> victores facti votum meriti solvimus.

> Suetonius Germanus with his wife Licinia, the vow which they had undertaken to Anna Perenna, that if they established themselves as victors they would place a marble altar, once again made victors, we deservedly repay the vow.
>
> *AE* 2003, 252[99]

The other has no heading or date, but is signed at the end 'Eutychides the freedman':

> votum sacratis quondam nymphis feceram
> boni patroni meritis ob victoriam
> C. Acili Eutychetis reddimus
> et esse sanctas confitemur versibus
> aramque gratis dedicamus fontibus.

> The vow [which] once I had made to the consecrated nymphs, who deserved it because of the victory of my good patron Gaius Acilius Eutyches, we pay; and we attest in verses that [the nymphs] are sacred, and we dedicate an altar to the welcome springs.
>
> *AE* 2003, 251

What sort of competition was this? The name of the victorious Acilius Eutyches may suggest an answer, if we compare an honorific inscription set up in 169 CE for the 'noble *archimimus*' Lucius Acilius Eutyches (perhaps his brother), who was 'honored by the tragic, comic, and all other corporations concerned with the stage'.[100] The competitiveness of such performers is well attested in the epigraphic record, as for example in a second-century statue-base from Rome:

> M. Ulpius Aug. lib. Apolaustus
> maximus pantomimus
> coronatus adversus histriones
> et omnes scaenicos
> artifices XII

Marcus Ulpius Apolaustus, freedman of the emperor [Trajan], crowned twelve times as the top *pantomimus* against the actors and all the professionals of the stage.

CIL 6.10114[101]

The dedicators of the two altars at the Piazza Euclide site used iambic *senarii*, the regular metre of dramatic dialogue. If they owed their victories to Anna Perenna and the nymphs, it may be because those divinities had a long history of association with the stage, and in particular with 'mime' in its various forms.[102]

The Piazza Euclide site was evidently in use from the first century CE to the late fourth. The lead curse-tablets and 'voodoo dolls' found in the pool may belong to the latter part of that long period, but the magical practices they attest were commonplace throughout antiquity. One of the lead cylinders containing one of the dolls bears fingerprints evidently of a woman.[103] There's not much one can do with this evidence, but it may be helpful to remember the witches Canidia and Sagana in Horace's satire, or the nameless old woman and her group of girls 'binding hostile tongues' in Ovid's account of the Feralia.[104] It seems that in that respect too, Anna Perenna was a deity for the Roman *plebs*.

From Carthage to Rome

1

Rivalry and Revelation: Ovid's Elegiac Revision of Virgilian Allusion*

Sarah McCallum

The poetry of Ovid teems with seemingly inexhaustible evidence of his engagement with Virgil. For Ovid, the impulse to compete with the monolithic achievement of his epic predecessor engendered a fiercely ingenious artistic rivalry, as exemplified by his striking celebration of Anna Perenna in the *Fasti* (*Fast.* 3.523–710). One pivotal question lurks beneath the surface of Ovid's treatment of Anna's mytho-legendary origins: who was the Carthaginian lover of Aeneas? The obvious answer, at least after the rise of the *Aeneid*, would be Dido, Aeneas's paramour in the widely acclaimed and imitated amatory narrative of Book 4 of Virgil's epic. But, as both Virgil and Ovid knew, there was an alternative version of the story, in which it was not Dido but her sister Anna who became erotically entangled with Aeneas. A comparative analysis of how Virgil and Ovid treated the figure of Anna reveals the divergent approaches to the question adopted by each poet, as I aim to show. I begin by demonstrating how Virgil negotiated with two competing traditions through concealment, as evidenced by allusive traces of the alternative Anna–Aeneas story within the narrative of *Aeneid* 4. Turning next to Ovid, I show that he not only recognized Virgil's allusive suppression of the Anna–Aeneas story but also responded to it through the Carthaginian aetiology of Anna Perenna in *Fasti* 3. By revealing what Virgil had concealed, Ovid lays bare the artistic process of his predecessor and his own poetic aims.

The Alternative Anna–Aeneas Tradition

Under the creative sway of Virgil, Dido becomes an integral figure in subsequent artistic accounts of the post-Iliadic wanderings of Aeneas. Her passionate love affair with Aeneas and its grave consequences are crucial to the narrative trajectory, aesthetic fabric and emotional impact of the *Aeneid*. Love compels Aeneas to linger with Dido in Carthage, delaying the hero's progress toward Italy. From banquet to pyre, the tale of erotic entanglement is a rich display of Virgil's extraordinary generic range and innovative engagement with literary predecessors. The grisly spectacle of Dido's suicide draws the episode to a violent and distressing conclusion, eliciting a conflicted emotional response rivaled only by the death of Turnus in the final lines of the poem. Indeed, Virgil's triumphant integration of Dido into the legendary history of Rome establishes her firmly within the subsequent literary tradition – after the *Aeneid* it seems virtually unimaginable that the story could unfold without her.

But despite the overwhelming success of Virgil's depiction of Dido and Aeneas, it stands in contrast to an alternative tradition, in which Anna, Dido's sister, played the role of Aeneas's erotic counterpart.[1] Two explicit references in the late antique Servian commentaries draw attention to the alternative version of the story recounted by Marcus Terentius Varro.[2] In relation to the dying words of Virgil's Dido, Servius Auctus provides the following insight: *Varro ait non Didonem, sed Annam amore Aeneae impulsam se supra rogum interemisse* (Varro says that it was not Dido, but Anna who, driven by love of Aeneas, killed herself on top of a pyre, Serv. Dan. *ad* Virg. A. 4.682.).[3] A second entry by Servius on the opening lines of *Aeneid* 5 indicates that the well-known version of Varro presented Anna as the ardent lover of Aeneas (*sane sciendum Varronem dicere, Aeneam ab Anna amatum*, certainly it must be known that Varro says that Aeneas was loved by Anna, Serv. *ad* Virg. A. 5.4).[4]

These two explicit references to the alternative Anna–Aeneas tradition also assist with the interpretation of more obscure allusions to Varro in the Servian commentaries. For example, the phrase *adludit ad historiam* (he alludes to history, Serv. *ad* Virg. A. 4.676)[5] is appended to a particularly puzzling aspect of Anna's final speech to her dying sister Dido in *Aeneid* 4: *hoc rogus iste mihi* (was it this that pyre of yours [was preparing] for me, Virg. A. 4.676).[6] The precise meaning of Anna's question has long confounded commentators, and Servius's annotation does little to clarify the issue.[7] But, as Sergio Casali has shown, the entry takes on new meaning when read in connection with the other Servian references to the alternative Anna–Aeneas tradition.[8] In effect, Anna's utterance *hoc rogus iste mihi* constitutes an allusion to the Varronian version of the story, in which the pyre was the setting for her own impassioned suicide:

> *Insomma, le note di S a 676 e SD a 682 sembrano essere residui di una lettura autoriflessiva del lamento di Anna, in cui il commentatore attento alle allusioni*

anfibologiche di Virgilio interpretava in chiave metanarrativa la rivendicazione a sé stessa del suicidio di Didone da parte di Anna.
In conclusion, the notes of Servius at line 676 and Servius Danielis at line 682 seem to be the remnants of a self-reflexive reading of Anna's lament, in which the commentator attentive to Virgil's amphibological allusions interpreted in a metanarrative way the claim for herself of Dido's suicide by Anna.

Casali. '*Ecce* ἀμφιβολικῶς *dixit*', 37[9]

Servius, perceptive to the metaliterary import of Anna's question, provides the comment *adludit ad historiam* to mark Virgil's allusion to Varro.[10] Thus, an apparently obscure commentary entry begins to reveal how Virgil engages with Varro: he incorporates subtle allusions to his predecessor, even as he innovates to focus on the figure of Dido. Taken together with the other more explicit examples, this Servian reference invites us to delve further into the traces of Varro that lurk beneath the surface of Virgil's depiction of Dido and her sister Anna. Indeed, as we will see, the alternative tradition provides answers for other narrative and textual problems awaiting resolution.

Virgil's *Anna Soror*

By turning now to a detailed exploration of Virgil's text, I aim to draw attention to further evidence of his allusive acknowledgment of the alternative Anna–Aeneas tradition presented by Varro. In this first section, I provide a brief overview of Anna's restricted narrative function within the *Aeneid*, before proceeding to discuss two key passages: Dido's request that Anna make a final plea to Aeneas on her behalf (Virg. *A.* 4.416–40); and Anna's final speech to her mortally wounded sister (Virg. *A.* 4.675–85). Within these two crucial passages, allusions to the alternative Anna–Aeneas tradition exist in productive tension with the primary storyline. Though often misinterpreted as narrative incongruities, the allusions recall Varro's version even as Virgil creates his own unique tale of passion gone awry.

Let us begin by considering the figure of Anna within the context of the *Aeneid*. By comparison to her sister Dido, whose narrative arc spans Books 1, 4 and 6, Anna plays a relatively small and supporting role within Virgil's epic. Within the erotic and tragic narrative of *Aeneid* 4, Anna functions as Dido's confidante, offering amatory encouragement that contributes to Dido's destruction. In this capacity, Anna recalls the nurse or confidante figure of tragedy, as well as Medea's sister Chalciope from Apollonius's *Argonautica*.[11] Though her role may seem somewhat limited, Anna shares the stage with Dido at pivotal moments. While Anna's encouraging conversation with Dido sets the plot of Book 4 in motion, her stricken speech to the dying queen brings the episode to its tragic conclusion. In other intervening passages, we see Anna deeply entrenched in the various stages of Dido's affair with Aeneas, privy to her sister's turbulent emotions and enlisted to act on her behalf. Anna's intimate connection with Dido and Aeneas creates opportunities for Virgil to allude to her own principal role in the alternative version of the story. Through such allusions, Virgil grafts the Varronian Anna onto the Dido–Aeneas affair, effectively creating a metaliterary love triangle.

In the first of the two passages to be discussed, Dido determines to make one final attempt to break the resolve of Aeneas, who is currently preparing for a hasty departure from Carthage. Rather than approaching Aeneas herself, Dido asks Anna to address him on her behalf:

> miserae hoc tamen unum
> exsequere, Anna, mihi; solam nam perfidus ille
> te colere, arcanos etiam tibi credere sensus;
> sola viri mollis aditus et tempora noras.
> i, soror, atque hostem supplex adfare superbum.
>
> Yet accomplish this one thing for me, Anna, in my wretchedness; for that faithless man ['respects', 'loves'?] you alone, and even entrusts his hidden feelings to you; you alone have known the times for approaching the man softly. Go, sister, and as a suppliant address the arrogant foreigner.
>
> Virg. A. 4.420–4

Dido's speech to Anna contains a most peculiar assertion; she strangely suggests that Anna shares a singular intimacy with Aeneas, an intimacy underscored by the repetition of *sola* (*solam*, Virg. A. 4.421; *sola*, 4.423) and *tu* (*te . . . tibi*, 4.422). Furthermore, according to Dido Aeneas affords special treatment to Anna and shares his secret feelings with her, while Anna alone knows when best to approach him. We may notice in particular Virgil's use of the word *mollis* ('soft'), a strong lexical marker of the elegiac genre, the 'softness' of which stands in contrast to *durus* ('hard') epic.[12] Given that Virgil nowhere else develops any sort of relationship between Anna and Aeneas, Dido's claims seem incongruous with the primary storyline and pose a striking problem of interpretation.

As R.G. Austin succinctly summarizes, 'These lines refer to something that Virgil has not told us'.[13] Attempts to resolve the apparent incongruity have generally been reductive and unsatisfactory. For example, Austin proposes that the audience should simply infer that Anna has been interacting with Aeneas on Dido's behalf behind the scenes,[14] while Richard Heinze allows that Virgil has left the truth of Dido's words to the imagination of the reader as a 'technique of drama'.[15] These suggestions might help to explain the narrative gap, but fail to take into account the erotic undertones of Dido's speech, which are suggestive of an intimacy between Anna and Aeneas that stands in stark tension with the story line presented by Virgil. In his seventeenth-century commentary, Juan de la Cerda asks whether something erotic lies hidden in the verb *colere* and discusses its use as a synonym for *amare*, then wonders whether Dido's words may betray a jealous suspicion indicative of Anna's status as a rival for the affections of the faithless Aeneas:

> An in verbo colere latet aliquid? Hoc verbum pro amare, interdum veteres dixerunt, sicut cultores, pro, amatores.... Ergo quis sciat, an hic Dido aliquid suspicetur de zelotypia, usaque sit obscuro verbo, & ambiguo, indicans Annae rivalitatem, quae ad se virum pellexerit? praesertim cum addat perfidus, perinde, in me perfidus, quia rivalis meus, & tui cultor.
>
> Is something lurking in the verb *colere*? Sometimes the ancients said this verb for *amare*, just as *cultores* for *amatores*.... Therefore who knows whether Dido suspects something out of jealousy, and used a verb both obscure and uncertain, revealing the rivalry of Anna, who had enticed the man to her? Especially since she adds *perfidus*, as in 'faithless to me', because my adversary in love and your lover.
>
> <div style="text-align:right">Ionnes Ludovicus de la Cerda, <i>P. Virgilii Maronis Aeneidos
Libri Sex Priores: Argumentis, Explicationibus et Notis Illustrati</i>
(Lyon: Horace Cardon, 1612), 451[16]</div>

De la Cerda's assertion that Dido may view Anna as an erotic opponent points to a problematic contrast between the undertone of the text and Anna's primary narrative role as supportive confidante. Like Austin, de la Cerda seems to see the lines as indicative of 'something Virgil has not told us', namely some erotic affair between Anna and Aeneas lurking beneath the surface.

But the observations of de la Cerda, when taken into account with our fragmentary evidence for the alternative Varronian tradition, leads to an attractive solution. Rather than a problematic narrative inconsistency, Dido's depiction of the intimacy between Anna and Aeneas subtly alludes to the alternative Anna–Aeneas tradition, as has been suggested by Anthony Barrett and Sergio Casali.[17] The verb *colere* can be used in the sense of 'admire' or 'respect', but can also be used as a virtual synonym for verbs of 'loving'.[18] The phrase *te colere* can thus be read as an allusive acknowledgement of Aeneas's relationship with Anna in the alternative tradition.[19] Furthermore, the epithet *perfidus*, which Dido applies to Aeneas here for the third and final time,[20] like the adjective *mollis*, derives from the lexicon of Latin erotic verse.[21] Within Dido's speech it functions in its erotic capacity as a term for the faithless lover – a subtle reference to Aeneas's extra-Virgilian dalliance with Anna. And, as noted by Barrett, the unmistakably erotic overtones of the formulation *sola viri mollis aditus et tempora noras* (you alone have known the times for approaching the man softly, Virg. *A*. 4.423) seems to hint at some sort of liaison between Anna and Aeneas.[22] Though jarring in the immediate narrative context, Dido's erotic description of Anna's interaction with Aeneas invites the audience to recall the alternative tradition. In effect, the subtle allusion allows the words of Dido to function on two levels simultaneously: as a request to the Virgilian Anna, her sister and confidante; and as a bitter acknowledgement of the Varronian Anna, her metaliterary rival.

When we turn to Anna's final speech to her mortally wounded sister, we find a similar superimposition of her Virgilian and Varronian incarnations. Rushing to the side of the dying Dido, Anna erupts with a frantic outburst:

> 'hoc illud, germana, fuit? me fraude petebas?   675
> hoc rogus iste mihi, hoc ignes araeque parabant?
> quid primum deserta querar? comitemne sororem
> sprevisti moriens? eadem me ad fata vocasses,
> idem ambas ferro dolor atque eadem hora tulisset.
> his etiam struxi manibus patriosque vocavi   680
> voce deos, sic te ut posita, crudelis, abessem?
> exstinxti te meque, soror, populumque patresque
> Sidonios urbemque tuam.'

'This, then, was that, sister? You were targeting me with your deception? Was it this that pyre of yours for me, this the fires and altars were preparing? What first shall I, abandoned, lament? Have you scorned by dying a sister's companionship? You should have summoned me to the same fate, the same sword-wrought agony and the same hour should have taken us both. With these hands I, too, built a pyre and called upon the ancestral gods with my voice, just so I could be away, cruel one, as you lay thus? You have killed you and me sister, and the people and the Sidonian fathers and your own city.'

Virg. *A*. 4.675–83

Much like Dido's earlier entreaty, Anna's speech has two coexisting levels of meaning: as a sorrowful accusation levelled by the Virgilian Anna against her dying sister; and as the metaliterary testimony of the Varronian Anna regarding her own impassioned suicide. As we have already seen, Casali detects within the phrase *hoc rogus iste mihi* (was it this that pyre of yours [was preparing] for me, Virg. *A.* 4.676) and its Servian annotation (*adludit ad historiam*, he alludes to history, Serv. *ad* Virg. *A.* 4.676) an allusion to Anna's own suicide atop a pyre in Varro.[23] Casali reinforces his observation by pointing out a second key allusion: when Anna says to Dido 'you have killed you and me' (*exstinxti te meque*, you have killed you and me, Virg. *A.* 4.682), she alludes to the deaths of each sister, one in Varro and one in Virgil.[24] The Servian commentary connects the phrase *exstinxti te meque* explicitly to the suicidal Anna of Varro, thus confirming the allusion (*Varro ait non Didonem, sed Annam amore Aeneae impulsam se supra rogum interemisse*, Varro says that it was not Dido, but Anna who, driven by a love of Aeneas, killed herself on top of a pyre, Serv. Dan. *A.* 4.682). Based on the strong testimony of these two examples, Casali suggests that other allusions may be found in Anna's speech, noting in particular her second reference to the pyre (*his etiam struxi manibus*, With these hands too I built..., Virg. *A.* 4.680) and her assertion that she should have shared Dido's terrible fate (*eadem me ad fata uocasses, | idem ambas ferro dolor atque eadem hora tulisset*, You should have summoned me to the same fate, the same sword-wrought agony and the same hour should have taken us both, Virg. *A.* 4.678–9).[25] Indeed, the triple repetition of *eadem*, *idem* and *eadem* underscores that both Dido and Anna suffer the same death, albeit in different sources. Thus, Anna's words recall the suicide of her Varronian doublet, even as she laments that of her sister Dido.

The examples discussed above illustrate the way in which Virgil encodes the two speeches of Anna and Dido with allusive references to the alternative Anna–Aeneas tradition. The question remains as to whether or not Virgil incorporates additional traces of the Varronian Anna elsewhere in *Aeneid* 4. Here I suggest that he does, by employing a technique of narrative gemination as a means of reinforcing his allusions to the 'other', Varronian Anna in *Aeneid* 4. In effect, Virgil creates scenarios in which Dido and Anna appear to perform precisely the same action twice, as we will see in the two examples to come. Through this sophisticated technique of allusion, Virgil is able to simultaneously acknowledge and suppress the alternative Varronian version of the story.

The first example of narrative gemination occurs in the depiction of Dido's emotional reaction as she watches the Trojans prepare for departure from Carthage. Virgil describes Dido's compulsion to try once again to change Aeneas's mind:

> ire iterum in lacrimas, iterum temptare precando
> cogitur et **supplex** animos summittere amori,
> ne quid inexpertum frustra moritura relinquat.

> She is compelled a second time to go to tears, a second time to try by entreating and as a suppliant to surrender her spirit to love, in order that she leave nothing untried about to die in vain.
>
> Virg. *A.* 4.413–15

Though Virgil suggests that Dido herself is compelled to take action by plying Aeneas with tears and entreaty as a suppliant, she rather surprisingly asks her sister Anna to approach Aeneas as a suppliant on her behalf: *i, soror, atque hostem* **supplex** *adfare superbum* (Go, sister, and speak to our arrogant guest as a suppliant, Virg. *A.* 4.424). Anna thus performs the very same action Virgil has already ascribed to Dido, thereby creating a sense of repetition and reenactment that is reinforced by the adverb *iterum* (*iterum . . . iterum*, a second time . . . a second time, Virg. *A.* 4.413). Furthermore, Dido's directive to Anna appears in a passage rife with allusions to the alternative Anna–Aeneas tradition, as already discussed above. On the one hand, Virgil's technique of narrative gemination reinforces the subtly allusive nature of his narrative – his lexical cues point the learned audience to the Varronian Anna buried beneath the surface. On the other hand, the technique is also fundamentally suppressive, allowing Virgil to showcase his own narrative focused on Dido.

Another even more striking example of narrative gemination occurs in relation to the construction of the pyre, which will serve as the site of Dido's impassioned suicide. Virgil clearly depicts Dido giving Anna specific instructions for building the pyre:

> tu secreta <u>pyram tecto interiore sub auras</u>
> **erige**, et a̱ṟm̱a̱ viri thalamo quae fixa **reliquit**   495
> impius e̱x̱u̱v̱i̱a̱sque omnis le̱c̱ṯu̱m̱que iugalem,
> quo perii, s̱u̱p̱e̱ṟ imponas.
>
> You in secret raise a pyre in the innermost courtyard beneath the sky, and place on top the arms of the man which he left hung in the bedchamber with no thought of duty and all the things he wore and the marriage bed, which has ruined me.
>
> Virg. *A.* 4.494–7

In the lines that follow, the unsuspecting Anna carries the instructions of Dido out to completion: *ergo iussa parat* (therefore she prepares the orders, Virg. *A.* 4.503).[26] But if Anna has already constructed a pyre as bidden, what explanation can be offered for the passage that immediately follows, in which Dido builds the pyre herself according to precisely the same specifications?:

At regina, <u>pyra penetrali in sede sub auras</u>
erecta ingenti taedis atque ilice secta,   505
intenditque locum sertis et fronde coronat
funerea; <u>super exuvias ensemque</u> **relictum**
effigiemque <u>toro</u> locat haud ignara futuri.

But the queen, when the pyre has been raised in the innermost part of her abode beneath the sky piled huge with pitch-pine and cut oak, hangs the place with garlands and crowns it with funeral foliage; on top she places on the bed the things he wore and the sword he left and an effigy, by no means unaware of what was to come.

Virg. *A.* 4.504–8

Notice the striking parallels of vocabulary and metrical arrangement in the corresponding passages: the almost identical description of the pyre's location (Virg. *A.* 4.494 and 504); matching forms of *erigo* and *relinquo* arranged in the same metrical position (**Virg.** *A.* **4.495 and 505;** *A.* **4.495 and 507**); repetition of *super* after the trihemimeral caesura (Virg. *A.* 4.497 and 507); and the same list of mementos including Aeneas's personal effects and the marriage bed (Virg. *A.* 4.495–6 and 507–8). At first glance, Virgil appears to create an incongruous surplus by having Dido and Anna build precisely the same pyre. But it is precisely through this technique of narrative surplus that Virgil is able to superimpose the intertextually related suicides of his Dido and Varro's Anna. In effect, Dido's actions and words repeatedly emphasize that she is reenacting the role of her Varronian sister. Indeed, her dying words contain one more example of narrative gemination: *moriemur inultae, | sed moriamur* (we will die unavenged, but let us die, Virg. *A.* 4.659–60). The plural verb form is especially striking here as Dido does not normally use the 'royal we' throughout the narrative of *Aeneid* 4 – in this example, the 'unecessary' plural verb echoes with the voices of two suicidal lovers. Thus, in *Aeneid* 4, the superimposed figures of Virgil's Dido and Varro's Anna die together. Taken together with the other *vestigia Varronis*, the examples of narrative gemination allow the different versions of Anna to coexist within Virgil's *Aeneid*; she is Dido's loving and concerned sister, her rival in love, and her suicidal doublet.

Virgil deviates from the alternative version of the story recounted by Varro, in which Anna, not Dido, falls victim to her passion for Aeneas. But although Virgil suppresses the alternative Anna–Aeneas tradition to focus on Dido, he allusively acknowledges the 'other', Varronian Anna in a series of allusions. Through marked language and instances of narrative gemination, Virgil subtly draws attention to his own innovation by recalling the literary path not taken.

Ovid's Allusive Program in *Fasti* 3

Up to this point, I have focused on the ways in which Virgil alludes to the alternative Anna–Aeneas tradition in his depiction of Dido and Anna in *Aeneid* 4. I turn now to an exploration of the impact of Virgil's allusive narrative on Ovid's aetiology of Anna Perenna in *Fasti* 3. Ovid has long enjoyed a reputation as a keenly perceptive reader of Virgil at every stage of his poetic career.[27] He identifies Virgilian passages that have potential for his elegiac poetry, and frequently subjects them to intertextual and intergeneric revision. With this in mind, I shift my focus to the intertextual connections between Virgil's Anna, the sister of Dido, in *Aeneid* 4 and Ovid's Anna Perenna, the fertility goddess, in *Fasti* 3. By analysing Ovid's lexical, generic and thematic interest in the Virgilian model, I aim to reveal his artistic process and his perception of, and relationship to, Virgil as poetic predecessor. As I will show, Ovid positions himself in direct competition with Virgil, adopting his allusive techniques to showcase his own virtuosity and distinguish his own poetic achievements.

In the third book of the *Fasti*, Ovid presents a series of *fabulae* that provide different explanations of the origins and qualities of Anna Perenna (Ov. *Fast.* 3.551–696), the lengthiest of which connects the goddess to Dido's sister Anna (*Fast.* 3.551–656). Ovid's insightful reading of *Aeneid* 4 informs his incarnation of the Carthaginian Anna. Crucial lexical and thematic correspondences between the two texts support two main points: first, Ovid's aetiology of Anna Perenna contains significant allusions to the treatment of Dido and Anna in *Aeneid* 4; and, second, these allusions are evidence of Ovid's recognition of, and response to, Virgil's suppression of the alternative tradition in which Anna, not Dido, was the lover of Aeneas. Hinds has suggested that Ovid capitalizes on the erotic part of Virgil's narrative that can be readily assimilated into his own elegiac Anna Perenna episode.[28] I argue, further, that Ovid exploits Virgil's allusive, fragmentary glimpse of the 'other' Anna within his comprehensive aetiological narrative.

Ovid's engagement with Virgil begins immediately in the proemial introduction to his aetiology of Anna Perenna. Following a short preamble about the merry festivities associated with Anna Perenna (Ov. *Fast.* 3.523–42), Ovid introduces his account of the goddess's origins with a brief programmatic statement: *quae tamen haec dea sit quoniam rumoribus errat, | fabula proposito nulla tegenda meo* (Since who this goddess is varies from rumor to rumor, no account must be buried in my enterprise, Ov. *Fast.* 3.543–4).[29] Latin poets typically utilize proems and introductory passages to establish their place within the existing literary tradition and to make self-conscious declarations of poetic identity and intent.[30] Ovid's introduction to the aetiology of Anna Perenna is no exception. His pointed declaration that no account must be concealed in recounting the origins of Anna Perenna (*nulla fabula tegenda*, Ov. *Fast*. 3.544), underscores the inclusivity of his narrative program. What precisely do I mean by inclusivity? Virgil, as already established, conceals the alternative Anna–Aeneas tradition in *Aeneid* 4, only acknowledging it through subtle allusion. Ovid's approach, by contrast to that of Virgil, is characterized by literary transparency, and he openly juxtaposes competing traditions from other sources like Varro and Virgil, as well as his own previous poetic works. Ovid presents an inclusive and comprehensive series of opposing traditions, and, in a further deviation from Virgil, focuses on the Carthaginian Anna, rather than giving precedence to her sister Dido.

Indeed, Ovid's brief commemoration of Dido immediately following the proem acknowledges Virgil's allusive suppression of the alternative Anna–Aeneas tradition and effectively dismisses Dido from his own narrative:

> <u>arserat</u> Aeneae Dido miserabilis **igne**, 545
>   <u>arserat</u> **exstructis** in sua fata <u>**rogis**</u>,
> compositusque cinis, tumulique in marmore carmen
>   hoc breve, quod **moriens** ipsa reliquit, erat:
> PRAEBUIT AENEAS ET CAUSAM MORTIS ET **ENSEM**:
>   IPSA SUA DIDO CONCIDIT VSA **MANV**. 550

Poor Dido had burned with fire for Aeneas, had burned on pyres built for her own doom, and her ashes were collected, and upon the marble slab of her tomb was this short epigram, which she herself left while dying: AENEAS GAVE BOTH THE REASON FOR DEATH AND THE SWORD: DIDO HERSELF FELL DEAD HAVING USED HER OWN HAND.

Ov. Fast. 3.545–50

The epitaphic passage contains a series of unmistakable lexical echoes of the passage from *Aeneid* 4 in which Anna makes her final speech to Dido:

> 'hoc illud, germana, fuit? me fraude petebas? 675
> hoc **rogus** iste mihi, hoc **ignes** araeque parabant?
> quid primum deserta querar? comitemne sororem
> sprevisti **moriens**? eadem me **ad fata** vocasses,
> idem ambas **ferro** dolor atque eadem hora tulisset.
> his etiam **struxi manibus** patriosque vocavi 680
> voce deos, sic te ut posita, crudelis, abessem?

exstinxti te meque, soror, populumque patresque
Sidonios urbemque tuam.'

'This, then, was that, sister? You were targeting me with your deception? Was it this that pyre of yours for me, this was what the fires and altars were preparing? What first shall I, abandoned, lament? Have you scorned by dying a sister's companionship? You should have summoned me to the same fate, the same sword-wrought agony and the same hour should have taken us both. With these hands I, too, built a pyre and called upon the ancestral gods with my voice, just so I could be away, cruel one, as you lay thus? You have killed you and me sister, and the people and the Sidonian fathers and your own city.'

Virg. A. 4.675–83

Through a series of direct repetitions and lexical parallels, Ovid echoes in his commemoration of Dido the words uttered by the Virgilian Anna in *Aeneid* 4: *ignis* (Ov. *Fast.* 3.545, Virg. *A.* 4.676); *rogus* (Ov. *Fast.* 3.546, Virg. *A.* 4.676); *moriens* (Ov. *Fast.* 3.548, Virg. *A.* 4.678); *manus* (Ov. *Fast.* 3.550, Virg. *A.* 4.680); *exstruo/struo* (Ov. *Fast.* 3.546, Virg. *A.* 4.680); *in sua fata/ad fata* (Ov. *Fast.* 3.546, Virg. *A.* 4.678); and *ensis/ferrum* (Ov. *Fast.* 3.549, Virg. *A.* 4.679). Ovid's imitative composition shows an intense engagement precisely with the speech of Anna in which Virgil superimposes the identical suicides of Dido and her Varronian sister, as discussed above. What is more, Ovid indicates in the opening couplet of his passage that he recognizes Virgil's technique of narrative gemination. His marked repetition of the verb *arserat* in the prominent first position of the hexameter and pentameter lines (*arserat* … | *arserat*, she had burned … | she had burned, Ov. *Fast.* 3.545–6), taken together with the plural phrase *exstructis rogis* (pyres built, Ov. *Fast.* 3.546), evokes the two identical pyres built by Anna and Dido in *Aeneid* 4. Ovid thus makes a deliberate and self-conscious allusion to Virgil's treatment of competing traditions, in order to underscore his own explicitly inclusive program.

Ovid further distinguishes his treatment of Anna from that of Virgil through the incorporation of the commemorative epitaph for Dido: PRAEBUIT AENEAS ET CAUSAM MORTIS ET ENSEM: | IPSA SUA DIDO CONCIDIT VSA MANV (AENEAS GAVE BOTH THE REASON FOR DEATH AND THE SWORD: DIDO HERSELF FELL DEAD HAVING USED HER OWN HAND. Ov. *Fast.* 3.549–50). Whereas Virgil conceals the 'other' Anna to focus on Dido, Ovid utilizes the epitaph to dismiss Dido decisively from his aetiological narrative. The couplet replicates directly the final couplet from Ovid's *Heroides* 7 (Ov. *Ep.* 7.195–6). In its original context of Dido's poetic epistle to *Aeneid*, the epitaphic couplet, resonant of death, functions as a strong closural marker. Ovid's inclusion of the couplet here in *Fasti* 3 not only underscores his program of inclusivity, yet another source incorporated into his tapestry, but also emphasizes his decision to focus on Anna: the epitaphic gesture effectively bids Dido *adieu* as Ovid prepares to write extensively about her sister.

Ovid's Carthaginian Anna

With his poetic aims established, Ovid proceeds to tell the story of Anna following the death of Dido. Throughout the lengthy narrative, Ovid incorporates aspects of Anna's Varronian and Virgilian counterparts, as well as her ill-fated sister Dido. Furthermore, Ovid's sustained thematic focus on sisterhood, recognition and erotic conflict hearken back to Virgil's allusive configuration of Anna and Dido as intertextual rivals for the affections of Aeneas. Two passages, in particular, exemplify Ovid's thematic and artistic engagement with the Virgilian Dido–Anna narrative in *Aeneid* 4: Anna's performance of funeral rites for Dido (Ov. *Fast*. 3.559–64); and Aeneas's recognition of Anna in Latium (Ov. *Fast*. 3.605–12).

After the death of Dido in *Fasti* 3, Iarbas invades Carthage, ever mindful of his spurned Virgilian self (*seque memor spretum*, remembering that he was spurned, Ov. *Fast*. 3.553).[31] When the Mauritanian king occupies the palace of Dido, Anna is driven from her home in tears:

> pellitur Anna domo, lacrimansque sororia linquit
>   moenia; germanae iusta dat ante suae.   560
> mixta bibunt molles lacrimis unguenta favillae,
>   vertice libatas accipiuntque comas,
> terque 'vale' dixit, cineres ter ad ora relatos
>   pressit, et est illis visa subesse soror.

> Anna is driven from home, and weeping she leaves the walls of her sister; first she performs funeral rites for her own sister. The soft ashes drink unguents mixed with tears, and they receive locks cut from the head as an offering, and three times she said 'Farewell', three times she drew the ashes back and pressed them to her lips, and her sister seemed to lie concealed in them.
>
> Ov. *Fast*. 3.559–64

As Ovid turns his focus to Anna, he avoids mentioning Dido by name, thereby fulfilling the programmatic promise of his proemial farewell to the Carthaginian queen. But his emphatic repetition of terms related to sisterhood – '*sororia*' (Ov. *Fast*. 3.559); '*germanae ... suae*' (3.560); '*soror*' (3.564) – serve as a persistent reminder of the kinship of Anna and Dido. Interactions between Anna and Dido in *Aeneid* 4, as I have already suggested, are precisely where Virgil tends to embed allusive traces of the Varronian Anna.

Ovid, in Anna's final farewell to Dido, uses additional lexical cues to link his account directly to the very passages in *Aeneid* 4 that feature Virgil's complex negotiation of the alternative Anna–Aeneas tradition. Ovid's repetition of the adverb *ter* (*ter*, three times, Ov. *Fast.* 563) in the description of the funeral rites undertaken by Anna is particularly significant. In *Aeneid* 4, *ter* appears in only two passages, which are precisely those in which Virgil's Dido and the 'other' Anna coexist, namely the planning and execution of suicide. The first passage depicts Dido performing rites immediately after constructing the 'second' pyre:

> stant arae circum et crinis effusa sacerdos
> **ter** centum tonat ore deos, Erebumque Chaosque
> **ter**geminamque Hecaten, tria virginis ora Dianae.
>
> The altars stand all around and the priestess with streaming hair invokes with thundering voice three hundred gods, Erebus and Chaos and threefold Hecate, the three faces of maiden Diana.
>
> Virg. *A.* 4.509–11

In the second, Dido repeatedly struggles to arise in the agonizing depiction of her final death throes:

> **ter** sese attollens cubitoque adnixa levavit;
> **ter** revoluta toro est.
>
> Raising herself three times and leaning upon her elbow she arose, three times she rolled back on the bed.
>
> Virg. *A.* 4.690–1

The similar duplication of *ter* in Ovid creates a verbal echo that strikingly confirms the intertextual connection between his Carthaginian sisters and their Virgilian antecedents. This strategic lexical choice serves two purposes: it prompts the learned audience to recall the Virgilian model; and, in doing so, it sparks a comparative and metaliterary interpretation of Ovid's text that ultimately reveals his innovative approach. Indeed, the intertextual resonance of Anna's ritual behaviour in *Fasti* 3 imbues the phrase *est illis visa subesse soror* (her sister seemed to lie concealed in them, Ov. *Fast.* 3.564) with two levels of meaning: it describes, on the one hand, the memory of Dido as embedded in her ashes; but it is also a metaliterary expression of Ovid's allusive recognition of the Varronian sister lurking beneath the surface of *Aeneid* 4.[32]

Ovid's subsequent description of Anna's naval journey is a dizzying display of intertextual virtuosity. Through her exilic flight, naval journey and shipwreck, Anna becomes a doublet for both the Virgilian Dido and Aeneas.[33] Her ultimate arrival in Latium and the recognition scene that follows provide Ovid with another opportunity to engage in metaliterary play with Virgil's suppressive allusions to the Varronian Anna in *Aeneid* 4. As Aeneas traverses the shores of Latium with his faithful companion Achates, he catches sight of the wandering Anna:

> litore dotali solo comitatus Achate
>   secretum nudo dum pede carpit iter,
> aspicit errantem, nec credere sustinet Annam   605
>   esse: quid in Latios illa veniret agros?
> dum secum Aeneas, 'Anna est!' exclamat Achates:
>   ad nomen voltus sustulit illa suos.
> heu, quid agat? fugiat? quos terrae quaerat hiatus?
>   ante oculos miserae fata sororis erant.   610
> Sensit et adloquitur trepidam Cythereius heros
>   (flet tamen admonitu motus, Elissa, tui).

While he, accompanied by only Achates, pursues a remote path with bare foot along the shore given as dowry, he sees her wandering, and cannot bear to believe that it is Anna: why would that one come into the domain of Latium? While Aeneas ponders to himself, Achates cries out 'It is Anna!' She raised her countenance(s) at her name. Alas, what should she do? Should she flee? What cleft in the earth should she seek? Before [Anna's/their/ our] eyes were the fates of her wretched sister. The Cytherean hero perceived her agitation and addresses her (yet he weeps moved by the reminder of you, Elissa).

Ov. Fast. 3.605–12

Ovid describes Aeneas as 'accompanied by only Achates' (*solo comitatus Achate*, Ov. *Fast.* 3.603) utilizing virtually the same formulation that appeared in *Aeneid* 1, when the shipwrecked Trojan commander traversed the lands of Carthage with Achates shortly before his fateful first meeting with Dido: *ipse uno graditur comitatus Achate* (he himself proceeds accompanied by only Achates, Virg. *A.* 1.312). Through the Virgilian reminiscence, Ovid acknowledges the very model he now reconfigures: Anna, not Aeneas, plays the role of stranded refugee; and Aeneas is about to encounter, not Dido, but her sister Anna.

Aeneas, initially unable to recognize the post-Virgilian Anna, ponders with great perplexity her arrival in Latium, until Achates confirms her identity: 'It is Anna!' ('*Anna est!*', Ov. *Fast.* 3.607). When Anna reacts to the sound of her name, Ovid borrows the Virgilian technique of narrative gemination, by having her raise not one but two countenances: *ad nomen voltus sustulit illa suos* (she raised her countenance(s) at her name, Ov. *Fast.* 3.608). In *Aeneid* 4, Virgil uses seemingly incongruous plural forms to superimpose his Dido on Varro's Anna, as I have already shown through the key example of *moriemur inultae | sed moriamur* (we will die unavenged, but let us die, Virg. *A.* 4.659–60). Ovid, in turn, adopts the same technique in his description of Anna's double countenance, thereby recalling the superimposed identities of Dido and Anna in the Virgilian model. Ovid's allusive play within the context of a passage focused on identity and recognition is a subtle, yet pointed, acknowledgment of and reaction to Virgil's treatment of the Carthaginian sisters. The inability of Aeneas and Anchises to recognize Anna corresponds to the disorienting effects of Ovid's multi-layered treatment of Anna, who variously reprises the roles of her Virgilian incarnation, Dido, and Aeneas himself.

In the lines that follow, a series of three questions plays further with the reconfigured identities of Anna, Dido and Aeneas in Ovid's narrative: *heu, quid agat? fugiat? quos terrae quaerat hiatus?* (Alas, what should she do? Should she flee? What cleft in the earth should she seek?, Ov. *Fast.* 3.609). The first of the three questions evokes Aeneas's distressed contemplation upon realizing that he must leave Dido in pursuit of Italy after the visitation of Mercury in *Aeneid* 4: *heu quid agat? quo nunc reginam ambire furentem | audeat adfatu? quae prima exordia sumat?* (alas, what should he do? with what speech now should he dare to solicit the raging queen? what first threads of speech should he begin with?, Virg. *A.* 4.283–4). Thus, Anna's agitated reaction to her reunion with Aeneas recalls his abandonment of Dido and the dissolution of the love affair that leads to the tragic end of *Aeneid* 4, the love affair in which Anna herself played the starring role in the alternative Varronian tradition. Ovid further stresses the connection to Virgil's narrative in the line that follows: *ante oculos miserae fata sororis erant* (before [Anna's/their/our] eyes were the fates of her wretched sister, Ov. *Fast.* 3.610). Before the eyes of Anna herself, of Aeneas and Achates and of Ovid's audience unfolds an encounter that reverberates with the memory of Virgil's Dido and the terrible fate she shared with her Varronian sister. True to form, Ovid adopts specific language and techniques to signal his recognition of, and poetic response to, Virgil's treatment of Dido and Anna in *Aeneid* 4.

In the speech that follows, Aeneas briefly outlines his affair with Dido (*Fast.* 3.613–24): his erotic loitering in Carthage; Dido's death; and his encounter with her shade in the underworld. By way of conclusion, I want to examine the final couplet of this speech in relation to Ovid's engagement with Virgil in *Fasti* 3. I have argued that Ovid, throughout his depiction of the Carthaginian Anna up to this point, engages in sustained engagement with Virgil. Ovid's own multi-layered and multi-generic narrative is a model of inclusivity, designed to respond to Virgil's allusive suppression of the Varronian Anna in *Aeneid* 4. Unlike Virgil, who relegates the alternative Anna–Aeneas tradition to his allusive backdrop, Ovid draws an explicit intertextual connection between his innovative new Anna and her Virgilian counterparts. Through the voice of the reminiscing Aeneas, Ovid once again makes an overt reference to Virgil's Dido and her narrative progression from lover of Aeneas to voiceless shade in *Aeneid* 1, 4 and 6. Within the final couplet of the speech, a pledge from Aeneas to Dido, Ovid once again allusively acknowledges the importance of his Virgilian model:

> multa tibi memores, nil non debemus Elissae:
> nomine grata tuo, grata sororis, eris.
>
> [Remembering/reminding] we owe many things to you, everything to Elissa: by your own name you will be beloved, beloved (by the name) of your sister.
>
> Ov. *Fast.* 3.623–4

Ovid here deploys the Virgilian technique of narrative gemination with intensified poet self-consciousness. The first-person plural *debemus* (we owe, Ov. *Fast.* 3.623) and the plural *memores* (remembering/reminding, Ov. *Fast.* 3.623) give the couplet a multidimensional resonance: the voice of Aeneas expresses a remembrance of the past and proclaims his indebtedness to both Anna and Dido, his two former lovers in the coexisting traditions; and the voice of Ovid declares his literary debt to the Virgilian Anna and Dido in a new version of the story that repeatedly reminds us of its intertextual engagement with the *Aeneid* and its sources.[34] In the final line of the speech, Aeneas assures Anna that she will be deemed *grata* (beloved) both on her own merit and that of her sister Dido. Through Aeneas's repetitive utterance (*grata … grata*, Ov. *Fast.* 3.624), Ovid likewise distinguishes his own Anna, while acknowledging the literary importance of her Virgilian sister.

My examination of key passages from *Aeneid* 4 and *Fasti* 3 demonstrates the ways in which Ovid encodes his aetiology with a poetic riposte to Virgil's technique of allusive suppression. Ovid adopts and repurposes Virgilian language and narrative gemination to assert his own artistic vision: his inclusive project exhumes what lies buried in the *Aeneid*. In my approach, I have been far from exhaustive, since a comprehensive survey of the Virgilian and Ovidian texts would far outstrip the confines of this chapter. Rather, my aim has been to unearth in *Fasti* 3 something of the fundamental nature of Ovid's engagement with Virgil, which may assist with the ongoing interpretation of the aetiology of Anna Perenna. Indeed, figures like king Battus, aware of the misfortunes of 'either sister' (*qui postquam didicit casus utriusque sororis*, who after he has learned of the downfalls of either sister, Ov. *Fast*. 3.571) and Lavinia, who is entreated by Aeneas to love Anna like a sister (*quam precor ut carae more sororis ames*, whom I beg you to love in the manner of a beloved sister, Ov. *Fast*. 3.632) even as she succumbs to a Dido-esque jealousy, seem to provide further evidence of the Ovidian strategies discussed here. Ovid's rivalrous and revisionary reinterpretation of the mytho-legendary Carthaginian Anna results in an echo chamber of multilayered allusions, reflecting back to Virgil's *Aeneid* and beyond. The intensely intertextual exposition of Anna is a revelatory achievement, which brings to light Ovid's own incisive and innovative poetics and those of Virgil before him.

2

Calendar Girl: Anna Perenna Between the *Fasti* and the *Punica**

James S. McIntyre

Anna Perenna is characterized by ambiguity and 'betweenness': she fits between Dido and Aeneas, Rome and Carthage, the human and the divine. Moreover, in Roman poetry, Anna fits between Virgil's imperial *Aeneid* and Ovid's more obviously subversive *Fasti*.[1] With his post-Augustan epic *Punica*, Silius Italicus draws upon this sense of 'betweenness' to insert his work into a Roman literary tradition that includes Lucan's historical epic on the civil war in addition to Virgil and Ovid. Following Ovid by sequelizing Virgil, Silius inserts Anna's story into the eighth book of his poem in an apparent digression describing the manner in which Anna of Carthage becomes the venerated Roman goddess of the new year. In this extended episode, Anna is sent by Juno to renew Hannibal's enthusiasm for war with the Romans prior to the battle of Cannae (Sil. 8.25–43; 202–41). The battle itself occupies a central point in the poem across the ninth and tenth books of Silius's seventeen-book poem, even though it takes place only in the second of seventeen years of the Second Punic War (218–201 BCE).[2] Cannae is the centrepiece of the poem and Anna is crucial in ensuring that it takes place, becoming prominent as the Romans reach their lowest ebb during the conflict. Yet despite her pivotal role and position, in many ways the Anna of the *Punica* remains unplaced and ambiguous, on the margins and in-between. Although clearly contextualized by her appearance in the *Aeneid*, dominant here is an Ovidian *Punica* that draws upon the *Fasti*'s playful subversion of Virgil 'in a dynamic interaction that … utilizes their contrasting poetics to add vigor, variety and a thematic complexity to his own belated epic'.[3] The long digression in *Punica* 8 on the means by which Anna Perenna came to be worshipped as a native Italian goddess is indicative of the interplay between Silius's literary antecedents, such as Virgil and Ovid, as well as the paradoxes, contradictions and ambiguities that characterize his own version of the war and its heroes. Through an intertextual engagement with the *Fasti*, Silius casts doubt on Rome's ascent to world power,[4] suggesting uncertainty, misinformation, faulty memory, misunderstanding and distrust. As such, the in-betweenness of Anna Perenna allows Silius to demonstrate a narrative and moral ambiguity that lies at the heart of Rome's victory over Carthage and ascent to world domination.[5]

Anna's In-Betweenness

Anna's role in the *Aeneid* appears minor, her in-betweenness signified by her role as an intermediary and confidante for Dido. She remains on the margins of surviving Roman literature: even when foregrounded, stories of the goddess's origins vary, with Ovid's *Fasti* famously relating several distinct versions. Even the details of Carthaginian Anna's relationship with Dido and Aeneas diverge significantly according to the sources.[6] Of the most extensive treatments that connect Anna of Carthage to the Roman goddess, the *Fasti* and *Punica* stand out;[7] Ovid's in particular for the vitality and variety of origins he provides for the goddess, and for the manner in which Anna facilitates an exploration of the Ides of March (Anna Perenna's festival day) and Caesar's murder.[8] Both the narratives of the *Fasti* and *Punica* show Anna incorporated into the story of the Trojans' establishment in Italy and embedded within Roman space. In a sense, despite her marginality and her Carthaginian otherness,[9] she becomes emplaced within the Roman landscape and according to the *Fasti* and the *Punica* perennial Anna becomes a figure of stability, a goddess of renewal connected to Rome's origins. The celebration of Anna's festival in a nearby grove made firm for ancient Romans and modern readers alike the goddess's place within the city;[10] yet at the same time, Ovid and Silius undermine the secure underpinnings of her identity and subvert the mythological and heroic narratives that associate her with Rome's foundation.

Unsurprisingly, the episode of the *Punica* in which Anna features is underexplored compared to Ovid's version,[11] yet it too offers opportunities to understand the place of paradoxical, perennial Anna, whose stability stands in contrast to her own variable and mixed identities, a Roman goddess and a Carthaginian sister.[12] Criticism has not been kind to Silius's poem: although praised by Martial,[13] Pliny's comment that the poem was written *maiore cura quam ingenio* has had greater influence amongst scholars and critics.[14] A common critical perception has been that the *Punica* represents a mundane celebration of Roman power, an inferior and prolix 'hymn to the goddess Rome' whose seventeen books represent a monotonous and uninspired reading of

Virgil's *Aeneid* that fails to go beyond that poem's apparent pro-Augustan level;[15] the work's singular nature gives rise not only to conflicting assessments of its aesthetic value, but also to disparate appraisals of its themes and ideological stance. Variously the poem has been judged to be unabashedly pro-Roman,[16] or subject to more ambiguous readings that suggest a subversive outlook on imperial expansion that challenges ideas of Roman greatness.[17]

More recent assessments of the *Punica* demand that the poem be appreciated for its place within the Roman historical epic tradition stretching back to Ennius, as well as for its broader intertextual importance. In the former sense, Silius can be understood to be at the very least a competent practitioner of a mode of literature for which we have little comparative evidence against which to judge his ability to innovate; moreover, the poem is unique among extant literature in being a versified adaptation of a prose historical source, in this case the third decade of Livy's *Ab Urbe Condita*.[18] On an intertextual level, as well as the clear relation to the poetry of Virgil and Ovid, Silius engages with the work of Lucan and the *Punica* functions to bridge – to go between – the mythological settlement of the Trojans in Italy which follows their quasi-civil war with the native Italians and the conflict between Caesar and the Roman Senate described in Lucan's *Bellum Civile*.[19] While ostensibly concerned with Rome's heroic victory in the Second Punic War, there is enough discord between the Romans to suggest that they have not a little in common with the more self-destructive late Republic. In this sense the *Punica* connects the murder of Turnus by Aeneas to Lucan's depiction of the death of the Republic with the rise of Caesar and his autocratic successors. Silius's portrayal of Anna's arrival in Italy, recently settled by the Trojans, directly connects the poem to the aftermath of the *Aeneid*, as well as to Aeneas's sojourn in Italy in the second book of Virgil's poem.

Although episodes within this long poem engender readings on pro-imperial lines, Silius's co-option of Anna Perenna and engagement with Ovid privilege a more equivocal reading of the work to suggest ambivalence and ambiguity as well as mistrust and misunderstanding among allies. While an apparent digression from the main narrative movement of the poem, Anna is a catalyst without whom Cannae – and subsequent developments in Roman history – will not take place. On the margins and yet in the middle of things, Anna performs a fundamental task for Juno with her encouragement of Hannibal, becoming responsible for ensuring that the battle takes place. Moreover, Anna and the celebration of her feast cannot easily be untangled from the murder of Julius Caesar on the Ides of March, 44 BCE and her presence in the poem is a reminder of more recent civil strife.[20] Book 8 of the *Punica* recognizes the means by which

Anna Perenna becomes embedded within the religious landscape of the city, but the goddess is made ambiguous by the wider connotations of her prior appearances in Roman literature and by the connection she establishes between the arrival of Aeneas in Carthage, the antagonism between the Romans and their most dangerous imperial competition, and the career and demise of the Trojan's most famous descendant.

Anna at Cannae

The *Punica* is poetically and thematically structured around Rome's defeat at Cannae,[21] and the battle is foreshadowed and takes place across books eight, nine and ten: the midpoint of his seventeen book epic.[22] Cannae becomes the central moment of Rome's historical narrative as well as Silius's poem, which occupies a place within an epic cycle of Roman history in-between Virgil's *Aeneid* and Lucan's concluding portrayal of Caesar's ascent to power in the *Bellum Civile*.[23] By bringing her into his narrative of the battle, Silius makes Anna an explicit link between (and in-between) the *Aeneid* and the establishment of the Trojans in Italy and the murder of Caesar on the Ides of March. In so doing, Anna herself becomes an intertextual marker denoting the place of the battle of Cannae in the schema of Roman history and connecting the battle to the wider mytho-historical framework detailing the origins of the Romans established through the *Aeneid* and refracted through the lens of Ovid's calendrical *Fasti*. Anna not only draws attention to the importance of the battle but as the tool of Juno she is fundamental to the occurrence of Cannae, a critical juncture between the foundation of Rome and the rise of its empire. Without Anna, there is no Cannae: indeed, Silius's wordplay embeds ANNA (encouraging her kinsman HANNibal) within the very battle of CANNAe itself:[24]

> praescia CANNArum Iuno atque elata futuris.
> namque hac accitam stagnis Laurentibus ANNAm...
>
> Juno foresaw Cannae and the future and took pride in things to come. Fetching Anna from the Laurentine river...
>
> Sil. 8.27–8

Picking up prior examples of wordplay from both the *Aeneid* and the *Fasti* adds emphasis to Anna and her role: in the *Aeneid* Virgil plays upon the names of ANNA and AENEAS in book 4 to establish Anna as a go-between for and counterpart to Dido and Aeneas;[25] while the *Fasti* juxtaposes Anna with Aeneas as a wandering exile.[26] Perennial Anna is a goddess of the year (*ANNus*) and a fitting subject for an extended etymological treatment in Ovid's *Fasti* – extended, at least, compared with the passing description of Caesar's death on the Ides of March.[27]

Ovid's *Fasti* narrates the tale of Anna's arrival in Italy at length, but it is an ambivalent and ambiguous account that problematizes the very notion of fixed and stable origins. Although pre-eminent in terms of length, the story of Dido's sister arriving in Italy is only one of several options characterized as rumours:

quae tamen haec dea sit, quoniam rumoribus errat,
   fabula, proposito nulla tegenda meo.

Yet who this goddess is, as rumours abound, my intention is to uncover her tale.

Ov. *Fast.* 3.543–4

After giving five varying origins for the goddess, of which the story of Anna Perenna and Dido is first and most extensive, Ovid commences his sixth version with an explicit claim that this final telling is the truth.[28] The true story is that Anna is an elderly woman from Bovillae who gave cakes to plebeians and who was honoured by them with a statue (Ov. *Fast.* 3.661–74), *haec quoque, quam referam, nostras pervenit ad aures / fama nec a veri dissidet illa fide* (Another story, which I will tell, has come to our ears that does not disagree with the truth, 3.661–2). Brief, dependent on hearsay and folk memory, this is the only version that Ovid credits as being closest to accuracy.

Although Silius claims to have narrowed the sources for Anna's origin down to a single myth, to be told in brief, he recalls Ovid by clearly signaling the depth and ambiguity of the tale:

multa retro rerum iacet atque ambagibus aevi
obtegitur densa caligine mersa vetustas,
cur Sarrana dicent Oenotri numina templo
regnisque Aeneadum germana colatur Elissae.
sed pressis stringam revocatam ab origine famam
narrandi metis breviterque antiqua revolvam.

Far in the past and concealed by thick gloom by the mystery of time, lies the reason why the Italians dedicate a temple to a Carthaginian goddess, and why the sister of Dido is worshiped in the kingdom of the Romans. But I will recall the story from its beginnings, draw tight limits and briefly recall antiquity.

Sil. 8.44–9

Adopting an Ovidian commitment to tell the story *ab origine* (and placing an emphasis on *fama*), Silius nevertheless foregrounds uncertainty and doubt, and acknowledges that there is a paradox in the Romans worshiping a goddess aligned with their greatest enemies. Silius engages in wordplay in this passage as he asks why Dido's sister (*germANA*) is worshiped by the Italians, despite being of Carthaginian origin (*SarrANA*):[29] AN[N]A is embedded among her family and the Romans, her adopted people. Anna herself acknowledges this identity crisis, obeying Juno's request but understanding that she also owes an allegiance to the Romans: *quamquam inter Latios Annae stet numen honores* (even though the deity of Anna stands among those honoured by the Romans, Sil. 8.43).

Given her ambiguous origins and conflicted loyalties, Anna may therefore seem an unusual figure for Silius to use to anchor Cannae within a Roman mythic narrative of *cosmos* and *imperium*. However, this note of ambiguity carries through to the battle of Cannae and Rome's ultimate victory in the Second Punic War and gives both their own ambivalence. Anna and Cannae become part of the teleological trajectory of Roman imperial history, and while this may ultimately offer the foundation for *imperium sine fine*,[30] Roman victory also suggests the seeds of the Republic's undoing.[31] Just as Anna has trouble defining her loyalties, the Romans too are characterized by paradox.[32] It is their weakest moments that validate their eventual victory:[33] *propriusque fuere periclo, / quis superare datum* (and they came closer to destruction, those to whom victory was given, Sil. 1.13–14).[34] The fight back against Carthage begins with a refusal to fight (and it is notable that the Anna's origins are described just as the Romans are discussing whether they should engage Hannibal, or if they should continue what has been a relatively successful strategy of delay as enacted in previous books by Fabius Cunctator). Moreover, although Jupiter has enough confidence in the Romans to make the claim that following this war against Hannibal, not even internal conflict can destroy them (Sil. 3.588–90),[35] he also claims that he is deliberately setting events that might destroy Rome in motion as a means of testing his favoured city. Finally, while the glory of the Roman army preserves the Republic, it lays the foundation for the accumulation of honours by individual soldiers and generals such as Scipio, leading inadvertently to the concentration of power and the struggles of the late Republic,[36] the civil wars and the rise of Caesar.

Even as they are ambiguous, origins are crucial to Silius's poem. The *Punica* has its roots in Virgil's portrayal of Juno's antagonism towards Rome in the face of Jupiter's desire to prove the city's superiority,[37] and this provides her motivation to dispatch Anna on her mission to give encouragement to Hannibal (Sil. 8.25–38).

As she does so the goddess gives explicit voice to her hatred for the Romans and desire to see them destroyed at Cannae, a scene parallelling her use of Allecto to foment discord between the Trojans and Italians in Book 7 of the *Aeneid*. Throughout the *Punica* Silius makes much of the Virgilian links between Rome and Carthage, and Aeneas, Dido and Anna.[38] In his first book Silius enumerates the historical motivation for the war (Sil. 1.1–16) before elaborating on the mythical origin of Roman and Carthaginian hostilities following Aeneas's betrayal of Dido in *Aeneid* 4 (Sil. 1.17–37). It is within the narration of these mythological *causae* that the *ira* of Juno triggers the action of the epic (*causus irarum*, Sil. 1.17),[39] as Juno sets herself and the city of Carthage against Rome (Sil. 1.26–33) and embeds the *Punica* firmly within the mytho-cosmic framework established by the *Aeneid*.[40] However, in what functions as a model for the conflicted response of Anna to the betrayal of her Roman worshipers in favour of her Carthaginian relations, Silius's Juno is self-contradictory: although indebted to a Virgilian model that attributes to the goddess the poem's motivation, the portrayal of Juno is inconsistent with the resolution of the *Aeneid* and the goddess's reconciliation with Jupiter and his ambitions for the Roman people (Virg. *A*. 12.829–42). According to Silius, Juno's antagonism is strongest after Rome's foundation and early expansion:[41] Juno admits that Rome's *imperium* may proceed, but only after the city has paid a price in blood and she foresees the disasters of the Ticinus, Trebia, Trasimene and Cannae (Sil. 1.45–55).[42] As such Silius sets Juno in parallel with her Virgilian precursor as a motivational force for the poem but intertextually exploits the tensions between the model offered by the conclusion of the *Aeneid* and the *Punica*'s presentation of her favour towards Carthage. Juno knows that she cannot win this battle with ordained fate: *hunc audet solum componere fatis* ([Hannibal] alone she dared to match against fate, Sil. 1.38–9).

Silius is clear that Juno is motivated by the events of the *Aeneid*, and this is reinforced by numerous textual parallels between the topography of Carthage in both poems. Yet Silius subverts the welcoming and attractive perspective that greets Aeneas at the grove and temple of Juno, recently founded by Dido. Aeneas arrives to find a *locus amoenus*: *Lucus in urbe fuit media, laetissimus umbrae* (In the centre of the city was grove, rich with shade, Virg. *A*. 1.441.). By the time of Hannibal's oath against Rome, the temple of Dido has become grim and murky:

> urbe fuit media sacrum genetricis Elissae
> manibus et patria Tyriis formidine cultum,
> quod taxi circum et piceae squalentibus umbris
> abdiderant caelique arcebant lumine, templum.

In the center of the city was a temple, sacred to the spirit of Elissa the foundress
and worshiped with native awe by the Tyrians, around which were yews and
pines with gloomy shade, which hid it and kept out the light of heaven.

Sil. 1.81–4

Aeneas and his followers find welcome in a landscape of most pleasant shade (*laetissimus umbrae*), but Dido's temple (standing at the very location where she killed herself, Sil. 1.85–6) is characterized by gloomy shade in which unknown and frightening noises escape from the underworld and are emitted from the earth (*squalentibus umbris*, Sil. 1.83; *immugit tellus rumpitque horrenda per umbras / sibila*, Sil. 1.95–6). In place of the ecphrasis in Juno's temple glorifying the Trojans' battle with the Greeks (Virg. A. 1.453–93), the temple of Dido instead recalls the gloomy history of Carthage's relations with Rome. Beneath the statue of Dido sits the Trojan sword, given to her by Aeneas and with which she killed herself (Sil. 1.91; Virg. A. 4.646–7, 664), and the statue itself sweats in the face of underworld spirits called by witchcraft (Sil. 1.97–8). The intense, hellish landscape surrounding them is a physical reminder of Juno's desire to move Hell in her service (*Acheronta movebo*, Virg. A. 7.312). Here, the witches in the service of Dido's temple have called Hell to the surface on her behalf (*Acheronta vocat*, Sil. 1.94), and here Hannibal's father encourages him to swear an oath against the Romans, providing the true genesis of his enthusiastic hatred of Rome (Sil. 1.100–5). In both the *Aeneid* and the *Punica* Juno attempts to delay the fated rise of Rome, yet Silius's poem is dependent on Juno having forgotten – or reneged upon – her commitment to Jupiter to change her mind (*adnuit his Iuno et mentem laetata retorsit*, Virg. A. 12.841). Anna, like Juno, appears to have questionable motives and despite both goddesses' veneration by Rome they are willing to sacrifice Romans in favour of Hannibal and his armies. Juno directly asks for Anna's help, whereupon her Carthaginian and Roman halves of her identity are put into conflict:[43]

tum diva Indigetis castis contermina lucis
'haud' inquit 'tua ius nobis praecepta morari.
sit fas, sit tantum, quaeso, retinere favorem
antiquae patriae mandataque magna sororis,
quamquam inter Latios Annae stet numen honores.'

Then the goddess, beside the sacred grove of the Indigenous God, replied: 'My duty is to obey your orders without delay. I ask only that I may keep the favor of my ancient homeland, and to carry out the great requests of my sister even though the deity of Anna stands among those honored by the Romans.'

Sil. 8.39–43

This passage physically locates Anna by the banks of the Numicius, close to the site of Aeneas's deification as the *Indiges* (and of a temple dedicated to Jupiter Indiges).[44] In the context of Juno's mission to Anna the reference to Numicius recalls Ovid's *Fasti* 3 and foreshadows the forthcoming aetiological narrative of Anna's own deification. Anna and Aeneas are doubles: both are Roman gods, and both inhabit the same landscape by the Numicius;[45] and, moreover, both are refugees fleeing the destruction of their home, shipwrecked, and washed up on the shores of a new kingdom.[46] Yet Anna, unlike Aeneas, breaks her compact with the Romans at Juno's prompting. Her response may be conflicted and her assistance to Juno may be appropriate, but it also serves her own self-interest: to maintain the goodwill of Carthage and Juno while also continuing to be venerated by the Romans.[47] Anna's willingness to help Juno and Hannibal, despite her position as a Roman goddess, reflects internal Roman dissent and potential internal strife.[48] While reiterating the centrality of the suicide of Virgil's Dido to the Second Punic War, Silius contextualizes Cannae as a fundamental event in the progress of Roman history, not only in terms of the Virgilian *telos* of *imperium sine fine*, but also towards internal discord and self-interest that will lead to civil conflict as depicted by Lucan's *Bellum Civile*.

Rewriting Anna

Silius narrates Anna's flight from Carthage, modelling his text closely on book 3 of the *Fasti*. In both poems, Anna departs Carthage and is subsequently shipwrecked in Italy, where despite her fears, she is welcomed by Aeneas (Ov. *Fast.* 3.545–600; Sil. 8.59–68). In both poems Anna seeks shelter with a king named Battus (Ov. *Fast.* 3.570; Sil. 8.57), and she is driven from shelter in each version by Battus's fear of Pygmalion (Ov. *Fast.* 3.574; Sil. 8.64). Yet Silius begins to diverge from his model: in the *Fasti* Anna is given safe haven on the island of Melite, off the coast of Libya, for three harvests (Ov. *Fast.* 3.557–8); in the *Punica* Anna hides in the Libyan city of Cyrene for two harvests (Sil. 8.61–2). Fleeing her refuge, Anna is then shipwrecked on Laurentine shores (*Laurens . . . litus,* Ov. *Fast.* 3.599; *Laurentes . . . oras*, Sil. 8.68). Anna then encounters Aeneas, described in both poems as having recently gained his kingdom (Ov. *Fast.* 3.601–2; Sil. 8.71–2). From this point, Silius maintains a broad narrative outline that is shared with the *Fasti*, but his Anna is allowed to tell her own version of the story (Sil. 8.79–159) whereas in the *Fasti* her words are not reported in detail: *errores exposuitque suos,* (. . . and she told of her wanderings, Ov. *Fast.* 3.626). Silius's

Anna is given a voice in direct conversation with Aeneas as she offers a first person account of Dido's anguish and suicide,[49] reacting with feeling as she lingers on the consequences of Aeneas's departure: *cui sic, verba trahens largis cum fletibus, Anna / incipit et blandas addit pro tempore voces* (So Anna then began, dragging her words with many tears and using flattering expressions suiting the occasion, Sil. 8.79-80). These details go unremarked in the *Fasti* where Anna's emotional response to the memory of Dido is confined to a single line: *ante oculos miserae fata sororis erant* (Her poor sister's end appeared before her eyes, Ov. *Fast.* 3.610).

Despite the welcome she receives in Italy, both Ovid and Silius report that Anna is disturbed in her sleep by the ghost of Dido who warns her that Aeneas's Italian wife Lavinia is plotting against her. Dido recommends that Anna escape (Ov. *Fast.* 3.639-44); Silius adds to Dido's speech an explicit exhortation that she should fly and join the nymphs of Numicius (Sil. 8.164-201) where – perhaps unexpectedly – she will henceforth be honoured as a goddess in Italy: '*aeternumque Italis numen celebrabere in oris*' ('and your deity shall be glorified forever in the land of Italy', Sil. 8.183).[50] This piece of crucial information is not provided to Anna in the *Fasti*, where her deification and sublimation into the landscape will be more suggestive of abduction and violence: *corniger hanc tumidis rapuisse Numicius undis / creditur et stagnis occuluisse suis,* (It is believed that horned Numicius stole her away in his swollen waves and hid her away in his waters, Ov. *Fast.* 3.647-8.). This compares with a more peaceful rendition of the scene in the *Punica*: *donec harenoso, sic fama, Numicius illam / suscepit gremio vitreisque abscondidit antris* (Until, as the story goes, Numicius received her into his sandy bosom and hid her in his glassy grottoes, Sil. 8.190-1).

Discrepancies between the version of Anna's arrival in Italy told in the *Fasti* and the *Punica* suggest key thematic choices. While in both poems Aeneas is welcoming and moved by Anna's story of hardship, in the *Punica* Anna is welcomed into Aeneas's home with no direct reference made to his new Italian wife, Lavinia (Sil. 8.73-5, 159-64). In contrast, Ovid's Aeneas has openly asked Lavinia to treat Anna with kindness: '*hanc tibi cur tradam, pia causa, Lavinia coniunx / est mihi: consumpsi naufragus huius opes*' ('Wife Lavinia, for me it is a duty that I hand her into your care; when I was shipwrecked I used her resources', Ov. *Fast.* 3.629-30). Despite this entreaty, the *Fasti* describes Lavinia as indeed developing and harbouring feelings of ill will, grounding Anna's fears in reality. Lavinia actively plots to harm her rival: *non habet exactum, quid agat: furialiter odit / et parat insidias et cupit ulta mori* (she had not yet decided what to do; she hated with *furor*, and she prepared traps, and longed to die avenged, Ov. *Fast.* 3.637–8).[51] A horrifying vision of Dido, with hair stained with blood, urges Anna to flee:

> nox erat, ante torum visa est adstare sororis
>   squalenti Dido sanguinulenta coma
> et 'fuge, ne dubita, maestum fuge' dicere 'tectum!'
>
> It was night, and before her sister's bed Dido appeared to stand, her hair covered in blood, seeming to say 'fly, do not be uncertain, fly from this ill-omened house!'
>
> Ov. *Fast.* 3.639–41

Silius omits any direct reference to Lavinia's plot against Anna, offering only Dido's report of her suspicion:

> surge, age, iam tacitas suspecta Lavinia fraudes
> molitur dirumque nefas sub corde volutat.
>
> Get up, quickly, now suspicious Lavinia plans secret deceit, and desires a dreadful crime in her heart.
>
> Sil. 8.176–7

There is duplicity in both poems: Ovid's Lavinia genuinely bears ill will towards Anna; Dido's warning goes unconfirmed by Silius and is only verified when reading the *Punica* with reference to the *Fasti*. The lack of confirmation, supplemented by the almost calm manner in which Dido instructs Anna to escape and submit herself to the Numicius, creates a sense of ambiguity surrounding Anna's fear and flight.

Silius's engagement with the *Fasti* therefore not only completes the gaps between his *Punica* and Ovid's poem, but it also complicates and subverts the arrival of the Trojans in Italy and more positive interpretations of Roman history more broadly. Silius's Anna draws upon her own literary antecedents, as well as those of Dido and Aeneas, making her an unreliable narrator of an incomplete history that is fully understood only with reference to the *Aeneid* as well as the Ovidian sequels in the *Metamorphoses* and *Fasti*.[52] In Silius's telling Anna and Aeneas both take a selective approach to describing their various interactions with Dido following Aeneas's departure from Carthage. In the *Fasti* Ovid declines to elaborate on the story Anna tells to Aeneas, and Ovid's Aeneas explicitly asks Anna not to describe the events that led to Dido's suicide. Describing his own encounter with Dido in the Underworld Aeneas makes it clear that he is well aware of the dire consequences of his actions: *ne refer! aspexi non illo corpore digna / vulnera Tartereas ausus adire domos* (Do not recall it. I saw the undeserved wounds on her body when I dared to visit the house of Tartarus, Ov. *Fast.* 3.619–20). Silius's Aeneas, on the other hand, openly asks Anna to tell the tale of Dido's death: *tum discere maesta / exposcit cura letum infelicis Elissae* (next with concerned sadness he asked about the death of unhappy Dido, Sil. 8.77–8). But notably, the Aeneas of the *Punica* – in contrast to Ovid's Aeneas, who reveals to Anna his encounter with Dido in the Underworld – completely omits to tell that he saw Dido following her suicide. Not even Anna's claim to have had a vision of Dido with Sychaeus prior to her sister's suicide prompts Silius's Aeneas to mention his own visit to the Underworld where he encountered Dido and her first husband (Sil. 8.122–3). Silius's Aeneas is silent on this crucial episode from Book 6 of the *Aeneid*, and this silence echoes another between Dido and Anna at *Aeneid* 4.420–3, where, having told Anna that she is the only one to whom Aeneas will tells his hidden feelings, neither Aeneas's secrets (or the reason why he entrusts them to Anna) are revealed to the audience. As Frederick Ahl notes, the 'reader is forced beyond the text of the *Aeneid*, into other traditions of Aeneas, Dido and Anna, for an answer'.[53] Silius replicates this effect. As a trio, Aeneas, Dido and Anna have form for deception, withholding personal information, and expecting each other (or the epic audience) to fill the gaps in the stories that they tell of themselves.[54]

Silius's Anna is also reluctant to give Aeneas a full picture of Dido's death and the curse placed by her sister upon Aeneas and the Romans in *Aeneid* 4 (Virg. *A.* 4.586–629). Both the *Aeneid* and the *Punica* depict Anna rushing to Dido (Virg. *A.* 4.672–85; Sil. 8.152–4); and, where Virgil has the dying Dido attempt to rise three times only to fall over again, Silius describes Anna attempting to throw herself on the Trojan sword three times, each time falling on the body of her sister (Sil. 8.155–6).[55] Virgil reports the curse pronounced by Dido on her deathbed (Virg. *A.* 4.618–20), but Silius's Anna omits this detail and chooses instead to relate that Dido, having previously called herself Aeneas's wife (Sil. 8.143), hoped to see Sychaeus in the Underworld:

nunc ad vos magni descendet corporis umbra.
me quoque fors dulci quondam vir notus amore
expectat curas cupiens aequare priores.

Now to you the shade of a great person shall descend. Maybe my husband [Sychaeus], whose love was once sweet to me, awaits, anxious to equally love me as before.

Sil. 8.145–7

Anna and Aeneas fail to report everything they know about Dido following the departure of the Trojans from Carthage but knowledgeable readers of the *Punica* are able to fill in the gaps by means of their readings of both the *Aeneid* and the *Fasti*. Silius's characters are guarded about the information they reveal to one another, remembering selectively and fostering an atmosphere of mutual suspicion.

Even in his report of Anna's flight from the Trojans Silius adapts and reconfigures the Ovidian narrative to subvert his readers' expectations. In the *Fasti* the threat of violence is palpable, and her deification has the coercive force of any similar event in the *Metamorphoses*. From the moment of Dido's warning, the very environment is heavy with threat as a blast of air slams the door, intensifying Anna's fear:

> sub verbum querulas impulit aura fores.
> exsilit et velox humili super arva fenestra
>   se iacit – audacem fecerat ipse timor –
> quaque metu rapitur tunica velata recincta   645
>   currit, ut auditis territa damma lupis.
> corniger hanc tumidis rapuisse Numicius undis
>   creditor et stagnis occuluisse suis.
>
> At [Dido's] word the wind pushed the protesting door. [Anna] leapt up and speedily she threw herself onto the ground from the low window – fear itself made her bold – and from where she is carried by dread, wrapped in her unfastened dress, she runs, as a frightened deer that hears the wolves. It is believed that horned Numicius stole her away in his swollen waves and hid her away in his waters.
>
> Ov. *Fast.* 3.642–8

It is not only that the river takes Anna; she is carried by fear, and compared to a frightened doe. Anna's dress is unfastened (*velata recincta*. Ov. *Fast.* 3.645), heightening the violent eroticism of the episode,[56] as she is swept away (*rapuisse*) by a horned and passionate river Numicius (*corniger . . . cupidis . . . Numicius*).[57]

Silius picks up on the tone of violence, initially prefacing his version of the episode with Juno's foreknowledge of the carnage that is to come at Cannae and Hannibal's own disturbed psychological state (Sil. 8.25–7, 207–9). Yet his version of Anna's story largely intimates brutality without enacting it. Instead of a violent disturbance of the air, Dido seems to disappear into it:

> sic fata in tenuem Phoenissa evanuit auram.
> Anna novis somno excutitur perterrita visis,   185
> itque timor totos gelido sudore per artus.
> tunc, ut erat tenui corpus velamine tecta,

prosiluit stratis humilique egressa fenestra
per patulos currit plantis pernicibus agros,
donec harenoso, sic fama, Numicius illam   190
suscepit gremio vitreisque abscondidit antris.

So uttered Dido, who vanished into thin air. Anna, terrified by this extraordinary vision, was shaken from sleep, and fear covered each limb with cold sweat. Then, just as she was, her body covered by a thin robe, she leapt up from bed, and, climbing out a low window, she ran across the open fields through hardy plants, until (as the story goes) Numicius received her into his sandy bosom and hid her in his glassy grottoes.

Sil. 8.184–91

Although Anna's robe is thin, she is covered (*tecta*), her night time flight is across open landscape and it lacks the erotic charge of the Ovidian version. As in Ovid, Anna escapes through a low window (*humili . . . fenestra*, *Fast.* 3.643, Sil. 8.188) into the fields, but when she reaches the river there is no hint of a struggle. In the *Punica* the Numicius is foremost Anna's protector as the river hides (*abscondidit*) Anna from the pursuers that she expects to be following her. Anna's metamorphosis is neither forced by the god of the river, nor is it unexpected, being the conscious result of Dido's advice and effort to escape the perceived threat of Lavinia and the Trojans. Numicius runs through a *locus amoenus* landscape; the river is described by Dido as a small, gentle spring that will provide safety: *haud procul parvo descendens fonte Numicus / labitur et leni per valles volvitur amne*, (not far from here Numicius glides down from a small well and meanders through the valleys with his smooth stream, Sil. 8.179–81). When she arrives at its banks Anna finds it sandy and shady (*harenoso . . . gremio, vitreisque . . . antris*). As demonstrated by the Numicius of the *Fasti* the waters of a *locus amoenus* can be suggestive of sexual violence,[58] but Anna's metamorphosis at the hands of Numicius in the *Punica* appears to be peaceful by comparison. Rather than being passively carried off by the river, Anna is instructed by Dido to carry herself away (*huc rapies, germana* Sil. 8.181); instead of a violent transformation, both Anna and Numicius consent to her sublimation into an Italian *locus amoenus* and incorporation into the Roman pantheon.[59]

In both poems Aeneas and his men find Anna following her metamorphosis into a river nymph. In the *Fasti* Anna is unaccompanied by the nymphs of the grotto when she is found by the loud and unruly party of Trojans searching for her in the fields (*magno clamore per agros*, 3.649). Silius too records the noisy Trojans searching for Anna (again, *magno . . . clamore per agrum*, 8.194), yet in the *Punica* Anna is in company, sitting with her sister Naiads (*inter caeruleas . . . sorores*, Sil. 8.198). In the *Fasti* the scene is one of calm in which the river hushes itself in order for Anna to be heard, in contrast to the energetic and eroticized manner in which the river has taken her:

> sustinuit tacitas conscius amnis aquas.
> ipsa loqui visa est 'placidi sum nympha Numici:
> amne perenne latens Anna Perenna vocor'.

> The knowing river held back and quietened his stream. She herself appeared to speak: 'I am a nymph of calm Numicius: concealed in the perennial river, I am called Anna Perenna'.
>
> Ov. *Fast.* 3.652–4

Silius too picks out this detail as the river holds itself back: *dumque inter se mirantur, ab alto / amnis aquas cursumque rapit*, (And while, between themselves, they looked in awe, the river seized the course of his waters to the sea, Sil. 8.196–7.). At this point Silius seems to reverse the energy of the Numicius and invert the trajectory of violence; only now are its previously calm waters constrained with what appears to be a degree of force (*rapit*).

Anna's short address to the Trojans is only articulated in the *Fasti*: in the *Punica*, Silius writes that Anna is seen sitting with the other nymphs and that she addressed the Trojans in a friendly manner but the words she uses are not repeated: *tum sedibus imis / inter caeruleas visa est residere sorores / Sidonis et placido Teucros affarier ore* (and then settled deep among her sister Naiads Anna appeared to sit and to speak to the Trojans with gentle speech, Sil. 8.197–9). The *Punica* invites the reader to recall the Ovidian predecessor and draws attention to Anna as she exists between the two texts, yet at the same time the reader is asked to confront the differences between the two poems: the different levels of violent energy between the two incarnations of the Numicius, which for Ovid has become calm (*placidi*) while the river of the *Punica* seems to have been stopped by force. Here it is Anna whose voice is calm (*placido ore*), in contrast to the now roiling waters of the river. In both poems Anna seems to be almost an apparition (*visa est*, Ov. *Fast.* 3.653 and Sil. 8.198), and she is visible to the Trojans even if they cannot fully interact with her (especially in the *Punica* where her speech is reported only). Perhaps Ovid and Silius both call into question the veracity of the report; perhaps she is not 'seen' but only 'seemingly' present. Each version appears necessary for a complete retelling, yet even so, uncertainty remains, only to be intensified once the two narratives are combined.

On a broad scale, Anna's deification continues the aetiological exploration of the tension between Rome and Carthage initiated by Virgil in the *Aeneid*. Yet within the structure of the *Punica*, Silius uses the narrative to foreshadow a Roman defeat at Cannae that is at least partially due to the Romans' own disagreements, misperceptions and rashness in the face of ill omens (Sil. 9.1–177). Like Rome's generals, Anna may be 'subverting Rome's interests and helping Carthage',[60] but Aeneas too employs subterfuge and partial recollections of the past. Anna and Aeneas are no straightforward expression of the dualism of Roman *fides* and Carthaginian *perfidia*;[61] Silius's deliberate evocation of the *Fasti* recalls the subversive potential of Aeneas in Ovid's poem,[62] and the duo's unreliability suggests the increasing Roman propensity to self-inflicted civil discord where individuals work to their own advantage and to the disadvantage of the common good.[63] Yet a final irony is that, unwittingly, Anna's role in ensuring that the battle of Cannae takes place is fundamental to Rome's ultimate destruction of Carthage: not only will this be the end of Hannibal's run of success, but in time it will be the end for his city as well.[64] In her message of hope, Anna unwittingly misleads her kinsman, making a promise that will be fulfilled, but not in the way that Hannibal hopes: *en, numen patrium spondet maiora peractis* (See! A goddess of our country promises our end will be famous, Sil. 8.239).[65]

By forming strong intertextual links with the *Aeneid* and Ovid's calendrical *Fasti*, Silius asserts that the centre of his epic, the battle of Cannae, is of fundamental importance to the Second Punic War as a pivotal existential moment for Rome,[66] foreshadowing both the greatness of the city as well as its decline into degeneracy. Cannae is accentuated in its importance by Anna, sister of Dido as the necessary facilitator of the battle, drawn from the *Fasti* where she is explicitly connected to events that precipitate the transition from Republican to Imperial Rome.[67] If Silius is not quite 'rewriting the origins',[68] he is certainly focusing attention on Cannae as fundamental to the course of Roman history.

Anna Perenna is a goddess of order and transition, and in the *Punica* she is a goddess that must sit in-between two warring nations and two identities. In the long term she may be loyal to Rome,[69] an example of 'cultural integration',[70] but Silius's version of Anna Perenna's origins puts the tension between Rome and Carthage and the battle of Cannae at the centre of Roman history to explore why Rome turned in on itself. By asserting the centrality of the events he narrates to the movement of the Roman story, Silius appropriates for his epic a position within the Roman mytho-historical cycle established by his predecessors, yet the poet does not unequivocally endorse a perception of history of which *imperium sine fine* is the *telos*. Engaging with a poem that subverts the ordered certainty of the Roman calendar allows Silius to engender an ambivalent attitude towards the actors in his narrative and the order that Anna herself is supposed to represent: Aeneas and his band of Trojans are not idealized, and perennial Anna's identity crisis prefigures a future for a Rome that forgets its own identity in the wake of prolonged, successful imperial expansion; an identity that was at its greatest realization in the disaster of Cannae, the event that paradoxically prepared the way for this Roman expansion and eventual decline into civil war and autocracy. Anna's utility as a multifaceted figure, associated with varied (and variant) mythological narratives, makes her particularly useful for Silius's project: the eternal goddess who sits at the centre of his epic, and at the centre of his own in-between Roman story.

3

Not Just Another Fertility Goddess: Searching for Anna Perenna in Art

Gwynaeth McIntyre

In Book 3 of the *Fasti*, Ovid outlines the possible identities for Anna Perenna, the goddess whose festival is celebrated on the Ides of March, suggesting that there are many rumours about who this goddess is and that *fabula proposito nulla tegenda meo* (no tale will be concealed by my purpose, Ov. *Fast.* 3.544).[1] Ovid's most descriptive account identifies Anna Perenna with Anna, sister of Dido, who underwent an *apotheosis* with the help of Numicius's waters. Following his mini-epic spanning over a hundred lines, which serves as a continuation, completion and replica of Virgil's *Aeneid*,[2] Ovid also lists Luna, Themis, the Inachian cow, a nymph (daughter of Azan) and even an old woman from Bovillae as other possibilities.

By underscoring Anna's problematic multiplicity, Ovid's literary account draws attention to the inherent challenge of identifying her particular characteristics and roles. Attempts to identify her securely in artistic sources are thwarted by her different identities, any of which might form the basis of visual depiction. Even a search narrowed to her most common roles as a nymph or fertility goddess is complicated by the fact that such entities share similar attributes, making differentiation difficult, if not impossible.

In order to explore the possible representations of Anna Perenna in art, this chapter focuses on Anna's identification with nymphs, a connection which is further strengthened when the inscriptional evidence from her sacred grove site is added to the literary accounts by Ovid and Silius Italicus. Anna's connection with nymphs and her importance in the mythic narratives of the Augustan period and after provides an avenue to explore the interpretation of two specific pieces of art, the south-eastern panel of the *Ara Pacis* and a comparable relief from Carthage.

The *Ara Pacis Augustae*

On 30 January 9 BCE, the *Ara Pacis Augustae,* was consecrated by the Roman Senate.[3] Taken as the epitome of Augustus's ideology and serving to promote Augustus's role in ushering a new 'golden age',[4] its panels, iconography, themes and religious and political connotations have been discussed and debated by modern scholars since its discovery and reconstruction in the nineteenth and early twentieth centuries.[5] The so-called fertility panel on the south-eastern corner of the monument has received the most scholarly attention in the last sixty years but despite the agreement that the iconography on this monument had considerable political and ideological value, no scholarly consensus has been reached on the identity of the central figure.[6]

In the centre of the panel, a female figure sits on what appears to be a rock or rocky ledge with two children in her lap along with an abundance of fruit. This figure exhibits many of the common features and attributes of female fertility goddesses which has led to much debate over her identification. It could be that this ambiguity was a deliberate action on the part of the artists, especially considering that although the fertility goddesses all share the same attributes, they also have many symbols which are specifically associated with them

Figure 3.1 South-Eastern Panel of the Ara Pacis. Photograph: Scala / Art Resource, NY.

Figure 3.2 Silver didrachm minted in Camarina; (reverse) Kamarina on a swan. British Museum: 1952,0409.2 © Trustees of the British Museum.

individually. Perhaps the identity of this figure was left ambiguous in order to allow for the viewers' own interpretation of the panel and their active participation in the scenes represented.[7] Since the symbols associated with the central figure do not help with a definitive identification, it is worth first addressing the other figures present in the scene.

The two flanking figures are depicted as semi-nude with the *velificatio* motif. On the left, the figure is found riding a swan or goose and is positioned over a stream, as represented by an overturned water jug and the river reeds. River nymphs (Naiads) are commonly associated with both geese and swans, as can be seen here on a coin depicting the Naiad Kamarina with a similar *velificatio* motif (Figure 3.2).[8] The overturned jug depicted on the *Ara Pacis* relief is also commonly associated with nymphs and the streams in which they rule.[9] This confirms that the figure on the left should be identified as a Naiad.

The figure on the right is riding a *ketos*, which rises out of the water. In his Natural History, Pliny describes Nereids as *supra delphinos aut cete aut hippocampus sedentes* (sitting upon dolphins, or *ketoi*, or hippocamps, Plin. *Nat.* 36.26) and they are commonly depicted in this way in art, as can been seen in Figure 3.3. Although the Nereid in Figure 3.3 is riding a hippocamp instead of a *ketos*, she is depicted displaying the same *velificatio* motif found in depictions of Naiads and the two flanking figures on the *Ara Pacis*.

Figure 3.3 *Terracotta relief of a Nereid on a hippocamp; Campania, 50 BCE–100 CE.* British Museum: 1805,0703.302 © Trustees of the British Museum.

In Greek myth, Nereids were goddesses of transition. They were responsible for ensuring one's safety while traversing the seas as well as the transition from life to death. They also appear to play some role in certain individuals' granting of immortality, a connection which will be discussed further below.[10] Supported by this comparable evidence, these figures are the most securely identified on the altar.[11]

The ewe and bull in front of the scene likely contribute to the overall scene of fertility and abundance but it is the central figure with the two children that has drawn the most attention from scholars. The elusive identity of this figure has led to much scholarly debate over the figure's characterization and her role within the artistic narrative of the altar.[12] First, the central figure is veiled and is sitting on a rock. Similar representations of fertility goddesses usually present them lounging on rocks, the ground, or on animals. Tellus or Terra Mater are the most common identifications for this figure in art history texts discussing this altar.[13] Yet, the panel lacks a *cornucopia*, the definitive symbol of Tellus, and the central figure is presented as veiled, whereas Tellus is always represented as bareheaded.[14] For example, a representation of Tellus on the breast plate of the Prima

Porta Augustus statue shows her reclining on the ground, holding a *cornucopia* and wearing a wreath of grain. The two children she is depicted with are on the ground in front of her, not on her lap.[15] Generally, children depicted in connection with a female goddess serve to represent the role of the goddess in human fertility.[16] Yet, traditionally these 'nursing' goddesses (*kourotrophoi*) are depicted with only one child or, as mentioned above, two children around the goddess but not sitting directly on her lap.[17]

One of the children seated in her lap offers her a fruit, most likely a pomegranate. This has been taken by some scholars to serve as proof for the interpretation of the central goddess as Demeter/Ceres, as the pomegranate was a central icon in her myths.[18] Nevertheless, the pomegranate does not provide such definitive confirmation. Pomegranates serve as a symbol of fertility as well as of some chthonic deities and are not conclusive evidence for one particular fertility deity.[19] In fact, it could be argued that there is a link between Anna (of Punic origin) and pomegranates (*punica poma*), as well as the fruit in the central figure's lap as making reference to Anna's grove, described by Martial as *pomiferum nemus*.[20]

If fertility goddesses are not commonly depicted seated on a rock and the two flanking figures are depicted as a naiad and a nereid, is it possible that the central figure is also a nymph, although one that is clearly of greater importance than her companions? Although commonly depicted riding on particular animals, as discussed above, nymphs are also depicted in a seated position on rocks. This helps to distinguish them from their fertility goddess counterparts which are more commonly depicted in a reclined position. If this central figure can also be identified as a nymph, it is worth turning the discussion away from the altar itself to examine the features of Anna's characterization and worship as a nymph to determine whether this might shed some light on the central figure's identification.

Anna and Her Nymphs

Ovid and Silius Italicus both identify Anna Perenna as Anna, sister of Dido, who underwent an *apotheosis* in the river Numicius to become the nymph Anna Perenna.[21] In both sources, we are told that a festival is then established in her honour and that she is worshiped throughout Italy.[22] In Ovid's narrative, the new nymph Anna Perenna is revealed seated alone. Yet, in Silius Italicus's narrative, which closely follows that of Ovid, she is found sitting among her 'sea-blue sisters' (*inter caeruleas visa est residere sorores*, Sil. 8.197–9).

Water serves as a focal point in the topography of Rome and its religious landscape, as well as the narrative landscape of many of the myths presented in literature from the Augustan age. For example, water – as represented by the sea, lakes, rivers and springs – plays an important role both in Virgil's narrative of Aeneas's journey to Italy and in Anna's own mini-epic journey to Italy as told in Ovid's *Fasti*.[23] Water deities have been shown to play an important part in the festivals celebrated in the regular Roman ritual calendar,[24] which may explain in part Anna's festival on the Ides of March as outlined in Ovid's narrative. Ovid's description of her festival celebrated on the banks of the Tiber river helps to identify Anna as a water deity and may suggest that her identity as the sister of Dido turned nymph through Numicius's transformative waters serves as the basis for her worship.

Although Ovid's poetic discussion of her festival day on the Ides of March identifies some of the key aspects of her worship (at least on this particular day),[25] the site of her sacred grove at the Piazza Euclide, discovered in 1999, which cannot be the site on which Ovid places the revelries of her festival day, provides more insight into the dedications and offerings made to her year-round. The focal point for this site was a spring and fountain, with two inscriptions and an altar embedded into the front of the fountain basin. The findings from this grove have been discussed in detail by Piranomonte,[26] but it is worth examining two aspects of Anna's worship at this site in more detail: first, the similarities between this site and a grotto site from Sicily dedicated to the worship of Anna and the *Paides*; and second, Anna's companions in worship as presented in the inscriptions found at both sites.

The site in Rome features not only the spring and inscriptions, but also what appears to be a sort of grotto. The grotto has led scholars to link this site with a similar grotto site possibly connected with Anna Perenna, the Sicilian cave cult of Anna and the *Paides*.[27] The Sicilian site, found near Buscemi, contains three rock-cut chambers of different sizes.[28] Although there are multiple spaces for dedicatory inscriptions, few inscriptions were actually found in the excavations.[29] Wilson argues that this possibly serves as evidence that this sanctuary was not in use for very long but also suggests that many of the blank tablets hanging on the walls could have been painted.[30] The surviving inscriptions themselves are all written in Greek and highlight the continued Greek practice of dating through reference to the priesthood of Zeus Olympios at Syracuse.[31] These inscriptions record the names of priests and priestesses of the cult of Anna and the *Paides* as well as offerings made to them and date to the late first century BCE and early first century CE.

From the inscriptions, we can see that the cult site was the focal point of pilgrimages by individuals and groups to the cave in order to participate in sacrifices and banquets. In some cases, there is evidence of votive offerings left in the cave, such as the mirror dedicated to Apollo, the *Paides* and Anna by Lucius Cornelius Aquila.[32] Although the name of the *Paides* comes first in most of the inscriptions, it appears that they play a secondary role to the figure of Anna. They have been identified as the equivalent of the *Korai* and other minor deities worshiped in Sicily, many of whom are often referred to as *Nymphai*.[33] There also appears to be some connection between Anna and other female deities, specifically Demeter and Magna Mater. Although the origins of this cult are unclear, Santini argues that Anna's legendary stay in Malta, an island not far from eastern Sicily, presented in Ovid's *Fasti* and Silius Italicus's *Punica*, may not simply be a literary construct, but that this legend may account for the cult of Anna and the *Paides* near Buscemi.[34] There is also a literary tradition for a Trojan connection to the island, and although this narrative might be deliberate political and cultural manipulation,[35] the stories create a link between the legends associated with the exodus of Aeneas and the Trojans and the cult practices found on Sicily.

The inscriptional evidence from Anna's grove site in Rome is much more explicit about the nature of her companions. Both inscriptions contain the dedication '*nymphis sacratis*'. In one, Gaius Suetonius Germanus made a dedication to the sacred nymphs of Anna Perenna.[36] The date of this inscription is unknown and the excavation publication notes that included on the stone is the faint image of a *simpulum* (ladle) and a *patera* (libation bowl), both of which are used in sacrifices for pouring wine and libations. The imagery on the inscription suggests the types of sacrifices made to Anna and further secures her religious connection with nymphs through the wording of the inscription itself. The second inscription is from the altar embedded in the fountain basin itself and is dedicated 'to the sacred nymphs' (*nymphis sacratis)*. This inscription can be securely dated due to the dating formula at the end of the inscription: 'Dedicated on the *nones* of April [April 5], when Silvanus and Augurinus were consuls [156 CE]'. This dedication was made by Suetonius Germanus and his wife Licinia but it is uncertain whether this is the same Germanus and the previous dedication or not. In any case, this inscription was set up in fulfillment of a vow: 'the vow to Anna Perenna which they had undertaken, that if they determined themselves as victors, they would set up a marble altar, once more made victors, we deservedly fulfill the vow'.[37] Whereas Blennow (Chapter 6 in this volume) examines these inscriptions in detail, I want to explore the worship of Anna within the broader context.

Although there is still some debate as to whether the Anna of Sicily is the same as the Anna worshiped in Italy, some common features of each cult suggest that they are performing similar functions within their respective spheres. Anna's connection with the *Paides*, figures generally interpreted as nymphs in Sicily, mirrors Anna's connection with nymphs at her grove site in Rome. The allocated space for dedications and dedicatory inscriptions highlight these locations as pilgrimage sites and places of worship for Anna. An inscription from Buscemi celebrates the dedication of a mirror to Apollo, the *Paides* and Anna by Lucius Cornelius Aquila on his own behalf as well as that of his mother and wife.[38] The inscriptions from Anna's grove site in Rome identify an altar itself being dedicated in response to their own vow, as discussed above. However, the grove site in Rome was in use for a significantly longer amount of time than the grotto at Buscemi and the excavations have uncovered votive offerings, coins and materials relating to magic.[39] In particular, deposits of pine cones and egg shells highlight Anna's role in overseeing fertility.

Anna's worship is, in part, consistent with other sites of nymph worship. Caves and grottos commonly serve as the sanctuary and the identification of particular sites with individual nymphs relies almost entirely on the votive deposits and dedicatory inscriptions.[40] From the votive evidence, it appears that visitors to most nymph sites are either coming for healing, especially to sites centred on springs, or in the case of girls, coming to make a *proteleia* (prenuptial dedication).[41] Although the site at Buscemi is likely influenced by other Greek sites of nymph worship, it is worth keeping in mind that Greek nymphs and Roman nymphs are not necessarily worshiped in the same way. However, the connection made with Apollo at this site does suggest a healing aspect to Anna's worship in Sicily. As a comparative Roman example, the cult sites to nymphs in the Three Gauls and in Narbonesis also appear to be healing sites where the nymphs are worshiped in connection with Apollo and the sites themselves focus in particular around hot water.[42] Thus, the Roman cult practices appear to also be concerned with the healing power of water.

In addition to their connection with healing, nymphs are also used as a way of claiming land and demonstrating fertility, as is particularly the case in the western communities of Magna Graecia. It is likely that the cult sites in Italy are further influenced by these traditions, and in Anna's case, the literary narratives which associate Anna with the river Numicius, the river responsible for her transition from Anna, sister of Dido, to Anna Perenna. The focal point of her grove site, a fountain, into which dedications were deposited, links Anna Perenna with water and fertility, aspects of which are both clearly depicted on the 'fertility' panel on the *Ara Pacis*.

The Fertility Panel in Context

The 'fertility' panel should not be interpreted in isolation as it would not have been viewed independently by its ancient audience. Although it is not my purpose to discuss or provide the identities of all the figures found on the various friezes associated with this monument, it is worth nevertheless discussing this panel within the context of the other images since this monument was envisioned as a whole.[43] My discussion of the other panels of the monument thus follows scholarly convention for the identifications of the other panels. If the monument is divided in cross-section through the west and east openings, one finds a distinct theme to the northern and southern halves. The northern panel of the western face depicts a heavily reconstructed image of Romulus, Remus and the she-wolf whereas the eastern face depicts the goddess Roma. Common images found on republican coinage, these images reflect Rome's past, its foundation and glorious Republic. The procession of senators found on the northern face of the altar links these two images. The southern half on the other hand focuses specifically on images relating to Augustus, his family and his ideology of ushering in a new age of peace and prosperity. On the western face, we find Aeneas, founder of the Julian gens, performing a sacrifice.[44] If the figure on the eastern face can be identified as Anna Perenna, she has an important connection to Aeneas, a connection further explored below. Finally, these two panels are connected through the procession of the imperial family found on the southern face.

Anna's role as nymph of the Numicius river directly links her to Aeneas.[45] The location of her *apotheosis* and the account of this event in the *Fasti* closely mirrors the account of Aeneas's own *apotheosis* in the river Numicius found in Book 14 of Ovid's *Metamorphoses*.[46] Ovid's use of this river as the site of Anna's *apotheosis* invites his reader to draw a connection with the Julian ideology.[47] This connection is made even more explicit by Silius Italicus, who introduces Anna as goddess, who is neighbour to the sacred grove of Indiges (*diva, Indigetis castis contermina lucis,* Sil. 8.39). His use of *diva* here, refers to individuals who have undergone *apotheosis*. Following the death of Julius Caesar, the title *divus* came to signify an individual, specifically a member of the imperial family, who had been deified after their death.[48] According to Servius, in his commentary on the *Aeneid*, the term is used for gods who have not always been gods, but have been created from men, whereas *deus* is the term for the immortals.[49] Although his interpretation of the terminology contradicts Varro's (who suggests the opposite), Servius is following the new terminology established by Octavian which served to identify the deified individuals in the ruling house.[50]

Silius's choice to use *diva* as opposed to *nympha* ties her directly to Augustan ideology and the deification of ancestors. Although the characterization of Anna in the *Punica* is problematic in that she, as an indigenous god to the Romans, is depicted as helping the Carthaginians,[51] Marks argues that in fact Anna is helping out the Romans since Hannibal's victory at Cannae ultimately leads to the overall supremacy of the Romans over the Carthaginians.[52] As mentioned above, her identification as *diva* within the text is also directly linked with Aeneas as the god Indiges. The importance of Aeneas as a divine ancestor for the Julii in Augustan ideology is also present in Horace's *Carmen Saeculare*,[53] further strengthening the connection between these deified individuals and Augustus's image of peace and the establishment of a new age.

As we have seen, figures who are important to the overall message of Augustan peace embodied a number of different characteristics and features and were not always so easily identifiable. We must also consider the ambiguity of the *Ara Pacis* itself. No dedication survives and it appears that the identity of the recipient of any sacrifice performed here was deliberately left ambiguous.[54] The processions themselves were most likely not meant to symbolize a specific act, although some scholars have argued that they represent the first procession at the consecration of the altar.[55] Instead, the procession friezes invite the viewer to be an active participant in the ritual associated with altar,[56] especially during periods when no sacrifices were taking place. The whole monument relies on viewer participation and the interpretations of the monument by those viewers.[57] One must also not forget that this altar was not just a decoration placed on the Campus Martius. It had a religious function and was the location of sacrificial ritual. In fact, the political message of the *Ara Pacis* appears to be reliant on the cultic themes inherent within it.[58]

The active participation of the viewer seems especially important since, in addition to the message that Augustus is responsible for ushering in this new age of peace and prosperity, the very act of viewing the sacrifices and processions invites the viewer to participate in the commemoration of the rites and symbols which celebrate Augustus's new age.[59] Images of fertility link to the past but also look forward to the future. The monument seems to also imply that participation in sacrifice can ensure the continuation of this prosperity. It once again leads us to think of sacrifices made to Anna Perenna to ensure prosperity and fertility for the coming year, both during her celebration on the Ides of March and through dedications made at her sacred grove. Rebirth and renewal is the ultimate goal and, as Anna was a mortal who underwent an *apotheosis* to become Anna Perenna and is now responsible for overseeing fertility and prosperity, she becomes an important figure for the promotion of Augustus's own 'Golden Age'. Anna's importance and association to other aspects of Augustus's own propaganda are further strengthened through her connection with Aeneas who also underwent a similar *apotheosis*. Augustus could connect himself with these deified individuals (and his deified father, Julius Caesar) and promote his own proximity to the gods, with the final step to divine status becoming a reality after his death and resulting *apotheosis*. Not only was Augustus responsible for ushering in this new peace and prosperity, but he alone could ensure that it would continue in the future.

Anna and the Carthage Altar

Anna's identification as a Carthaginian princess and the sister of Dido, explicitly noted within the literary traditions (see Chapters 1, 2 and 4 in this volume), may shed some light on a relief from Carthage that shares many similar features to the south-eastern panel of the *Ara Pacis*.

Figure 3.4 Relief from Carthage. Altar © RMN-Grand Palais / Art Resource, NY.

It is likely that the central figure here depicts the same nymph/fertility goddess as on the *Ara Pacis* although some of the other features of the panel are different. Although the exact nature of this monument is unclear, two panels (one now in the Louvre, the other in the museum in Algiers) embody Augustan ideology and present many of the same images and themes found on the *Ara Pacis* in Rome. The city of Carthage itself, founded as a colony under Augustus, has a marked presence of Augustan ideology and seems to embody the ideology of an Augustan colony.[60] The connection between this new city and the story of Aeneas and his own journey to Carthage is drawn through Virgil's own narrative of Dido's city.[61] Not to be dismissed as literary fiction, Virgil's catalogue of buildings in Dido's city looks very much like the Augustan colony (minus the walls).[62] Thus, it should not be surprising to find Augustan influences throughout the city during the Julio–Claudian period, and more specifically for the purposes of the current study, monuments that embody Augustan virtues and ideology and highlight the important myths and themes central to the *gens Iulia*, although it is still unclear how these images are being transferred.[63] The question thus remains whether the central figure of this panel could also be interpreted as representing Anna Perenna.[64]

The panel has a central figure with two small children on her lap and a cow and a sheep at her feet in an identical configuration to that on the *Ara Pacis*. The water jug on the left part of the Carthage relief and the *ketos* on the right also mimic the bottom of the Ara Pacis relief. Although the panel is not as well preserved as that of the *Ara Pacis*, the same ambiguity of symbols suggests a similar type of reading for this monument. Examinations of the artistic representations of some of the more local fertility goddesses (such as Astarte) do not shed any more light on the discussion, and it could be that, as was the case with the panel on the *Ara Pacis*, the ambiguity could have been intentional and thereby invited the viewers (in this case, those who found themselves in Carthage) to actively participate in rendering meaning for the monument through their own interpretations.

The Carthaginian panel differs from the *Ara Pacis* in the flanking figures accompanying the central figure: on the Carthaginian panel the female nymphs which flank her on the *Ara Pacis* are replaced by a male figure rising out of water on the right, surrounded by a sea monster and dolphins, and a female figure with a torch on the left, above a water jug, water bird and reeds. There has been much debate in modern scholarship over the identities of these figures as well, an issue made more complicated by the poor condition of the top left section of the panel. The most common identification for the male figure is a triton or as some kind of sea divinity, although he has also been identified as Sol.[65] If Galinsky and de Grummond are correct in their identification and the figure on the right is Sol, this also fits in with the characterization of Anna as detailed by Ovid, as Perennial Anna, or Anna who oversees the seasons, growth of crops and the flourishing of vegetation. In addition, Galinsky identifies a link between Sol and the god Indiges (the deified Aeneas),[66] further strengthening the connection between Anna, Aeneas and Augustan ideology.

The female figure on the left has been interpreted as being the moon, Diana Lucifera, a manifestation of the sky, Persephone, or Caelestis.[67] As with all the other figures on this panel, it is not possible to come to a definitive identification. The discussion of possible identities for this figure is made even more difficult as the top half of this figure does not survive. In any case, scholars seem to have reached at least some consensus, stating that this deity has at least some connection with the moon. As with all fertility goddesses, Anna also has some connection with the moon, and Ovid even attributes the moon to one of her possible identities.[68] Similar to the figure of Sol, her connection with the moon is a result of her role as overseer of the seasons, and specifically because it completes the year by the months (*quia mensibus impleat annum*). Whether the female on the left represents the moon, or the sky more generally, these two flanking figures together could symbolize either the sky and sea, or perhaps the movement of time, both of which serve as features of Anna's own influence (along with many of the other fertility goddesses).[69] The panel taken as a whole seems to promote symbols of peace and prosperity both on land and sea, and throughout the year, much like the similar panel on the *Ara Pacis*.

The other panel associated with this altar confirms the importance of Augustan ideology here in this city as well.[70] None of these figures are explicitly connected to Carthage but rather to Augustus's role in bringing peace and prosperity to the empire, thereby directly linking this monument with the *Ara Pacis* in Rome. However, Anna's own importance within Augustan literature as well as her legendary connection with Carthage might suggest that her presence on this monument served to unite these myths and these two communities. The variation in the two 'fertility' panels found on the Carthaginian altar and on the *Ara Pacis* suggests not only that the overall themes of Augustan ideology were adopted by communities in the provinces but also that local interpretations could be incorporated into the art.

The elusive identity of Anna, her multiple characterizations and the generic depictions of nymphs and fertility goddesses in art all contribute to the difficulty in identifying the artistic representations of Anna. This is further complicated by the lack of cult images or other representations of her in her places of worship. However, her position as a nymph/goddess who was not only responsible for overseeing prosperity and fertility for the coming year but was also inherently linked to Augustan ideology through the shared location of her *apotheosis* with Aeneas. Her association with nymphs, continued worship in Rome as well as the votive offerings donated at her grove mark her importance as a fertility deity. The central figure of both the *Ara Pacis* and the Carthaginian altar, clearly intended by the artists to be the same individual, highlights the importance of promoting the continued peace and prosperity ushered in by Augustus's reign. Although we can never know for certain, the central figure of both the *Ara Pacis* and the Carthaginian altar, whose identification has proved as elusive to any scholar attempting such an analysis, may in fact be the very figure who embodies not only the problematic ambiguity and multiplicity of the overseers of fertility and prosperity but also the permanence and stability that comes with Augustus's new age.

Anna and Her Nymphs

4

Anna, Water, and Her Imminent Deification in *Aeneid* 4*

David J. Wright

In Book 3 of the *Fasti*, Ovid gives several *aitia* for the cult of Anna Perenna. The first and longest *aition* indicates that she is in fact the sister of the Carthaginian queen Dido (3.545–654). Several scholars have questioned the validity of this origin story and have suggested that Ovid made it up.[1] I, however, argue that Ovid did not invent this tradition.[2] A close reading of *Aeneid* 4 suggests that Virgil is in fact aware of this *aition* that associates the goddess with the sister of Dido. I present this case by showing Anna's close association with *lympha*, a word for 'water' which was connected to *nympha* through popular etymology. An acrostic, hitherto unnoticed by scholarship, also suggests a connection of Anna with her divine counterpart. There is also a passage with a covert reference to the second part of her name, *Perenna,* and another passage that addresses Anna with hymnic language as though she were a goddess. These connections between Anna and her future status as a nymph show the popularity of the goddess during the late first century BCE and allow the audience to further draw parallels between herself and another tragic figure in the poem, Juturna.

One of the main ways in which Virgil alludes to Anna Perenna in the construction of Anna's character is through subtle references to Anna Perenna's status as a nymph. While Ovid provides many differing identities for Anna, he explicitly refers to her as a *nympha* of the river Numicius (*Fast.* 3.653). Besides the Dido story, another one of his identifications suggests that she was thought of as a nymph:

invenies qui te **nymphen** Atlantida dicant
   teque Iovi primos, Anna, dedisse cibos.

You will find those who call you the **nymph** daughter of Atlas, and say that you, Anna, gave the first food to Jupiter.

Fast. 3.659–60

While Virgil does not directly use the word *nympha* in his depiction of Anna, he does associate her with the closely related word *lympha*. Varro states that the word *lympha* comes directly from the Greek *nympha* (*L.* 7.87).[3] The root *lymph-* appears to have a connection to nymphs in archaic Latin literature. Cicero records a fragment of Pacuvius which describes Hesione as 'moved at heart as though possessed by nymphs or stirred up by the rite of Bacchus' (*flexanima tamquam **lymphata** aut sacris Bacchi / commota*, fr. 422 R apud Cic. *Div.* 1.80). *Lymphata* here appears to be a translation of νυμφόληπτος ('seized by the nymphs'), which can indicate insanity caused by possession of the nymphs.[4] The mention of Bacchus in these lines provides further association with nymphs since they were frequently his attendants.[5]

Catullus plays with the potential anthropomorphic connotation lympha can have:

> Minister vetuli puer Falerni
> inger mi calices amariores,
> ut lex Postumiae iubet magistrae
> ebrioso acino ebriosioris.
> at vos quo lubet hinc abite, **lymphae**
> vini pernicies, et ad severos
> migrate. hic merus est Thyonianus.

> Attendant boy of little old Falernian, pour me more bitter cups as the law of the mistress Postumia, drunker than the drunken grape, bids. But depart to where it pleases, **waters** (or nymphs), the bane of wine, and go of to the strict ones. Here is the pure Thyonian!

> Catul. 27

In this skolion, the speaker wishes for unmixed wine and wine that is stronger. Notably, he addresses the water directly with *lymphae* (line 5). Both Putnam and Cairns see the *lymphae* here as personified.[6] Cairns maintains that lines 5–7 refer to an *aversio*, a form of religious ritual to cast away evil. The referent is usually a human. Cairns posits that the *lymphae* must refer to the nymphs that normally accompany Bacchus/Dionysus who appears at the end of the poem (*Thyonianus*, 7).[7] In Catullus 64, the adjectival form of *lympha* is used. The followers of Bacchus who approach Ariadne are described as 'raging with minds possessed by the nymphs' (***lymphata** mente furebant*, 254).[8]

The Augustan poets in particular engaged with wordplay *lympha* and *nympha*. A passage of Propertius provides good example. In an attempt to persuade his mistress that an unadorned love is best, the speaker gives examples from nature to make his point:

aspice quos summittat humus non fossa colores,
   ut veniant hederae sponte sua melius,
surgat et in solis formosius arbutus antris,
   et **sciat** indocilis currere **lympha** vias.

Behold what colours the ground sends forth without furrows so that the ivy comes better by its own volition and the arbutus grows better in remote glens, and the **water knows** how to run in untaught paths.

Prop. 1.2.9–12

In line 12, *lympha* is given anthropomorphic tendencies. The water is made sentient: it 'knows' how to run (*sciat*). Another telling example appears in Horace when the poet, in a very Epicurean fashion, recommends composure to Dellius when times are hard and moderation when times are good. He goes on to suggest that nature works for mankind's enjoyment, and so he might as well have a good time while he can:

   ... Quid obliquo **laborat**
lympha fugax trepidare rivo?
Why does the **fleeing water strive to bustle about** with its winding stream?

Hor. *Carm.* 2.3.11–12

As with the Propertius passage, we observe more anthropomorphic traits surrounding the word *lympha*. This water displays traits more typical of humans. As Nisbet and Hubbard note, *fugax* (fleeing) could easily describe both a river and an escaping nymph.[9] The fact that the water 'strives to bustle about' (*laborat / ... trepidare*) further suggests human-like qualities.[10] In addition to the examples outlined above, this anthropomorphizing of *lympha* appears in several other poems that predate or are contemporaneous with the composition of the *Aeneid*.[11] In these cases, the poets of Augustan period clearly recognize the connection of *lympha* to *nympha* and engage in wordplay by anthropomorphizing *lympha* allowing the audience to imagine a nymph in its place.

It is through this association of *lympha* and *nympha* that Virgil implies a connection between Anna, Dido's sister, and the Roman goddess. The word *lympha* appears six times in the *Aeneid*.[12] Two of these occurrences are in Book 4, and both times it is used in close connection to Anna. The instances of *lympha* outside the two in Book 4 do not overtly suggest *nympha*, but a closer look at them does indicate that the word is often loaded with meaning in Virgil. The first occurrence is in Book 1. During the famous banquet scene at the end of the book, servants bring out food and water: *dant manibus famuli* **lymphas Cererem** *que canistris / expediunt* (the servants pour **water** on their hands and bring out **bread** in baskets, Virg. A. 1.701–2). On the surface, *lymphas* means 'water'. What is striking is that the word is placed directly next to the goddess of grain (*Cererem*) which the poet uses as a metonym for 'bread'. Though *lymphas* means 'water', and *Cererem* means 'bread', the juxtaposition of these two words, which in other contexts indicate deities, could cause the audience to contemplate the dual meanings of these two words.

In Book 9, the word appears in a divine context. After seeing a vision of Iris, Turnus goes down to the river to pray:

> processit summoque hausit de gurgite **lymphas**
> multa deos orans, onerauitque aethera votis.
>
> He (Turnus) went forward and drew water from the stream as he prayed for many things from the gods. He loaded the sky with prayers.
>
> Virg. A. 9.23–4

As in the passage from Book 1, there is no pronounced reference to nymphs. But perhaps the context of the divine vision (9.21–2) and Turnus's prayer suggest that the *lymphas* is no ordinary *aqua*. Nymphs, especially in this poem, were closely associated with rivers.[13] In the next book, we observe *lympha* in a fluvial context as well. Here, Mezentius, suffering a wound dealt by Aeneas and not yet aware of his son Lausus's death, finds brief respite near a river:

> Interea genitor **Tiberini** ad fluminis undam
> vulnera siccabat **lymphis** corpusque levabat.
>
> Meanwhile the father was drying his wounds by the waves of the Tiber and was refreshing his body with **water**.
>
> Virg. A. 10.833–5

Again, *lympha* appears in a natural setting in close connection to a river, the haunt of nymphs. The mention of Tiberinus is significant. Servius tells us that Tiberinus is the title for Tiber the god that is used specifically in sacral contexts.[14] After seeing the Tiber's cult title, the audience might pause when it comes to *lymphis* in the next line since that word can connote simply water or divine beings.[15] What is more, Lymphae, the deities, were in particular connected to healing.[16] Nymphs might more naturally come to mind after an allusion to Tiberinus.

The final occurrence of *lympha* in the *Aeneid* is in Book 12. After Aeneas is wounded by an arrow, the healer Iapyx tries heal him. After Iapyx is unsuccessful, Venus clandestinely puts the healing herbs in Iapyx's washbasin:

hoc Venus obscuro faciem circumdata nimbo
detulit, hoc fusum labris splendentibus **amnem**
inficit occulte medicans, spargitque salubris
ambrosiae sucos et odoriferam panaceam.
fovit ea vulnus **lympha** longaevus Iapyx
ignorans,

Venus veiled in a dark cloud brought this (the herb) and she, secretly treating it, put **water** fused with it into the sparkling basins. She sprinkled the juice of healthy ambrosia and redolent panacea. Aged Iapyx, though unaware, takes care of the wound with this **water**.

Virg. A. 12.416–21

Tarrant notes the highly poetic nature of these lines and remarks that Virgil tends to do this when the subject matter is mundane.[17] One of the words in this 'high' language is *amnem*, 'water' though it more usually means 'river'. The use of this word perhaps looks forward to a few lines later where the word for water is transformed into *lympha*. As we saw in the last two examples, *lympha* can have a close association with rivers, so the proximity of *amnis* and *lympha* is likely not coincidental. Furthermore, as with the last example of Mezentius, but more prominently here, *lympha* is placed in a context of healing. Again, *lympha* most directly means 'water', but one wonders whether the image of the healing nymphs was a natural association for the ancient audience. Though in none of these examples *lympha* has the sense of 'nymph', Virgil plays with the polysemous possibilities of the word.

Now, to return to the cases of *lympha* connected to Anna in the *Aeneid*. The first occasion appears in Book 4 just after Dido has made the decision that she wishes to die. She summons her nurse Barce and gives her very specific orders:

'**A**nnam, cara mihi nutrix, **huc** siste **sororem**:
Dic corpus properet **fluviali** spargere **lympha**,
Et pecudes secum et monstrata piacula ducat.
Sic veniat, tuque ipsa pia tege tempora vitta'.

'Nurse dear to me, bring my **sister** Anna here and bid that she rush to sprinkle her body with **river water** and that she bring with her the flocks and the appeasements which have been shown. In this way, may she come, and you, cover your temples with a holy fillet'.

Virg. A. 4.634–6

In this passage Anna and *lympha*, a metonym for nymph, are juxtaposed. What is more telling is the fact that Virgil specifies that Anna must use water from a river (*fluviali*), an apt adjective since Anna Perenna was connected with the Numicius River. Furthermore, a word referring to Anna, *sororem* ('sister' 634), is placed directly above the word for nymph, *lympha* (635).[18] They both also possess the same metrical quantity and occupy the prominent final position of their respective lines.

There is an acrostic which has gone unnoticed in these lines.[19] This acrostic also hints at Virgil's awareness of the tradition of Anna's future deification. The first letters of each of the verses from this passage spell out ADES, 'Be present'. This vertical imperative corresponds well with the other horizontal imperatives in this passage; *siste* (634), *dic* (635), *tege* (636). The acrostic is well integrated with the context here. On a superficial level, *ades* is appropriate since Dido is giving a command for Anna to be present. On a deeper level, since Virgil is aware of Anna's status as a goddess, *adesse* especially fitting since it is very often used in prayer formulae (*OLD* s.v. 13). The beginning of this passage also contains the word *huc*. This '*huc*' essentially completes the thought of the acrostic. *Huc ades* is especially prominent in prayer formula.[20] There is also a precedent for having part of the prayer in an acrostic. In her recent article in *Mnemosyne*, Kronenberg argues that there is an intentional acrostic, AUDI ME, in Tibullus's prayer to Apollo in 2.5.16–27 in alternating lines.[21]

Lympha appears for its second and only other time in this book immediately after Dido has stabbed herself on the pyre. Anna rushes out and reproaches her dying sister for her earlier ruse. At the end of her speech, however, she devotes her words to a more pressing task:

> '… date, vulnera **lymphis**
> **abluam** et, extremus si quis super halitus errat,
> ore legam …'

> Let me **wash** the wounds with **water** and, if any last breath wanders over her, let me catch it with my lips.

Virg. A. 4.683–5

Anna requests water to ritually wash the body of Dido, as was customary in Greco-Roman burial practices.[22] In this scene we finally see Anna providing the water that Dido requested in the passage recently discussed (4.634–5). Since Anna will be a water nymph, the audience will recognize her connection to ritualistic baths with which nymphs are so often associated in the Greco-Roman world.[23] What is more, the verb *abluere* is of great significance. The verb elsewhere in Latin literature has connotations of a ritualistic *lavatio* in a natural body of water.[24]

This verb is used only two other times in the entire *Aeneid*. The first use of *abluere* in the poem is in Book 2 when Aeneas finally decides to flee Troy. He just recently engaged in futile combat with the Greeks and returns to his home with bloodied hands. He gives these instructions to his father:

> 'tu, genitor, cape sacra manu patriosque penatis;
> me bello e tanto digressum et caede recenti
> attrectare nefas, donec me flumine vivo
> **abluero**.'
>
> 'You, father, take these sacred objects and ancestral *penates* in hand. It would be against the will of the gods for me to touch them, after I just returned from so great a skirmish and fresh carnage, until **I wash** myself in a living river'.
>
> Virg. A. 2.717–20

Here, as with the passage from Book 4, the verb *abluere* is associated with a river, as well as with water used in a ritualistic context. Horsfall remarks that these lines are the standard language of ritual purification, which requires water from a natural, running water source.[25] He cites Serv. Dan., who glosses *vivo* as *perenni*, the word which Ovid will later connect to Anna's second name (*amne perenne*, Ov. *Fast.* 3.654). The only other instance in which Virgil uses this term is with Turnus at the very end of Book 9. The Rutulian hero makes his escape from the Trojan camp by jumping into the Tiber:

> ... ille suo cum gurgite flavo
> accepit venientem ac mollibus extulit undis
> et laetum sociis **abluta** caede remisit.
>
> And that one (the Tiber) received him as he came with its tawny stream and raised him up with its soft waves and sent him back happily to his friends while **washing** off the slaughter.
>
> Virg. A. 9.816–18

One again, the verb *abluere* appears to have a strong connection to rivers, and it has a ritual connotation since Turnus himself is in a sense being 'purified' by the river.[26]

This reading also may shed light on an old crux of Book 4. When Dido learns of Aeneas's decision to leave Carthage, she asks Anna to try to stop him. Her words have puzzled commentators:

> miserae hoc tamen unum
> exsequere, Anna, mihi; **solam** nam perfidus ille

te colere, arcanos etiam **tibi** credere sensus;
sola viri mollis **aditus** et tempora **noras**.

Anna nevertheless perform this one thing for poor me. For that treacherous one was **cherishing/worshiping you alone**, was entrusting his secret feelings even to you. **You alone know** the soft **means to access** the man and the proper times.

Virg. A. 4. 420–3

Two questions that arise are: (1) Why does Dido imply that Anna is closer to Aeneas than she is? (2) What exactly does *colere* mean? Some scholars have posited that this passage refers to the alternate tradition mentioned above that *Anna*, and not Dido, fell in love with Aeneas.[27] Swallow has postulated that it alludes to Aeneas and Anna as kindred spirits because they were both very 'practical'.[28] Not ruling out an allusion to the tradition of Varro (as Virgil often alludes to contradictory versions of the myth),[29] I argue that this passage may also refer to Anna Perenna. The verb *colere* is often thought to mean 'cherish' or 'attend to' (*OLD* s.v., 7), indicating the affair of Aeneas and Anna. Another meaning, however, is 'worship' (*OLD* s.v., 6). This sense coincides well with the audience's knowledge of Anna's future deification. Furthermore, this passage also exhibits the typical *topoi* of Greco-Roman hymns, the so-called *du-Stil* coined by Norden.[30] This passage contains several components of hymnic formulae: (1) the repetition of the second person personal pronoun in multiple cases (*te ... tibi*, 422); (2) asyndeton (*colere ... credere*, 422); (3) the listing of the deity's spheres of influence or concern (*sola viri mollis aditus et tempora noras*, 423);[31] and (4) the indication that the deity can have no rival in these spheres of influence and concern (*solam ... sola*, 421–3).[32] In essence, Dido here composes her own miniature hymn to Anna Perenna. The potentially sexual connotations of *aditus* and *noras* could also speak to the erotic nature of Anna Perenna's festival in addition to the tradition of Aeneas and Anna's affair.[33] This hymnic language further suggests that Virgil is evoking the divine qualities of the nymph Anna Perenna.

Given that Virgil has used subtle hints such as the acrostic in 4.634–6 discussed above, I would like to propose one more subtle hint of Virgil playing with the Anna Perenna tradition. Another indicator of Anna's godhead is her full name hidden in her first speech of the poem:

Anna refert: 'o luce magis dilecta sorori,
solane **perpetua** maerens carpere iuventa
nec dulcis natos Veneris nec praemia noris?'

Anna says, 'Oh one who is cherished by her sister more than light, will you waste away sad and alone in **everlasting** youth? Will you know neither the sweet sons of Venus nor her rewards?'

Virg. A. 4.31–3

The passage cited above contains a subtle allusion to the goddess's name. The first part of the goddess's name is present at the beginning of line 31 (*Anna*). It also seems striking since *perpetua* is a synonym of *perennis*. Forms of these two words (or roots of these two words) appear on several occasions in close proximity to suggest a similarity in meaning. In a passage of Plautus's *Persa*, the scheming parasite Saturio speaks to his daughter:

> Quae res bene vortat mi et tibi et uentri meo
> **perennitati**que adeo huic, **perpetuo** cibus
> ut mihi supersit, suppetat, superstitet.
>
> May this matter turn out well for me and you and my belly and also this **perpetuity** so that food may exist, be at hand, and remain for me **forever**.

Pl. Pers. 329–31

The two synonymous words, *perennitati* and *perpetuo*, though differing in parts of speech, are not without purpose placed in the same line. The similarity of their meaning is highlighted by the rapid-fire, alliterative list of synonyms in the next line: *supersit, suppetat, superstitet*.[34] In Cicero's *De Natura Deorum*, the speaker Balbus argues for the intelligence and divine nature of the stars themselves. In his description, the adjectives are juxtaposed:

> earum autem **perennes** cursus atque **perpetui** cum admirabili incredibilique constantia declarant in his vim et mentem esse divinam, ut haec ipsa qui non sentiat deorum vim habere is nihil omnino sensurus esse videatur.
>
> Their (the stars') **unending** and **ceaseless** courses with wonderful and unbelievable harmony, however, makes clear that in them there is a divine power and mind to the end that anyone who does not feel these things have the power of the gods seems that they would utterly feel nothing.

Cic. N.D. 2.55

In this passage, it seems that *perennis* and *perpetuus* are indistinguishable. A third and final example from Ovid's *Remedia Amoris* proves this. The speaker uses an aquatic analogy to suggest that the best way to end a love affair is slowly, in gentle stages: *Flumine* **perpetuo** *torrens solet altior ire / Sed tamen haec breuis est, illa* **perennis** *aqua* (A torrent is likely to go higher than an everlasting river, but nevertheless the former is short-lived, the latter is unending water, 651–2.). Once again, it is clear that these words are interchangeable. Furthermore, it is of note that both words are used in fluvial context. Because of the apparent connection between *perpetuus* and *perennis*, I argue that Virgil's use of *perpetua* in 4.432 is a subtle reference to Anna's divine alter ego, Anna Perenna, since Ovid explicitly connects Perenna to *perennis* (*Fast.* 3.654). The placement of *perpetua* right below the line and to the right of *Anna* in the line above (431), further strengthens the intentionality of this wordplay.[35] A covert allusion to Anna's full name is unsurprising. As O'Hara discusses in his book on etymological wordplay, Virgil often suppresses the name, which the audience must supply to complete the wordplay.[36] He takes the idea of suppression from Servius himself who notes that Virgil suppresses the name of the *felix malum* at *Georgics* 1.126.[37] Here Virgil does say Anna Perenna directly, but the learned audience member will recognize this allusion.

Now that the allusions to the goddess Anna Perenna in the *Aeneid* are clear, the greater resonances this connection has for the epic as a whole can be explored.[38] Turnus also has a sister, Juturna, who is both a helper figure and a water nymph. In her first, albeit brief, appearance in the poem, she advises Turnus (10.439–40) to help Lausus, the pitiable son of Mezentius who soon will be vanquished by Aeneas. She plays a much more significant role in Book 12. The nymph, at the behest of Juno (12.139–60), provides aid to her brother. In order to save Turnus from single combat with the martially superior Aeneas, she causes the treaty struck between the Latins and Trojans to be broken and renews the fighting (12.222–69). Later in the book, she leads Turnus away from the fighting by taking on the guise of his charioteer Metiscus (12.468–99) and further attempts to save Turnus's life by fetching his sword for him (12.783–5). Eventually realizing her cause to be lost, she delivers an impassioned speech highlighting her own suffering and calling into question the benefit of her own divinity (12.872–84).

Scholars have drawn comparisons and explored the correspondences between Anna and Juturna.[39] Grace West (1979) and Victor Castellani (1987) have noted the intratextual echoes that form a link between the two. Firstly, the two sisters receive the epithet *maesta soror* ('the sad sister'). This appellation appears in the poem only twice, one time for Anna (4.476) and one time for Juturna (12.682).[40] The other verbal echo involves Anna and Juturna disfiguring their bodies in the act of mourning. In both of these cases, the grieving sisters address their ill-fated siblings in the subsequent lines. Virgil uses the exact same line for both the sisters: *unguibus ora soror foedans et pectora pugnis* (Virg. *A.* 4.673).[41] These words are used of Anna when she realizes that Dido has killed herself on the pyre that Anna had helped to construct (4.673). The exact same line is applied to Juturna when she sees the ill-omened bird sent by Jupiter and realizes that Turnus's cause is doomed (12.871). West and Castellani maintain that these verbal echoes invite parallels to be drawn between Anna and Juturna and that these parallels suggest they are tragic figures.[42]

My reading demonstrates how this parallelism of Anna and Juturna is strengthened by Juturna's status as a water nymph and the audience's knowledge of Anna's eventual transformation into one. A passage of Cicero gives us an alternate name for Juturna, 'Diuturna' (*Clu.* 101), which recalls in its meaning, 'eternal', the second half Anna *Perenna*. These two goddesses also share in common their path to godhead. Juturna achieves her divine status as compensation for her rape by Jupiter.[43] Similarly, Anna was a mortal who was granted immortality in her lifetime. She, like Juturna, becomes a goddess through a rape by a god:[44]

> corniger hanc **cupidis rapuisse** Numicius undis
> creditur et stagnis occuluisse suis.
>
> It is believed that the horned Numicius **snatched** her **up** in his **lustful** waves and hid her in his streams.
>
> Ov. Fast. 3.647–8

Here, instead of describing the Numicius strictly as a natural body of water, Ovid has the anthropomorphized river 'snatch her up' (*rapuisse*). The elaboration that waves are 'lustful' further stresses the violent, sexual nature of her encounter. Anna appears again in the next few lines declaring her divine status: *placidi sum nympha Numici* ('I am a nymph of the tranquil Numicius', 3.653–4). Therefore, it is clear that Anna's newfound immortality is a direct result of this rape.

Furthermore, this connection between Anna and Juturna is even more solidified with the knowledge that they are both associated with the same River Numicius, a river near Lavinium.[45] Servius tells us that there was a spring to Juturna near the River Numicus [46] and, as mentioned above, Anna meets her end in this same river. In addition, the aquatic nature of both Anna and Juturna perhaps adds a sacrificial connotation to the people they 'wash' since both the Numicius and Juturna's spring in Lavinium were frequently used in sacrificial rites at Rome.[47] Anna literally washes the body of Dido after her ritual suicide, which some have seen as perverted sacrifice (*A.* 4.683–5).[48] As for Juturna, she does not literally wash Turnus, but she is present just before his death in her capacity as a water nymph. Just before she plunges into the river, she performs an action that seems ritualistic: *caput glauco contexit amictu* (she covers her head with a grey cloak, Virg. A. 12.885).[49] The idea of Turnus as a sacrifice is not a new concept,[50] but I suggest that my reading further lends validity to this notion.

As mentioned above, the verbal and thematic parallels between Anna and Juturna highlight their tragic role in the *Aeneid*. Anna and Juturna both attempt in vain to aid a sibling who has suffered at the hands of the Aeneas. There is a certain irony in their failures as well in light of their realms of influence as nymphs. The waters from the springs associated with Juturna, both the one near the Numicius, and the famous *Lacus Iuturnae* in the Roman Forum, were known for their salubrious properties.[51] Furthermore, Juturna has another connection to salvation through her association with the Dioscuri. It was alleged that they appeared at her fountain in the Forum to water their horses on two occasions in Roman history in which they had aided Rome in a battle.[52] Her primary goal throughout her appearances in the poem is to save the life of her brother. In spite of all of her attempts to save Turnus, none of them prove fruitful. Juturna essentially fails in the one area that her public cult was known for.

In the same vein, Anna fails in a similar tragically ironic manner. Anna Perenna is a goddess of fertility. This is clear from the lascivious nature of her festival and her association with water.[53] In the *Aeneid*, Anna's relationship with fertility clearly displays itself in her speech that strongly argues for sex and marriage as stated above. Dido's most common epithet in the entire poem, however, is *infelix*.[54] On one level, Dido receives this epithet because she is ill starred: we the audience know that her relationship with Aeneas cannot last. At the same time, this word can also mean 'sterile' or 'unfruitful'. Pease maintains that it can also suggest 'childlessness', as it clearly does, since Dido tragically will bear no children.[55] Anna, in a sense, does partially complete her goddess function: she does facilitate Dido engaging in sexual activity with Aeneas. She does not, however, fulfill completely her function as fertility goddess and Dido does remain *infelix*.

In conclusion, I have shown that Virgil connects his Anna to Anna Perenna and alludes not just to the goddess herself, but to the other elements of her festival. This association enriches our understanding of how Virgil crafts his poetry by drawing upon alternate forms of the myth.[56] Finally, there is a strong connection between Anna and Juturna through their statuses as water nymphs and their association with the River Numicius. The twinning of Anna and Juturna highlight their similar, tragic plight. A stronger parallelism between Anna and Juturna also suggests a more striking link between to two other figures who suffered at the hands of Aeneas: Dido and Turnus.[57]

5

How to Become a Hero: Gendering the Apotheosis of Ovid's Anna Perenna

A. Everett Beek

Ovid's *Fasti* relates a wide variety of apotheosis narratives, from the catasterisms of characters such as Callisto and Orion to the assumption of Romulus. Throughout the *Fasti*, most of the narratives of supernatural transformations are some species of apotheosis (in contrast to the *Metamorphoses*, in which most supernatural transformations are punitive transformations into subhuman forms), and moreover most of these transformations are catalyzed by violence.[1] In particular, the apotheoses of female characters tend to be prompted by sexual assaults; for example, Lara is raped by Mercury in her transformation into the goddess Tacita, and Chloris is raped by Zephyrus before she is promoted from a minor nymph to become the powerful goddess Flora.[2] Apotheosis in the *Fasti* is not a pleasant process, and is fraught with the potential for irreversible violence.

Anna Perenna stands out among the apotheoses in the *Fasti* because she is one of the few female characters who achieves apotheosis without suffering a sexual attack (either before or during her apotheosis). To escape some of the confusion of the mutually contradictory multiple aetiologies Ovid's *Fasti* provides for Anna Perenna, for this paper I will be focusing on the self-contained narrative of the travels and apotheosis of Dido's sister (Ov. *Fast*. 3.545–656), reading the character as a continuation of Virgil's Anna from *Aeneid* 4.[3] Ovid conflates the nymph Anna Perenna with Dido's sister,[4] and in doing so presents her as a political figure, specifically the leader of a band of Carthaginian refugees. In Ovid's narrative, Anna survives the collapse of Carthage, seeks refuge with Aeneas, is attacked on Lavinia's orders and saved from this attack via apotheosis. The audience sees more of her leadership role than her role in sexual or romantic drama.

Anna's transformation into Anna Perenna, as presented in the *Fasti*, reflects masculine more than feminine experience.[5] Typically, female characters in

Ovid's works occupy narrative roles that highlight their sexual identity; specifically, the stories of female characters who are apotheosed in the *Fasti* almost always involve a sexual attack.[6] Throughout Anna's narrative, her sexual identity and role in sexual or romantic drama is minimized; meanwhile, she instead takes on responsibilities in traditionally masculine spheres such as political leadership. Within the *Fasti*, Anna is a heroic character who performs epic – and traditionally masculine – deeds by leading the Carthaginian refugees and seeking a new place for them to settle. In this way she makes a strong contrast to typical female characters in Ovid's works. She even contrasts her sister's role in the *Aeneid*. Although Dido occupies a political (i.e., traditionally masculine) role in Carthage up until the moment Aeneas arrives, throughout the time she is onstage in Vergil's epic, she is nevertheless defined in terms of her sexual identity,[7] and allows her sexual identity to overrun her political responsibilities, in a way that is conventionally associated with women.[8] As I will illustrate, the sexual aspect of Anna's identity is downplayed within Ovid's quasi-epic narrative, which casts her as a less feminine, more masculine character, in substantial contrast to other women in the *Fasti*.

Anna is not an epic hero in the sense that she exemplifies masculine virtues through her achievements in warfare and combat. Even so, Ovid is notoriously unconventional in his construction of epic.[9] In the *Metamorphoses*, Ovid pushes back against the traditional generic constraints and expands the genre by incorporating voices and experiences that were avoided by earlier epic poets, especially feminine voices and experiences, as has been explored in articles by Mairéad McAuley and Carole Newlands.[10] Female characters are more often cast in heroic, leading roles, as Newlands articulates: 'In the *Metamorphoses* women impinge on traditionally masculine, heroic spheres … When they transgress onto traditional male territory, the women of the poem challenge conventional notions of epic femininity as passive, modest, and domestic'.[11] Although Ovid's *Fasti* is difficult to classify generically,[12] the adventures of Anna present a typically epic scenario, one that recalls the travels of Odysseus or Aeneas.[13] This epic is decidedly Ovidian: gender roles are less restrictive and women can be successful in heroic roles. Anna's narrative in many ways marks her as an epic hero, as far as the elegiac genre and the brevity of her story allow.

The epic that Anna's travels mirror most directly is the travels of Aeneas, as Porte describes: 'Le lecteur des *Fastes* découvre qu'Ovide a composé une *Énéide* en miniature, dont Anna est, cette fois, l'héroïne!'[14] In introducing Anna, Ovid seems to pick up where Virgil left off in describing the history of

Carthage and the relationship between Dido and Aeneas, and within this paper I construe Ovid's character Anna as carrying the history and characterization of the same character from the *Aeneid*. To evoke the Virgilian background to his story, Ovid efficiently summarizes many crucial events from Dido's story in the *Aeneid*: the fatally intense passion, the interference of Rumor and Iarbas, Dido's bitter suicide, and even Aeneas's address to Dido in the underworld. After this synopsis of familiar events, Ovid shows Anna undertaking new adventures, which, even though they have not been reported in previous literature, will no doubt sound familiar because they make Anna the avatar of Aeneas in a transposed *Aeneid*.[15] Anna's home city is destroyed by invaders; she gathers a small group of survivors to lead to a new home;[16] she is hospitably received by a foreign king (Battus of Melite), but is forced to leave that refuge due to an attack; she suffers a dangerous storm at sea;[17] and finally, she lands in Italy, where she is apotheosed by the river Numicius. In the *Metamorphoses*, Ovid also relates the apotheosis of Aeneas at the river Numicius,[18] which associates Anna not only with Aeneas, but with the long line of apotheosed heroes and political leaders in the *Metamorphoses*: Hercules, Romulus and Julius Caesar.[19]

Aeneas, nonetheless, is not Anna's only model. In the *Aeneid*, when Dido and Aeneas first meet, Dido famously remarks on the similarity of her difficulties to those of Aeneas: *me quoque per multos similis fortuna labores / iactatam hac demum volvit consistere terra* (I also was driven through many similar difficulties, until Fortune at last brought me to a stop in this land, Virg. *A.* 1.628–9).[20] While Ovid makes self-conscious literary allusions to link Anna with Aeneas, it is clear that both of these characters share affinities with Dido as well: McKeown, in the comparison between the *Aeneid* and Anna's adventures in the *Fasti*, casts Anna sometimes in the role of Aeneas, sometimes in that of Dido.[21] Dido also flees from a threat in her home city with a band of supportive compatriots, and leads them to settle in a new town, as described briefly by Venus (Virg. *A.* 1.340–68). The conclusions of these narratives, however, mark a crucial divergence between Dido's story and Aeneas's: Aeneas is ultimately rewarded with apotheosis, while Dido is driven to suicide, and, according to the *Fasti*, her city collapses immediately in the wake of her death. While Anna has two political leaders before her as potential role models, it should be clear to the reader which one has the more enviable fate.

Throughout her abbreviated journey, Anna's adventures resemble Aeneas's more than Dido's. Unlike Anna and Aeneas, Dido meets no storm at sea, and receives hospitality from no foreign king. She does not flee Tyre on account of an invading army, and she is not apotheosed. The allusions in her story to previous epic heroes are minimal. Although Anna's journey invokes both Aeneas's and Dido's as literary antecedents, Aeneas's is the more direct model.

Still, it is Dido who establishes precedent for Anna's role as a woman taking on traditionally masculine responsibilities. Dido in the *Aeneid* is cast from the outset as a boundary-breaking character in terms of her gender. It is unusual *per se* for a woman to be a founder figure, even rarer than it is for a woman to be head of state. Female heads of state are generally viewed with suspicion in the ancient world,[22] and once Aeneas arrives in Carthage, Dido quickly plays out the fears embedded in this suspicion: she is easily distracted from her obligations by an attractive man, she attempts to compel her lover's affection by exercise of her political authority, and she is so consumed by infatuation that it leads to her suicide, which, according to the *Fasti*, is disastrous for the state that depends on her.[23] When attempting a conventionally masculine role, Dido is ultimately ruled by stereotypically feminine weaknesses, to her sorrow. Such weaknesses are not evident in Ovid's Anna – she is not distracted from her responsibilities by an infatuation – which gives her a more masculine identity.

Angeline Chiu has discussed Anna's story as a 'demilitarized' (and consequently de-epicized) version of Aeneas's epic.[24] While I concede that Anna as doublet of Aeneas lacks the military accoutrements that he prominently displays, Anna's achievements as a political leader still mark her with traditionally masculine qualities that are important for an epic hero.[25] Compare, for example, the point in *Aeneid* 2 when Venus orders Aeneas to abandon the fight against the Greeks and instead flee the city: at that juncture, his skills as a leader of refugees are more important to the epic than his skills as a warrior. Creusa's shade reinforces the importance of his leadership skills by prophesying his future *regnum* in Italy.[26] Although Anna's story in the *Fasti* may be demilitarized, I would hardly agree that it is thereby de-epicized.

The connection between Anna and Aeneas is reinforced by the similarity between Anna's escape from Lavinia, and Aeneas's escape from Troy. Both escapes are precipitated in the same way: after going to sleep, they receive a supernatural warning of an impending attack.[27] After Lavinia develops an intense hatred of Anna, Anna sees Dido's shade in a dream:

> nox erat: ante torum visa est adstare sororis
>   squalenti Dido sanguinulenta coma
> et 'fuge, ne dubita, maestum fuge', dicere 'tectum';
>   sub verbum querulas impulit aura fores.

It was night: Dido, blood-soaked and with filthy hair, seemed to stand before her sister's bed, saying: 'Flee this grim house without hesitation', and following close upon the words, a wind rattled the doors with a groan.

Ov. Fast. 3.639–42[28]

Aeneas likewise receives a nocturnal warning, given in more detail:

> in somnis, ecce, ante oculos maestissimus Hector   270
> uisus adesse mihi largosque effundere fletus,
> raptatus bigis ut quondam, aterque cruento
> puluere perque pedes traiectus lora tumentis . . .
> squalentem barbam et concretos sanguine crinis
> uulneraque illa gerens, quae circum plurima muros
> accipit patrios. ultro flens ipse uidebar
> compellare uirum et maestas expromere uoces . . .   280
> ille nihil, nec me quaerentem uana moratur,
> sed grauiter gemitus imo de pectore ducens,
> 'heu fuge, nate dea, teque his' ait 'eripe flammis'.

In my dream – look! – most wretched Hector seemed to stand before my eyes and pour forth tears, just as he once looked when he was dragged by a chariot, darkened with bloody dust, with the reins pierced through his swollen feet . . . He had a filthy beard, and hair clotted together with blood, and those many wounds that he received around the walls of his ancestral city. I myself, weeping, seemed (in the dream) to beseech the man and force out miserable words . . . He did not respond, nor did he wait for me while I asked useless questions. Instead, dragging a deep groan from the bottom of his heart, he said, 'Alas, flee, goddess-born, and save yourself from these flames'.

Virg. A. 2.270–3, 277–80, 287–9

The fact that supernatural intervention arrives to rescue both Aeneas and Anna from some ostensibly terrible fate implies that their lives carry weighty significance. Aeneas is sent to re-found Troy and continue Trojan culture in spite of the sack; Anna is seeking a safe haven for her people, but this endeavour is threatened when Anna apparently is about to suffer some horrible fate, possibly death, at the hands of Lavinia's henchmen. The fact that Anna is supernaturally warned in time to escape leads the audience to expect that she might continue following Aeneas's precedent and lead her people elsewhere, although this possibility is averted by her sudden apotheosis; she does not have the opportunity to pursue her leadership role on earth as long as Aeneas does. The similarity to Dido's dream of Sychaeus is also noteworthy, although it is told indirectly and in less detail: *in somnis inhumati venit imago coniugis . . . celerare fugam patriaque excedere suadet* (the shade of her unburied husband visits her in a dream ... he persuades her to escape hurriedly and leave her country, Virg. A. 1.353–4.357). Like Aeneas, Dido here uses her admonitory dream-vision as a springboard to take on the heroic role of leading a population to a new home. It is remarkable, however, that these characters have substantially different degrees of success in pursuing their heroic roles: while Aeneas successfully founds his city and achieves apotheosis, Dido and Anna are divided: Dido only founds the city without apotheosis, whereas Anna is apotheosed before she can re-settle her population in a new city.

The adventures of Anna in the *Fasti* are capped by Anna's apotheosis, a final confirmation of her heroic role, and a significant link to Aeneas. Unlike the majority of the apotheosed women in Ovid, Anna undergoes an apotheosis that is not a compensation for a rape that she has suffered at the hands of the gods, and in fact has no apparent connection to rape.[29] Rather, her apotheosis is effected as a salvation from imminent, life-threatening violence, sparing her from the ambush that Lavinia has laid for her:

>   omnia promittit falsumque Lavinia volnus
>   mente premit tacita dissimulatque metus;
>   donaque cum videat praeter sua lumina ferri   635
>   multa, tamen mitti clam quoque multa putat.
>   non habet exactum quid agat: furialiter odit,
>   et parat insidias et cupit ulta mori.
>   nox erat: ante torum visa est adstare sororis
>   squalenti Dido sanguinulenta coma   640
>   et 'fuge, ne dubita, maestum fuge' dicere 'tectum';
>   sub verbum querulas impulit aura fores.
>   exsilit et velox humili †super ausa† fenestra
>   se iacit (audacem fecerat ipse timor),
>   cumque metu rapitur tunica velata recincta   645
>   currit ut auditis territa damma lupis,
>   corniger hanc cupidis rapuisse Numicius undis
>   creditur et stagnis occuluisse suis.
>   Sidonis interea magno clamore per agros
>   quaeritur: apparent signa notaeque pedum;   650
>   ventum erat ad ripas: inerant vestigia ripis;
>   sustinuit tacitas conscius amnis aquas.
>   ipsa loqui visa est 'placidi sum nympha Numici:
>   amne perenne latens Anna Perenna vocor'.

Lavinia agreed to everything, and she disguised in her quiet mind how she mistakenly perceived an affront, and she hid her fear; although she saw many gifts carried before her eyes, she thought that many others were also sent in secret. She had not planned what she would do: she hated [Anna] wrathfully, and she prepared an ambush and desired to die avenged. It was night: Dido, blood-soaked and with filthy hair, seemed to stand before her sister's bed, saying: 'Flee this grim house without hesitation', and following close upon the words, a wind rattled the doors with a groan. [Anna] jumped up and, having thrown herself quickly over the low windowsill, she cast herself down (fear itself made her daring), and because she was seized by fear, she ran dressed in her girded-up tunic, just as a frightened sheep runs from wolves that she has heard, and the horned Numicius is believed to have snatched her in his desirous waves and to have hidden her in his waters. Meanwhile, the Sidonian [Anna] was sought in the fields with a great commotion, and the marks and signs of her feet were found; they came to the banks [of Numicius]: there were footprints on the banks; the knowing river smoothed his calm waters. She herself seemed to speak: 'I am a nymph of quiet Numicius: eternally hiding by the river [*amne perenne*], I am called Anna Perenna'.

Ov. *Fast.* 3.633–54

Throughout her adventures in the *Fasti*, Anna survives numerous disasters from which she is not saved. She suffers considerably when she is (for the second time) driven out of her home by political upheaval and forced to resettle, losing family members and loved ones in the process. She finds refuge among the people of Aeneas's Italian city, whom she learns too late to be untrustworthy. Having been attacked and driven from her bedroom, she flees in the night, and her rapture by the river Numicius prevents her death at the hands of Lavinia's henchmen. But she is at last spared from rape, the typical initiatory experience for apotheosed women in the *Fasti*.

Insofar as Anna Perenna's apotheosis serves as a salvation from death, she is comparable to Julius Caesar in the *Fasti*,[30] and set apart from the raped women such as Chloris. While the raped women suffer violence first and are ostensibly compensated for this violence with apotheosis or other supernatural transformation, Anna Perenna is transformed, and thereby saved, before she suffers such violence. In this case, Anna's apotheosis is prompted not by the completed violence of a rape, but by threatened violence so immediate that death is inevitable. While apotheoses in the *Fasti* are typically precipitated by violence, in this case the threat of violence has become surrogate for the violence itself. Though Anna is spared from this ultimate danger, her long narrative of disasters and suffering in the *Fasti* ultimately builds the theme, inescapable in Ovid, that apotheosis is not an enjoyable process, possibly not even a desirable process.

At this point we should examine the connections between Anna's and Aeneas's apotheosis. Although though this event is not directly narrated in either the *Aeneid* or the *Fasti*, it is described in detail in the *Metamorphoses*:

> litus adit Laurens, ubi tectus harundine serpit
> in freta flumineis vicina Numicus undis.
> hunc iubet Aeneae quaecumque obnoxia morti   600
> abluere et tacito deferre sub aequora cursu.
> corniger exsequitur Veneris mandata suisque
> quidquid in Aenea fuerat mortale repurgat
> et respergit aquis; pars optima restitit illi.
> lustratum genetrix diuino corpus odore   605
> unxit et ambrosia cum dulci nectare mixta
> contigit os fecitque deum, quem turba Quirini
> nuncupat Indigetem temploque arisque recepit.

> [Venus] approached the Laurentian shore, where the Numicus, shaded with reeds, flows through its fluid waves into the nearby streams. She ordered Numicus to remove from Aeneas whatever is subject to death and to wash it away in its placid stream to the sea. The horned god [Numicus] carried out the orders of Venus and cleaned away whatever was mortal in Aeneas and sprinkled him with his waters; he retained his best part. His mother anointed his purified body with a divine fragrance and applied to his mouth ambrosia mixed with sweet nectar and made him a god, whom the Romans call Indiges, and they received him with a temple and altars.[31]
>
> Ov. Met. 14.598–608

Not only are both Anna and Aeneas transformed from their mortal state, but both Anna and Aeneas are transformed by the same agent: the river Numicius. The process of apotheosis is, within the works of Ovid, strongly associated with famous heroes. Although it is known to befall more inconspicuous characters such as Arethusa or Io, the best-known apotheoses from the *Metamorphoses* are those of heroes: Hercules, Aeneas, Romulus and Julius Caesar. Anna as a political leader is likewise associated with this august company.

I must address one possible objection to my argument. I have argued that Anna is spared from rape, but a careful reading of the passage opens this statement to interpretation. Overall, Anna's narrative is told briefly, and with minimal detail. Aeneas not only does not request an explanation for Anna's appearance in his realm, he actively urges her to refrain from telling the story of Dido's death.[32] Likewise, there is minimal elaboration over Anna's transformation. When she flees Lavinia, she becomes a nymph. The slamming of a door gives little indication of what Lavinia's henchmen had planned, what danger threatened Anna, or why Numicius felt it was essential to save her. In fact, the details are so vague that one may ask whether Anna's transformation actually spares her from any violence. While she is rescued from the attack arranged by Lavinia, her rescue itself may open up the potential for other violent acts. In lines 3.645–8 above, she is 'snatched away' (*rapuisse*) by the 'desirous' (*cupidis*) waves of the river Numicius, and is changed into a *nympha Numici*. There may be more violence latent in this narrative than is apparent on the surface.

This description, including the simile to a frightened animal fleeing a predator, is evocative of the many rapes that gods in the *Fasti* commit against mortal women. For this reason, most scholars assume that Anna Perenna's apotheosis has a sexual element, to the effect that Anna Perenna's salvation from Lavinia's henchmen is dependent upon a marriage-type arrangement between her and the river god.[33] In this case, her apotheosis would be much more similar to the rape narratives of Lara or Chloris. Still, no sexual contact between Anna Perenna and Numicius is specified, and no children are mentioned, in contrast to the rape-transformations of Lara and Chloris, which clearly foreground the stories' sexual element. In Lara's story, Ovid's description of the rape is unambiguous: *[Mercurius] vim parat ... [Lara] frustra muto nititur ore loqui, fitque gravis,* ([Mercury] threatens violence ... [Lara] struggles in vain to speak with a silent mouth, and she becomes pregnant, Ov. *Fast.* 2.613–15). Chloris also describes her own rape in brief but clear terms: *[Zephyrus] insequitur, fugio: fortior ille fuit. et dederat fratri Boreas ius omne rapinae ... vim tamen emendat dando mihi nomina nuptae,* (Zephyrus pursued; I fled, but he was stronger. Boreas granted his brother every right to rape ... but he atoned for his rape by giving me the name 'bride', Ov. *Fast.* 5.202–5). Even though Anna's transformation is not the fully unsexualized event granted to Aeneas in the *Metamorphoses*, the sexual language is merely hinted at, rather than stated outright as Ovid does in the stories of women whose apotheosis is precipitated by rape. In effect, Anna's apotheosis takes on sexualized, typically feminine language, while still remaining essentially unsexualized. In Ovid's stories, rape is such a common element of female transformation that language evocative of rape appears even in stories that are ostensibly rape-free. Although Anna throughout her travels has been presented as a more masculine political leader, her story still takes on feminine language at the end. Even if a sexual element is being hinted at in Numicius's actions, it is significant that Anna Perenna is being saved by Numicius from her would-be assassins, and her encounter with Numicius is presented as an alternative to death. In the rape stories the rape itself is the primary threat; the rape victims are not simultaneously menaced by mortal danger.

As a secondary point, Anna's apotheosis makes a remarkable contrast with the transformations of fleeing women in the *Metamorphoses*. There are a plethora of women who flee from libidinous or simply violent attackers in Ovid's poetry, but in the *Metamorphoses*, most commonly these stories are resolved in a way that deprives the women of agency or protection: they are transformed into a plant, a spring, a bird, an island, or some subhuman form. In the *Fasti*, a different pattern emerges, in which pursued women are typically promoted to divinity and thereby invested with power.[34] Accordingly, Anna's transformation to a nymph invests her with more power than she had as a mortal. She is not only safe from her mortal attackers, but she also is able to exercise divine power as a goddess, and what sets her apart from other female characters' apotheosis stories in the *Fasti* is that her divine power is illustrated in a subsequent narrative, in which Anna Perenna plays a role in divine society and uses her position to deceive Mars.

I would like to make a final point regarding an event that is deeply loaded with gender significance: Lavinia's attack on Anna. Lavinia attacks Anna because she perceives Anna to be a threat to her marriage, despite Anna's limited involvement with Aeneas. It may seem rash and unreasonable for Lavinia to assume that any female refugee or diplomat who consults her husband is a threat to her marriage. One may, however, trace Lavinia's line of reasoning by following the argument in John Heath's article on Diana's understanding of Ovid's *Metamorphoses*.[35] Heath argues that Diana's attack on Actaeon, while frequently read as an overreaction to the limited danger that Actaeon could pose to the goddess, is in fact precipitated by the numerous assaults that have occurred in various *loci amoeni* previously in the poem. Diana, Heath argues, has observed or otherwise been made aware of these assaults, and for that reason chooses to preemptively attack Actaeon rather than suffer an attack herself. Likewise, Lavinia may be an attentive reader of the relevant background to Anna's arrival: Aeneas's Carthaginian adventures in the *Aeneid*. If she knows that Aeneas's stay in Carthage led to the romance between Dido and Aeneas, which directly led to the complete collapse of Carthage, her interference with Anna may be driven by fears for her marriage, as well as for the stability of her home. In this concern, Lavinia fears not that Anna will become another Dido, but rather that Anna will become another Aeneas: the foreign interloper who fascinated the head of state and led to the city's destruction. Lavinia acts quickly to cut off this possibility, and in doing so actually precipitates Anna's apotheosis at the river Numicius, shadowing Aeneas's heroic career before Aeneas reached such achievements himself.

There is a long-established discussion of Aeneas's depiction as a hero within the *Aeneid*, and how his version of epic masculinity is deliberately separated from that of his predecessors, especially Odysseus. When Ovid writes of Anna's epic adventures, he not only builds on Virgil's reframing of the epic hero, but also Ovid's own expansion of the epic genre following the *Metamorphoses*. The gender of Anna the epic hero, though modelled most closely on that of Aeneas, does not strictly follow any conventions, and marks her as a strongly independent and self-defined character.

6

Instability and Permanence in Ceremonial Epigraphy: The Example of Anna Perenna

Anna Blennow

Epigraphy is often viewed as related to the eternal preservation of text and monument, to the materiality of history and to the perpetualization of memory and of powerful individuals. As a consequence, inscriptions are regarded as signifiers of the stability of a public space and of the individuals whose existence becomes interwoven into the urban structure and the visual landscape. In this chapter, I argue that epigraphy in fact tells us not primarily about stability, but about change. With the three votive inscriptions from the Anna Perenna sanctuary at Piazza Euclide as focal points, I set out to investigate how change motivates and interferes with epigraphic monuments as the decisive driving force for the making of the same monuments, and how this change is communicated in the epigraphic text. I will introduce the theory that an inscription almost always is created as a result of change, closely connected with transitional phases of individuals, groups of individuals and even objects. As I will show, also the location of an inscription is of vital importance for understanding the nature of change that lies behind the creation of an inscription.

Initially, I will present the three votive inscriptions in the general context of votive epigraphy. Then, after an introduction to previous theories on epigraphic habit, I will give an overview of the theory of epigraphy and change, and how the Anna Perenna inscriptions can be understood in a new way through this theory. What kind of change is signified through the inscriptions, their content and their location? And what can they actually tell us about the cult to Anna Perenna? By studying the inscriptions of the Arval Brethren as a comparative case, I will also analyse the role of epigraphy as ceremonial writing in extra-urban cult places, such as the Anna Perenna sanctuary and the sacred grove of the Arval Brethren, and in what ways change is expressed in their epigraphic evidence. Lastly, I will show how epigraphic writing as part of the entire vow process can be illustrated through the votive inscriptions together with the *tabellae defixionum* found in the Anna Perenna sanctuary.

The Inscriptions

When the fountain of Anna Perenna was found and excavated in 1999, three inscriptions were found on the site.[1] They were located on two marble votive bases and one marble altar, built into the late-antique retaining wall of the fountain. The inscriptions played a decisive part in identifying the site as a sanctuary to Anna Perenna, a goddess previously known mainly through literary references, and they constitute the first known examples of inscriptions in Rome dedicated to Anna Perenna and her nymphs.[2] Thus, these inscriptions greatly enhanced our knowledge of the activities and whereabouts of the Anna Perenna cult. But what can they tell us? In the following, I will relate the content of the inscriptions, as well as give an account of votive inscriptions in general.

The three inscriptions in the sanctuary of Anna Perenna belong to a period when the site had already been in use for several hundred years: the mid-second century CE. A consular dating to 156 CE is found on one of the inscriptions, and the other two inscriptions are for stylistic reasons believed to be dated to approximately the same period.[3] The present location of the objects is secondary, since they were built into the wall of the fountain in the late antique period. At that point in time, the votive gifts that are supposed to have been placed on the two bases were probably also removed, and thus it is not clear of what they consisted. The inscriptions are not the only text-based evidence on the site: several *tabellae defixionum*, leaden curse tablets, were also found inside the fountain, most of them placed inside oil lamps. A reference to nymphs is found on one of the *tabellae* (and an invocation to *sacras sanctas* on another, taken to refer to the nymphs), which made Marina Piranomonte assume a continued connection between the nymphs, Anna Perenna and the fountain also in the later period of use; Jürgen Blänsdorf has underlined that the name of Anna Perenna is absent from the curse texts, and that the nymphs may have replaced her as addressees in the sanctuary. To judge from the extant material, the main activity of textual practice at the sanctuary over time was concerned with curse tablets, and not with votive or altar inscriptions, although much epigraphic material may of course have been lost.[4]

The first inscription is situated on a marble base, broken in two pieces but reunited when incorporated in the late antique wall.

96　　　　　　　　　　　　　*Anna Blennow*

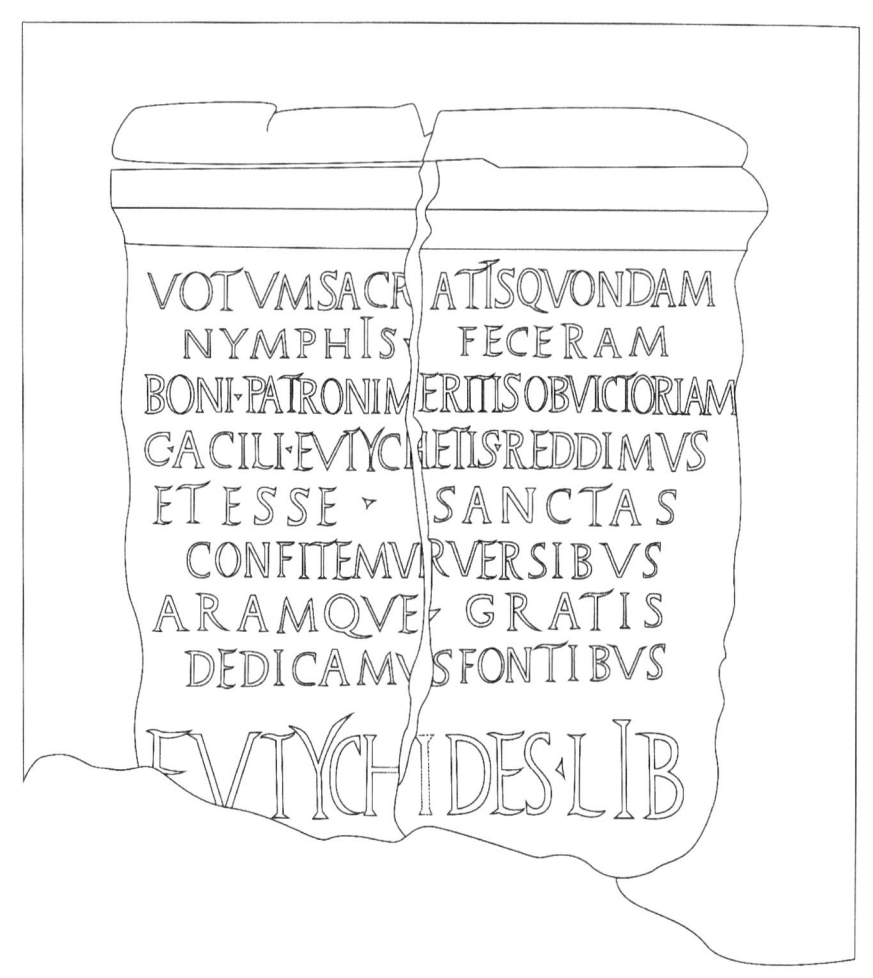

Figure 6.1 *Inscription of Eutychides libertus.* Drawing: Lisa Trentin.

The text describes a dedication by the freedman Eutychides to the nymphs of Anna Perenna on grounds of a victory of his *patronus* Gaius Acilius Eutyches. The text consists of five iambic *senarii*; the signature *Eutychides libertus* on the last line, in much larger size than the rest of the text, is not part of the metrical scheme:

Votum sacratis quondam
nymphis feceram
boni patroni meritis ob victoriam
C(aii) Acili Eutychetis reddimus

> et esse sanctas
> confitemur versibus
> aramque gratis
> dedicamus fontibus.
> Eutychides lib(ertus).

> The vow [which] once I had made to the consecrated nymphs, who deserved it because of the victory of my good patron Gaius Acilius Eutyches, we fulfil, and we confess in verse that they are sacred, and we dedicate an altar to the precious springs. Eutychides, freedman.

AE 2003:251[5]

The second inscription is placed on a marble altar, decorated with balusters and rosette-finials, and a *patera* and a *culter* on the damaged tympanum.

> On the upper element:

> Nymphis sacratis

On the front of the base:

> Suetonius Germanus cum
> Licinia coniuge
> Annae Perennae votum
> quod susceperant si se victo-
> res statuerent, aram mar-
> moream se posituros denuo
> victores facti votum me-
> riti solvimus.
> Ded(icata) non(is) Apr(ilibus), Silvano et Augurino
> co(n)s(ulibus).

> To the consecrated nymphs. We, Suetonius Germanus with his wife Licinia, again made victors, deservedly fulfilled the vow; the vow to Anna Perenna that they had undertaken, that if they had established themselves as victors, they would place a marble altar. [The altar was] dedicated April 5, during the consulship of Silvanus and Augurinus [156 CE].

AE 2003:252[6]

The third inscription, on a votive base in marble, is somewhat fragmentary.

> C(aius) Suetonius Germ[anu]s
> nymphis sacra[tis]
> Annae Perennae d(ono) d(edit).

98 Anna Blennow

Gaius Suetonius Germanus gave [this] as a gift to the consecrated nymphs of Anna Perenna [or: to the nymphs (and) to Anna Perenna, or: to the nymphs consecrated to Anna Perenna].

AE 2003:253[7]

Thus, all three inscriptions refer to votive gifts to the consecrated nymphs,[8] and two of them explicitly mention victories of an unspecified kind as the reason for

NYMPHIS SACRATIS

SVETONIVS GERMANVS CVM
LICINIA CONIVGE
ANNAE PERENNAE VOTVM
QVOD SVSCEPERANT SI EVICTO
RES STATVERENT ARAM MAR
MOREAM SE POSITVROS DENVO
VICTORES FACTI VOTVM ME
RITI   SOLVIMVS
DED NON APR SILVANO ET AVGVRINO
COS

Figure 6.2 *Inscription of Suetonius Germanus and Licinia.* Drawing: Lisa Trentin.

Instability and Permanence 99

```
C SVETONIVS GER[
NYMPHIS SACRA
ANNAE PERENNAE D·D
```

Figure 6.3 *Inscription of Suetonius Germanus.* Drawing: Lisa Trentin.

the gifts. Gaius Suetonius Germanus occurs in two inscriptions, together with his wife Licinia in one of them and alone in the other.[9] In the first inscription, the freedman Eutychides has made a vow for the victory of his *patronus* Gaius Acilius Eutyches. Germanus and his wife, to judge from the plural form in all of the verbs, made both the vow and the votive donation together. Eutychides, on the other hand, seems to have made the vow himself (singular in *feceram*), while the votive gift was given by both the freedman and his *patronus* (*reddimus, confitemur, dedicamus*). The vows are described as made to the consecrated nymphs in the Eutychides inscription, and to Anna Perenna herself in the inscription of Germanus and Licinia. The Eutychides inscription also makes clear that the nymphs symbolize or equal the *grati fontes* (precious springs), since the vow was made to the nymphs while the altar was dedicated to the springs. The ambiguous wording in the shorter of the Germanus inscriptions might mean that the votive gift was given by Germanus either to the nymphs of Anna Perenna (if her name is interpreted as in the genitive), to the nymphs consecrated to Anna Perenna (if her name is taken as dative), or to the nymphs and to Anna Perenna (if the name is understood as in the dative and the conjunction 'and' is implied). The mentions of the nymphs, the springs and of Anna Perenna herself seem to suggest a sort of conglomerate deity, where vows and offers can be made equally to all three versions.

A vast number of votive altars and votive inscriptions like these are preserved from the Roman world, with an absolute height in production from the mid-second century CE to around 230 CE. This coincides both with the phenomenon of 'epigraphic habit', to which we will return shortly, and with a partly new concept of 'personal' altars set up by individuals as a manifestation of the votive practice. Often, as in the Anna Perenna inscriptions, a person could erect several altars at the same sanctuary. Votive altars are rarely found *in situ*, and are seldom dated.[10] The votive inscriptions are usually highly formalized, and typically contain the name of the deity and the donor, together with a dedicatory, often shortened, formula such as *v(otum) s(olvit) l(ibens) m(erito)* (solved the vow willingly and deservedly). Only rarely, as in our examples, are the motives behind the vow explicitly stated, and votive objects are seldom mentioned or preserved. A vow was a form of legal contract between an individual and a god, and could for example concern questions of health, safety, well-being and success. Nicole Belayche has described the vow as 'a regular means to keep control of the future', and as a dynamic and reciprocal relationship between humans and gods.[11]

In the process of a vow, a wish was initially announced (*nuncupatio*) together with a promise of offerings, for example of a small altar; when the wish had been granted, the vow was solved (*solutio*) through formal offerings. The absolute majority of votive inscriptions concern the second part of the process, namely the fulfillment of the vow, when both the individual and the god were 'freed' from the votive contract, hence the formula *votum solvit*. As pointed out by Ton Derks and Alison Cooley, a votive inscription would be a costly donation that not all members of society could afford. Thus, it comes rather naturally that the investment in an altar and/or an inscription was made only when the contract of the vow had been successful. The first phase of the vow, the *nuncupatio*, was probably also made in written form, but on perishable materials, such as lead or wooden tablets, or in the form of graffiti on the walls of a sanctuary. Derks has argued that a quote from Pliny the Younger (*Ep.* 10.35) seems to suggest that these vows often were sealed, and probably they had to be kept in the sanctuary for the duration of the votive process. We cannot know for certain whether writing in some form accompanied every single vow, although both Cooley and Derks assume that it might have. Cooley has also underlined the general practice of writing as crucial for negotiating the relationship of the vow, as has Mary

Beard. Writing was both an important part of the ritual itself and a means to show that the individual was keeping his or her part in the vow.[12]

As seen from this overview, the three Anna Perenna inscriptions conform to the epigraphic votive context: they mention the names of the deity and the donors; they contain votive formulas such as *votum feceram*, [*votum*] *reddimus, aram dedicamus, votum susceperant, votum solvimus* and *donum dedit*; and they are dated within the period when altar dedications and inscriptional vows were most frequently produced. Two of the inscriptions even contain more information than usual, since they also give the circumstances of the vow: victories won by individuals or groups of individuals. But, as Rudolf Haensch has underlined, even if epigraphic sources often, as in this case, are crucial for our knowledge of Roman religion and rituals, yet the evidence is often not detailed enough for reconstructing the rituals and ceremonies with certainty.[13]

Earlier research on the inscriptions has focused mainly on the fact that they confirm a cult to Anna Perenna and to her nymphs on the site. However, some discussion has been dedicated to the fact that the sanctuary in Piazza Euclide does not conform with the information given by the *Fasti Vaticani* for the Anna Perenna festival, as located at the first milestone on the via Flaminia.[14] Ovid states in his *Fasti* only that the location is near the Tiber, and Martial mentions vaguely that Anna's 'fruit-bearing grove' can be seen from the Gianicolo.[15] But what do the inscriptions tell us about the sanctuary and the cult?

The mentions of victories in the Anna Perenna inscriptions have no parallels in the literary sources, and the nature of the contest that Gaius Acilius Eutyches won, and that Gaius Suetonius Germanus and Licinia won twice, cannot be deduced from the epigraphic texts themselves.

Since the cult of Anna Perenna, according to Ovid's *Fasti*, was connected with drinking rituals, Rosanna Friggeri suggested that these drinking games may have developed into more or less formalized contests.[16] The reference to the nymphs – only found in the epigraphic evidence, not in the literary sources – made Peter Wiseman suggest a hypothesis about choruses of girls dancing at the festival of Anna Perenna, and that the nymphs, or impersonations of them, might have had connections with Bacchic cults with satyrs and nymphs as *dramatis personae*.[17]

Wiseman also introduced the idea that the competition mentioned in the inscriptions could refer to *ludi* with dancers and/or actors, and that the persons mentioned in the inscriptions, except for the *patronus* of Eutychides, all may have been professional mime actors. Wiseman meant that the use of iambic *senarii* in the inscriptions, 'as if an actor were speaking', would point to the fact that the victories referred to were won by 'performers in competition'.[18] It may, though, safely be stated that iambic *senarii* could be used for many types of inscriptions, and not only those that were connected with actors and performance.[19] Friggeri has suggested that the conclusions that with certainty can be drawn from the epigraphic evidence are that there was a cult to sacred nymphs connected with Anna Perenna at the fountain, and that this cult must have been connected with a competition. The winners of this competition had to be publicly attested, the participants could compete as a couple, and women could compete, though perhaps only together with a man, and the same person could win several times. The winners offered a votive gift, probably most often an altar, and offerings were made to Anna Perenna and the nymphs. Friggeri correctly underlined, though, that theories about games to Anna Perenna at her festivity can only remain hypotheses without further evidence.[20]

Thus, despite the fact that the inscriptions only relate the vows to Anna Perenna and the nymphs, and give no information at all regarding the nature of the competitions, previous research has assumed that the contests were connected with the festival of Anna Perenna.[21] It has also been presupposed that the festival of Anna Perenna took place in the vicinity of the sanctuary at Piazza Euclide, although the location of the sanctuary does not conform entirely with the information given in the literary sources. In the following discussion, I will try to show that it may be possible to discern several layers of importance in the textual information of an inscription, and how the respective value of these layers could be understood from a new theory of epigraphy as primarily a signifier of change. By reading the texts of the Anna Perenna inscriptions in the light of this theory, I will argue that the references to contests or games in fact should not be regarded as the main reason why the inscriptions were put up in the sanctuary to Anna Perenna, and further, that the nature and location of the contests cannot be proved from the epigraphic evidence as being linked to the Anna Perenna festival.

Epigraphic Habit and the Change Theory

The core for understanding any epigraphic monument is to single out the specific incentive for its production. Previous research in this field has focused on the concept 'epigraphic habit', as coined by Ramsay MacMullen in the early 1980s, and further developed by Elizabeth Meyer and Greg Woolf.[22] McMullen discussed phenomena such as 'Romanization' and 'sense of audience' as driving forces for the making of inscriptions, and argued that epigraphy must be understood as an expression of culture rather than of practical necessity. Meyer elaborated the idea of inscriptions as a way of expressing status and Roman identity, and preserving the memory of the individual for eternity. Producing inscriptions was a characteristic of the Roman culture, and when 'Romanization' spread to larger groups in society and new parts of the empire, epigraphic habit came with it. Woolf provided a vital contribution to this discourse when pointing out that epigraphic monuments preserve the memory of 'momentary events of lasting significance', thus turning attention to the very event that preceded the making of the monument, rather than focusing on a general, culturally induced, epigraphic practice.

In discourse on epigraphy, inscriptions are habitually defined as text on non-perishable materials for the sake of durability.[23] Hence, epigraphy is often being related to the eternal preservation of text and monument, to the materiality of history and to the perpetualization of memory and individuals. Inscriptions are seen as signifiers of the stability of a public space and of the individuals whose existence becomes interwoven into the urban structure and the visual landscape. In the construction of a theoretical framework behind the concept 'epigraphic habit', the main focus has hitherto been to explain why an inscription is being made, and to understand why this practice suddenly became very intensified in the Roman world during the first centuries CE. McMullen underlined that the second century CE, characterized by an enormously increased epigraphic activity, was a period of profound social and cultural change. Yet, he discussed epigraphic habit by only indirectly referring to these changes – rather, he saw the habit as driven by social factors, connected with the extended Roman citizenship during this period. Even though the theories on epigraphic habit as described above have made significant contributions to the understanding of the factors behind the creating of inscriptions, aspects of change as a motivator for epigraphy has hitherto not been investigated.

In the following, I will argue that epigraphy and epigraphic monuments primarily manifest change, not stability, and that an inscription almost always is created as a result of change closely connected with transitional phases of the individual, of groups of individuals, and even of objects. As I will show, these changes could concern for example the transition between life and death, between offices, change of ownership, or transition between vow and fulfillment. After a general introduction to epigraphy and change, I will focus my argument on the three Anna Perenna inscriptions, with two other groups of inscriptions as comparative cases: the *tabellae defixionum* found in the Anna Perenna sanctuary, and the ceremonial inscriptions of the Arval Brethren.

The basic underlying message of an inscription is always that it is intended for an eternal afterworld, with never-ending generations of readers. This fact shapes the way the contents of an inscription are formulated and expressed, how the reader is addressed, and how the sender of the message is perceived. Several of the main epigraphic functions depend upon this: the circumstance that the sender of the message always is absent, either by distance or by death, makes it possible for a monument or an inscription to take on the voice of the sender, and create so-called speaking objects. The stable setting in the urban, architectural or monumental context of an inscription, too, constructs a possibility for the language and message of the inscription to be elliptical, and only completed by the existence of the same context – the inscription on the Pantheon, for example, needs its monument to make the text understandable: *M(arcus) Agrippa co(n)s(ul) tertium fecit* (Marcus Agrippa built [this] when consul for the third time, *CIL* VI.896). But these are aspects connected with the stability and permanence of epigraphy. What happens if we instead turn to questions about epigraphy and change?

All epigraphic categories in some way or another relate to, and are products of, change. They expose major transformations of individuals or of society, and the need for a material manifestation of the new order, even though the very formulation, execution, and intention of the epigraphic monument serve to underline the permanence of this new state of existence. Funerary inscriptions, the most commonly occurring of all types of epigraphic monuments, obviously signify the transition of the individual from life to death, or from this world to another. Honorary inscriptions, as for example inscriptions on statue bases, concern a change of power, office, connections and collaborations on the personal level for the person to whom the monument was created, or change on a more general or contextual level: a new emperor, a new legislation, and so on. An honorary inscription to a benefactor, for example, would be preceded by a specific action of change as a donation or the like. Buildings carry inscriptions that are connected to changes and transitional phases such as construction, reconstruction or consecration. Inscriptions, it could be argued, are also often found on structures that in themselves are connected with change, movement or transition – such as temples, bridges and milestones. Inscriptions on triumphal arches are directly connected with a change both in the military relationship between Rome and the rest of the world, and a change in the merit-list of the individual. Religious inscriptions signify changes in the relationship between individuals (or the society as a whole) and the gods. Inscriptions on domestic objects, such as *fibulae*, cups or other everyday goods, often signify the transition of the objects into the ownership of the person who made the inscription or had it made, and an artisan would mark the production of a new object by inscribing a signature on it.

An important observation is that the choice of location for an epigraphic monument is closely connected with the change that motivated the production of the inscription, and furthermore often with the final phase of a change process. A funerary inscription is placed at the grave as the terminal point for the process from death to burial. Honorary inscriptions are located in public spaces associated with display of individual status and power, such as important civic areas or building structures. Building inscriptions naturally point to a change in the building itself, and religious inscriptions are located near the divinity that is of importance for the change concerned. Significantly, inscriptions on triumphal arches are located at the triumphal procession route, which constitutes the final phase of the military campaign and the honour bestowed upon the victorious commander. Thus, if we pay close attention to the location of an inscription, we can actually obtain a deeper understanding of the core of its message.

Epigraphic monuments can also bear trace of multiple changes over time – an inscription put up in a later time, or replacing an older monument, is made because of change. A change of power, wealth or ideological orientation of a person or group of persons, or simply the destruction of the old monument in a fire or the like, calls for making a new, better, more beautiful or more modern monument, sometimes with palimpsests of the earlier changes still visible. The inscription on the arch of Septimius Severus on the Roman Forum provides a good example, where the *damnatio memoriae* of Publius Septimius Geta expressed in the erasure of his name from the inscription shows how change affects already existing epigraphic monuments.[24]

To establish the validity of the theory over time, it is important to add that in the Middle Ages, we can trace the same functions, where epigraphic habit is tied to transitional phases of individuals. Connections with the eternal afterlife are underlined: epigraphy is found mainly at church doors, on baptismal fonts and on tombstones – the three most important spaces concerning transition from earthly existence to salvation and afterlife. Also the transition or creation of objects is highlighted by epigraphy: a name in runes on a domestic object signifies the transition of ownership; an inscription above a church door memorizes the decision and funding for the building of the church.[25]

Epigraphy and Change: The Case Studies of Anna Perenna and the Arval Brethren

Let us now return to the Anna Perenna inscriptions. How can change be understood from this epigraphic evidence, and how do change and location contribute to a deeper understanding of both their textual content and the context of the sanctuary?

As previously shown, the three inscriptions in the sanctuary belong to the typological category of votive inscriptions. Thus, the change connected to the production of the inscriptions is to be found in the votive process. The two longer inscriptions explicitly mention the same type of process, namely a solemn vow followed by the grant of the wish, and the consequent fulfillment of a vow through votive donations and inscriptions. The freedman Eutychides made a vow to the nymphs for the victory of his *patronus*, and when the wish had been granted, the inscription was made at the *solutio* of the vow. Germanus and Licinia had made a similar vow to Anna Perenna with a wish for victory, and when this had been granted, they fulfilled the vow by putting up an altar with an inscription. Also the third inscription, which mentions Germanus and his gift to the nymphs, must be regarded as belonging to the *solutio* of a vow, even if the nature of the vow is not specified in the text.

The initial vow in itself cannot be regarded as a change of a situation. Rather, it is a suggestion to the gods to enter a sacred contract containing a wish for an outcome of future events, and a promise of compensation to the gods if the wish is granted. The wish for victory has then been granted to the vow-givers, but their personal change of status as winners is not the main driving force behind creating the inscriptions. Instead, it is the fulfillment of the vow that calls for the creation of the inscriptions, and the display of the names of the individuals at the sanctuary, visible to all visitors, is to be seen as a secondary effect of the inscriptions. We have seen that the absolute majority of votive inscriptions are made when the vow has been fulfilled at the *solutio*, which makes it possible to trace the established epigraphic practice of the votive process. The fulfillment of the vow is the major change that needs to be marked out epigraphically, and constitutes the final phase of a process of change that contains a vow, a wish and the granting of the wish.

None of the three inscriptions are located *in situ*, but it could be presupposed that they were originally placed close to the fountain, since nymphs and a spring explicitly are mentioned in the inscriptions, and since the nymphs also are referred to in the *tabellae defixionum* found in the fountain.[26] In his study on religion and votive inscriptions in Roman Gaul, Ton Derks included a reconstruction of a sanctuary in Deneuvre, dedicated to Hercules and consisting of three stone basins, fed by water systems, as ritual *foci*, where a large number of votive altars and inscriptions are arranged around or in the immediate vicinity of the basins.[27] The arrangement at the Anna Perenna sanctuary may have been similar.

The location of the inscriptions next to the sanctuary tells us that the vicinity to the sphere of the gods has been seen as the most important factor for the choice of place, and this also leads to the conclusion that the sacred vow as a process of change has constituted the incentive for the creation of the inscriptions. The fact that two of the vows concerns victories in a contest cannot, thus, be linked to the immediate context of the sanctuary – in theory, the vows could have concerned any wish, and their location at the sanctuary would still have been the same. Therefore, the theories of among others Friggeri and Wiseman about the contests as connected with the festival of Anna Perenna, and furthermore that the festival took place in the vicinity of the fountain,[28] cannot be proven from the epigraphic evidence. It should be underlined here that it of course cannot be excluded that the contests were related to the cult of Anna Perenna – especially the fact that a couple, Suetonius Germanus and his wife, are referred to as winners could point in this direction, as Ovid mentions that the festival of Anna Perenna was celebrated in pairs. My point is, however, that we cannot draw any conclusions about the nature of the contests from the location and content of the inscriptions – what they testify is, instead, the belief that the deity connected with the fountain had the power to grant vows.

To further illustrate how change can be traced in the location of inscriptions, not only in their textual content, I will now turn to the inscriptions of the Arval Brethren as a comparative case.[29] The sacred grove of the Arval Brethren and the nature of their cult have been described as parallel in several cases to the sanctuary of Anna Perenna as an extra-urban sanctuary, tied to users from the city of Rome through mythical construct, and also connected with writing rituals. The Arval grove is also one of the best-explored extra-urban cult areas in Rome, thanks to the detailed epigraphic evidence.[30]

The Arval inscriptions derive from the time of Augustus and up to the beginning of the fourth century CE, and contain descriptions of the ceremonial activities of the Arval Brethren. The inscriptions are believed to have been ritually cut once a year as a form of annual documentation, and located in the sacred grove of the Brethren, where also a temple to Dea Dia was situated – a goddess known from the Arval inscriptions only, connected with agriculture and central for the Arval cult.[31] As Mary Beard has argued, it is highly probable that the inscriptions were not primarily made to be of practical use as an epigraphic archive, but instead for symbolical reasons.[32] That the very act of writing was regarded as religious practice and formed part of the ceremonial practice is shown for example by the fact that the stone-cutting tools had to be ritually handled and that the grove had to be expiated each time inscriptions had been made. Beard described the aim of the 'epigraphic habit' of the Arval Brethren as offering 'permanent presence' to the ceremonial acts of the Brethren through the inscriptions. She meant that the Arval inscriptions were not primarily meant to be read and used for practical purposes, but instead to offer symbolic permanence to the content of the laws.

I agree on the point that the function of the Arval inscriptions is to a large extent symbolic, but in line with the theory of epigraphy and change I would further argue that the main aim of putting up the inscriptions at their location is to manifest an act of change. It would be easy to conclude that the change in question here was constituted by the many ceremonies, such as processions and offerings, that were performed by the Arval Brethren year by year, but that would not be in line with the location of the inscriptions in the sacred grove outside the city. The fact that the inscriptions had to be located in the grove near the Dea Dia temple instead points to that the very act of writing was the main change motivating the inscriptions: the ritual closing of the preceding year by writing down all the activities performed during the year. Change in the form of a new year was a motivator for putting up the inscriptions, and it might be argued that this change was the main motivator, rather than giving permanence to the acts of the Brethren. This could also explain the sometimes absurd detail of the inscriptions, as for example notices about a tree falling in the grove: the reason for including this in the inscription was probably not a wish to always remember the falling of the tree, but instead the need to 'close the case' about the events of the past year. Thus, the Arval inscriptions show that religious inscriptions connected with change often can be related to writing as a ceremonious act of negotiating the relationship with the gods, exactly as the Anna Perenna inscriptions, and that this fact is underlined by the location of the inscriptions.

Lastly, I will also make a comparison with the *tabellae defixionum* found in the fountain of Anna Perenna, since they form part of the epigraphical evidence and ceremonial writing of the sanctuary.[33] The function of *tabellae defixionum* in general was to grant a wish, often, for example, that an enemy would be cursed. Springs, sanctuaries to chthonic deities and tombs were popular places in which to locate the *tabellae*, so that they would be physically proximate to the infernal powers that they evoked. The deposition of the tablets was surrounded by rituals and prayers, and the language in the *tabellae* is often of a magical and/or incomprehensible nature. Jürgen Blänsdorf has shown that nymphs were seen as belonging to the infernal world, and therefore were commonly evoked in *tabellae*, as also in the Anna Perenna case.[34] How does change interfere in this kind of documents? In fact, the *tabellae* belong to the same process of vows that the Anna Perenna inscriptions illustrate, but refer instead to the initial vow. While the inscriptions regarding the *solutio* of the vow were placed in full visibility in the sanctuaries, the *tabellae* were instead usually deposited in springs and the like, and were probably often sealed, as discussed above. The *tabellae*, located at the very heart of the sanctuary, seems to have been regarded as infused with the power of the deities in order to realize the wish – the secret text in the *tabellae* was seen as actively working for the change, rather than manifesting it when fulfilled. Thus, if votive inscriptions can be seen as the end point of change and the concluding of a process, *tabellae* instead constitute more dynamic documents, active makers of change over a period of time. Proximity to the gods is of single importance to the *tabellae*, not readability or public display. Further studies in this field may elucidate how specific locations became invested with sacral power, and how epigraphic activities in these locations both confirmed and reaffirmed the sacredness of the location, something that would deepen our understanding of religious epigraphy. In the case of the *tabellae defixionum* in the Anna Perenna sanctuary, they serve to illustrate the whole vow process from the aspect of writing – even if the *tabellae* are dated later than the three votive inscriptions, it is highly probable that the vows to the nymphs and Anna Perenna made by Eutychides, Germanus and Licinia also were manifested in writing and deposited in the basins of the sanctuary.

In this chapter, I have used the epigraphic evidence from the Anna Perenna sanctuary, as well as the inscriptions of the Arval Brethren, as empirical cases for showing how change is the main motivator for the making of epigraphy, rather than, or parallel to, the epigraphic function of permanence and preservation of memory. As Mary Beard has argued regarding the Arval inscriptions, other functions than the mere utilitarian must be assumed for epigraphy, and especially for ceremonial inscriptions. The theory of epigraphy and change presented in this chapter can develop this view further by showing that the process of change behind the creation of an inscription, crucial for understanding of epigraphy, is traceable both in the text of an inscription, and also, importantly, in its location. The choice of place for an inscription, as the evidence from the Anna Perenna sanctuary shows, can signify either the end point in a newly completed process of change – as the three votive inscriptions – or form part of an ongoing process of change, as in the *tabellae defixionum*.

This chapter has shown that through the textual material at the Anna Perenna sanctuary, the whole epigraphic process of a vow is illustrated, from the deposition of inscribed lead tablets containing vows to the materialization of the completed contract of the vow by solemn inscriptions in stone. Also, the importance of ceremonial writing in Roman religion has been underlined through the inscriptions from both the sanctuary of Anna Perenna and the sacred grove of the Arval Brethren. However, as I have argued, the three votive inscriptions studied in the chapter do not furnish us with any proof of a drinking or acting contest connected with the festival of Anna Perenna, nor of where her festival was located. What they do attest is that a cult to Anna Perenna and her nymphs existed in the place where the inscriptions were found, and what the textual content of the inscriptions point to is the act of change interwoven in the vow process, and the ability of the goddess and her nymphs to grant vows. The content of the inscriptions also shows the fleeting borders between the Anna Perenna, her nymphs and the sacred spring, since vows could be made and altars and votive gifts could be put up on a seemingly equal scale to any of the three.

In closing, the present chapter has addressed previously unexplored questions concerning epigraphy as a signifier of instability and change; and thus, hopefully, provided a richer understanding of actions and strategies of ceremonial communication in public space, as well as a deeper understanding of the epigraphic evidence of the cult to Anna Perenna.

Champion of the Plebs

7

Ovid's Anna Perenna and the Coin of Gaius Annius*

Teresa Ramsby

Might a likely depiction of Anna Perenna on a coin from 82 BCE provide us insight to her Late Republican identity? This chapter explores the depiction that appears on the coin of the proconsul of Spain, Gaius Annius, minted at the time he was ordered by Sulla to march into Spain to confront and depose the formidable general Quintus Sertorius.

The woman who appears in profile on the coin's obverse, wearing a diadem, and often appearing with scales in front of her and a caduceus behind her, was identified as Anna Perenna as early as 1854, though since then some have questioned the identification and have sought to re-identify the woman or leave her identity undetermined.[1] By taking into account our few existing literary sources on Anna Perenna, the information we have about Late Republican numismatic portraiture and the frequent use of paronomasia on coins, as well as the context of civic realignment, civil war and rebellion that defines the time period in question, I argue that a strong case can be made for identifying the figure on the coin as the goddess of the Ides of March, featured in Book 3 of Ovid's *Fasti*.

Ovid's Anna: Goddess of the Plebs

There is considerable literary evidence that ties Anna Perenna to the plebeian class of Rome, a class significant to the identity of Gaius Annius. As has been demonstrated elsewhere in this volume, Ovid's *Fasti* is an important source for the plausible identities associated with Anna Perenna.[2] The poet's sixth aetiology of Anna (*Fast.* 3.661–74) associates her with an old woman from Bovillae who became a goddess honoured by the plebs for her involvement in the first plebeian

Figure 7.1 Denarius of Gaius Annius depicting Anna Perenna on obverse, Victory in quadriga on reverse 82–81 BCE (RRC 366.1.1). © Trustees of the British Museum.

secession of 494 BCE. Ovid tells us that Anna of Bovillae prepared rustic cakes for the Roman plebs as they camped out on the Sacred Mount.[3] Intriguingly, there is an apparent precedent for a figure who prepares bread or simple cakes to feed hungry Romans. John Lydus, a sixth-century Byzantine scholar, speaks of a custom on the Kalends of March in which bakers of coarse loaves would send their goods to members of the nobility to commemorate a moment in legendary history when Romulus sent whatever bread he could find to his soldiers (*De mens.* 4.43). This ritual does not appear in Ovid or our other extant calendrical sources, or in the graphic charts of the year (*laterculi fasti*) produced by Furius Dionysius Filocalus and Polemius Silvius that Lydus used in his compilation.[4] Could it be that a rite known to us only by way of Lydus was long ago conflated with the plebeian event upon the *Mons Sacer*? This tradition regarding food for Rome's earliest soldiers and the associated ritual of feeding the nobility may have been co-opted by the plebs into their own narrative of survival and protest, a narrative that eventually acquired religious associations.[5]

Ovid grants considerable authority to this story: *haec quoque, quam referam, nostras pervenit ad aures / fama, nec a veri dissidet illa fide* (this report also, which I will recount, has reached our ears, and does not reside far from the credibility of truth, Ov. *Fast.* 3.661–2).[6] The people's gratitude for her industrious generosity, he goes on to report, led them to put up a statue in her honour: *pace domi facta signum posuere Perennae, / quod sibi defectis illa ferebat opem* (when peace reigned at Rome, they put up a statue to Perenna because she relieved their deprivation, Ov. *Fast.* 3.673–4).[7] Ovid does not make it clear how soon afterwards she was deified, but that eventually she received the honour.[8]

Ovid then points us to an association between Anna of Bovillae and the trickster goddess figure who deceives and humiliates Mars (*Fast.* 3.675–96), a story that likely has connections to the prior existing mime by Decimus Laberius, from which we have only four words, but words that a recent commentator cautiously connects to the Anna–Mars episode.[9] This story of Anna tricking Mars works nicely in concert with the role of Anna Perenna who, as deity of the civic new year, ushers out the prior year. In Ovid's account, there is a description of a *pompa* that may depict this 'ushering out' by way of festival-street-theater: *occurrit nuper (visa est mihi digna relatu) / pompa: senem potum pota trahebat anus* (recently the procession took place – to me it seemed worthy of mention – a drunk old woman leading away a drunk old man, *Fast.* 3.541–2). E.H. Alton interpreted these lines to describe a theatrical representation of the leading away of the old year (possibly known as Mamers or Mamurius Veturius) by Anna on her feast day.[10] The suggestion that the *pompa* in 3.542 is a theatrical procession specific to Anna's festival is intriguing in light of Ovid's comment that plebeian revelers sing lyrics from the theatre at her festival: (*plebs venit*) ... *illic et cantant quicquid didicere theatris, / et iactant faciles ad sua verba manus* (there they sing whatever they have learned from the theater, and they clap in rhythm to the words, *Fast.* 3.535–6).[11] Ovid's description reflects a festive atmosphere surrounding Anna's celebration, perhaps linked to annual performances of Laberius's mime or later adaptations of it. A picture emerges of a festival in which the plebeian class celebrated Anna in ribald fashion for her trickery both in leading away the old year and in deceiving the god Mars in the bedroom.[12] The plebs may have viewed her trickery with particular fondness since she, once, as 'Anna of Bovillae', allegedly applied her clever resourcefulness to help the plebs withstand the difficulty of their secession against the nobility.[13]

Indeed, Geraldine Herbert-Brown has indicated the myriad ways that the Anna Perenna story and many other narratives within the *Fasti* favour plebeian causes and plebeian traditions over aristocratic ones.[14] In the already festive atmosphere of the *Fasti*, Anna Perenna stands out as a goddess whose identity is associated with both the festive 'acting out' of the plebeian class against the stricter *mores* of the upper class (the festival on the Tiber involves public drinking and sex) and a more somber historical moment of 'acting up' when the plebs seceded from the state in 494 BCE due to various political and social grievances. Thus, two major aspects of Anna Perenna come to the fore. First, she has close ties to Latium, and second, as Ovid makes clear, she is celebrated in a festive manner by the plebs primarily. Anna is perceived by the Romans in Ovid's narrative as a goddess of the common folk, and one with the power to renew the year and make it prosperous by her blessing. Whatever story it was that originally inspired plebeian dedication to her, Ovid offers this story of Anna feeding the plebs, and in doing so within the context of the Conflict of the Orders 'creates a vignette that de-prioritizes male political prominence and lofty rhetoric in favour of Anna, her sympathy with the *plebs*, and her resistance to established civic authority', as Angeline Chiu has suggested.[15] The coin in question, to which I will now turn, was produced before the mime by Laberius, and if the woman who appears on it is indeed Anna Perenna, then the coin may serve as evidence that associations between her and plebeian loyalty were made much earlier than Ovid's elegiac calendar.

The Coin of Gaius Annius

Gaius Annius, before setting out on Sulla's orders to his proconsular assignment in Spain, took the opportunity of his coincident position as moneyer at Rome to mint the silver denarius coins in question (see again Figure 7.1).[16] The various iterations of the coin were struck in the period 82–81 BCE under the supervision of each of the two quaestors who also accompanied him to Spain, Lucius Fabius and Gaius Tarquitius, and the name of each appears on the reverse of their respective coins. There are twenty-nine hoards that contain the coins with some variation in letter-marks and details of imagery, but the key images are consistent, despite the fact that some coins were struck in Italy, and others in Spain. On the obverse, along with Annius's name, appears the head of a woman facing right, wearing a diadem, with her hair gathered in the back. In some portraits she wears a pearl necklace and elaborate earrings. On most coins, scales appear in front of her, and in some coins a caduceus appears behind her. Below her portrait there is typically a control mark, though the symbol varies depending on the coin. The coin shown here, minted in Hispania, features a carnyx, or Celtic war trumpet. On the reverse of the coin, Victory in a *quadriga* consistently appears, along with the name of the relevant quaestor, Fabius or Tarquitius.

The numismatist Celestino Cavedoni identified the woman as Anna Perenna or Themis in 1854, and several consecutive publications, most notably by Hans Grueber and E.A. Sydenham, have offered support to the interpretation of the goddess as Anna Perenna.[17] By contrast, S.W. Stevenson states that the goddess depicted is Juno Moneta or Aequitas, while Michael Crawford simply asserts that no secure identification is possible.[18] The identification of Anna Perenna on this coin is compelling for several reasons. First, these identifications of the goddess as Juno or Aequitas do not match the numismatic evidence. Juno is frequently depicted on coins in the republican period, often with the legend ISMR (*Iuno Sospita Mater Regina*).

Figure 7.2 Denarius of Lucius Thorius Balbus depicting Juno Sospita on obverse, 105 BCE (RRC 316.1.1). © Trustees of the British Museum.

In many other coins, she wears a diadem, but also often a veil;[19] she also often carries a sceptre, either positioned over and against her shoulder, and so protruding behind her head, or held aloft in her hand as she charges in a *quadriga* (as she sometimes appears on the reverse of coins) – the sceptre does not resemble a caduceus, as seen on Annius's coin, but a pole consisting of dots, and sometimes Juno wields a spear.[20] Furthermore, when Juno Moneta is depicted, she typically has the word *Moneta* inscribed behind her.[21] The goddess on the coin of Annius does not possess these distinctive features to make it clear that she is Juno, and for that reason we would expect an inscription to identify her as such, but there is none.

An identification of Annius's goddess as Aequitas or Themis has its merits with regard to the representation of scales on many of the variants of the coin, a symbol commonly associated with the two goddesses, but representations of personified virtues, like Aequitas, are found more often among imperial coins and less often in the Republic, with the exception of Victoria who appears quite frequently for reasons tied to the military roles of many republican moneyers.[22] Furthermore, when more obscure goddesses appear on republican coins, they tend to do so with an identifying legend, such as Concordia and Fides;[23] indeed, as I stated above, even Juno, a well known goddess, often appears with an acronym.

The absence of a legend that directly names the goddess on the coin of Annius is neatly explained by the name of Annius himself, with *ANNI* or *ANNIVS* prominently displayed on all the variants of the coin on the right side of the obverse. This use of paronomasia, punning, that linked family names to deities or legendary figures, was a common practice among families during the Late Republic.[24] To illustrate this, I offer several examples. In the same year as Annius's mint, 81 BCE, Quintus Caecilius Metellus Pius, the soon-to-be governor of Farther Spain from 79 to 71, featured Pietas on the obverse of his coin.

Figure 7.3 Denarius of Quintus Caecilius Metellus Pius depicting Pietas on obverse, 81 BCE (RRC 374.1.1). © Trustees of the British Museum.

The choice of Pietas was relevant to Metellus's *agnomen* 'Pius' that was granted to him as a young man because of his well known efforts to obtain his father's recall from exile in 99.[25] It is significant that on the coin the name of Pietas does not appear on the obverse with the goddess's image because the minter's name on the reverse would have succinctly clarified the image. We are made more certain that this is the case because a stork, the animal associated with Pietas, also appears beside her as a helpful identifier. Going further back in time, the link made between the Julii and the goddess Venus is well known, and attested on coinage as early as 129 BCE.[26] Around 114, the Fonteius family issued a coin depicting the Janiform head of either Janus or his son Fons (or Fontus), the son of Janus and Juturna.[27] The moneyer Decimus Iunius Silanus, a descendant of the praetor Silanus, struck a denarius around 91 BCE displaying the bearded mask of Silenus on the obverse (see Figure 7.4).

Contemporaneous also with Annius, in 82 BCE, the moneyer Lucius Marcius Censorinus placed the god Marsyas, a master of augury, on his coin's reverse with Apollo on the obverse.[28] Intriguingly, the pose of Marsyas on the coin is reminiscent of the statue of Marsyas placed in the Comitium at Rome in the fourth century to celebrate plebeian *libertas*, making it possible that in this period there existed a desire among at least two minters (Censorinus and Annius) to associate their families with figures associated with plebeian loyalties.[29] Lastly, in 46 BCE, Gaius Antius Restio depicted Hercules, the father of Antiades, his family's alleged ancestor, on the obverse of his coin.[30] In the same way, the presence of the inscription on the coin of Annius points to the play on his name with that of the goddess Anna.[31]

The bulk of these divine and ancestral references on coins focus on male divinities. Even so, female ancestors of history and legend do appear among the first-century coins, as noted on the coins of the Julii that depict Venus.[32] Harriet Flower, in her discussion of Roman ancestry, mentions at least three

Figure 7.4 Denarius of Decimus Iunius Silanus depicting Silenus on obverse, 91 BCE (RRC 337.1.1). © Trustees of the British Museum.

Figure 7.5 Aureus of C. Clodius Vestalis depicting the vestal Claudia on reverse, 41 BCE (RRC 512.1.1). © Trustees of the British Museum.

prominent statesmen who featured mortal female figures on coins.[33] In 58 BCE Aemilius Lepidus featured Aemilia the Vestal virgin.[34] The second representation features the Vestal Aemilia again on the aureus of the moneyer L. Livineius Regulus in honour of the triumvir Aemilius Lepidus in 42.[35] The third, the aureus of C. Clodius Vestalis minted in 41, features two women: on the obverse appears Flora, goddess of flowers and spring and erotic theatrical shows, and on the reverse appears the Vestal Claudia Pulchra, daughter of Appius Claudius Pulcher, holding her *culullus*. Of course these three examples all appear after the coin of Annius, but the cluster of female images decades after Annius signals a notable rise in the interest of semi-prominent families, like that of Annius, in establishing themselves through divine or legendary, female, predecessors.[36]

It is also important to note that on all of Annius's coins Victory appears on the reverse, as shown in Figure 7.1. The representation of Victory on coinage in general either celebrates a completed military victory or inspires confidence in a military venture about to take place under the leadership of the moneyer or a member of his family. Annius minted this coin at the time he was awarded *imperium* and assigned a hostile province as his jurisdiction; I interpret this to mean that he wished to convey on his coin, to his soldiers and to the Roman people, that he was prepared for the task, and was optimistic that he would succeed. Victory appears frequently on republican coins, and often the goddess is shown in proximity to the conquered weapons to signify defeat of an enemy army. For example, the coin by Decimus Iunius Silanus with Silenus on the obverse, shown earlier and dating to 91 BCE, depicts on the reverse Victory *in quadriga* with a carnyx, or Celtic war trumpet, lying under the feet of the horses (see again Figure 7.4). There and on many other coins, the carnyx typically lies among other captured weapons and accoutrements of battle characteristic of the Celtic tribes of Gaul and Spain.[37] On many (though not all) variants of Annius's coins, a carnyx appears not with Victory, but under Anna's portrait. It is possible that Annius selected this placement to distinguish his coin's imagery from that of Silanus, but possibly also to suggest that his leadership, under the protection of his family's tutelary deity, will lead to success. Though Victory on the coin may forecast the defeat of the foe, it is Anna Perenna who receives the spoils as divine representative of Annius and his family.[38]

The caduceus that appears behind Anna's head on most of the Annius coins is a symbol of peace, which may refer to the prospective benefits of Annius's leadership in Spain.[39] It is notable that Sulla minted a coin in 82/81, contemporaneous with Annius, which depicts on its reverse a triumphator in *quadriga*, holding a caduceus, while being crowned by a winged Victoria; the two coins thus both associate victory with peace.[40] The scales on Annius's coin signify law and justice, a symbol associated with the goddess Aequitas on coins in the imperial period, but that may here refer to Anna's role in overseeing a smooth transition from the old civic year to the new one, at the same time that armies venture forth on campaigns.[41] Though there is no clear evidence of a statue of Anna Perenna from any Roman site, there is the possibility that the portrait on the coin reflects the appearance of the statue of Anna if it existed as Ovid stated.[42] As I mentioned above, a statue of the god Marsyas was erected in the Comitium at Rome in the fourth century BCE to represent plebeian *libertas*;[43] there may have been an Anna Perenna statue somewhere among Rome's neighbourhoods to represent plebeian identity or solidarity.

Annius and Sertorius: A Struggle for Plebeian Loyalty

Relevant to an association with Anna Perenna, Gaius Annius came from a prominent plebeian family of consular rank. His father was T. Annius Rufus, the plebeian consul of 128 BCE, and the grandson of T. Annius Luscus, the plebeian consul of 153 who was an enemy of Tiberius Gracchus.[44] We have a historical reference to the family as far back as the fourth century, when, according to Livy (8.3–6), a praetor named Gaius Annius from the town of Setia in Latium led a Latin delegation to Rome in 340. At a meeting on the Capitoline Hill, in a fit of patriotic, Latin zeal, this Annius denounced the Roman Senate for interfering with the rights of the Latin people to engage in treaties and battles as circumstances required. He demanded that Latins populate one half of the Senate and fill one consular position annually, though to no avail.[45] It is possible to suggest that the family had a history of advocating for the under-represented.

As for Gaius Annius, he had led troops before; in 108, under orders from Caecilius Metellus during the Jugurthine war, he led four Ligurian cohorts to aid the Roman loyalists of Leptis Magna and served there as governor for a time.[46] Twenty-five years later, Annius, who had worked closely with the Metelli, a clan well known for their support of the optimates, was being sent to depose Sertorius, a prominent Marian supporter with a loyal military following. Annius's coin can be seen, I argue, as an effort to draw on knowledge of his prior leadership, his family's status and history, and to make a perhaps crucial connection between his family and the Latin goddess adored by the plebs. Furthermore, Anna presided over a significant, plebeian festival that takes place in March, the same month notably associated with martial activity, and the part of the year in which Annius would be expected to have arrived in Spain and begin his campaign to unseat Sertorius.

In late 83 or early 82, the Sabine *novus homo* Quintus Sertorius, one of the most experienced and talented warriors of Rome and a chief supporter of the Marian faction against Sulla, was passed over for a consulship that, by most accounts, was due to him.[47] Likely in response to this, and to the failing prospects of the Marian faction under Gnaeus Papirius Carbo, Sertorius took the opportunity to exercise his proconsular powers over Hispania, the province that had been delegated to him in recent years after serving as praetor.[48] Plutarch tells us he sought to establish himself in Spain where he could fulfill his obligations and set up a refuge for Roman defectors, who, like himself, had become disillusioned with the senatorial elite (*Sert.* 6.2). While proconsul in Spain, Sertorius distinguished himself among the diverse tribes of Celts and Iberians as a relatively fair and just leader (*Sert.* 6.3–4):[49] operating in the nearer province of Hispania, he reportedly removed several onerous taxes and punished Roman collectors and officers who treated the Spaniards unfairly. In less than a year, Sertorius gained the overall trust of the Spanish tribes who had experienced many decades of abusive treatment from previous Roman governors (*Sert.* 6.4).

Meanwhile, back in Rome, Sulla achieved victory over the remaining Marian supporters and Sertorius's name appeared on the proscription list after the battle of the Colline Gate in November of 82 BCE.[50] Sulla sought to settle matters in Spain by removing Sertorius and placing his own man there.[51] In late 82 or early 81, Sulla sent Gaius Annius to Spain with three or four legions to unseat Sertorius and take back the position of governor.[52] Sertorius anticipated this action and sent in advance his lieutenant Livius Salinator who was instructed to keep Sulla's men from entering Spain. Salinator was effective, and Annius was forced to wait for a time in the foothills of the Pyrenees until an officer named Calpurnius Lanarius assassinated Salinator.[53] Calpurnius was likely a member of Salinator's own retinue, and may have been persuaded to switch sides either by the reluctance to face an army sent by Sulla or by material means.[54] With Salinator dispatched, Annius was able to enter Spain, and Sertorius, having a much weaker force than the interloper, was forced to flee his position. He fled first to Nova Carthago, and then to Mauretania on the coast of Africa to avoid a loss of his forces, though he later rallied, reinforced by allies, and re-entered Spain in the summer of 81.

Before he set out for Spain, Annius no doubt faced a dilemma. He was being sent out to hostile territory to drive out Sertorius who was, as Plutarch tells us, a powerful Roman general and a man who held the allegiance of many Roman troops. By contrast, Annius was working for Sulla whose dictatorship later manifested a disdain for political agency among the plebeian class. Admittedly, Sulla had an appeal among the legions that defied classist tensions, evidenced by at least two indicators: the refusal of soldiers in Asia to fight Sulla's legions despite the pleading of their commander C. Flavius Fimbria in 85 BCE, and by their willingness to march on Rome twice under Sulla's leadership.[55] Yet despite Sulla's prowess as a military leader, his initial march on Rome in 88 and his violent re-entry into Rome with proscription in 82 would surely have embittered many veterans who felt that the political leadership of Sulla and his supporters had devolved into tyranny and chaos. It is not out of the question that Annius was calculating that he would need to establish his *bona fides* with plebeian society, the class from which Rome obtained the vast majority of its rank and file soldiers. A decade later, according to Sallust, the tribune C. Licinius Macer delivered a blistering speech to the plebs about the overreach of the nobility and prefaced his ideas with a reference to the Struggle of the Orders that took place in the fifth, fourth and third centuries BCE, demonstrating that the history of the struggle maintained its relevance and served to rally the plebs.[56] Annius had various means to win the hearts and minds of his troops, one of which was to strike a coin that depicted his ancestral deity, Anna Perenna. Even though Roman commanders possessed an array of punitive options to deal with disciplinary issues, outright mutiny, or desertion, they depended a great deal on the support of their soldiers. For example, the *contio*, a system of communication via assembly of commanders and rank and file soldiers, was frequently used in the Roman army for the explanation of plans, exhortations of the troops, and necessary reproaches.[57] The *contio* was also an opportunity for lower-class members of the military to make their demands or desires known to their commanders, though occasionally the situation could deteriorate into violence. In 89 during the Social Wars, in a *contio* called by Aulus Postumius Albinus to clear the air of soldiers' grievances, the unarmed troops who attended stoned their commander to death, either for his cruelty toward them, or his anti-plebeian politics.[58] In early 81, Annius would need a symbol to broadcast who he was, what connections he had to Rome's history and legend, and, perhaps more importantly, what deity he counted on as protector.

For these reasons the selection of Anna Perenna on the silver denarius would be highly appropriate. The average Roman soldier, drawn primarily from the plebeian class and non-aristocratic, Italian allies, would expect to have many of the newly minted coins in his possession at the dispensation of his annual *stipendium*, and the coin would appropriately reflect the goals and significance of the army's commander.[59] Furthermore, Annius could have minted a coin that promoted his plebeian roots without fear of reproach from Sulla. To speak of anti-plebeian policies and measures in Sulla's regime would be premature in early 81 BCE when Sulla's dictatorship was just beginning. Annius's coin bearing Anna's image would then broadcast his pride in the longstanding plebeian values of his family, tied allegedly to this goddess who once aided the plebs in their secession. To the soldiers accompanying him into Spain, Annius presents himself as the appropriate choice for leading a transition of power in Spain from the old Marian faction, represented by Sertorius, to the new Sullan regime. To those soldiers already in Spain, uneasy about open rebellion against Rome, Annius presents himself as a legitimate alternative to Sertorius. Even though Sertorius had not yet embarked on his campaign against Rome, his immediate resistance to Sulla's desire to remove him from office, going so far as to send Salinator to the Pyrenees to block Annius, must have signaled to all an inevitable clash of armies and ideologies. It is even possible that in the assassination of Salinator at the Pyrenees, if Calpurnius did indeed turn against Sertorius and his lieutenant in favour of Annius, we see the first fruits of Annius's overall strategy to win those Roman soldiers who initially sympathized with the Marian faction and with Sertorius – a strategy in which, as argued here, the coin played a small part.[60]

The plebeian general who featured on his coinage his patron goddess Anna Perenna either died in Spain or returned to Rome and led the rest of his life in obscurity.[61] Anna Perenna did not fade into obscurity, however, but lived on as an object of plebeian dedication, and in, perhaps, the mime of Laberius, and surely in Ovid's *Fasti* remained a potent symbol of *libertas* and humor at the expense of the elite. As I have shown, the evidence neatly confirms Anna's significance as a goddess of the plebs, ritualized in Ovid's literary calendar, and, if G. McIntyre is correct in this volume (Ch. 3), portrayed as a Julian goddess on the Ara Pacis. The coin of Gaius Annius suggests that Anna's special association with the plebs extended as far back as the early first century BCE, when an ambitious proconsul saw fit to honour his patron goddess on a coin to endear him to the Roman army and sanction a victory on behalf of Sulla, ironically one of Roman republican history's most anti-plebeian rulers.

8

Infiltrating Julian History: Anna Perenna at Lavinium and Bovillae (Ovid, *Fast.* 3.523–710)

Carole Newlands

Today, the Ides of March generally evokes the assassination of Julius Caesar. However, in Ovid's poem on the Roman calendar, the *Fasti*, the Ides of March is also given as the festival of Anna Perenna, an ancient goddess. Curiously, the poet devotes more lines to her licentious festival and to speculation about her origins (3.523–696) than he does to the new event on the Ides, Caesar's assassination and apotheosis (3.697–710). The mysteries that surround this goddess, apparent from the finds at her recently discovered cult site in Rome at the Piazza Euclide, are not clarified by the account in the *Fasti* but are instead compounded.[1] Why does Ovid's poem highlight Anna Perenna on the Ides of March? Her cheerful, free-spirited festival, 'a spectacle for the common people' (*spectacula volgi*, 3.539), where festival-goers pitch tents and devote themselves to heavy drinking, dancing, music and love-making (3.525–42), contrasts sharply with the sombre imperial commemoration. Temporal continuity is disrupted on the Ides as the distant Roman past and the imperial present are juxtaposed. This contrast is also articulated along generic and gendered lines: a female deity associated with fertility and popular, comic celebration versus a new male deity associated with tragic death, civil war and patriarchal hierarchy.

This chapter will attempt to address the curious aspects of Anna's representation in Ovid's *Fasti*, in particular the seemingly disproportionate emphasis on her cult, the insistence on her original mortal status, and the fictive aetiological narratives that attempt to explain how she became a goddess. As Jacqueline Fabre-Serris has argued, the *Fasti* plays an extremely subtle game between the constraints owed the calendar and liberty in the choice, and interpretation, of narratives.[2] I will argue that in the comically irreverent fictions that Ovid tells about Anna, he enters the creative, licentious spirit of her festival. At the same time, through a virtuosic, intertextual engagement with his literary predecessors, Virgil and Callimachus, and with his own earlier poetry, Ovid demonstrates the generic range of the elegiac *Fasti* and the multiplicity of its perspectives on Rome's traditional founding narratives. Furthermore, in the *Fasti* issues of political and literary authority are closely intertwined. Ovid's treatment of the Ides of March is a key episode in his critical engagement with political as well as literary hierarchies, with both his poetic predecessors and the ruling imperial house. In particular, by making the goddess Anna Perenna originally a mortal, either Dido's sister from Virgil's *Aeneid* or an old woman from Bovillae, the poet provocatively connects Anna Perenna with one of the major discourses of early imperial rule, deification. The two events commemorated in Ovid's poem on the Ides of March, while apparently so different, here converge. Augustus's right to rule was based in important part on the prospect of deification since he could claim divine descent from the newly deified Julius Caesar, who traced his lineage back to Venus, mother of Aeneas.[3] While we may not learn from Ovid's poem much about Anna's role in Roman religious practice, she acts as a key figure in the *Fasti* in revealing the creative fictions that surround both ancient Roman cult and the new imperial cult initiated by the deification of Julius Caesar.

In a paper written some years ago I applied Bakhtin's ideas of the carnival to Ovid's treatment of the Ides of March, suggesting that Anna's populist festival constituted a licensed, temporary subversion of the new imperial hierarchy in Rome under Augustus.[4] This seems to me now too narrow a view of the episode's function in Ovid's poem. As Natalie Zemon Davis has argued, for instance, it is not necessarily the case that 'a world-upside-down' can only be righted, not changed. Rather, festive inversion can undermine as well as reinforce social norms; women can act the social critic, not only the *dominatrix*.[5] Ovid's Anna embodies resistance to, or at the very least, offers alternative perspectives upon, Rome's dominant narratives of nationhood and divinization as articulated in literature and in contemporary media, including the Roman calendar. The *Fasti* was composed during 2–8 CE but was subsequently revised when Ovid was sent into exile; it should therefore be regarded as a work reflective of the late-Augustan and early Tiberian era, a period that was less a new Golden Age than a time of hardening autocracy.[6] As we shall see, Ovid's Anna does more than preside over a temporary period of festive license; she tests gender norms and also acts as social and political critic.[7]

Ovid's choice of the calendar as the basic framework for his *Fasti* was a provocative one, for it involved him in an implicit conflict of authority with the *princeps* over control of Roman time and Roman history. As *pontifex maximus* (high priest of Rome), Augustus had oversight of the Julian calendar. In its commemoration of historical, religious, and political events, the calendar was a key instrument in shaping ideas of what it meant to be 'Roman'.[8] Augustus extensively altered the public calendar to reflect his dynastic interests by adding new festivals honouring himself and the family.[9] As Denis Feeney points out, for the first time the public calendar was tied to the actions of great individuals: 'After centuries in which no human being was named on the calendar, the imperial family is now everywhere... Births, deaths, apotheoses...'.[10] The lengthy discussion in the *Fasti* of the festival of Anna Perenna, an ancient Roman deity, suggests resistance to the new imperial chronology, to Augustus's public 'authoring' of new Roman memories and their sense of cultural identity.[11] The Roman calendar provided an ideal framework for Ovid's Callimachean aetiological project, allowing him to span temporalities while grounded in late Augustan Rome; it also provided the cultural basis on which Ovid could attempt to put his individual stamp on both literary history and his own 'times'.

Anna is mentioned first at the start of Book 3, which is devoted to the month presided over by Mars. The treatment of the first day of March includes a discussion of early calendars, and Romulus's mistaken notion that there were only ten months to the year. Anna Perenna is associated with natural time, with the old Roman calendar that began the year in March, in spring therefore, a time of fertility and renewal (Ov. *Fast.* 3.145–6). Julius Caesar, on the other hand, is praised for regularizing the year by instituting the twelve-month calendar, although, in a hint of the political self-interest underlying the Julian calendar, his main motive is said to be his desire for foreknowledge of the heavens that will be his future home (Ov. *Fast.* 3.155–66).

In the *Fasti* the Ides of March begins not with the notorious event of Caesar's murder, but with the celebration of Anna's festival. There is no mention of a fountain-shrine, the form of her newly discovered cult site in Rome, or of song competitions.[12] Rather, the festival is described as a free-spirited, outdoor event where couples of all ages pitch tents and enjoy sex, heavy drinking, dancing, and songs:

> Plebs venit ac virides passim disiecta per herbas 525
>   potat, et accumbit cum pare quisque sua.
> Sub Iove pars durat, pauci tentoria ponunt,
>   sunt quibus e ramis frondea facta casa est;
> pars, ubi pro rigidis calamos statuere columnis,
>   desuper extentas imposuere togas. 530
> Sole tamen vinoque calent annosque precantur

   quot sumant cyathos, ad numerumque bibunt.
Invenies illic qui Nestoris ebibat annos,
   quae sit per calices facta Sibylla suos.
Illic et cantant quicquid didicere theatris,   535
   et iactant faciles ad sua verba manus,
et ducunt posito duras cratere choreas,
   cultaque diffusis saltat amica comis.

The common folk come and scattered all over the green grass they drink and lie down each with his partner. Some rough it under the sky, a few pitch tents, for others a leafy hut has been made from branches; some, when they've set up reeds as sturdy pillars, have stretched out togas and put them on top. They grow warm with the sun and the wine, and they pray for as many years of life as the cups they take, and they drink up to that number. There you will find someone who could drink in number the years lived by Nestor, and a woman become a Sibyl measured by her cups. There they sing songs learned in the theatre, and they beat time to the words with their nimble hands; setting aside the bowl they dance clumsily while an attractive girlfriend twirls around with streaming hair.

Ov. Fast. 3.525–38

Ovid authenticates his description by presenting himself as an eye-witness of the drunken crowd staggering home at the end of the day:

cum redeunt, titubant et sunt spectacula volgi,
   et fortunatos obvia turba vocat.
Occurrit nuper (visa est mihi digna relatu)
   pompa: senem potum pota trahebat anus.

On their way home they stagger drunkenly, a spectacle for people to behold; the crowd calls those it meets 'blessed'. Recently I encountered the procession. It seems something worthy of the telling: a drunken old woman was pulling along a drunken old man.

Ov. Fast. 3.539–42

The alliterative 'p's' of the last line suggest drunken hiccupping. The drunken old woman dragging along a drunken old man is an inversion of conventional hierarchical order that marks in a comic register the dominance of the female in this festival.[13] The relaxing of social restraints is emphatically marked too at the start by the festive 'architecture', where makeshift tents are constructed of leaves, or with supports of reeds in place of columns (527–30). Emily Gowers points out that Vitruvius (2.1.2–3) describes the earliest human dwellings as huts that used leaves and sticks in their construction; the festival of Anna Perenna is a prime example of what Gowers calls 'vertical comparisons' between the civilized state of modern Rome and the festivals that commemorate Rome's earliest origins.[14] In *Aeneid* 8, the founding of the Ara Maxima is celebrated in the pastoral setting of proto-Rome with song and feasting (Virg. *A.* 8.280–305). But in contrast to the festival of Anna Perenna, the celebration is highly formalized. The song is a ritual hymn performed by the Salian priests and by choruses of old and young men; women play no part. In Ovid's description of the informal setting for Anna's festival, the slender, pliant *calamus*, a word that also means both a writer's pen and a pipe associated with pastoral music, stands in opposition to the aristocratic columns whose epithet, *rigidis*, suggests unbending, top-down rules and codes of conduct.[15] These festive *ad hoc* structures firmly dissociate Anna's festival from Augustan Rome's city of marble. The *calamus* marks the continuing and widespread importance of poetry and song from Rome's earliest origins.

Anna's festival is thus described in such a way as to mark a collision of social and cultural values on the Ides of March. By contrast, Ovid's Ides of March ends with a goddess of a very different character, Vesta, Rome's goddess of chastity and guardian of the hearth that symbolized the state. During Augustus's rule she became closely associated with the emperor, who installed her in a shrine in his palace on the Palatine, thus elevating her as a major imperial deity along with Palatine Apollo.[16] Ovid elsewhere marks her close association with the emperor by naming her *Caesarea ... Vesta* (Caesar's Vesta, *Met.* 15.865). In the *Fasti*, she ends the episode of the Ides of March by asserting her own agency in the rescue and apotheosis of Julius Caesar. Ovid claims that 'he was about to omit telling of the swords aimed against the *princeps*' (*praeteriturus eram gladios in principe fixos*, 3.697); it is not clear whether his reticence comes from a sense of the contradictions of Caesar's murder with Anna's festival, from reverence for the Caesars, or from a willful silence. The reference to Julius Caesar as *princeps* (3.697), however, is striking. As Bömer points out, Ovid is the first writer after Cicero to call Julius Caesar *princeps*, and this is the only occasion he does so in his works.[17] *Princeps* was chosen by Augustus to define his position as 'first man in the state', a title with a democratic gloss. The reference to Julius Caesar as *princeps*, however, emphasizes his dynastic importance for Augustus. His deification legitimated Augustus's rule and virtually guaranteed that Augustus too, as Caesar's adoptive son, would after death become a god.

It was widely believed that Julius Caesar was declared a god at his funeral games, when the people interpreted a bright comet in the sky as a sign of his deification (Plin. *Nat.* 2.23.94).[18] In the *Fasti* Vesta, having reprimanded the poet for his silence, offers a different version of Caesar's deification in which she plays the starring role: first she rescued Caesar from the assassins and then she took his soul heavenwards (3.699–703). Ovid's account of Caesar's deification, with Vesta in the double role of Caesar's saviour from murder and his vehicle for heavenward ascent, is unique and compressed into one simultaneous event. Two 'home-grown' gods, but of very different character, are thus provocatively commemorated on the same day, Anna Perenna and Julius Caesar.

The majority of Ovid's account of Anna Perenna focuses on the origins of this goddess, origins that the poet makes more vexed than seems necessary. Multiple explanations were a feature of Roman ritual exegesis, but Ovid's accounts of how Anna became a goddess are far from the mark.[19] The most popular – and probable – explanation of antiquity was that she was an ancient Roman fertility goddess, associated with the prosperity of the year *(annus)*.[20] Ovid follows this explanation of Anna at the start of *Fasti* 3 when he associates her with new, fecund beginnings in spring (145–6). But on the Ides he makes Anna originally a mortal and provides two unfounded, alternative explanations for the identity of Anna Perenna and her route to becoming a goddess.[21] He thus uniquely inserts Anna Perenna into the new ideology of deification, both associating and contrasting her with Julius Caesar.

The first explanation (Ov. *Fast.* 3.545–656), that Anna Perenna is Dido's sister Anna from Virgil's *Aeneid*, emphasizes Ovid's densely intertextual and intratextual literary ambitions in the *Fasti*.[22] Ovid writes a unique sequel both to Virgil's *Aeneid* 4 and to his own seventh *Heroides*, Dido's elegiac letter to Aeneas that, through her tragic and exclusive perspective, suggests the moral tensions within Virgil's text. The story of Anna in the *Fasti*, which examines the aftermath of the Trojan withdrawal from Carthage through Dido's surviving sister, reinforces the critical reading of *Aeneid* 4 offered by the *Heroides* but goes beyond it by bringing Carthaginian Anna to Italy and placing her within a politicized Roman context focused upon deification.

As Sara Myers comments of Ovid's reworking of Virgil's *Aeneid* in the *Metamorphoses* (Ov. *Met.* 13.623–14.573), 'issues of literary continuation, appropriation and repetition are central'.[23] Likewise, complex repetition is at the core of the sequel in the *Fasti*. Anna shifts between the roles both of Dido and of Aeneas with, however, a dramatic change of focus from the tragic context of the *Heroides* and the *Aeneid*. Ovid's sequel takes a parodic approach to the *Aeneid* in the sense that it forms 'an ironic but not necessarily disrespectful revisiting and recontextualising of an earlier work ... (it is) a form of repetition with ironic critical difference, marking difference rather than similarity'.[24] As Margaret Rose argues, parody accommodates both admiration and laughter.[25] Thus parody is appropriate to a festive occasion and allows the poet to offer fresh angles on Virgil's canonical epic, revisiting its characters with an ironic, even comic gaze, and privileging female experience. As Rose furthermore comments, the reader is invited to decode the relationship between the parody and the parodied text: 'the embedding of the parodied text within the text of the parody both contributes to the ambivalence of the parody which derives from its ability to criticize and renew its target as a part of its own structure and ensures some continued form of existence for the parodied work'.[26] Ovid's sequel to Virgil's *Aeneid* thus also demonstrates the widening of the poet's horizons in this late elegiac work from amatory affairs to matters that strike deep at the heart of the Roman state. Through parodic continuation of the well-known Dido and Aeneas story, elegy and epic are mutually revitalized.

The narrative of Anna, Dido's sister, begins analeptically. One couplet refers back to the end of *Aeneid* 4, with Dido's death on the funeral pyre (Virg. *A.* 4.642–7), and the two following couplets repeat word-by-word Dido's epitaph that concludes *Ep.* 7:

> PRAEBUIT AENEAS ET CAUSAM MORTIS ET ENSEM.
> IPSA SUA DIDO CONCIDIT USA MANU.
>
> Aeneas provided the reason for her death and the sword. Dido herself fell by her own hand.
>
> *Fast.* 3.549–50; *Ep.* 7.195–6

While the epitaph acts as a seal for the narrative of Dido in *Ep.* 7, it is now, in the expansive Roman world of the *Fasti*, a dividing mark for the continuation of the Carthaginian story through Dido's sister Anna. The epitaph, repeated in this new context, marks Ovid's renewed bid for authorial control over Virgil's poem in the fragmentation of its teleological narrative. In so doing, he gains the cooperation of his established readers, who would recognize the repetition of the epitaph from the *Heroides* and would remember its condemnation of Aeneas as treacherous and responsible for Dido's suicide. Thus already at the start of this continuation of Book 4 of the *Aeneid* the reader's disposition is shaped towards suspicion of the Aeneas of the *Fasti*. And, as Sarah McCallum shows in this volume (Ch. 1), Ovid's Anna also carries the ambiguity of Virgil's Anna who incorporates memories of the well-known alternative tradition, that she, rather than Dido, was Aeneas's lover.[27]

As Dido's sister, Anna is a virtual double of Dido, but she is also in many respects a double of Aeneas.[28] For, according to Ovid's parodic narrative, like the Trojan hero she has to flee from Carthage after Dido's suicide; she also, like him, wanders in exile searching for a home, and suffers shipwreck after a terrible storm (Ov. *Fast.* 3.551–600). Anna's journey, however, lacks divine guidance or intervention. This repetition with a female protagonist of Aeneas's journey to Carthage and Italy in the *Aeneid* is a masterpiece of elegiac compression of epic themes. Ovid had repeated Aeneas's episodes of exile and storms previously with another character, his Diomedes in the *Metamorphoses* (*Met.* 14.476–9). Thus in the *Fasti* too we are invited to read Anna's Aeneas-like wanderings through an Ovidian lens with perhaps, as Stephen Hinds suggests, 'its own vestigial claims to set its own agenda'.[29]

On Anna's arrival in Italy, the doubling, and indeed reversal, of roles becomes more complex as Anna shifts between the roles of Dido and of Aeneas, depending on the internal focalization of the characters. In the *Aeneid* Aeneas was shipwrecked on Carthaginian shores and was welcomed by Dido; in the *Fasti* Anna is shipwrecked on the shore of Italy, very close to Lavinium, Aeneas's new settlement in Italy, and is welcomed by Aeneas as an exile, like his former self in need of hospitality (Ov. *Fast.* 3.601–36). To Aeneas's wife Lavinia, however, Anna appears as Dido's double and thus her hated rival. Ovid coins the new adverb *furialiter* (in the manner of a Fury, 637) to describe Lavinia's mad jealousy of Anna. Lavinia, whose main role in the *Aeneid* was to appear as the silent object of desire for the two rival males and whose marriage to Aeneas was the lynchpin of reconciliation between Italians and Trojans, now appears in a different light as a divisive, destructive Fury intent on killing Anna. Mad with fear and hatred at her betrayal by Aeneas (Ov. *Fast.* 3.633–8), she herself has become in a further complicated reversal like Virgil's Dido at the end of *Aeneid* 4 (Virg. *A.* 4.474–665), or her fiancé Turnus who became possessed by jealousy and anger after he was maddened by the Fury Allecto (Virg. *A.* 7.406–74).

The narrative comes to a melodramatic climax with the appearance of Dido's bloodied ghost urging Anna to flee from Lavinia's murderous intent (Ov. *Fast.* 3.638–42). In a burlesque scene the scantily clad Anna jumps from her bedroom window and runs to the river Numicius (642–8). There 'the horned river god Numicius, with swollen waters is believed to have raped her/rescued her and hidden her in his deep pools' (*corniger hanc tumidis rapuisse Numicius undis/ creditur et stagnis occuluisse suis*, 647–8).[30] From union with the river god, Anna becomes the goddess Anna Perenna, and the *aetion* comes to a peaceful close: *placidi sum nympha Numici: / amne perenne latens Anna Perenna vocor*, (I am a nymph of the peaceful Numicius; concealed in a perennial river I am called Anna Perenna, Ov. *Fast.* 3.653–4), or at least so 'she seemed to say' (*ipsa loqui visa est*, 653).

This rather salacious story of Anna's deification provides an alternative ending to the hatred between Carthage and Rome thematized in the *Aeneid*. Dido's sister Anna is now domesticated on Italian soil as a peaceful goddess associated with the constant fertile flow of the river.[31] The discovery of the fountain and dedications to the nymphs at the Piazza Euclide suggests that Anna Perenna was indeed a deity associated with water. But apart from that kernel of authenticity, the reader's attention is drawn to Ovid's creative engagement with literary tradition in the matter of Anna's deification by skeptical qualifiers such as *creditur* (648) and *visa est* (653).

The main Roman model for rescue by a river-god and marriage was Ennius's epic account in the *Annales* (xxxix Sk.) of Ilia, mother of Romulus and Remus who, with Venus's help, is saved from her murderous uncle by union with the river Anio. Ovid retells that story in *Am.* 3.6 with a decidedly erotic cast, and marks the literary heritage of his version with *dicitur* ('people say', *Am.* 3.6.81–2), a reference to Ennius that points to the poet's transformative, elegiacizing hand.[32] Book 3 of the *Fasti* opens with a prominent allusion to Ennius through a recasting of Ilia's dream of impregnation by Mars (*Fast.* 3.11–86). In the *Fasti* Anna, therefore, has another double, Ilia, mother of Romulus, the founder of the city of Rome. The importance of Ennius in Ovid's construction of Anna's myth is perhaps hinted at in Anna's final words announcing her immortality, *amne perenne latens Anna Perenna vocor* (hiding in a perennial river, I am called Anna Perenna, *Fast.* 3.654). *Latens*, a word that signposts etymological word play, points to the virtual anagram of the new goddess's name in *amne perenne*.[33] Furthermore, Ovid, I suggest, also alludes to Lucretius's pun on Ennius's name (1.117–18): *Ennius ut noster cecinit, qui primus amoeno /detulit ex Helicone perenni fronde coronam* (as our Ennius sang, who was the first to bring down from pleasing Helicon a garland of perennial foliage). As Denis Feeney comments, 'Lucretius shows how time is built into Ennius's very name', claiming for the poet immortality.[34] Ovid audaciously appropriates the pun and its implicit claims of immortality for Anna Perenna, using the adjective with which he makes his own claims to immortal fame.[35] Through allusion to Ennius and his own elegiac poetry, Ovid emphasizes his professional and ambitious command of his literary sources, even as he gives them, under the lighter embrace of elegy, a comic turn. At the same time he challenges the teleological version of Roman history of his literary forebears, Ennius and Virgil. Together, Ilia and Anna offer another way of looking at Rome's foundational narratives, one that suggests the importance also of female figures and female sexuality in shaping Roman values and origins. Sharon James has recently argued that the many mythic as well as Roman rapes in Ovid's poetry would have been implicitly associated, for Ovid's Roman readers, with Roman politics and Roman foundation narratives, to which rape was central.[36] But in the case of Anna, rape – or union with the river Numicius – *saves* her from a greater evil, from the murderous house of Aeneas and Lavinia, and from civic politics; she founds a peaceful, fertility cult, and unlike Ilia, she has no sons to carry forward the burden of Rome's imperial future. All the same, in modelling Anna's deification on Ilia's rescue by the Anio, Ovid also edges Anna close to Julian history.

There is another politically charged model for deification in play here, and that is Aeneas's own. Anna is said to become a goddess in the very river, the Numicius, which will soon be the site of Aeneas's deification (Ov. *Met*. 14.581–608).[37] Aeneas's deification is foretold in the *Aeneid* but not described (*A*. 1.259–60 and 12.794–5).[38] It is the *Metamorphoses* that provides another sequel to the *Aeneid* by recounting how, through Venus's command, the river Numicius purifies Aeneas of his mortal elements (600–5). Aeneas thus is made a god by the very waters that, by lascivious means, sheltered Anna from Aeneas's treacherous household and made her a goddess.

In the *Metamorphoses* Aeneas's deification forms part of a sequence of the deification of rulers culminating with the apotheosis of Julius Caesar; Hercules (*Met*. 9.250–72) precedes Aeneas, and Romulus with his wife Hersilia (*Met*. 14.805–51) follows Aeneas. These rulers provide paradigms of apotheosis for Julius Caesar and his heir Augustus. Ovid's epic plots a narrative of dynastic, divine destiny for Augustus, but in the *Fasti* Anna disrupts that narrative. A Carthaginian who becomes a Roman goddess, she is a foreign element in the Julian line of descent; yet, hidden deep in an immortal river, associated with the deification of Aeneas, she has become integrated into the Italian landscape, a partial forerunner of Romulus's mother Ilia. Ovid's account of Anna is full of comic ironies. She compromises the masculine-driven, teleological narrative of the *Aeneid*; and she is now an unsettling part of Julian history too.

Indeed, Ovid rather daringly associates Anna's deification with Julius Caesar's also. In both accounts, rescue from murder and deification are connected. The verb used to describe the method by which Anna became a goddess, *rapuisse* (647), has the sense of both 'rape' and 'rescue' and finds a provocative echo in Vesta's words describing her rescue of Julius Caesar from the assassins:

Ipsa virum rapui simulacraque nuda reliqui:
    quae cecidit ferro, Caesaris umbra fuit.

I myself snatched away the man and left behind a naked image; it was Caesar's shade that fell by the sword.

Ov. *Fast*. 3.701–2

We can translate the phrase *virum rapui* as 'I snatched away the man', but there is an underlying ironic association with 'rape' as the goddess of chastity leaves behind on earth a strangely 'naked image' of her 'man' (*simulacraque nuda*, 701) and ensures his divinity through the precedent set by Numicius.[39]

As Alessandro Barchiesi comments, the involvement of Vesta in Caesar's apotheosis is entirely novel, and it contradicts Ovid's account of the deification of Julius Caesar in *Metamorphoses* 15 (843–51), where it is Venus who, as maternal founder of the Julian line, rescues Caesar.[40] Here too the language is comically and sexually risqué (Ov. *Met.* 15.844–5): *suique/ Caesaris eripuit membris . . . /recentem animam* (she snatched her Caesar's freshly minted soul from his limbs). Not only does *eripuit* carry connotations of sexual predation, *membris* also can connote the 'male member'.[41] Moreover, when Caesar turns into a comet he is so hot that Venus has to release him from her bosom:

> dumque tulit, lumen capere atque ignescere sensit
> emisitque sinu.
>
> And while she carried it, she felt it spark light and catch fire and she released it from her bosom.
>
> Ov. *Met.* 15.847–8

As Adams comments, *sinus* can mean 'womb' as well as 'bosom'.[42] Not everyone may accept this eroticized reading, of course, even for the goddess of love and of sexual generation, though the two possible meanings of *sinu* conflate her erotic and dynastic roles. But as Barchiesi argues, a characteristic of Ovid's poetry is its insistence that 'every work of art is open to deviant interpretations'.[43] Ovid's cross-referencing of his two accounts of Caesar's apotheosis in the *Fasti* and the *Metamorphoses* points up the contingency of deification narratives, their status as creative, even comic, fictions that nonetheless acknowledge the political necessities and self-interests underlying imperial ruler cult.

Ovid's treatment of ruler deification in the *Metamorphoses* and the *Fasti* challenges the traditional idea that divinization of mortals rested on merit. As Fabre-Serris argues, Ovid makes favouritism and family connections the basis for the apotheosis of Rome's new rulers. In the *Metamorphoses* Venus pleads with Jupiter for the divinization of her descendant Julius Caesar, gaining a guarantee of Augustus's future apotheosis also (Ov. *Met.* 15.760–842); in the *Fasti* Vesta saves Caesar for, as *pontifex maximus*, he was head of her cult. With these two different accounts of Caesar's apotheosis, Ovid advertises the poet's transformative hand and lays bare the usefulness of apotheosis as a political tool for legitimating a dynasty, while the deified Anna also reveals its usefulness as a stimulus for creative literary fictions.[44]

With his first aetiological story about Anna, Ovid brilliantly incorporates into his Ides of March a work that had achieved canonical status in Augustan Rome, Virgil's *Aeneid*.[45] But his sequel offers fresh ways of reading that text that suggest the multiple tensions within Virgil's poem. Here in the *Fasti* Aeneas appears in a poor light, inept, as in *Aeneid* 4, at social relations, and unable to control his wife. He is introduced to the narrative walking on the beach he acquired as a dowry (*litore dotali,* 603); that is, his ownership of Italian land is presented as acquired by marriage, not by heroic, military victory. Gender norms are inverted. While his wife Lavinia rules the house, he strolls barefoot on the beach with his friend Achates (Ov. *Fast*. 3.603–6). He is, moreover, referred to here by the rare expression *Cythereius heros* (611). While the epithet associates Aeneas with his mother Venus, often called *Cytherea*, the particular, rarer spelling *Cythereius* appears earlier only at Cicero, *Att*. 15.22, where it describes Antony under the influence of his courtesan Cytheris.[46] Aeneas appears in this narrative as a weak ruler, prone to repeating in Italy his earlier woman trouble in Carthage.[47] In particular, in Ovid's sequel he fulfills Dido's damning prediction in *Ep*. 7 of what will happen when he arrives in Italy:

> scilicet alter amor tibi restat et altera Dido;
> quamque iterum fallas altera danda fides.
>
> I suppose that a second love lies in store for you, and a second Dido; a second pledge to give, and a second time to prove false.[48]
>
> Ov. *Ep*. 7.17–18

If anyone is heroic and thus deserving of deification in Ovid's Virgilian sequel, it is surely Anna, who shows *pietas* to her sister and courageously survives exile, shipwreck and attempted murder.

Ovid's first *aetion* of Anna demands to be read not only in a post-Virgilian context but also in a post-Ovidian one. Its significance is sharpened by its engagement with Ovid's other works so that the *Fasti* appears here as a dynamic continuation both of Virgil's account of Rome's early history and of Ovid's own. In particular, Ovid's parodic *aetion* suggests the possibilities offered by Virgil's story of Dido and Aeneas for creative rewriting even when brought into the imperial present, where deification had become a live issue. On the Ides of March Ovid revisits in a differently gendered mode a literary and a political tradition dominated by masculine perspectives. The ironic subversion of the Virgilian tradition is, moreover, a vehicle of literary self-aggrandizement. Ovid's continuation of the Carthaginian drama, which begins with Dido's epitaph from the *Heroides* and ends with allusion to the *Metamorphoses*, is thus framed by Ovid's own unique interventions into Virgil's narrative of Aeneas and the foundation legends of Rome. The main narrative arc is Ovidian, and it demonstrates the rich generic capabilities of Ovid's mature elegy.

In the second main explanation that the poet provides of Anna's origins there is a clear link between merit and deification. Ovid here draws on a historical occasion (Ov. *Fast.* 3.661–74), the secession of the plebs in 494 BCE, which led to the creation of the office of the tribune of the plebs (Liv. 2.23–33). Like Livy, Ovid places the secession on the Mons Sacer, and not on the Aventine. Otherwise, however, the role of Anna here seems to be a fabrication.[49] According to Ovid, Anna was an old woman from the town of Bovillae (just over ten miles from Rome), who distributed her home-baked cakes to the commoners when they were starving during their secession from Rome.[50] When peace was agreed upon, a statue was erected in her honour and she was made a goddess. Until the imperial age, it was highly unusual for a Roman woman to have a public statue erected in her honour. Livy (2.13.6–11) records only one woman from the distant past, a certain Cloelia who was awarded an equestrian statue (*novo genere honoris*, a new type of honour, Liv. 2.13.11) for her bravery in time of war. Leading a band of women hostages, she escaped from Etruscan captivity by heroically swimming to safety across the Tiber.[51]

With this story of the elderly Anna, Ovid looks from off–centre at an iconic event of successful social struggle that, as Lisa Mignone has argued, was embedded in the cultural memory of the Roman people for generations and had been handled with narrative dynamism by the historiographers Livy and Dionysius.[52] The emphasis on the old woman comes at the expense of silence about Livy's hero of the event, the plebeian leader Agrippa Menenius, with his fable about the Belly and the Limbs enjoining the need for all parts of the body (and the body politic) to work together (Liv. 2.32.8–12); it comes also at the expense of the creation itself of the plebeian tribunate. Ovid's version is essentially Hellenistic in its attention not to the main political event but to a humble old woman and domestic details.

The deification of an elderly, working woman is certainly an oddity, and Bömer claims that there is no parallel for the story of Anna of Bovillae.[53] A possible model, I suggest, is Callimachus's *Hecale*, as has also been suggested recently by Angeline Chiu.[54] This epyllion is centred on the figure of the hospitable old woman who enjoys extraordinary honours after death. The *Fasti* announces its Callimachean credentials in its programmatic first three words, *tempora cum causis* (times with their causes), *causae* being the Latin version of Greek *aitia*, stories of origin. A few of the narratives in the *Fasti* draw overtly on Callimachean models, most notably the tales of the disobedient raven (Ov. *Fast.* 2.243–66) and of Orion (Ov. *Fast.* 5.493–536), but Anna Perenna has been overlooked.[55] The eponymous protagonist of Callimachus's epyllion *Hecale* is a poor, elderly woman living in the country, who is an example of unstinting hospitality. On the eve of Theseus's fight with the Marathonian bull – at a moment of crisis, therefore – Hecale puts her guest up overnight. Like Hecale, who 'sets out for her guest loaves in abundance taken from a bread bin' (ἐκ δ' ἄρτους σιπύηθεν ἅλις κατέθηκεν ἑλοῦσα, fr. 35 Hollis), Anna is an old woman who serves 'country cakes in abundance' (*rustica liba, copia grata, Fast.* 3.670) to the needy plebs who are starving away from home. In Callimachus's poem Theseus institutes honours in memory of Hecale after her death (fr. 81–3 Hollis): an annual banquet at her tomb; a deme named after her; and institution of her cult in the precinct of Zeus Hekaleios.[56]

These elaborate honours granted Hecale find some counterpart in the unprecedented granting of a statue for the old woman Anna:

> pace domi facta signum posuere Perennae,
>   quod sibi defectis illa ferebat opem.
>
> When peace was made they set up a statue to Perenna, because she brought them help when they were in need.
>
> Ov. *Fast.* 3.673–4

Ovid severely compresses Anna's final honours. Nonetheless, the statue, along with the title 'Perenna', seems to signify Anna's deification for an act of hospitality that extends beyond one person to an entire political class. In the *Hecale*, the focus on the old woman, rather than the epic hero Theseus and his fight with the Marathon bull, finds some correspondence in the disproportionate emphasis on Anna over Julius Caesar. Yet unlike Callimachus's Hecale, Anna of Bovillae is given political import. For according to Ovid's poetic calendar, a humble old woman, who displays her populist, Republican sympathies by performing an act of charity for the *plebs*, is honoured as a deity on the same day as Julius Caesar. The *Hecale* is an innovative poem that invites the questioning and transgression of generic and gender boundaries. In this second story of Anna's origins, Ovid has grafted Callimachus's Hecale onto Anna of Bovillae and boldly inserted her not only into an elegiac context but also into a Roman historical narrative where her act of generosity, not family connections, has political effect and earns her deification.

Scholars have wondered why Ovid made this elderly Anna come from the specific locale of Bovillae, a small town some ten miles south of Rome near the Alban lake.[57] It seems implausible that an old woman would travel seven miles or so to the Mons Sacer to feed the plebs. A well-established theory holds that Ovid is spinning off a central feature of the following festival of the Liberalia, where old women hawked sweet cakes in the streets.[58] I suggest that there may also be a punning allusion to the *Hecale* in the 'bullish' name of Anna's town, which was believed to have been founded on the spot where a bull fleeing sacrifice was captured. Maltby reports an ancient etymological tradition deriving the name Bovillae from a bull (*bos*); for instance *Schol. Pers.* 6, 55 reports: *nam . . . ab ara fugiens taurus . . . ibi conprehensus est, unde Bovillae dictae* (Bovillae is named after a bull that was captured there, after fleeing from the altar).[59] Callimachus's Hecale welcomes Theseus to her cottage on the eve of his fight with the monstrous bull on the nearby plain of Marathon; Ovid situates his old woman in a town whose very name means 'bull'. The connection with the *Hecale* may therefore be wittily signalled by the 'bovine' in Bovillae.

There are surely also political reasons for the choice of town. Bovillae had a major connection with Julius Caesar and his ancestral family.[60] Bovillae was closely associated with Trojan foundation-legends. It was an offshoot settlement of Alba Longa, which was traditionally founded by Aeneas's son Iulus. One of the most complete examples of the *Tabulae Iliacae*, the *Capitolina*, was found at a villa not far from Bovillae. Dating from the mid-Augustan period, it is carved with scenes from the Trojan war and shows Aeneas boarding a ship, testimony to the importance of Trojan legends in this area near Rome. As David Petrain argues, 'there are undeniable points of contact between the contents of its reliefs and the religious traditions of the city'.[61] These traditions closely involved the Julians. After Alba Longa was destroyed early in Rome's history (Liv. 1.27–30), Bovillae seems to have become the centre of cultic activity by the Julian family, in Ovid's day the ruling Trojan family in Rome. A Republican altar found outside the theatre in Bovillae in 1826 and probably dating to the latter half of the second century BCE, names with archaic orthography members of the Julian family.[62] David Petrain suggests that it perhaps preserves an old epigraphic record of the Julians' cultic activity at Bovillae; if so, it testifies to the antiquity of the Julian family's association with Bovillae.[63] During the Augustan period, the town was given a monumental city centre with the construction of a theatre, a circus, and a monumental tomb. Tacitus tells us that the emperor Tiberius in 16 CE dedicated a *sacrarium* (a sanctuary) with a statue to the deified Augustus; the *sacrarium* was a possible centre for the *sodales Augusti*, the priests in charge of Augustus's deified cult (*Ann.* 2.41.1; *Ann.* 15.23.15). It was at Bovillae two years earlier that Augustus's body, on its way back from Nola for cremation in Rome, was formally received by a deputation of Roman knights, who conducted it to the city (Suet. *Aug.* 100). Bovillae in short was Julian family heartland. Here they held special games and festivals in honour of their ancestors and family members.[64]

Thus Ovid's association of Anna with Bovillae is bold. Once again, as in the first, Virgilian story, Anna Perenna is associated in time and in place with the Julian family. But Ovid's invented tradition about Anna of Bovillae represents different principles. In the popular memory, according to Ovid's narrative, her sympathies are on the side of the plebs. She earns deification, moreover, through merit. By contrast, as Jacqueline Fabre-Serris points out, Ovid makes the deification of Julius Caesar a matter of family politics and favouritism, *not* a matter of merit; Vesta saves Caesar for the stars because 'he was my priest' (Ov. *Fast.* 3.699). And in the *Metamorphoses* Ovid writes that Caesar had to become a god for dynastic reasons – so that Augustus could become one too: *ne foret hic igitur mortali semine cretus/ ille deus faciendus erat* (in order that he [sc. Augustus] might not be a creature of mortal seed/ he [Julius Caesar] had to be made a god, *Met.* 15.760–1).[65] In Ovid's origins of Rome, Anna shares both place and time with the Julian family, yet is a reminder of different foundational values. Her sympathies are republican and plebeian, not autocratic.[66] Her festival is celebrated by the general populace, not by the elite, and her traditional roots are in music, dance and song. She is associated with festive fun, with charity and honest labour, with female authority, and, as the final story about her makes clear, with freedom of speech.

This final narrative, a farcical tale that most likely draws from mime (Ov. *Fast.* 3.677–94), explains why young girls sing racy songs at her festival: *nunc mihi, cur cantent, superest, obscena puellae, /dicere* (now it is left for me to explain why girls sing obscenities, 3.675–6). The paradoxical juxtaposition of *obscena* with *puellae* emphasizes the relaxation and inversion of social conventions at the festival with regards to speech; even young girls, the most carefully guarded category of femininity, can sing without constraint. Earlier Ovid mentioned that the celebrants sing songs learned at the theatre (3.535). A fragment of a mime entitled *Anna Peranna* by Decimus Laberius survives, and thus there may well be a connection here to the songs sung at Anna's festival, as well as to this final story about her.[67] The mimes of Laberius and his fellow dramatists included topical satire, and interestingly, Laberius, an equestrian, was known for the political edginess of his mimes.[68] A Roman reader of Ovid's final story about Anna may have understood that its connection with mime did not simply entail farce but also offered social and political bite.

It has not always been recognized that the Anna of this final story is Anna of Bovillae, and that this story therefore forms a sequel to her role in the secession of the *plebs*.[69] For instance, she appears here as a freshly minted goddess, *nuper erat dea facta* (she had lately become a goddess, 677). She is clearly not Dido's deified sister, for the god Mars, who uses Anna as a go-between in his passion for Minerva, identifies her as a kindly old woman who is skilled at bringing people together:

> Effice, di studio similes coeamus in unum:
>   conveniunt partes hae tibi, comis anus.
>
> Facilitate the union of two deities alike in their interests; this type of job suits you, kindly old woman.
>
> Ov. *Fast.* 3.683–4

Mars here makes an oblique reference to Anna's part in engineering peace between the warring classes during the plebeian secession, but he perverts her charitable role to serve his own erotic interests. Anna however tricks Mars and frustrates his adulterous sexual plans, thus making the divine father of Romulus the butt of a joke that Venus, Mars's partner, particularly enjoys:

> ridet amatorem carae nova diva Minervae,
>   nec res hac Veneri gratior ulla.
>
> The new goddess laughs at the lover of his beloved Minerva, nor was anything more pleasing to Venus than this.
>
> Ov. *Fast.* 3.693–4

Here, provocatively, Anna of Bovillae, an elderly woman and a figure of Republican, plebeian sympathies, hoodwinks the great warrior god and father of Romulus. Given the reputation of Laberius's mimes for political satire, a Roman readership or audience would probably have appreciated the come-uppance of one of the chief founding deities of Rome's ruling class.

In the festive mix of narratives on the Ides of March, Ovid has moved from Virgil's *Aeneid* to low-level mime. Yet the central plot of the mime and of Ovid's Virgilian sequel is similar: suspected and foiled adultery. Furthermore, in all three stories Anna retains the moral high ground. She is hardly 'the procuress of the gods' that Barchiesi calls her.[70] The final comic turn on Rome's founding deities, Mars and Venus, is overtly used to validate joking and liberty of speech on the Ides of March. Significantly, Anna's trick on Mars is described in terms of speech: *et iuvat hanc magno verba dedisse deo* (and it is a pleasure to have hoodwinked a great god, Ov. *Fast.* 3.696). In translation I have used a common visual metaphor for deception; the Latin metaphor, however, is verbal. Literally meaning 'gave words to', this expression emphasizes the power of women's speech at Anna's festival to challenge social and gender norms and mock patriarchal structures.[71]

On the Ides of March, Ovid ironically underlines the diversity of his rewritings of Rome's past. Narratives of Anna's origin are told through a network of different traditions, epic, historiography, theatre and mime.[72] The poem also offers the reader three possible, different identities for Anna Perenna: the elite princess who is also a refugee from North Africa; the honest working woman of low social class; and the goddess who also performs the even lower social role of *lena* in the farcical passion of Mars for Minerva. This richly varied social tapestry offers a new perspective on Roman origins from the Virgilian narrative, for instance. It draws attention to the importance not only of women but also of different levels of society in constructing the Roman state. Interestingly, although the three identities of Anna Perenna are separate as regards social class, they all are provocatively associated with Julian history.

By contrast with the freedom of speech in song and mime on Anna's festival, the poet's speech is bridled with regards to the assassination of Julius Caesar, as if the imperial hierarchy demanded words of the utmost discretion.[73] The poet claims he was about to pass over (*praeteriturus*, 697) the topic when Vesta ordered him to include it in his poem. As Richard Thomas comments, a *praeteritio* 'is a device which purports to minimize, but in fact creates emphasis'.[74] There is a stark contrast between the liberal speech at Anna's festival and the poet's commissioned speech for Caesar, which ends with a sober reminder that the dead at the battle of Philippi were left unburied, and with the unsettling claim that the conspirators' deaths were nonetheless deserved:[75]

> morte iacent merita: testes estote Philippi,
>   et quorum sparsis ossibus albet humus.
> hoc opus, haec pietas, haec prima elementa fuerunt
>   Caesaris, ulcisci iusta per arma patrem.
>
> They (sc. the conspirators) lie in deserved death: be witness, Philippi, and the ground that is white with their scattered bones. This was Caesar's task, his act of piety, his first building blocks of power, to avenge his father through righteous arms.
>
> Ov. *Fast.* 3.707–10

The Ides of March ends with unresolved tension between the 'unburied dead' and 'their deserved death' through Augustus's 'righteous arms'. Whatever one might think of Caesar's *pietas* to his murdered father, the grim image of scattered, desiccated bones sits oddly with the earlier festive spirit and with the *pietas* of Anna of Bovillae to the *plebs*.

Barchiesi claims that Ovid's juxtaposition of the two different events on the Ides of March 'guarantees' that there will always be two options for commemoration available on the Ides of March.[76] Yet until the recent stunning discovery of Anna Perenna's fountain at the Piazza Euclide, this goddess was largely forgotten outside readers of the *Fasti*; the Ides was Caesar's day. Interestingly, the date of Anna's festival seem to have been changed, possibly under Tiberius, from the Ides of March, as recorded in the first century CE *Fasti Vaticani* (*Insc. Ital.* 13.2.23), to 18 June, the recorded date in the fourth century calendar, the *Fasti Filocaliani*. The place where the festival was celebrated seems to have been changed also from the ideologically charged location near Augustus's Mausoleum, where Ovid apparently situates it, to the more politically neutral site by the present day Piazza Euclide. Scholars have argued that these changes happened for political reasons, in order to move Anna Perenna physically and metaphorically away from prime Julio–Claudian space.[77] Whatever the truth of the matter, Ovid's treatment of the Ides of March in the *Fasti* is calibrated in such a way as to advertise the difficulty of resisting the gravitational pull of Augustan control over the calendar. The account of Caesar's murder and apotheosis is a short speech voiced or mandated by Vesta that brings the Ides to a close. As such, it advertises the importance of deification as a dynastic strategy to the ruling house, regardless of its self-conscious fictiveness.

However, the poet's strategy is different with the next important day in the calendar, March 17, which also commemorates two different types of event, the people's festival of the Liberalia (Ov. *Fast.* 3.713–90), whose very name advertises 'liberty', at least in the popular imagination,[78] and the battle of Munda, Caesar's final victory in the civil war in Spain.[79] Munda is recorded in the contemporary *Fasti* from Caere.[80] But our poet remains silent on this battle, a sign of his continual negotiation in the *Fasti* with the Caesars for cultural and literary authority over the calendar.

Nonetheless, through his divided treatment of the Ides of March, Ovid invites comparison between the old and the new deity and their different systems of value. Anna's imagined association with Julian history, moreover, offers the reader the opportunity to revisit the past from a differently gendered point of view. As Victor Turner has argued, festivals and games are situations with innovative potential; they are not therefore auxiliary to the main structures of society.[81] In a period when Augustus was reshaping the public calendar to suit his dynastic needs, Ovid's literary version of the calendar offers a view of Roman 'times' that emphasizes the pluralism of Roman historical practices and values. With its annual reenactment of ancient customs, the festival of Anna Perenna suggests that the past is a repository of valuable traditions that are subject always to creative renewal. Anna presides over fertility in a physical and metaphorical sense. Free expression in the form of music, dance and poetry are represented on Anna's day as central to Roman cultural identity and deep-rooted in its earliest traditions.

Furthermore, on a day owned by Caesar's calendar perhaps more than any other, Ovid shows as poet of the innovative new poem the *Fasti* that he too has an important voice in the debate around deification, shaping and contesting its fictions.[82] The deification of a mortal Roman was a new, controversial idea in Rome, for it was regarded as an Eastern practice, the prerogative of Pharaonic and Ptolemaic royalty. It was met with a good deal of scepticism on the part of the elite, and with creative fascination by Rome's poets.[83] The deification of women was even more controversial.[84] As a new phenomenon in Rome, deification was always up for negotiation, and also, as we have seen in the *Fasti*, for imaginative representation. Much has been written lately about Ovid's active, and slippery, participation in the debate over deification, and his subtle invitation to his readers to consider the possibility of alternative, resistant responses to official compliment. As Olivier Hekster argues, under Augustus deification, while crucial for legitimizing the new regime, was not a clearly articulated, stable concept but rather was 'a process of trial, error, and success in defining the proper ways to integrate Julian divine ancestry into the new balance of power'.[85] The *Fasti* exploits these uncertainties by suggesting that the Julian hold over deification was not in fact unique, that deification of mortals in Italy had a long tradition that included women as well as men, and different social classes, not only the elite. Rome's early history therefore was rooted in multiple, divergent histories in which communitarian values, human sexuality and artistic creativity played an important, determining part.

To conclude, on the Ides of March Ovid provides new festive stories of deification for Anna that fall, however, within the orbit of Julian history, unsettling the patrilineal narrative and offering a broader, more diverse view of Rome's founding values. While adding little to our understanding of the actual practices involved in the goddess's cult, Ovid's highlighting of Anna Perenna on the Ides of March importantly contributes to the debate around imperial deification. Through Anna, moreover, Ovid makes a call for the perennial importance of his 'elegiac' values and the centrality of art, highbrow and lowbrow, to Roman cultural identity. The focus on relations of power that are so important in Ovid's *Fasti* should not occlude the aesthetic dimension that was also so important for our poet. His claim to cultural authority over his 'times' is interleaved with his bid for literary supremacy. His ambitious display of intertextual and intratextual virtuosity closely aligns contemporary politics with superb artistry. In tandem with the poem's resistance to a conventional top-down focus on Rome and the Julian narrative of divine destiny, its creative fictions about Anna Perenna resist the gravitational pull of Virgil's *Aeneid*; they also, as we have seen, give a Roman, political stamp to Callimachus's generic play with non-epic themes and tropes.

When our poet hesitates to mention Julius Caesar's assassination on the Ides of March, Vesta commands our poet *ne dubita meminisse* (don't hesitate to remember, Ov. *Fast*. 3.699). The *Fasti* raises the question of what a society should remember and who has the authority to make those decisions. In his work on cultural memory, Jan Assmann discusses how the stock of memories stored up in the medium of writing quickly surpasses the horizons of knowledge that can be put to immediate use.[86] Augustus's reshaping of the Roman calendar and thus of the cultural memories of the Roman people showed how remembering can become a powerful political tool in that it means making distinctions and pushing into the background or even obliterating other memories. As Denis Feeney comments:

> Augustus over the years created a profound reconfiguration of the systems of representing the past time of the city. This reconfiguration centred on his own person and that of his heir, in the process forging links with Rome's divine origins and creating a new imperial dating era. The Republican time systems appear to be still in place, but by the end of Augustus's reign their symbolic power, iconography, and resonance have been compromised and redrawn.[87]

My contention in this paper has been that Ovid's aim in the *Fasti* was to expand the horizon of cultural memories that Augustus was foreclosing. With his multivocal and virtuosic treatment of Anna Perenna on the Ides of March, Ovid boldly mounts a challenge to both temporal and literary authority. With Anna Perenna, 'the politics of poetry' and the 'poetics of empire', to use the phrasing of Iannis Ziogas, overtly collide, but also partly converge, in a dynamic contest between poet and *princeps* over the interpretation and representation of Roman 'times'.[88] Indeed, in almost his last words from exile, Ovid writes:

> Di quoque carminibus (si fas est dicere) fiunt,
> tantaque maiestas ore canentis eget.

> If it is permitted to say this, gods too are made by poetry and their great majesty needs the poet's voice.
>
> Ov. *Pont.* 4.8.55–6

The Afterlife of Anna Perenna

9

Riverrun: Channelling Anna Perenna in *Finnegans Wake*

Justin Hudak

The 'the' that ends *Finnegans Wake* – or rather, the 'the' with which that work denies its ending[1] – brings us back to the dactylic 'riverrun' (*FW* 03.01) that opens the floodgates of James Joyce's magnum opus.[2] This 'the', afloat upon iambic waves of 'a' ('a way a lone a last a loved a long the', *FW* 628.15–16), on the one hand challenges us to define a prodigiously polysemous text, and on the other defies such definition.[3] Strictly speaking, this definite article need not take dominion over the entire *Wake*; its referential scope, insofar as it has one, may be limited to the word 'riverrun'. Without seeking to assign a definitive meaning either to this neologism or to the *Wake* as a whole, I do strive, in the following meditation upon influence, to demonstrate one salient strand of the word's and the work's artfully concealed Ovidianism.

In his most recent monograph on the subject, Harold Bloom defines influence simply as 'literary love, tempered by defense'.[4] Here, as in the title of the work from which this definition is culled (*The Anatomy of Influence*), Bloom eschews the word 'anxiety'. And who could blame him? Ever since his earlier work on the subject was first published in January of 1973, scholars have been (weakly) misreading it.[5] Particularly relevant to the concerns of this chapter is a misreading produced by the Joyce scholar and biographer Richard Ellmann, according to whom the author of the *Wake* 'exhibits none of that anxiety of influence which Harold Bloom has recently attributed to modern writers'.[6] What Ellmann here and others elsewhere have failed to understand, is that, at least for Bloom and his critical adherents, influence anxiety manifests itself not necessarily in the creators of imaginative literature but, far more crucially, in their creations. And yet, even when readers have turned their attention to influence anxiety as manifested in texts, too often interpretative injustice has been done. Consider, for example, the following assertion by Theodore Ziolkowski: 'Joyce has found his spiritual forefather in Ovid, a kinship inherent in [*A Portrait of the Artist as a Young Man*] since Ovid plays no such major role in either of Joyce's subsequent works'.[7] While it is true that neither of the Irish writer's prose epics flaunts its Ovidian heritage as flagrantly as does the *Bildungsroman* that takes for its epigraph a line from the Roman poet's tale of Daedalus and Icarus (*et ignotas animum dimittit in artes*, Ov. Met. 8.188), both *Ulysses* and *Finnegans Wake* are more profoundly shaped by the works of Joyce's spiritual forefather than has hitherto been appreciated.

Hence this chapter, in which I argue that the river of Ovidian influence running through the *Wake* not only exists but has a name: Anna. This palindromic personage, who represents both the river upon whose banks Dublin was founded and the mother in the narrative's archetypal family, is nothing short of influence personified. Her full name is Anna Livia Plurabelle (ALP), and it is my contention that this riverine figure is in large part derived from the similarly fluminal Anna Perenna of Ovid's *Fasti*. Derived from, yes, but hardly unoriginal, for Joyce executes a sort of *clinamen* in relation to his forerunner. I borrow this term from my own critical forerunner, Bloom, who takes it from Lucretius, in whose *De Rerum Natura* the word denotes a change-enabling 'swerve' of the atoms. According to Bloom, 'A poet swerves away from his precursor . . . as a corrective movement in his own poem, which implies that the precursor poem went accurately up to a certain point, but then should have swerved, precisely in the direction that the new poem moves'.[8]

Criticism, too, often involves corrective swerves, and in this tripartite act of appreciation I make three such manoeuvres, one each in relation to the three influential scholars whose names I have already mentioned. Parting ways first with Ziolkowski, I set the stage for my central argument by demonstrating that the Ovidian oeuvre continues to exert its influence on the Joycean corpus well after the publication of *A Portrait of the Artist as a Young Man*, and that the *Fasti* enjoys a particularly persistent and pervasive resurgence in the *Wake*. Next, though willing to accede to Ellmann's claim that Joyce himself felt no anxiety of influence, I reveal how the *Wake*'s ALP nevertheless tallies that anxiety.[9] Finally, in what I hope amounts to a pious gesture, I attempt to bear upon my shoulders the theory of influence which has hitherto borne me. To Bloom's six revisionary ratios – those mechanisms of defence that a writer, in the throes of literary love, may be induced to take against a precursor – I add a seventh, a unique *modus defendendi* exemplified in and through ALP. Call it reverse osmosis or complete absorption, meta-*clinamen* or metempsychosis, an(n)astomosis or what you will – that which Joyce achieves through ALP is an appropriation not only of this or that Ovidian textual gesture but of something more fundamental: Ovid's own influence anxiety and characteristic modes of defence.

'Merus Genius to Careous Cassius!' (*FW* 167.23–4)

It is all too easy – especially in this era of digital humanities – for literary scholars to reduce the study of influence to mere source-hunting, to follow, say, a Joycean river to an Ovidian origin, and then by way of explanation to appeal to either the 'intention'[10] or the 'death'[11] of the author, leaving behind, like so much flotsam and jetsam in their wake, such terms as 'allusion' and 'intertext'.[12] However, just as for strong writers influence involves more than the production of echoes, so, too, does its detection by critics demand more than just a bat-like echolocation or a simple tap-tapping into a search engine. And so, though I do eventually attend to matters of 'camparative accoustomology' (*FW* 598.23–4), I first move beyond echoes by stating at the outset what I perceive to be the more essential connection between my two favourite authors. What Ovid and Joyce share is a virtually infinite curiosity, a totalizing impulse, a Casaubonesque absorption of all mythologies, a Luciferian refusal to serve, a comic vision, a linguistic playfulness, a stylistic exuberance, an etymological splendor, a tendency to wander wilfully beyond established limits or else to be carried away by unbridled enthusiasm.[13] If forced to sum up these qualities in a single word, one could do worse than 'ingenuity'. Indeed, what the first-century rhetorician Quintilian said of Ovid – that he was *nimium amator ingenii sui* (too much a lover of his own genius, Quint. *Inst.* 10.1.88) – suits Joyce perhaps even better than it does the Augustan poet.

And yet, as much as Joyce was a lover of his own genius, by the time he began his career as a writer that genius was no longer purely his, no longer *merus*, for it had already been diluted by, or infused with, wit of the finest Ovidian vintage.[14] Throughout his literary life Joyce was enamoured of his Roman precursor. In the diary entry at the end of *A Portrait of the Artist as a Young Man*, Stephen Dedalus, invoking his Ovidian namesake, writes, 'Old father, old artificer, stand me now and ever in good stead' (*P* 253). Just as Stephen is a stand-in for his author, so, too, is the artificer mentioned here a stand-in for his own authorial progenitor, with the result that these words flow also from Joyce to Ovid. That the Irish writer's prayer is answered is a fact to which his later work, the *Wake*, lovingly (albeit with a characteristically defensive evasiveness), attests: 'yet am I *amorist*, I love him, I love his old *portugal's nose*' (*FW* 463.18–19; my emphases throughout this paragraph). These words evoke not only Ovid's amatory elegies (the *Amores* and cognomen (Naso, an oblique form of the Latin noun meaning 'nose'), but also the fact that in Joyce's semi-autobiographical novel the protagonist 'recalled the shrewd northern face of the rector who had taught him to construe the Metamorphoses of Ovid in a courtly English' and 'learnt what little he knew of the laws of Latin verse from a ragged book written by a *Portuguese* priest' (*P* 179). That it was Ovid's ingenuity, in particular, which attracted the Irish writer can be gleaned from reference, in *Ulysses*, to 'fables such as that of the Minotaur which the *genius* of the elegant Latin poet has handed down to us in the pages of his Metamorphoses' (*U* 14.994–6).

The transformative effect of Ovid's epic upon Joyce's later works (especially *Ulysses*) is hardly uncharted territory.[15] This chapter, however, is primarily concerned with the influence of another Ovidian work, the *Fasti*, upon Joyce's final opus, the *Wake*. Although he nowhere names his precursor's calendar poem outright (as he does the *Metamorphoses* in the just-cited passage of *Ulysses*),[16] Joyce was intimately acquainted with this work. In a 1921 interview with the American writer Djuna Barnes, he recounted the fascinating myth, reported in the fifth book of the *Fasti*, according to which Orion derives his name as well as his very being from *urina* (urine).[17] But it was not just Orion, whose constellification was commemorated on the eleventh of May, that Joyce knew about; he was interested in the 'complete anniums of calendarias, gregoromaios and gypsyjuliennes' (*FW* 553.16–17). At least once in the *Wake*, he folk-etymologizes the names of those six months for which Ovid had composed his six books of the *Fasti*: January to June are rendered as 'the doorboy, the cleaner, the sojer, the crook, the squeezer, the lounger' (*FW* 142.09–10).[18] While Joyce does refer to festivals drawn from throughout these months,[19] he seems preoccupied with the month of March, referring on one occasion to the 'calends of Mars' (*FW* 85.27), on another to 'the twentysecond of Mars' (*FW* 134.12). But it is the date of Julius Caesar's assassination, the Ides of March, thinly veiled as 'thides of marse' (*FW* 366.29–30) and 'hydes of march' (*FW* 603.15), upon which the *Wake* fixates. Indeed, the wonderful episode of 'Burrus and Caseous' – butter and cheese on the one hand, Brutus and Cassius on the other – would not exist were it not for the events that transpired in Rome on March 15, 44 BCE.

'by a commodious vicus of recirculation' (*FW* 003.02)[20]

Less well known than Caesar's assassins, however, is another figure associated with the Ides of March: Anna Perenna, whose annual festival marks the beginning of the new and recurring year. In his calendar entry for the fifteenth of March, Ovid devotes a whopping 174 verses to Anna and just fourteen to Caesar. Thus is the former described by William Warde Fowler in the second volume of the eleventh edition of the *Encyclopædia Britannica* (1910–1911), a reference work Joyce is known to have scoured in the seventeen years that he spent composing *Finnegans Wake*:

> ANNA PERENNA, an old Roman deity of the circle or 'ring' of the year, as the name (*per annum*) clearly indicates. Her festival fell on the full moon of the first month (March 15), and was held at the grove of the goddess at the first milestone on the Via Flaminia. It was much frequented by the city *plebs*, and Ovid describes vividly the revelry and licentiousness of the occasion (*Fasti*, iii.523 foll.). From Macrobius we learn (*Sat.* i.12.6) that sacrifice was made to her 'ut annare perannareque [*sic*] commode liceat', *i.e.* that the circle of the year may be completed happily. This is all we know for certain about the goddess and her cult; but the name naturally suggested myth-making, and Anna became a figure in stories which may be read in Ovid (*l.c.*) and in Silius Italicus (8.50 foll.). The coarse myth told by Ovid, in which Anna plays a trick on Mars when in love with Minerva, is probably an old Italian folk-tale, poetically applied to the persons of these deities when they became partially anthropomorphized under Greek influence.
>
> W.W. Fowler, *Encyclopædia Britannica*, 11th edn, s.v. 'Anna Perenna',
> New York: Encyclopædia Britannica, 1911

It is perhaps worth mentioning that the encyclopedia entry immediately before this one is given to Anna Leopoldovna (also known as Anna Karlovna), who appears to lie behind the *Wake*'s 'nana karlikeevna' (*FW* 331.25). In any case, I shall circle back to Anna Perenna's entry at the end of this section. For now, suffice it to say that even in reduced, encyclopedic form this old Roman deity bears a distinct resemblance to Joyce's ALP: both bring things (whether the year or the *Wake*) full circle; both are associated with the moon; both inspire myth-making and gossip; both are pranksters. Nor am I the first to point out this connection: in *The White Goddess*, Robert Graves claims *en passant* that Joyce 'playfully celebrates Anna's universality in his Anna Livia Plurabelle'.[21] While Graves does make several dubious claims in what T.S. Eliot famously dubbed a 'prodigious, monstrous, stupefying, indescribable book',[22] this is not one of them. And while Joyce's ALP has hundreds of sources, Ovid's Anna Perenna is arguably this figure's single most significant *fons et origo*. Nonetheless, for more than three-quarters of a century her presence in the *Wake* appears to have escaped the notice of all but Graves and a few stray voices in the blogosphere. Attending to both large-scale narrative patterns and small-scale allusive details, I seek to uncover this presence. Focusing primarily upon the *Wake*'s ALP chapter, which Joyce had originally intended to publish in a journal called, perhaps not coincidentally, *The Calendar of Modern Letters*,[23] I show how the *Wake*'s riverwoman echoes the *Fasti*'s, and how our attunement to these echoes can serve to deepen our understanding not only of the *Wake* itself but of Joyce's lifelong engagement with his Roman precursor, an engagement too often thought of as diminishing post-*Portrait*.

In the first verse of the *Fasti*'s 188-line entry for March fifteenth, Ovid calls Anna's feast a *festum geniale* (a joyous feast) celebrated by wine-bibbing commoners not far from the banks of the Tiber (Ov. *Fast.* 3.523–6).[24] In these respects, it is akin to the 'grand funferall' (*FW* 013.15) celebrated in the *Wake*, and to the ALP chapter which its author characterized as 'a chattering dialogue across the river by two washerwomen'.[25] These two washerwomen exchange sordid tales about Anna Livia, much as at Anna Perenna's feast *cantent obscena puellae* (girls chant obscenities, Ov. *Fast.* 3.675). In addition to its riparian setting and its gossiping women, the *Wake*'s ALP chapter also shares with the *Fasti*'s account of Anna its totalizing impulse. The former, before weaving into its fabric the names of several hundred rivers,[26] fans out into its famous delta (*FW* 196.01–04): 'O / tell me all about / Anna Livia! I want to hear all / about Anna Livia'. Similarly, the *Fasti*'s narrator declares: *quoniam rumoribus errat, / fabula proposito nulla tegenda meo* (since erroneous rumours abound, no tale is to be covered up by my account, Ov. *Fast.* 3.543–4), and then proceeds to offer six different explanations of who Anna Perenna is. The first explanation given, and by far the longest, is that the Anna worshiped on the Ides of March is the sister of the Carthaginian queen Dido, who died by her own sword after Virgil's Aeneas had abandoned her in pursuit of Lavinian shores. Ovid's account picks up where the *Aeneid* had left off, back in Carthage, where to her dying sister Anna *terque 'vale' dixit* (thrice said 'farewell', Ov. *Fast.* 3.563). This valediction twice finds anagrammatic expression in the *Wake*'s final chapter: first with 'whereinn once we LAVE 'tis ALVE and VALE' (*FW* 600.07), and again with ALP's own 'AVELAVAL. My LEAVes have drifted from me' (*FW* 628.06).

Once Ovid's Anna bids adieux to Dido and to Carthage, she acquires the status of *exul Phoenissa* (Phoenician exile, Ov. *Fast.* 3.595). Ovid and Joyce were themselves exiles, a fact to which their literary output amply attests.[27] Though many scholars have examined the Ovidian artificer behind *A Portrait*'s Stephen Dedalus, relatively few have recognized the profound influence that Ovid's other exiles exert on Joyce's later works. Central to *Ulysses*, for instance, is Pythagoras, who in the final book of the *Metamorphoses* expounds the doctrine of metempsychosis. Like Joyce, Ovid's Pythagoras was an *exul sponte* (a voluntary exile, Ov. *Met.* 15.61–2). In the *Wake*, it is not the *Metamorphoses*' Daedalus or Pythagoras, but the *Fasti*'s Anna Perenna who seems to capture Joyce's exilic imagination. Of course, Anna is not just any exile; she is, more specifically, a Phoenician exile,[28] which perhaps helps to explain why Joyce repeatedly represents ALP – both in the *Wake* itself and throughout his various notebooks and personal letters – with the Greek letter *delta*, derived (as Joyce well knew) from the Phoenician letter meaning 'door' (*dalet*).[29]

After Ovid's Phoenician exile flees her native shores, it is far from smooth sailing. Though kindly received by Aeneas, Anna is, on her first night in Italy, visited in a dream by her deceased sister, who warns her to flee without delay (Ov. *Fast.* 3.639–46). This Anna does, and it is believed, says Ovid, that she is subsequently swept away in the swelling waves of the Numicius; it is because Anna hides in this *amnis perennis* (perennial stream) that she comes to be called Anna Perenna (Ov. *Fast.* 3.647–52). What does Joyce make of this Ovidian material? While it is true that he attaches to his Anna neither the Latin epithet *perennis* nor the English adjective thence derived, he does provide her with an equivalent descriptor (*FW* 104.01): 'Annah ... the Everliving'. A little later, we find the phrase **Amnis Limina Permanent** (the thresholds of the river remain, *FW* 153.02). Figuratively, too, Anna Perenna remains in this acrostic (itself but one of many such acrostics in the *Wake*): hiding, again anagrammatically, in *PERmANENt* is 'Perenna'. Names aside, just as Ovid's Anna Perenna disappears into the waters of the Numicius River, so does Joyce's ALP appear to disappear into the river Liffey at the very end of the *Wake* (*FW* 627.35–628.01): 'I'll slip away before they're up. They'll never see ... I go back to you, my cold father'.

Thus far, we have seen how the Roman poet's first version of Anna Perenna – an exile, a Phoenician, and a river-nymph – corresponds to the Irish expatriate's ALP, the river-woman whose presence permeates the *Wake*. But Ovid presents five further versions of Anna as well. 'There are some people', he reports, 'for whom she is the moon, since the moon fills up the year with her months' (Ov. *Fast.* 3.657). It is in one of Joyce's working notebooks (VI.B.18.258), rather than in the *Wake* itself, that we find the most tantalizing evidence for his acquaintance with Anna's lunar aspect. On a single page appear not only the crossed-out names of the 'month-men' who do end up in the *Wake* ('the doorboy, the cleaner, the sojer', and those others mentioned earlier), but also two uncrossed-out items which do not: 'mensural', probably referring to both month (*mensis*) and measurement (*mensura*); and 'calendar lunatic'. R.J. Schork suspects that Joyce is offering 'a personal comment not only on a calendar in which the months are calculated according to the phases of the moon (*luna*) but also on the ridiculously complicated computations involved in reconciling ancient solar and lunar calendars'.[30] This may be the case. I, however, suspect that Joyce is here coming to terms with Anna Perenna's lunar aspect in Ovid's calendar poem, especially since it is from this very source that he appears to have derived the names of his month-men.

According to the *Fasti*, Anna Perenna, if she is not Dido's sister or the moon, could also be one of the following: Themis, the titaness representing divine justice; Io, who was ravished by Jupiter; or a nymph who gave Jupiter his first food (Ov. *Fast.* 3.658–60). Ovid disposes of these three versions of Anna in a mere three verses, and while Themis and Io do make appearances in the *Wake*, nowhere do they appear to be meaningfully associated with ALP.[31] The same cannot be said of the sixth and final version of Anna presented in the *Fasti*. There was, says Ovid, a certain Anna born in suburban Bovillae, a poor but industrious old woman (Ov. *Fast.* 3.661–74). In the early days of the Roman Republic, before the plebeians were represented by their own tribunes, this Anna used to make cakes and distribute them to fellow commoners. In return for her generosity she was worshiped in life and deified in death. It is what Anna does after her deification that leads to her being commemorated with obscene songs on the Ides of March. At the bidding of Mars, in whose month she is celebrated, Anna becomes, like ALP, a proxenete, a marriage-broker. When asked to unite Mars and Minerva (war-god and war-goddess), Anna promises to do so. But when the day of the wedding arrives, Anna does not actually summon the desired deity; instead, she veils her own face (*tegens voltus suos*, Ov. *Fast.* 3.690) and steps toward the expectant groom, who, just as he is about to kiss the bride, recognizes her and waxes wroth. Anna simply laughs (*ridet*, Ov. *Fast.* 3.693).

Echoes of this final Ovidian version of Anna can be heard throughout the *Wake*'s ALP chapter, in which Joyce's Anna is not only a 'proxenete' (*FW* 198.17), but also a 'prankquean' (*FW* 21.15). As one washerwoman tells the other (*FW* 206.06–08): 'So she said to herself she'd frame a plan to fake a shine, the mischiefmaker, the like of it you niever heard'. As was the case with Anna Perenna's, ALP's ruse results in laughter (*FW* 207.14–16): 'O gig goggle of gigguels. I can't tell you how! It's too screaming to rizo, rabbit it all! Minneha, minnehi minaehe, minneho!' In his commentary on these lines, Roland McHugh notes an allusion to Hiawatha's girl Minnehaha, whose name is commonly taken to mean 'laughing water'. He also detects the Danish word *minne* (love) and the German word *Ehe* (marriage).[32] But might not all the 'min-' variations sounded here remind us also of *Mi*n*e*rva, Anna's impersonation of whom precipitated the laughter (*ridet*) described in the *Fasti*, as well as, perhaps, the 'rizo' and the giggles found here? Although the decked-out ALP is generally compared (and rightly so) to Hera and Pandora in all their finery, the 'fishnetzeveil' that she dons 'for the sun not to spoil the wrinklings of her hydeaspects' (*FW* 208.10–11) may also recall Anna Perenna's veiled visage in the *Fasti*.

After Ovid has presented his sixth and final version of Anna Perenna, he coyly adds, 'I was about to skip over the swords that pierced the *princeps*' (Ov. *Fast.* 3.697). For the March fifteenth entry of his calendar poem this would have constituted a grave omission indeed! Whereas Ovid here avoids referring to Caesar by name, Joyce inches somewhat closer to doing so. Once the Irish writer's washerwomen have gotten out their giggles, one begs the other, 'Ogowe presta! Leste, before *Julia sees her*!' (*FW* 207.24, my emphasis). Just as in these words lurks 'Julius Caesar', so, too, behind the ALP chapter as a whole lurks the Ovidian narrative, which culminates, however begrudgingly, with a reference to the Roman leader.

To conclude this exercise in source-hunting, let us return briefly to the encyclopedia entry with which I began this section. There, William Warde Fowler cites Macrobius's claim that Anna is celebrated in order 'that the circle of the year may be completed happily [*commode*]'. In 1936, Joyce added to the opening lines of his work in progress the phrase 'by a commodious vicus of recirculation' (*FW* 03.02). As nearly every commentary on the *Wake* indicates, 'vicus' refers to Giambattista Vico, whose theory of history's cyclical nature (*corsi e ricorsi*) fascinated Joyce and imparted to the *Wake* its four-book structure. Glosses for 'commodious', on the other hand, tend to be far less illuminating, referring as often as not to what H.G. Wells called Joyce's 'cloacal obsession'.[33] Though I would not rule out a pun here on 'commode', I suggest that this adjective owes its presence first and foremost to Joyce's intimate acquaintance with Anna Perenna, and that the river running through the *Wake* – indeed, through Joyce's entire corpus – is ingeniously Ovidian.

'from swerve of shore to bend of bay' (*FW* 03.01–02)

I previously referred to Anna as a 'palindromic personage' and as 'influence personified'. I maintain that she is both, and here add that influence is itself palindromic, figuratively and in the etymological sense of the word (< Greek *palin* 'again, back' + *dromos* 'a running'). It is not simply a force exerted by an earlier text and passively received by a later one, but a 'two-way process'[34] through which a later text can redound as a flood on the precursor from which it sprung.[35] In the *Wake*, Anna *qua* influence runs both ways, coursing forward from the *Fasti* and 'ricocoursing' (*FW* 609.14) back to the *Aeneid*. If one were keen on viewing this influence in a linear fashion, one could say that Virgil's Anna gives rise to Ovid's Anna Perenna, who gives rise, in turn, to Joyce's Anna Livia Plurabelle. But to regard the later Annas as mere accretions (or, for that matter, the earlier Annas as mere alluvia) would be to insult the creative processes of their authors; more gravely still, it would be to confuse that which belongs to discursiveness and history and reality (words, images, other such *quidditas*) with that which belongs to literature and artistry and the imagination (a voice, a vision, a distinctive relation to *quidditas* which we may call *quomoditas*).

In the foregoing discussion I have been concerned largely with *quidditas*, with discrete particles of verbal matter (sounds and letters) that bond the *Fasti* to the *Wake*. But what truly sets ALP apart from other specters of literary influence is not so much the resemblance that she bears to Anna Perenna as the very manner in which she inundates Joyce's prose epic, a manner uncannily similar to that in which her Virgilian analogue floods Ovid's calendar poem. Expressed somewhat differently, the *clinamen* which the *Wake*, via ALP, executes in relation to the third book of the *Fasti* mimics the *clinamen* which the *Fasti*, via Anna Perenna, executes in relation to the *Aeneid*. To appreciate more fully the former swerve we must also attempt to understand the latter.

Ovid's defence against Virgil is, at its core, a destabilization, a deviation, an ambiguating undulation.[36] The wielder of the stateliest measure offers readers what purports to be a definitive account of Rome's foundation. Ovid then challenges this account by re-entering the world of the *Aeneid*, reanimating one of its characters, and giving us six Annas where formerly there was one, thereby transforming his precursor's would-be 'the' into just another 'a'. This is a strategy which he deploys again and again throughout his oeuvre, and it is a strategy which Joseph Solodow, the scholar who first welcomed me into the Ovidian fold, skilfully analyses and elegantly describes. After comparing the storm described in the first book of the *Aeneid* to the flood described in the first book of the *Metamorphoses*, Solodow concludes:

> The world of the *Metamorphoses* marks its difference from that of the *Aeneid* so sharply that it amounts to a criticism of it. Many features of Ovid's narrative seem to call into question the premises of Virgil's. The connected imagery of the horses which patterns the story of Aeneas implies that history has a wholeness

and a unity. The political imagery imposes a political meaning on events. But through the way he constructs his own narrative, Ovid in effect raises objections. Are human events connected to form significant units? Is their significance chiefly political? Do not such views disregard the individual person and the uniqueness of events, in which lies perhaps the possibility of manifold meanings? ... The unswerving tone of the *Aeneid* is spotlighted by the ever-varying tone in the *Metamorphoses*. This too carries an implicit criticism. It is human after all to have conflicting views of something or to change one's views from one time to another. To assume a single view implies an impossible fixity in both the observed and the observer. We may admire such firmness but we are also right, with Ovid, to be suspicious of it. He liberates us from the tyranny of an 'authoritative' viewpoint.

J.B. Solodow, *The World of Ovid's Metamorphoses,* Chapel Hill: University of North Carolina Press, 1988, 126[37]

Polysemy and polyphony – these are the destabilizing mechanisms that Ovid employs to defend himself against his prime precursor. They are also the strategies employed against him by Joyce.

What, then, distinguishes the defensive stance of the Irish writer from that of his Roman predecessor? Their swerves differ, I suggest, in degree rather than in kind, in depth rather than in direction. Let two examples suffice. First, consider the similar manner in which Ovid and Joyce develop Anna's fluminal associations. In the fourth book of the *Aeneid*, Dido's sister is connected to *lympha* (water) on two separate occasions: first when the Carthaginian regent tells Anna to sprinkle herself with river water (*fluviali spargere lympha*, Virg. A. 4.635), and again when Anna tries to wash her moribund sister's wounds (*date, vulnera lymphis / abluam*, Virg. A. 4.683–4). I suggest that Ovid playfully elaborates upon the connection latent in Virgil's text. Via the later writer's adoption of a popular etymology,[38] the lymph-bearing Anna of the *Aeneid* becomes the *nympha Numici* of the *Fasti* (Ov. *Fast.* 3.653).[39] The *Wake*, too, contains several *lymph-* and *nymph*-onyms,[40] but the verbal particulars are not germane to my larger point about influence, which is that both Ovid and Joyce cause that which flows in their precursors' works to overflow in their own.[41] Thus, the devious *nympha Numici* of the *Fasti*, though extravagant in relation to her Virgilian analogue, looks positively tame beside the riverrun of the *Wake*.

A second example of such effluence can be seen in ALP's anagrammatic valedictions, which, it turns out, flowed in Virgil before they overflowed in either Ovid or Joyce. Thus are the expiring Dido's final actions described: *ter sese attollens cubitoque adnixa levavit, / ter revoluta toro est*, (thrice leaning on her elbow she struggled to lift herself, thrice she rolled back upon the bier, Virg. *A.* 4.690–1). Ovid appropriates these anaphoric verses, compressing them into a single (overflowing) line: *terque 'vale' dixit, cineres ter ad ora relatos / pressit,* (thrice she said 'farewell', thrice she carried back the ashes and pressed them to her mouth, Ov. *Fast.* 3.563–4). Virgil's *ter . . . aDnIXa LEVAvIT* corresponds to Ovid's *terque 'VALE' DIXIT,* as does the former's *ter REvoLuTA tORO eSt* to the latter's *ter ad ORA RELATOS*. Such anagrammatical wordplay is a hallmark of Ovid's linguistic playfulness and ingenuity. And yet, even it pales in comparison to the *Wake*'s verbal high jinks, which feature anagrams and portmanteaux, 'punns and reedles' (*FW* 239.35–6) on every page.

As the comparisons above only begin to adumbrate, Joyce takes to a new extreme the 'manifold meanings' and 'ever-varying tone' which Solodow rightly identifies as hallmarks of his Ovidian precursor. The later writer's effluence is even reflected in the quasi-cognomen that he gives to his Anna: *Plu*rabelle, among whose roots is to be counted a form of the Latin word *plus* (more). ALP is a more concentrated form of Anna Perenna. Similarly, the fundamental qualities of the *Wake* in many ways represent an intensification of those already found in the *Fasti*. The former work is more totalizing: with the Roman's *fabula proposito nulla tegenda meo* (Ov. *Fast.* 3.544), compare Joyce's mountainous Everyman HCE and riverine Everywoman ALP, each of whom contains multitudes. It is more comic: while the *Fasti* is at times quite humorous (as when Anna Perenna throws herself out a window, Ov. *Fast.* 3.643–4), the *Wake* 'can make us laugh aloud on nearly every page'.[42] It is more carried away: whereas in the *Fasti* Ovid observes at least some limits (as when he gives to Caesar what is Caesar's, Ov. *Fast.* 3.697–710), in the *Wake* Joyce continually refuses to curb his enthusiasm. All this may sound like a negative judgment of Ovid, but it is not. Untrammeled in a way that his precursor was not, Joyce could slake his thirst in the boundless ocean of the *Encyclopædia Britannica*; could access, if not the key to all mythologies, then at least books about many of them; could declare *non serviam* without fear of relegation; could draw on the resources of more than sixty languages; could, in short, dismiss his mind into arts unknown to Ovid.

The mode of defence that I have been at pains to describe could be called by a variety of names. At the outset of this chapter, I proposed a few possibilities. Reverse osmosis, 'the process by which water or other liquid tends to flow across a membrane from a region of high solute concentration to one of lower concentration (the opposite direction to natural osmosis) when subjected to a hydrostatic pressure greater than the osmotic pressure' (*OED* s.v.), is not a standard trope for literary influence, but rather a water purification technology. As I have attempted to demonstrate, the *Wake* is, among other things, a highly concentrated Ovidian solution. Lest he drown in his precursor's wake, Joyce applies the hydrostatic pressure of ALP to overcome the osmotic pressure exerted by Anna Perenna. The solvent with which we are left is Joyce's own genius, ostensibly purged of Ovidian influence. Of course, the very process responsible for isolating this genius can itself occur only after what I previously referred to as complete absorption. Before the Irish writer redounds as a flood on his Roman precursor, he is first inundated – inundated, but not sunk beneath the watery floor, for Joyce absorbs the energy of the Ovidian waves that strike him. In time, he also absorbs the forces (largely Virgilian) that transfer to these waves their own energy and individuating rhythms. It is for this reason that I have proposed the term meta-*clinamen* to describe Joyce's mode of defence, which absorbs and magnifies that of his precursor, much as one wave is impelled and enlarged by the wave that precedes it. So thorough, indeed, is Joyce's absorption of his forerunner that metempsychosis may, in the end, seem to be the best model for explaining the Irishman's kinship with Ovid.

There is, however, a fifth term, which I introduced earlier to describe this kinship: an(n)astomosis. Thus is this word – which occurs in the *Wake* as 'annastomoses' (*FW* 585.22–3) and 'anastomosically' (*FW* 615.05) – described in the eleventh edition of the *Encyclopædia Britannica*, just a few pages before the 'Anna Perenna' entry that we have already seen:

> ANASTOMOSIS (a Greek word in which the second *o* is long, from *anastomoun*, to furnish with a mouth or outlet), the intercommunication between two vessels; a word used in vegetable and animal anatomy for the communication between channels (arteries and veins) containing fluid, and also for the crossing between the veins or branches of leaves, trees, insect-wings or river-connexions, and by analogy in art-design.
>
> H. Chisholm, *Encyclopædia Britannica*, 11th edn, s.v. 'Anastomosis', New York: Encyclopædia Britannica, 1911

There are at least three reasons for preferring the term 'anastomosis' to the other four that I have proposed: first and foremost, it seems to have been the *Wake*'s own way of inserting itself into the literary tradition (much as 'metempsychosis' was *Ulysses*' way of doing the same);[43] secondly, it stresses the bidirectionality of the influence process, without privileging one direction over another; and finally, it already applies to literal river connections, whence it is not a large leap to literary ones.

The 'the' that (b)ends *Finnegans Wake* comes, crucially, from Anna's *stoma* (mouth). This definite article's connection to the work's opening 'riverrun' is thus one sort of an(n)astomosis. The word 'riverrun' is another, for it connects Annas (Anna Perenna and ALP), annals (the *Fasti* and the *Wake*), and annalists (Ovid and Joyce). Although this chapter has focused, in its own meandering way, on channelling Ovid's Anna Perenna in *Finnegans Wake*, I would like now, in closing, to open the floodgates even further by proposing that the influential figure that we have seen running 'anastomosically' between Ovid's calendar poem and Joyce's dream-drama begins her literary life, not in Virgil's epic but in what is perhaps the most fitting place imaginable: in Ilia's dream in Ennius's *Annales* (34–50 Skutsch). Nita Krevans has already analysed the connections between this dream and Dido's nightmares in the fourth book of the *Aeneid*.[44] No one, however, appears to have made explicit how Dido, while recounting her nightmares to Anna ('*Anna soror*', Virg. *A.* 4.9), quite literally echoes the words with which Ilia recounts her dream to her unnamed sister ('***germana soror***', Enn. *Ann.* 40).[45] Swerving from Ennius's *germana* to Virgil's Anna, from Ovid's Anna Perenna to Joyce's Anna Livia Plurabelle, Anna qua influence is a 'Bringer of Plurabilities' (*FW* 104.02). She defies definition as steadfastly as the *Wake* itself denies an ending, overflowing not from the 'the', but from '-*ana*'.

Notes

Introduction: Anna and the *Plebs*: A Synthesis of Primary Evidence

1. Erasmus, *De ratione studii ac legendi interpretandique auctores*, Paris 1511, in *Desiderii Erasmi Roterodami Opera omnia*, ed. J.H. Waszink, (Amsterdam 1971), vol. I 2, 79–151: *in primis ad fontes ipsos properandum*.
2. *AE* 2003, 251.7–8.
3. *ILLRP* 9 = *Inscriptiones Italiae* 13.2, 1–28. The *terminus post quem* is the last date on the consular list that accompanied the calendar; the *terminus ante quem* is Caesar's calendar reform.
4. Gaia was evidently Gaia Taracia or Fufetia, reported in *annales antiqui* as a Vestal Virgin who was honoured by the Roman People for bequeathing the Campus Martius to them in her will: see Plin. *Nat.* 34.25; Gel. 7.7.1 (at Plu. *Publ.* 8.4 she is named Tarquinia). Not to be confused with Gaia Caecilia, who was identified with queen Tanaquil (Plin. *Nat.* 8.194; Fest. 85L; cf. Plu. *Quaest. Rom.* 30).
5. Cited from Σκιαμαχία περὶ τύφου by Gel. 13.23.4, who was interested in the vocative *Nerienes* (instead of *Nerio*). Cicero makes Varro describe his Menippean satires as an early work (Cic. *Ac.* 1.8: *in illis veteribus nostris*).
6. On March as the original first month of the Roman year. Some MSS read *perennareque*, but I think *perannareque* is preferable as the *lectio difficilior*.
7. (August. *C.D.* 4.22.1); translation by P.G. Walsh.
8. August. *C.D.* 6.3.4 = Var. *Antiquitates divinae* fr. 4 Cardauns (cf. frr. 87–203 Cardauns for the surviving items of his list).
9. August. *C.D.* 7.2.3, 7.3.1 = Var. *Antiquitates divinae* fr. 95 Cardauns.
10. See for instance August. *C.D.* 3.4.1 (*vir doctissimus*), 3.17.22 (*magna peritia Varronis*), 4.1.3 (*vir doctissimus et grauissimae auctoritatis*), 4.31.3 (*auctor acutissimus et doctissimus*), 6.2–9 *passim* for use of the *Divine Antiquities*, 7.9.5 and 7.34.2 for use of *De cultu deorum*, 18.2–23 *passim* for use of *De gente populi Romani*.
11. August. *C.D.* 4.11.3 (*in illa turba quasi plebeiorum deorum*), 6.1.7 (*ex illa turba vel quasi plebeiorum vel quasi procerum deorum*), 7.2.1 (*illam quasi plebeiam numinum multitudinem minutis opusculis deputatam*); cf. 7.3.1 on Vitumnus and Sentinus, each described as *obscurus et ignobilis*. For the *di praecipui atque selecti* see Varro, *Antiquitates diuinae* frr. 4, 229 Cardauns (August. *C.D.* 6.3.4, 7.2.1).
12. Var. *Antiquities divinae* fr. 2b, Cardauns (August. *C.D.* 7.3.8).

13 Lactant, *Inst.* 1.6.7; August. *C.D.* 7.35.2.

14 Censorinus, *DN* 3.2 (on Genius and Lar); Arn. 3.8 (on the *di nouensiles*); cf. Macr. 1.18.4 (on Apollo and Liber).

15 Prisc., *Inst.* 6.73 (*G.L.* 2.257 Keil); Macr. 1.9.11, 1.17.62; cf. [Caes.] *B. Alex.* 42–3 (Q. Cornificius, Caesar's *quaestor pro praetore* in Illyricum); Cic. *Fam.* 12.17.3 (Q. Cornificius's *summum ingenium* and *studia optima*).

16 Cic. *Corn. I* fr. 48 Crawford = Asconius 76C (*propter nimiam dominationem potentium*); Sal. *Hist.* 1.11M (*iniuriae validiorum*); cf. Liv. 2.23.1–8 for an example.

17 Cic. *Rep.* 1.31 (*mors Tiberii Gracchi et iam ante tota illius ratio tribunatus divisit populum in duas partes*).

18 Vell. 2.3.2–3 (*hoc initium in urbe Roma civilis sanguinis gladiorumque impunitatis fuit*); App. *BC.* 1.1.1, 1.2.4–5; cf. D.H. 2.11.2–3, who dates the turning point a decade later.

19 Cic. *S. Rosc.* 135, 138 (*causa nobilitatis*), cf. 142 (*victoria nobilium).*

20 Cic. *Sest.* 96 (*qui ea quae faciebant quaeque dicebant multitudini iucunda volebant esse*).

21 Those opposing terms appear in various combinations at Sal. *Cat.* 39.1; *Jug.* 5.1, 27.1, 30.3, 31.2, 31.20, 40.3–5, 41.5–7, 42.1; *Hist.* 3.48.28M. For the oligarchy (*pauci potentes, paucorum potentia*), see *Cat.* 20.7, 58.11; *Jug.* 3.4, 31.19; *Hist.* 1.12M, 3.48.6M; also Caes. *Civ.* 1.22.5 (*populum Romanum factione paucorum oppressum*); Hirt. *Gal.* 8.50.2 (*contra factionem et potentiam paucorum*).

22 Sal. *Jug.* 31.6, 17 (Memmius); *Hist.* 1.55.23M (Lepidus), 3.48.1, 15M (Macer); *Cat.* 33.3 (Manlius). For a discussion of Anna of Bovillae's connection to the secession of the plebs, see Newlands (Chapter 8) in this volume.

23 Suet. *Jul.* 5, cf. 11 on Caesar in the mid–60s (*conciliato populi favore . . . adversante optimatium factione*).

24 Cic. *Catil.* 4.9 (*is in re publica viam quae popularis habetur secutus est*); D.C. 37.37.2 on the election (ἐν τῷ πλήθει τὴν ἐλπίδα αὑτῆς . . . λάβων).

25 Translation by B. Perrin.

26 Translation by T.J. Luce.

27 Cic. *Agr.* 2.18; *Amic.* 96.

28 Vell. 2.12.3; Suet. *Nero* 2.1 (*lex Domitia*); D.C. 37.37.1 (Sulla).

29 Asconius 79C; Plu. *Caes.* 7.1. Close ally: Plu. *Sull.* 6.5 (Pius and Sulla consuls together, 80 BCE). Loyal son of Q. Metellus Numidicus: D.S. 36.16; V. Max. 5.2.7. Arrogant optimate: Sal. *Jug.* 64.1 (*inerat contemptor animus et superbia, commune nobilitatis malum*); Cic. *Sest.* 37; V. Max. 4.1.13 (opposition of *populares*).

30 Suet. *Jul.* 46; cf. Mart. 12.18.2 (*clamosa Subura*); Juv. 11.51 (*ferventi Subura*).

31 cf. 37.38.1 on the goodwill of οἱ πολλοί towards Caesar.

32 Cic. *Fam.* 7.11.2 (53 BCE); Macr. 2.6.6 (Clodius's aedileship in 56); Laberius died in 43 (Jerome, *Chronica* on Olympiad 184.2). For further discussion on Anna as a god for the plebs, see Ramsby (Chapter 7) and Newlands (Chapter 8) in this volume.

33 So spelt in the sources: Gel. 16.7.10; Non. 129L (Laberius frr. 2–3 Panayotakis).
34 The *fasti Verulani* (*Inscriptiones Italiae* 13.2, 166–7) mark the Ides of March as *feriae Iovi*.
35 Themis was the mother of Evander in the Greek tradition (D.H. 1.31.1–3, 1.32.3).
36 Ov. *Fast.* 1.56; Macr. 1.15.15 (sacred to Jupiter); Paus. 8.4.2–3 (Azan), 8.38.2 (infancy of Zeus).
37 Serv. *A.* on Virg. *A.* 4.9 (*cuius filiae fuerint Anna et Dido, Naevius dicit*); cf. *A.* 1.621 for Belus (Phoenician Baal) as Dido's father, but elsewhere (on *A.* 1.343) Servius names him as Mettes.
38 For a discussion of this alternate tradition where Anna is Aeneas's love interest, see McCallum (Chapter 1) in this volume.
39 Var. *Antiquitates humanae* frr. 2.6–18 Mirsch, esp. fr. 12 (Serv. Dan. *ad* Virg. *A.* 3.349); cf. Var. *R.* 2.pref.6 for his command ('from Delos to Sicily').
40 For Virgil's use of Naevius, see Macr. 6.2.31; Serv. Dan. *ad* Virg. *A.* 1.198.
41 See n. 22 above.
42 *Origo gentis Romanae* 17.6; cf. 9.6, 10.4, 11.3, 15.4–5, 16.4, 17.3, 18.5, 20.3 for L. Caesar's *Pontificalia* as one of the anonymous author's sources, and Liv. 1.30.2 for the Julii as one of the *gentes* that came to Rome from Alba.
43 Tac. *Ann.* 2.41.1, 15.23.2; *CIL* 14.2387 = 1^2.1439 = *ILLRP* 270.
44 Cf. Cic. *Fam.* 7.11.2 for the sort of scenario Laberius liked. See Newlands (Chapter 8) in this volume.
45 Linked to the first by *nuper erat dea facta* at Ov. *Fast.* 3.677.
46 (August. *C.D.* 4.5.1, 4.5.7, 4.5.2): translation by P.G. Walsh.
47 August. *C.D.* 4.31.1, 6.5.5–6.7.5 *passim*, esp. 6.6.3 (*di poetici theatrici ludicri scaenici*), 6.7.1 (*theologia fabulosa theatrica scaenica*).
48 Var. *Antiquitates divinae* fr. 7 Cardauns = August. *C.D.* 6.5.2 (*ut di furati sint, ut adulterarint, ut servierint homini*).
49 cf. Lucr 4.978–83 for music and dancers on stage at the *ludi scaenici*.
50 Poll. 4.141 (τὰ δ' ἔκσκευα πρόσωπα Ἀκταίων ἐστὶ κερασφόρος ...).
51 Rhinthon *PCG* T 1–2 = *Suda* R 171, 4.295 Adler (Ταραντῖνος κωμικός, ἀρχηγὸς τῆς καλουμένης ἱλαροτραγῳδίας, ὃ ἐστὶ φλυακογραφία); St.Byz. 603.1 (Ταραντῖνος φλύαξ, τὰ τραγικὰ μεταρρυθμίζων ἐς τὸ γελοῖον). It was also called 'Italian comedy' (Ath. 9.402b).
52 Rhinthon *PCG* T 5: = Bas. in *Grammatici Latini* 6.312 Keil, Euanthius, *De fabula* 4.1; Don. *De comoedia* 6.1; Don. on Ter. *Ad.* 7; Lyd. *Mag.* 1.40.
53 Cic. *Q. Rosc.* 23; cf. Gel. 1.3.3 for Dionysia as a *notissima saltatricula*.
54 Sen. *Con.* 3.pref.10, 16; Macr. 2.7.12–19; Jer. *Chron.* Ol. 189.3 (22–21 BCE); Luc. *Salt.* 34 (Augustus's time); D.C. 54.17.4–5 (18 BCE).
55 Ath. 1.20e (ἡ δὲ Βαθύλλειος ἱλαρωτέρα); Plu. *Mor.* 711f; cf. Pers. 5.123 (*ad numeros satyrum moveare Bathylli*).

56 August. *C.D.* 6.6.5 (*maiestati indigna divinae*); cf. 4.27.1 (*multa de diis fingantur indigna*), 6.1.1 (*falsa atque indigna*), 6.7.1 (*indignitatis et turpitudinis plena*), 6.8.4 (*de diis indigna*).

57 Prop. 4.9.32 (*et iacit ante fores verba minora deo*); Ov. *Fast.* 2.586 (*multa tulit tanto non patienda deo*).

58 Ov. *Fast.* 4.326 (*mira, sed et scaena testificata loquar*), on the arrival of Magna Mater.

59 August. *C.D.* 4.26.1–3, 4.27.5; presumably from Varro, who is cited at 4.31.1.

60 V. Max. 2.10.8; Sen. *Ep.* 97.8. Cato and Caesar: Caes. *Civ* 1.3.4 (*veteres inimicitiae*); for details cf. Plu. *Cat. Mi.* 23.1–2, 24.1–2, 31.3, 32.1–2, 33.1–3, 43.5, 49.1, 51.1–52.4, 58.6, 64.5, 72.2.

61 V. Max. 2.10.8 (*priscum morem iocorum*); Sen. *Ep.* 97.8 (*Florales iocos*); Mart. 1.pref. (*iocosae . . . sacrum Florae*); Ov. *Fast.* 4.946 (*scaena ioci morem liberioris habet*), 5.183 (*mater ades florum, ludis celebranda iocosis*), 5.331–2 (*quare lascivia maior | his foret in ludis liberiorque iocus*). Showgirls: *Fast.* 5.349 (*turba meretricia*), 352 (*plebeio choro*).

62 Ov. *Fast.* 1.396 (*di quicumque iocis non alienus erat*), 2.304 (*traditur antiqui fabula plena ioci*), 6.320 (*est multi fabula parva ioci*); 3.735 on Silenus's discovery of honey (*non habet ingratos fabula nostra iocos*).

63 Ov. *Fast.* 1.393–0 (a Greek festival of Bacchus), 2.269–82 (Faunus as Pan), 6.321–324 (Cybele's festival on Mount Ida).

64 Ov. *Fast.* 6.692 (*et canere ad veteres verba iocosa modos*), cf. 704–8 on Marsyas. Pipers played at the *ludi scaenici*: *Fasti* 6.659 (*cantabat tibia ludis*), 667 (*quaeritur in scaena cava tibia*).

65 Ov. *Fast.* 3.675–6 (*puellae*), 695 (*inde ioci veteres obscaenaque dicta canuntur*), cf. 653 and 659 on Anna as a *nympha*. For a discussion of Anna's link with nymphs, see G. McIntyre (Chapter 3) and Wright (Chapter 4) in this volume.

66 Ov. *Fast.* 5.18–20 (*par erat omnis honor | . . . ausus de media plebe sedere deus*); cf. *Met.* 1.595 (Apollo to Daphne, 'nec de plebe deo'). Polyhymnia and *pantomimus*: *Anthologia Palatina* 9.505.17–18 (cf. 504.7); Nonn. *D.* 5.104–7.

67 Cf. also Mart. 8.49.3–4 (*qua bonus accubuit genitor cum plebe deorum | et licuit Faunis poscere vina Iouem*).

68 Ov. *Met.* 1.172 (*atria nobilium*), 176 (*magni Palatia caeli*); cf. 1.200–5 for the explicit parallel with the Augustan Senate.

69 Ov. *Met.* 1.173 (*plebs habitat diversa locis*).

70 Ov. *Fast.* 5.197–212 (Flora); Virg. *A.* 12.139–42 (Juturna); cf. also Ov. *Met.* 14.623–41 (Pomona as a nymph pursued by satyrs, Pans, Silenus and Priapus); Var. *L.* 7.45 = Enn. *Ann.* 118 Skutsch (*flamen Pomonalis*, implying divine status).

71 Ov. *Fast.* 3.673 (*signum posuere Perennae*), cf. 677 (*nuper erat dea facta*).

72 Ov. *Fast.* 3.663 (*nullis etiam nunc tuta tribunis*).

73 Caes. *Civ.* 1.2.7–8, 1.5.1–5, 1.7.2–8.1; D.C. 41.1–3. Cf. Cic. *Att.* 11.7.1: Caesar regarded as invalid all senatorial resolutions made after the expulsion of the tribunes.
74 As admitted even by the optimate Cicero: *Att.* 7.3.5, 7.7.6, 8.3.4, 10.4.8 (December 50 – April 49 BCE); cf. App. *BC* 1.4.16 on Caesar as δημοτικώτατος.
75 *RRC* 480.19; *Inscriptiones Italiae* 13.1, 182–3 (*fasti Ostienses* on 44 BCE: *Caesar pare[ns patriae occisus]*). Or *pater patriae*: *ILLRP* 407–8; App. *BC* 2.106.442, 2.144.602; D.C. 44.4.4.
76 App. *BC* 1.4.17, 2.147.613–14, 3.60.247.
77 Aug. *RG.* 1.4, 2; cf. App. *BC* 3.95.392 (assassins condemned by due legal process), 4.7.27 (triumvirate set up by a tribunician law), 4.8.31 (triumvirs elected ἁρμόσαι καὶ διορθῶσαι τὰ κοινά).
78 D.C. 47.18.3–4, cf. 51.22.2 for its dedication in 29 BCE.
79 D.C. 47.18.5–6; *Inscriptiones Italiae* 3.2, 188–9 and 208 (*fasti Amiternini* and *fasti Antiates ministrorum*, 12 July).
80 Translation by J.C. Rolfe; also D.C. 47.19.1.
81 Cic. *Att.* 12.3.1; *Phil.* 2.31; V. Max. 1.5.7, 1.8.8, 3.1.3, 6.4.5, 6.8.4; Tac. *Ann.* 4.34.3; Flor. 2.17.1.
82 *Inscriptiones Italiae* 13.2, 172–3, 255 (*fasti Vaticani* and *fasti Farnesiani*).
83 Ov. *Fast.* 6.697 (*praeteriturus eram gladios in principe fixos*), 698–702 (Vesta), 703–4 (divinity), 705–10 (piety and vengeance).
84 Aug. *RG* 10.1 (granted 'by law'); Tac. *Ann.* 1.2.1 (*ad tuendam plebem*).
85 Ov. *Fast.* 3.524 (*non procul a ripis, advena Thybri, tuis*); *Inscriptiones Italiae* 13.2, 172–3 (*fasti Vaticani*). It makes no significant difference whether the road was measured from the 'golden milestone' in the Forum (Plu. *Galb.* 24.4) or from the nearby Porta Fontinalis below the north-eastern slope of the Capitol (cf. Fest. 97L for a gate as the start of a road).
86 *AE* 2003, 251–3. For further discussion of the inscriptions from Anna's grove, see Blennow (Chapter 6) in this volume.
87 Translation by D.R. Shackleton Bailey; *longo Ianiculi iugo* is at line 3.
88 (August. *C.D.* 4.11.4, 6.9.7); cf. also *C.D.* 7.24.7; Lactant. *Inst.* 1.20.36. For *virgineus cruor* in a bridal context, cf. Claudian, *Nupt. Hon. et Mar.* 4.27; Aus. *Cent. Nupt.* 118.
89 Fest. 142L (*sacellum . . . de quo aris sublatis balnearia sunt facta domus*).
90 Translation by D.R. Shackleton Bailey; the word he elaborately avoids using is *mentula*.
91 Ov. *Fast.* 6.223–4: *post sacras monstratur Iunius Idus | utilis et nuptis, utilis esse viris.*
92 *Inscriptiones Italiae* 13.2, 248–9 (*fasti Furii Filacali*).
93 Petron. 133.3 (*nympharum Bacchique comes . . . Dryadumque voluptas*); *Priapeia* 33 (*Naiadas antiqui Dryadasque habuere Priapi . . .*).

94 *Musa Lapidaria* 155.13–22 Courtney; inscribed on a phallic herm dedicated to the *Genius numinis Priapi* by an imperial freedman whose name, Julius Agathemerus, gives the approximate date.
95 See J. McIntyre (Chapter 2) in this volume.
96 Excursus: Sil. 8.44–199. Details: 8.190-1 (*Numicius illam | suscepit gremio vitreisque abscondidit antris*), 8.198 (*inter caeruleas visa est residere sorores*).
97 25 CE: Tac. *Ann.* 4.34–5 (trial of Cremutius Cordus). 41 CE: J. *AJ* 19.166–87 (Senate), 19.227–8 (opposition of Senate and People).
98 Tac. *Ann.* 1.8.6 (*aliis pessimum aliis pulcherrimum facinus*): translation by A.J. Woodman.
99 The third line is four syllables short. See Blennow (Chapter 6) in this volume.
100 *CIL* 14.2408 = *ILS* 5196: *L. Acilio L.f. Pompt. Eutyche[ti] nobili archimimo, commun. mimor. adlecto, diurno parasito Apoll., tragico comico et omnibus corporib. ad scaenam honor., decurioni Bovillis . . .*
101 *ILS* 5184. Cf. *ILS* 5185–94 for further examples: each inscription honours a *hieronica* or *hieronica coronatus*, '(crowned) victor in the sacred contest'.
102 Var. *Antiquitates divinae* fr. 3 Cardauns (August. *C.D.* 4.22) for nymphs in mime; Laberius's play *Anna Peranna* was of course a *mimus*. Priapus appeared in mime too (August. *C.D.* 6.7.2).
103 Museo Nazionale Romano, sezione epigrafica, inv. no. 475549.
104 Hor. *Sat.* 1.8.23–45, cf. 1.8.10 for the setting (*hoc miserae plebi stabat commune sepulcrum*); Ov. *Fast.* 2.571–82.

1 Rivalry and Revelation: Ovid's Elegiac Revision of Virgilian Allusion

* I presented the first version of this chapter at the 2014 Annual Meeting of the Classical Association of Canada at McGill University in Montréal. It was there that I had the great fortune of meeting Gwynaeth McIntyre and Jamie McIntyre, two people who shared my interest in Anna Perenna and with whom I formed a special panel on Anna Perenna at the 2015 Annual Meeting of the Classical Association in Bristol. I wish to thank Gwynaeth and Jamie, who have been enthusiastic and encouraging companions in the pursuit of Anna Perenna. My sincere gratitude also extends to the audience members and fellow participants from the aforementioned conferences, as well as those from the 2016 Annual Meeting of the Classical Association of Canada at the Université Laval in Québec City, for their incisive questions and invaluable feedback. And last, but certainly not least, I am grateful to Alison Keith, Suzanne Lye and my Thiasos gang (Zoa Alonso Fernández, Lauren Curtis and Naomi Weiss) for offering generous feedback on the various incarnations of this material.

1 On the lack of evidence for the existence of the Dido–Aeneas tradition prior to the composition of the *Aeneid* see M.M. Odgers, 'Some Appearances of the Dido Story', *The Classical Weekly* 18.19 (1925, pp.145–8). Odgers points out that Timaeus makes no mention of Aeneas in his account of Dido's story and that there is no certain reference to the Dido–Aeneas story in the extant fragments of Naevius's *Bellum Punicum*.

2 Marcus Terentius Varro (116–27 BCE) produced a body of work astonishing in both size and scope, including poetry of various genres and a vast *oeuvre* of prose devoted to the study of history, geography, antiquarianism, philology, rhetoric, law, religion, philosophy and science. For a detailed and helpful overview of his life and work, see G.B. Conte, *Latin Literature: A History* (Baltimore and London: The John Hopkins University Press, 1994), 210–21. His *Antiquitates Rerum Humanarum et Divinarum*, the loss of which is frequently and justifiably lamented, would certainly have informed Virgil's composition of the *Aeneid*. See also Odgers, 'Some Appearances', 145.

3 G. Thilo and H. Hagen, eds., *Servii Grammatici qui feruntur in Vergilii carmina commentarii*, 3 vols. (Hildesheim, Zurich, New York: Georg Olms Verlag, 1986), 1.580. Translations of Latin excerpts throughout this chapter are my own.

4 Thilo and Hagen, *Servii Grammatici*, 1.588.

5 Thilo and Hagen, *Servii Grammatici*, 1.580.

6 All excerpts from Virgil's *Aeneid* in this chapter are taken from R.A.B. Mynors, ed. *P. Vergili Maronis Opera* (Oxford: Oxford University Press, 1969).

7 The difficulty of the line is evidenced by the variation of proposed translations: R.G. Austin, ed., *P. Vergili Maronis Aeneidos Liber Quartus* (Oxford: Oxford University Press, 1955), 193 *ad* Virg. A. 4.675–6, 'This it was that that pyre of yours had in store for me?'; R.D. Williams, ed., *The Aeneid of Virgil: Books 1–6* (London: Macmillan, 1972), 391 *ad* Virg. A. 4.675–6, 'This was what your pyre was for, was it (*mihi*)?'; R. Fitzgerald, trans. *Virgil: The Aeneid* (New York: Vintage Classics, 1990) 120, 'The pyre meant this?'; F. Ahl, trans. *Virgil: Aeneid* (Oxford: Oxford University Press, 2007) 98, 'That's what the pyre meant for me?'.

8 S. Casali, '*Ecce* ἀμφιβολικῶς *dixit*': allusioni 'irrazionali' alle varianti scartate della storia di Didone e Anna secondo Servio' in *Servio: stratificazioni esegetiche e modelli culturali*, ed. S. Casali and F. Stok (Bruxelles: Éditions Latomus, 2008), 24–37.

9 Casali also explores the possibility that *adludit ad historiam* refers to the version of Timaeus, in which Dido does not encounter Aeneas but commits suicide on a pyre to avoid marriage with Iarbas and remain faithful to Sychaeus: see Casali, '*Ecce* ἀμφιβολικῶς *dixit*', 33–6. I wish to give sincere thanks to Sergio Casali, whose generous correspondence provided helpful guidance regarding the English rendering of the excerpted passage, as well as further clarification of the crucial aspects of his discussion in '*Ecce* ἀμφιβολικῶς *dixit*'.

10 See M.L. Delvigo, '*Per transitum tangit historiam*: Intersecting developments of Roman identity in Virgil' in *Augustan Poetry and the Roman Republic*, ed. J. Farrell and D. Nelis (Oxford: Oxford University Press, 2013), 19–39, who provides an

insightful discussion of the ways in which Virgil dealt with *historia* ('a term that 'includes the sense of 'myth', 'legend' and that of 'history', and, more particularly, 'Roman history', p. 25) and the Servian commentary notes about the incorporation of *historia* (including formulations like *adludit ad historiam*, which 'underline the skilfully implicit use of history, and explicitly identify this procedure as one that is habitual and well known in Virgil', pp. 26–7).

11 See A.S. Pease, ed., *Publi Vergili Maronis Aeneidos Liber Quartus* (Cambridge: Harvard University Press, 1935), 91 *ad* Virg. A. 4.8; Austin, *Liber Quartus*, 28 *ad* Virg. A. 4.8; Williams, *Aeneid of Virgil: Books 1–6*, 28 *ad* Virg. A. 4.8; R. Heinze, *Virgil's Epic Technique,* translated by H. and D. Harvey and Fred Robertson (Berkeley: University of California Press, 1993), 126–9; D. Nelis, *Vergil's Aeneid and the Argonautica of Apollonius Rhodius* (Leeds: Francis Cairns, 2001), 136–45.

12 See *TLL* 5.1.2310.55–60 s.v. *durus* (*in arte poetica*: Prop. 2.1.41 *duro . . . versu i.hexametro epico [opp. mollis de elegiae versibus.]*) and 8.1376.80–1377.10 s.v. *mollis* (*de poesi elegiaca*). For discussion of the elegiac significance of *mollis*, see Pichon s.v. *mollis*; F. Cairns, *Virgil's Augustan Epic* (Cambridge: Cambridge University Press, 1989), 148; and D.F. Kennedy, *The Arts of Love: Five Studies in the Discourse of Latin Love Elegy* (Cambridge: Cambridge University Press, 1993), 32–3. See also S.L. James, *Learned Girls and Male Persuasion: Gender and Reading in Roman Love Elegy* (Berkeley: University of California Press, 2003).

13 Austin, *Liber Quartus*, 129 *ad* Virg. A. 4.421. See also Pease, *Liber Quartus*, 350–1 *ad* Virg. A. 4.421, with further bibliography.

14 Austin, *Liber Quartus*, 129 *ad* Virg. A. 4.421: 'Anna must have been acting for Dido in some way: and Dido [speaks] miserably (not necessarily out of jealousy)'.

15 Heinze, *Virgil's Epic Technique*, 135.

16 On *colere* as a synonym for *amare* and other verbs of 'loving', see *TLL* 3.1693.26–1693.59 s.v. *colo*. For a discussion on how the use of the verb *colere* may hint at Anna's future as a divinity, see Wright (Ch. 4) in this volume.

17 A.A. Barrett, 'Anna's Conduct in *Aeneid* 4', *Vergilius* 16 (1970, pp. 21–5), 23–4. See also Casali, 'Ecce ἀμφιβολικῶς *dixit*', 34–5.

18 Barrett, 'Anna's Conduct in *Aeneid* 4', 23–4. By contrast, Pease, *Liber Quartus*, 351 *ad* Virg. A. 4.421 asserts: 'The word [*colere*] is ambiguous in meaning and may refer to nothing more than attention or respect'.

19 Barrett, 'Anna's Conduct in *Aeneid* 4', 23.

20 Dido addressed Aeneas using the vocative *perfide* at Virg. A. 4.305 and 366.

21 The erotic valence is already noted in Servius *ad* Virg. A. 4.366 (*amantum verbo eum increpat*, she accuses him with a lovers' word): Thilo and Hagen, *Servii Grammatici*, 1.529. For the term *perfidus* used of the unfaithful lover in erotic verse, particularly elegy, see also: de la Cerda, *P. Virgilii Maronis*, 451; Pease, *Liber Quartus*, 283 *ad* Virg. A. 4.305; Pichon *s.v. perfidi*; Barrett, 'Anna's Conduct in *Aeneid* 4', 23–4.

22 Barrett, 'Anna's Conduct in *Aeneid* 4', 24.
23 Casali, '*Ecce* ἀμφιβολικῶς *dixit*', 33–7.
24 Casali, '*Ecce* ἀμφιβολικῶς *dixit*', 36.
25 Casali, '*Ecce* ἀμφιβολικῶς *dixit*', 36–7.
26 On the half-verse, see: Pease, *Liber Quartus*, 413 *ad* Virg. *A.* 4.503; and Austin, *Liber Quartus*, 150 *ad* Virg. *A.* 4.503.
27 'Ovid shows himself to be one of Virgil's most sympathetic and perceptive readers. His interest is not just in Virgilian words and themes, but in the very roots of Virgil's poetry': S. Hinds, 'Generalizing about Ovid', *Ramus* 16 (1987, pp. 4–31), 16. For discussion of Ovid as a keen reader of Virgil, see also: G.B. Conte, *Memoria dei poeti e sistema letterario: Catullo, Virgilio, Ovidio, Lucano* (Turin: Giulio Einaudi Editore, 1974); S. Hinds, *The Metamorphosis of Persephone: Ovid and the Self-Conscious Muse* (Cambridge: Cambridge University Press, 1987); J.J. O'Hara, 'Vergil's Best Reader?: Ovidian Commentary on Vergilian Etymological Wordplay', *CJ* 91.3 (1996, pp. 255–76); B.W. Boyd, *Ovid's Literary Loves: Influence and Innovation in the Amores* (Ann Arbor: University of Michigan Press, 1997); R.A. Smith, *Poetic Allusion and Poetic Embrace in Ovid and Virgil* (Ann Arbor: University of Michigan Press, 1997); S. Hinds, *Allusion and Intertext: Dynamics of Appropriation in Roman Poetry* (Cambridge: Cambridge University Press, 1998); R.F. Thomas, *Virgil and the Augustan Reception* (Cambridge: Cambridge University Press, 2001).
28 S. Hinds, '*Arma* in Ovid's *Fasti* Part 1: Genre and Mannerism', *Arethusa* 25.1 (1992, pp. 81–112), 108–12.
29 All excerpts from Ovid's *Fasti* are taken from E.H. Alton, D.E.W. Wormell and E. Courtney (eds.), *P. Ovidi Nasonis Fastorum Libri Sex* (Leipzig: BSB B.G. Teubner Verlagsgesellshaft, 1978).
30 On the 'literary code' of the proem, see G.B. Conte, 'Proems in the Middle', *YCIS* 29 (1992, pp. 147–59).
31 On Ovid's deployment of the vocabulary of memory in his allusions, see G.B. Conte, *The Rhetoric of Imitation: Genre and Poetic Memory in Virgil and Other Latin Poets*, ed. C. Segal (Ithaca: Cornell University Press, 1986) and J.F. Miller, 'Ovidian Allusion and the Vocabulary of Memory', *MD* 30 (1993, pp. 153–64).
32 As a side note, Ovid's reference to the locks of Dido's hair (*vertice libatas accipiuntque comas*, and they receive locks cut from the head as an offering, Ov. *Fast.* 3.562) also looks back to the final scene of *Aeneid* 4 (Virg. *A.* 4.693–705), in which divine intervention releases Dido to death through the clipping of her tresses. This Virgilian scene, when taken together with Aeneas's words to Dido in the Underworld of *Aeneid* 6 (*invitus, regina, tuo de litore cessi*, unwilling, queen, I departed from your shore, Virg. *A.* 4.460), comprises a complex allusion to Catullus 66 and its Callimachean model: for a detailed discussion of the interpretive problems posed by the allusion, see N. Horsfall, *Virgil: Aeneid 6* (Berlin and Boston: De Gruyter, 2013),

344–6 *ad* Virg. *A*. 6.460. Ovid, in his description of one sister mourning another, seems to activate a layered recollection of Catullus's 'sisterly locks' (*comae sorores*, Cat. 66.51) and the *coma Didonis* in Virgil.

33 See Beek (Ch. 5) and Newlands (Ch. 8) in this volume.

34 On the vocabulary of memory, see note 31 above.

2 Calendar Girl: Anna Perenna Between the *Fasti* and the *Punica*

* This chapter originated as a section of the doctoral thesis I completed at the University of St Andrews in 2008, with a version presented as part of the panel on Anna Perenna at the 2015 Annual Meeting of the Classical Association in Bristol. The decision to revisit Anna Perenna came after a fortuitous meeting between Sarah McCallum, Gwynaeth McIntyre and I at the conference of the Classical Association of Canada in 2014. I have greatly appreciated Gwynaeth and Sarah's commentary and suggestions, as well as those of the comments of the audience members in Bristol. I am deeply grateful to Karla Pollmann, Emily Greenwood and Carole E. Newlands who have generously given their time and thoughts on many incarnations of the work since its original composition over a decade ago.

1 Political readings of the *Aeneid* are not unproblematic, but whether positive or pessimistic, the poem is deeply concerned with Rome's imperial situation and the Augustan settlement; see S.J. Harrison, 'Some Views of the *Aeneid* in the Twentieth Century' in *Oxford Readings in Vergil's* Aeneid, ed. S.J. Harrison (Oxford and New York: Oxford University Press, 1990), pp. 1–20; R. Tarrant, 'Poetry and Power: Virgil's poetry in contemporary context' in *The Cambridge Companion to Virgil*, ed. C. Martindale (Cambridge and New York: Cambridge University Press, 1997), 169–87, 177–87 for an overview.

2 F. Ahl, M.A. Davies and A. Pomeroy, 'Silius Italicus', *Aufstieg und Niedergang der Römischen Welt* 32, no. 4 (1986, pp. 2492–561), 2501–11; C. Santini, *Silius Italicus and his view of the Past* (Amsterdam: J.C. Gieben, 1991), 7.

3 M. Wilson, 'Ovidian Silius', *Arethusa* 37, no. 2 (2004, pp. 225–49), 226; cf. S. Hinds, *The Metamorphosis of Persephone: Ovid and the Self-conscious Muse* (Cambridge and New York: Cambridge University Press, 1987), 14–17 on the complex relations between Ovid's Anna episode in the *Fasti* and both the *Georgics* and *Aeneid*.

4 C.E. Newlands, 'Transgressive Acts: Ovid's Treatment of the Ides of March', *CP* 91, no. 4, (1996, pp. 320–38), 328.

5 R. Marks, 'Reconcilable Differences: Anna Perenna and the Battle of Cannae in the *Punica*' in *Ritual and Religion in Flavian Epic*, ed. A. Augoustakis (Oxford and New

York: Oxford University Press, 2013) 289, 297 on Anna as a figure of transition and change, as well as of coherence and order.

6   For instance, Varro's depiction of Anna as Aeneas's lover (Serv. *A* 4.682, 5.4), discussed by McCallum in Chapter 1 of this volume.

7   Silius's Anna narrative is told from 8.25–241, which includes a passage of some eighty lines, 144–224, which have had their authenticity contested by a number of scholars. Understanding the *Punica*'s transmission and reconstructing a stemma for the poem is problematic, and there are compelling arguments on both sides of this discussion. I will not discuss the issue in depth here, but note the problem and direct the reader to some of the bibliography on the issue. It is impossible to make sense of Silius's Anna narrative without them. Given that scholarship has established that the style is credibly Silian and there is a plausible means of transmission for the lines, I discuss them here. However any interpretation of the *Punica* that depends on these lines remains open to debate. See: W.E. Heitland, 'The "Great Lacuna" in the Eighth Book of Silius Italicus', *The Journal of Philology* 24, no. 48, (1896, pp. 188–211), 191–5; G.P. Goold, 'Observationes in Codicem Matritensem M. 31', *RhM* 99 (1956, pp. 9–17), 10–12; J. Volpilhac, P. Miniconi and G. Devallet, *Silius Italicus – Tome II: Livres V–VIII* (Paris: Belles lettres, 1981), 126–7; P. McGushin, *The Transmission of the Punica of Silius Italicus* (Amsterdam: Adolf M. Hakkert, 1985), 1; Ahl, Davies and Pomeroy, 'Silius Italicus', 2497; F. Spaltenstein, *Commentaire des* Punica *de Silius Italicus (livres 1 à 8)* (Genève: Droz, 1986), 508–14; J. Delz, *Silius Italicus:* Punica (Stuttgart: Teubner, 1987), lxviii; Santini, *Silius Italicus*, 54–6; G. Brugnoli and C. Santini, *L'Additamentum Aldinum di Silio Italico* (Roma: Accademia Nazionale dei Lincei, 1995), 17–51.

8   A. Barchiesi, *The Poet and the Prince: Ovid and Augustan Discourse* (Berkeley and Los Angeles, Ca.: University of California Press, 1997), 124–30; M. Pasco-Pranger, *Founding the Year. Ovid's* Fasti *and the Poetics of the Roman Calendar* (*Mnemosyne* Supplementum 276) (Leiden and Boston: Brill, 2006), 204; Newlands (Chapter 8) in this volume.

9   A. Augoustakis, *Motherhood and the Other: Fashioning Female Power in Flavian Epic* (Oxford and New York: Oxford University Press, 2010), 138.

10 Mart. 4.64; cf. T.P. Wiseman, 'The cult site of Anna Perenna: documentation, visualization, imagination' in *Imaging Ancient Rome: Documentation – Visualization – Imagination*, ed. L. Haselberger and J. Humphrey (*Journal of Roman Archaeology* Supplement 61) (Portsmouth, Rhode Island: *Journal of Roman Archaeology*, 2006), 55 on Anna's grove and changes to its location in the early imperial period.

11 Recent examinations include W.J. Dominik, 'Rome Then and Now: Linking the Saguntum and Cannae Episodes in Silius Italicus' *Punica*' in *Flavian Poetry*, eds. R.R. Nauta, H-J van Dam and J.J.L. Smolenaars (Leiden: Brill, 2006), 113–27; Augoustakis, *Motherhood and the Other*, 146–4; M. Fucecchi, 'With (a) God on Our Side: Ancient Ritual Practices and Imagery in Flavian Epic' in *Ritual and Religion in Flavian Epic*, ed. A. Augoustakis (Oxford and New York: Oxford University Press, 2013), 23–7;

Marks, 'Reconcilable Differences', 287ff; C. Stocks, *The Roman Hannibal: Remembering the Enemy in Silius Italicus' Punica* (Liverpool: Liverpool University Press, 2014), 91-6; A. Keith, 'Sisters and Their Secrets in Flavian Epic' in *Family in Flavian Epic*, ed. N Manioti (Leiden: Brill 2016), 268-71.
12 On the complexities of Anna's identity see Marks, 'Reconcilable Differences', 288; Fucecchi, 'With (a) God on Our Side', 25-7.
13 Mart. 4.14; 7.63; 8.66.
14 Plin. *Ep*. 3.7.5.
15 D.W.T.C. Vessey, 'Flavian Epic' in *The Cambridge History of Classical Literature Vol. 2.4: The Early Principate*, ed. E.J. Kenney (Cambridge and New York: Cambridge University Press, 1982), 95; D.C. Feeney, *The Gods in Epic: Poets and Critics of the Classical Tradition* (Oxford and New York: Oxford University Press, 1991), 311.
16 Feeney, *The Gods in Epic*, 302, 311; Vessey, 'Flavian Epic', 95.
17 R. Marks, 'Silius Italicus' in *A Companion to Ancient Epic*, ed. J.M. Foley, (Oxford: Blackwell Publishing Ltd, 2005), 530-6; Ahl, Davies and Pomeroy, 'Silius Italicus', 2519.
18 Marks, 'Silius Italicus', 531-2.
19 Ahl, Davies and Pomeroy, 'Silius Italicus', 2501 suggest that the *Punica* falls between the *Aeneid* and the *Bellum Civile* both chronologically and ideologically; W.J. Dominik, 'Hannibal at the Gates: Programmatising Rome and *Romanitas* in Silius Italicus' *Punica* 1 and 2' in *Flavian Rome: Culture, Image, Text*, eds. A.J. Boyle and W.J. Dominik (Leiden and Boston: Brill, 2003), 471; Marks, 'Silius Italicus', 529.
20 J.C. McKeown, '*Fabula Proposito Nulla Tegenda Meo*: Ovid's *Fasti* and Augustan Politics' in *Poetry and Politics in the Age of Augustus*, eds. T. Woodman and D. West (Cambridge and New York: Cambridge University Press, 1984) 169; Marks, 'Reconcilable Differences', 296.
22 Ahl, Davies and Pomeroy, 'Silius Italicus', 2505-10; Stocks, *Roman Hannibal*, 94.
22 Dominik, 'Rome Then and Now', 115-17.
23 D.C. Feeney, *A Commentary on Silius Italicus Book 1* (Unpublished Dissertation. Oxford: University of Oxford, 1982), 365; B. Tipping, *Exemplary Epic: Silius Italicus' Punica* (Oxford and New York: Oxford University Press, 2010), 1-7; R.T. Ganiban, 'Virgil's Dido and the Heroism of Hannibal in Silius' *Punica*' in *Brill's Companion to Silius Italicus*, ed. A. Augoustakis (Leiden and Boston: Brill, 2010), 82-3.
24 F. Ahl, *Metaformations: Soundplay and Wordplay in Ovid and Other Classical Poets* (Ithaca and London: Cornell University Press, 1985), 311.
25 Ahl, *Metaformations*, 310.
26 Cf. Ahl, *Metaformations*, 313 on Ov. *Fast*. 3.607: *Dum secum A[E]N[E]AS, 'AN[N]A Est!' exclamat Achates*.
27 Ahl, *Metaformations*, 315.
28 T.P. Wiseman, *Roman Drama and Roman History* (Exeter: University of Exeter Press, 1998), 65.

29 Ahl, *Metaformations*, 311.
30 Virg. *A.* 1.279; Marks, 'Reconcilable Differences', 296.
31 Dominik, 'Rome Then and Now', 114.
32 Ahl, Davies and Pomeroy, 'Silius Italicus', 2504; Dominik, 'Hannibal at the Gates', 489, 497. Figures such as Hercules and Juno, as well as cities such as Saguntum, also have a paradoxical nature, D.W.T.C. Vessey, 'Silius Italicus and the Fall of Saguntum', *CP* 69, no. 1 (1974, pp. 28–36), 34.
33 And empire: Sil. 3.582–90.
34 Cf. Liv. 21.1.2; 21.29.4; Tipping, *Exemplary Epic*, 6–7.
35 Marks, 'Reconcilable Differences', 299.
36 Sil. 10.657–8: *haec tum Roma fuit. post te cui vertere mores / si stabat fatis, potius, Carthago, maneres.* Cf. Sil. 3.570–629: Jupiter claims that the empire gained by the great Romans of Silius's narrative cannot be destroyed even if their descendants are degenerate, before summarizing the early Principate and the Flavian dynasty; a subtle connection is established between 'degeneracy' and the Principate. Also Sil. 9.352–3; 14.684–8; 15.124–7. F. Spaltenstein, *Commentaire des* Punica *de Silius Italicus (livres 9 á 17)* (Genève: Droz, 1990), 338; Ahl, Davies and Pomeroy, 'Silius Italicus', 2556–7); Dominik, 'Hannibal at the Gates', 495; Tipping, *Exemplary Epic*, 10.
37 3.163–7, 571ff.; Feeney, *The Gods in Epic*, 306; A. J. Pomeroy, 'Silius Italicus as '*Doctus Poeta*' in *The Imperial Muse: Ramus Essays on Roman Literature of the Empire*, ed. A.J. Boyle (Bendigo, Victoria: Aureal Publications, 1990), 126; Ahl, Davies and Pomeroy, 'Silius Italicus', 2553.
38 Stocks, *Roman Hannibal*, 92.
39 Cf. Virg. *A.* 1.8–11.
40 Marks, 'Silius Italicus', 529.
41 Sil. 1.29–33; cf. Spaltenstein, *Commentaire 1–8*, 7–8.
42 Cf. Virg. *A.* 7.293–322; Feeney, *Silius Italicus Book 1*, 39–40.
43 On the reconciliation of these identities, Fucecchi, 'With (a) God on Our Side', 26–7; Marks, 'Reconcilable Differences', 300; Augoustakis, *Motherhood and the Other*, 138. D.T. McGuire, *Acts of Silence: Civil War, Tyranny, and Suicide in the Flavian Epics* (Hildesheim: Olms–Weidmann, 1997), 128 characterizes Anna as a 'double-agent'; cf. Santini, *Silius Italicus*, 38.
44 Cf. Liv. 1.2.6; Ov. *Met.* 14.595–608; Spaltenstein, *Commentaire 1–8*, 501. Ahl, *Metaformations*, 312–15; Newlands, 'Transgressive Acts', 329.
45 According to Ovid, both deified in the waters of *Numicius undis*: Aeneas, Ov. *Met.* 14.599; Anna, Ov. *Fast.* 3.647. Ahl, *Metaformations*, 311–14 on Anna as a double for both Dido and Aeneas; also Beek (Chapter 5) and Newlands (Chapter 8) in this volume.
46 C.E. Newlands, *Playing with Time: Ovid and the Fasti* (Ithaca and London: Cornell University Press, 1995), 61.

47 Keith, 'Sisters and Their Secrets in Flavian Epic', 271.
48 Cf. Sil. 8.253–7. McGuire, *Acts of Silence*, 127; Marks, 'Reconcilable Differences', 295–6 on the blurred categories of 'Roman' and 'Carthaginian' at Cannae.
49 Stocks, *Roman Hannibal*, 94.
50 Marks, 'Reconcilable Differences', 294 on Dido's warning that there will never be peace between Rome and Carthage (Sil. 8.171–5).
51 Cf. Barchiesi, *The Poet and the Prince*, 164–6; Newlands, 'Transgressive Acts', 329.
52 Cf. Ahl, *Metaformations*, 203–4.
53 Ahl, *Metaformations*, 203.
54 Cf. K.P. Bednarowski, 'Dido and the Motif of Deception in Aeneid 2 and 3', *TAPA* 145, no. 1 (2015, pp. 135–72), 136–9.
55 Cf. Virg. *A.* 4.690–2; Spaltenstein, *Commentaire 1–8*, 509.
56 Wiseman, *Roman Drama*, 69.
57 Cf. C. Segal, *Landscape in Ovid's* Metamorphoses: *A Study in the Transformation of a Literary Symbol* (Wiesbaden: Franz Steiner Verlag, 1969), 8–19; H. Parry, 'Ovid's *Metamorphoses*: Violence in a Pastoral Landscape', *TAPA* 95 (1964, pp. 268–82), 282 on violence in otherwise attractive and peaceful landscapes; Wright (Chapter 4) in this volume. Beek (Chapter 5) in this volume argues that the depiction of Anna's apotheosis in the *Fasti* lacks the sexual violence of other Ovidian transformations.
58 Cf. Arethusa and Alpheus, Ov. *Met.* 5.572–641: Alpheus's waters are described as calm in the episode, but Arethusa resists his sexual advances and is pursued by the river; Segal, *Landscape in Ovid*, 55–7.
59 See Chapters 4 and 5 in this volume for further discussion about this transition.
60 McGuire, *Acts of Silence*, 129; Augoustakis, *Motherhood and the Other*, 144.
61 Cf. P. Hardie, *The Epic Successors of Virgil: A Study in the Dynamics of a Tradition* (Cambridge and New York: Cambridge University Press, 1993), 80; Ahl, Davies and Pomeroy, 'Silius Italicus', 2510.
62 Cf. McKeown, 'Ovid's *Fasti* and Augustan Politics', 172–7; Newlands, 'Transgressive Acts', 325–7.
63 Cf. McGuire, *Acts of Silence*, 135.
64 Dominik, 'Rome Then and Now', 119.
65 Augoustakis, *Motherhood and the Other*, 143–4.
66 Ahl, Davies and Pomeroy, 'Silius Italicus', 2493–501; Vessey, 'Flavian Epic', 95–6; Pomeroy, 'Silius Italicus', 126; D.W.T.C. Vessey, 'Silius Italicus: The Shield of Hannibal', *AJP* 96 (1975, pp. 391–405), 405 on the *locus amoenus* represented on the shield of Hannibal: 'The shield as a whole fixes the Punic Wars in the perspective of eternity'.
67 Ov. *Fast.* 3.697–710; cf. Newlands, 'Transgressive Acts', 321.
68 Cf. Barchiesi, *The Poet and the Prince*, 110ff.
69 Marks, 'Reconcilable Differences', 301.
70 Fuecchi, 'With (a) God on Our Side', 25.

3 Not Just Another Fertility Goddess: Searching for Anna Perenna in Art

1. For a discussion on how this account is linked to astronomical cycles of fertility and rebirth, see L. Magini, *Astronomy and Calendar in Ancient Rome: The Eclipse Festivals* (Rome: <<L'Erma>> di Bretschneider, 2001), 46–58.
2. A. Barchiesi, *The Poet and the Prince: Ovid and Augustan Discourse* (Berkeley: University of California Press, 1997), 21. McKeown argues that Ovid might be subverting Virgil's version by granting Anna her own epic journey. For references and the intertextual analysis between the journeys of Aeneas and Anna in Virgil's *Aeneid* and Ovid's *Fasti,* see J.C. McKeown, 'Fabula Proposito Nulla Tegenda Meo: Ovid's *Fasti* and Augustan politics' in *Poetry and Politics in the age of Augustus*, ed. T. Woodman and D. West (Cambridge: Cambridge University Press, 1984), 171. This type of study has also been taken up more recently by P. Murgatroyd, *Mythical and Legendary Narrative in Ovid's* Fasti (Leiden: Brill, 2005).
3. This day, and a presentation of the ideology of the altar itself, is presented by Ovid in his *Fasti* (1.709–22).
4. For a discussion of the artistic development of the *Ara Pacis*, its Greek influences, and the way in which it embodies the ideology of the Roman state, see D. Castriota, *The Ara Pacis Augustae and the Imagery of Abundance in Later Greek and Early Roman Imperial Art* (Princeton: Princeton University Press, 1995).
5. For an excellent summary of the scholarship and debate of the iconography found on the altar, see B. Spaeth, 'The Goddess Ceres in the Ara Pacis Augustae and the Carthage Relief', *AJA* 98 (1994, pp. 65–100), 66–8.
6. The identities proposed for this figure include Tellus (M. Schäfer, 'Zum Tellusbild auf der Ara Pacis Austustae', *Gymnasium* 66 (1959, pp. 288–301)), Italia (E. Strong, 'Terra Mater or Italia', *JRS* 27 (1937, pp. 114–26)), Venus (K. Galinsky, 'Venus, Polysemy, and the Ara Pacis Augustae', *AJA* 96 (1992, pp. 457–75)); A. Booth, 'Venus on the Ara Pacis', *Latomus* 25 (1966, pp. 873–9), Rhea Silvia (L. Berczelly, 'Ilia and the Divine Twins: A Reconstruction of two Relief Panels from the Ara Pacis Augustae', *Acta ad archaeologiam et artium historiam pertinentia* 5 (1985, pp. 89–149)), Pax (N. de Grummond, 'Pax Augusta and the Horae on the Ara Pacis Augustae', *AJA* 94 (1990, pp. 663–77)); P. Zanker, *The Power of Images in the Age of Augustus,* A. Shapiro (trans.) (Ann Arbor: The University of Michigan Press, 1990), 175–6; S. Weinstock, 'Pax and the Ara Pacis', *JRS* 50 (1960, pp. 44–58), and Ceres (Spaeth, 'The Goddess Ceres'). For a full bibliography, see Spaeth, 'The Goddess Ceres'. More recent discussions and bibliography are presented in P. Rehak, *Imperium and Cosmos: Augustus and the Northern Campus Martius* (Madison: The University of Wisconsin Press, 2006).

7 Elsner argues that it is the relationship between viewer and art-object that creates the 'dialogue' out of which the meaning is created (J. Elsner, 'Cult and Sculpture: Sacrifice in the Ara Pacis', *JRS* 81 (1991, pp. 50–61) 53.
8 Spaeth, 'The Goddess Ceres', 79.
9 For a discussion of the symbols associated with nymphs see *RE* 17.2 (1937) s.v. Nymphai.
10 Nereids were responsible for bringing immortality to Ino, sister of Semele. She plunged into the sea (in part to save herself from the Furies sent by Juno because she was nursing the god Bacchus) and became the Nereid Leukothea (Ov. *Fast.* 6.499–506).
11 Although Galinsky, 'Venus, Polysemy, and the Ara Pacis Augustae' (and earlier in K. Galinsky, 'Venus in a Relief on the Ara Pacis Augustae', *AJA* 70, 1966, pp. 223–43) suggests that the central figure is Venus, and the flanking figures represent different aspects of the goddess and de Grummond, 'Pax Augusta and the Horae' suggests that they are the Horae, attending to Pax, these interpretations are largely disregarded in the more recent scholarship.
12 Spaeth, 'The Goddess Ceres' and Rehak, *Imperium and Cosmos,* have clearly outlined the various interpretations of this central figure and it is not my purpose to present all these identities here, although some will be discussed through the course of my analysis.
13 Although the scholarship putting forth this identification dates to the mid-twentieth century (Schäfer, 'Zum Tellusbild', 294–301), this is the identification that is most commonly found in general resource books of Roman art and architecture.
14 Berczelly, 'Ilia and the Divine Twins', 93–5. Anna, on the other hand, is veiled in Ovid's account of her tricking Mars (Ov. *Fast.* 3.690), demonstrating that at least in some instances she can appear veiled. Unfortunately, a possible image that depicts this scene (and another possible artistic representation for Anna although the interpretations of these friezes are extremely contentious), does not depict her veiled but instead wearing some kind of headscarf (J.-M. Moret. 'Le feste dei nani' in *Nani in Festa. Iconografia, religione e politica a Ostia durante il secondo triumvirato,* ed. C. Bocherens (Bari: Edipuglia, 2012), 77–9).
15 Zanker, *The Power of Images*, 176 (Figure 137).
16 Spaeth, 'The Goddess Ceres', 73.
17 For a catalogue of all types of 'nursing' goddess figures (*kourotrophoi*) with children in the Greek tradition, see T.H. Price, *Kourotrophos: Cults and Representations of the Greek Nursing Deities* (Leiden: Brill, 1978).
18 Spaeth, 'The Goddess Ceres', 72–3. Likewise, the poppies and wheat ears were also were used to identify the figure as Demeter/Ceres as these are attributes most commonly associated with her. However, these symbols were also appropriated by other fertility goddesses such as Magna Mater and even Venus and so do not prove as conclusive as scholars would like (Castriota, *The Ara Pacis Augustae*, 142).

19 S. Perea, 'Anna Perenna: Religión y ejemplaridad mitica', *Espacio, Tiempo y Forma. Serie II, Historia Antiqua* 11 (1998, pp. 185–219), 191–2.
20 Mart. 4.64.18. (*et quod virgineo cruore gaudet | Annae pomiferum nemus Perennae.* And Anna Perenna's fruitful sacred grove, which rejoices in virgin blood). Various interpretations for what might be meant by *virgineo cruore* are laid out in R. Moreno Soldevila (ed.), *Martial, Book IV. A Commentary* (Leiden: Brill, 2006), 441–3 although a new interpretation has been put forth by A. Mastrocinque, *Bona Dea and the Cults of Roman Women* (Stuttgart: Franz Steiner Verlag, 2014), 144–5 which suggests this is directly linked to initiatory rites associated with a girl's first menstrual cycle. Magini, *Astronomy and Calendar*, 58–9 also links Anna's festival to menstrual blood. A connection has been drawn between this passage and the passage in Ovid's *Fasti* relating to the obscene songs performed by young girls at her festival, which has led to some conjectures about the manuscript and the substitution of *virgineo canore* or *rubore; virginea cohorte;* and *virgine nequiore* for *virgineo cruore* (Moreno Soldevila, *Martial, Book IV*, 441). Some other interpretations include a reference to an archaic version of Anna's festival and human sacrifice (T.P. Wiseman, *Roman Drama and Roman History* (Exeter: University of Exeter Press, 1998), 65), although he argues against this interpretation in T.P. Wiseman, 'The Cult Site of Anna Perenna: Documentation, Visualisation, Imagination' in *Imaging Ancient Rome: Documentation – Visualisation – Imagination,* ed. L. Haselberger and J. Humphrey (Portsmouth: Journal of Roman Archaeology Supplementary Series 61, 2006), 60; H.J. Rose, 'A Misunderstood Passage in Martial', *CR* 38 (1924, pp. 64–5); the sexual 'misconduct' during the festival as described by Ovid (Moreno Soldevila, *Martial, Book IV*, 441); a ritual to eradicate plagues performed by menstruating women (Col. 10.357–68; Moreno Soldevila, *Martial, Book IV*, 441); a reference to the Aqua Virgo aqueduct which provided water to her cult site (E. Assmann, 'Zu Martialis 4,64', *Rheinisches Museum für Philologie* 60 (1905, pp. 637–9); Moreno Soldevila, *Marital, Book IV*, 442); and a connection drawn between her grove (*pomiferum nemus*) and pomegranates (*punica poma*), the trees of which have been described as having blood-coloured blooms (Col.1.1.242–3; F. Ahl, *Metaformations: Soundplay and Wordplay in Ovid and Other Classical Poets* (Ithaca: Cornell University Press, 1985), 317–18).
21 Sil. 8. 190–1 tells us that she was hidden in Numicius's glassy grottos (*vitreisque abscondidit antris*). Ovid describes her *apotheosis* and Anna's own self-identification (Ov. *Fast.* 3.653–4: *placidi sum nympha Numici: | amne perenne latens Anna Perenna vocor,* (I am a nymph of calm Numicius: in this perennial stream, I am called Anna Perenna).
22 Sil. 8.200–1; Ov. *Fast.* 3.655–6.
23 I. Edlund-Berry, 'Hot, Cold, or Smelly: the Power of Sacred Water in Roman Religion, 400–100 BCE' in *Religion in Republican Italy,* ed. C.E. Schultz and P.B. Harvey Jr. (Cambridge: Cambridge University Press, 2006), 173; Ov. *Fast.* 3.567–654.

24 Edlund-Berry, 'Hot, Cold, or Smelly', 168 with further bibliography.
25 Ov. *Fast.* 3. 523-44; 675-96.
26 M. Piranomonte (ed.), *Il santuario della musica e il bosco sacro di Anna Perenna* (Roma: Mondadori Electa, 2002); M. Piranomonte, 'The Discovery of the Fountain of Anna Perenna and its Influence on the Study of Ancient Magic' in *The Wisdom of Thoth: Magical Texts in Ancient Mediterranean Civilisations*, ed. G. Bąkowska-Czerner, A. Roccati, and A. Świerzowska (Oxford: Archaeopress Publishing Ltd, 2015).
27 Mastrocinque, *Bona Dea*, 147; U. Egelhaaf-Gaiser, 'Roman Cult Sites: A Pragmatic Approach' in *A Companion to Roman Religion*, ed. J. Rüpke (Chichester: Wiley-Blackwell, 2011) 213; Perea, 'Anna Perenna', 195-9; M. Guarducci, 'Il culto di Anna e delle Paides nelle iscrizioni sicule di Buscemi e il culto latino di Anna Perenna', *Studi e materiali di storia delle Religioni* 12 (1936, pp. 25-50). R.J.A Wilson, *Sicily under the Roman Empire: The Archaeology of a Roman Province, 36 BC–AD 535* (Warminster: Aris & Phillips, 1990), 280 argues against making this kind of a connection but does not defend his position (and also argued this point before the grove in Rome was uncovered) as does K. Latte, *Römische Religionsgeschichte* (München: C.H. Beck, 1960), 138, n.1.
28 For a discussion of this cult site see G. Pugliese Carratelli, 'Sul culto delle Paides e di Anna in Acre', *La parola del passato: Rivista di studi antichi* 6 (1951, pp. 68-75); B. Pace, *Arte e civilita della sicilia antica. III. Cultura e vita religiosa* (Roma: Societa anonima editrice dante Alighieri, 1945), 483-6.
29 See *SEG* 42.825-36 for texts.
30 Wilson, *Sicily under the Roman Empire*, 280. There is also evidence of an inscription on an *aedicula* which was set up to the *Paides* and to Anna, with the dating formula 'in the priesthood of the *Paides* and Anna of ...' with the rest left blank (*SEG* 42.825). Wilson suggests that this was carved in advance so that it was ready for when an individual wished to make a dedication but was never completed (Wilson, *Sicily under the Roman Empire*, 280).
31 Wilson, *Sicily under the Roman Empire*, 318. The use of Syracusian dating may be a result of the community of Acre having been founded by Syracuse (R.K. Sherk, 'The Eponymous Officials of Greek Cities V: The Register: Part VI: Sicily', *ZPE* 96 (1993, pp. 267-95) 267).
32 *SEG* 42.836. Translation and image in Wilson, *Sicily under the Roman Empire*, 280-1.
33 J. Larson, *Greek Nymphs. Myth, Cult, Lore* (Oxford: Oxford University Press, 2001), 222; Wilson, *Sicily under the Roman Empire*, 280; Pace, *Arte e civilita della sicilia antica*, 486. There also appears to be a connection between the *Paides* and *Nymphai* in *SEG* 42.832 and *IG* 14.204 (also see Pugliese Carratelli, 'Sul culto delle Paides e di Anna in Acre', 70-3).
34 C. Santini, *Silius Italicus and his view of the Past* (Amsterdam: Gieben, 1991), 43-4.

35 K. Galinsky, *Aeneas, Sicily, and Rome* (Princeton: Princeton University Press, 1969), 102.

36 Piranomonte (ed), *Il santuario della musica*, 29. *AE* 2003:253. *C(aius) Suetonius Germ[anu]s / nymphis sacra[tis] / Annae Perennae d(ono) d(edit).* G(aius) Suetonius Germ(anu)s, gave (this) as a gift to the sacred nymphs of Anna Perenna (or to nymphs devoted to Anna Perenna/to the sacred nymphs (and) to Anna Perenna).

37 *AE* 2003:252. *Nymphis sacratis / Suetonius Germanus cum / Licinia coniuge / Annae Perennae votum / quod susceperant si se victo- / res statuerent, aram mar- / moream se posituros denuo / victores facti votum me- / riti solvimus. / Ded(icata) non(is) Apr(ilibus), Silvano et Augurino / co(n)s(ulibus).* To the sacred nymphs. Suetonius Germanus with his wife, Licinia, the vow to Anna Perenna which they had undertaken, that if they determined themselves as victors, they would set up a marble altar. Once more made victors, we deservedly fulfill the vow. Dedicated on the Nones of April [5 April]. When Silvanus and Augurinus were consuls [156 CE]. The connection between nymphs and theatrical performances has been discussed in detail by Wiseman, 'The Cult Site of Anna Perenna', 55.

38 *SEG* 14.836.

39 For a detailed discussion of the offerings, see Piranomonte (ed), *Il santuario della musica*. A brief summary is also given in Piranomonte, 'The Discovery of the Fountain of Anna Perenna'.

40 For a discussion of the caves sanctuaries of nymphs in the Greek world, see Larson, *Greek Nymphs*, 226–67.

41 Larson, *Greek Nymphs*, 229.

42 M.-C. Lhote-Birot, 'Les nymphs en Gaule Narbonnaise et dans les Trois Gaules', *Latomus* 63 (2004, pp. 58–69), 58.

43 Most of the scholars attempting to identify the figure on this panel have presented a holistic approach to the monument. See Spaeth, 'The Goddess Ceres', and Rehak, *Imperium and Cosmos*, for a full bibliography.

44 P. Rehak. 'Aeneas or Numa? Rethinking the Meaning of the Ara Pacis Augustae', *The Art Bulletin* 83 (2001, pp. 190–208) has argued for a reinterpretation of the Aeneas panel as instead representing Numa. He bases this interpretation on a holistic approach to the monument and suggests that the artists present Romulus and Numa as representative of two aspects of Augustus, war-like founder and peaceful lawgiver. The crux of this argument is that Aeneas is not depicted with a beard in art although this assertion is further complicated in two ways. First, Numa is not regularly depicted in art and so it is difficult to determine artistic conventions for his depiction. Second, the physical appearance of Aeneas himself is not clearly defined. Griffith discusses these different depictions (whether Greek, Etruscan or Roman, differing hair lengths, bearded or un-bearded, etc.) and concludes that the audience

may view Aeneas however he or she chooses (M. Griffith, 'What does Aeneas Look Like?', *CP* 80 (1985, pp. 309–19), 318–19).

45 Within his discussion of wordplay by classical poets, Ahl also sees a connection between the two, specifically identifying Anna as the female counterpart to Aeneas's masculinity, and, within Silius's narrative, her hostility to Rome as a counterpart to Aeneas's friendliness (Ahl, *Metaformations*, 315).

46 Ov. *Met.* 14.596–608.

47 C. Newlands, 'Transgressive acts: Ovid's Treatment of the Ides of March', *CP* 91 (1996, pp. 320–38), 329.

48 For a discussion of the terminology of deified individuals, see G. McIntyre, *A Family of Gods: The Worship of the Imperial Family in the Latin West* (Ann Arbor: The University of Michigan Press, 2016), 17.

49 Serv. *A.* 5.45, quoting and opposing Var. *L.* fr. 424.

50 For example, Augustus gets the title *divus* after his funeral in 14 CE. The first woman to be deified, Caligula's sister Drusilla, gets the feminized title, *diva,* in 38 CE.

51 Ganiban follows the argument that by inciting Hannibal to fight, Anna is ensuring that her sister is avenged, thereby making Hannibal Dido's *ultor*. In the description of Hannibal's shield, Hannibal is found praying and making sacrifices to fight against the Romans (2.426-8; this passage immediately follows the depiction of Dido committing suicide as Aeneas sails away. Unlike the description of the future glories of Rome as depicted on the armor of Aeneas in Virgil's *Aeneid,* Hannibal's shield instead focuses on the avenging of past wrongs (R.T. Ganiban, 'Virgil's Dido and the Heroism of Hannibal in Silius' *Punica*' in *Brill's Companion to Silius Italicus,* ed. A. Augoustakis (Leiden: Brill, 2010), 88).

52 R. Marks, 'Reconcilable Differences: Anna Perenna and the battle of Cannae in the *Punica*' in *Ritual and Religion in Flavian Epic,* ed. A. Augoustakis (Oxford: Oxford University Press, 2013), 287–302.

53 K. Galinsky, 'Sol and the "Carmen Saeculare"', *Latomus* 26 (1967, pp. 619–33), 626-7. The Carmen Saeculare (29–32) has been employed as evidence in favour of identifying the goddess on the panel as Tellus but this interpretation is extremely problematic and is (rightly) dismissed by Spaeth, *The Goddess Ceres*, 77.

54 J. Elsner, *Art and the Roman Viewer: The Transformation of Art from the Pagan World to Christianity* (Cambridge: Cambridge University Press, 1995), 194. Castriota notes the disturbing nature of this type of conclusion, but suggests that in reality, the ambiguity may have served to better connect this monument with its audience and promote the main theme of the monument – peace and prosperity – through demonstrating the divine concord of these fertility goddesses (Castriola, *The Ara Pacis Augustae,* 71). Kleiner discusses the *Ara Pacis*'s ability to display the major themes of Augustus's principate by maintaining the hint of ambiguity allowing for multiple interpretations thereby allowing everyone to find the significance in their

own interpretations (D.E.E. Kleiner, 'Semblance and Storytelling in Augustan Rome' in *The Cambridge Companion to Augustus,* ed. K. Galinsky (Cambridge: Cambridge University Press, 2005), 197–233). Some scholars argue that because this is the *Ara Pacis*, Pax must be present somewhere, leading to the identification of the figure on the southeastern panel as Pax herself (an interpretation most recently put forth by Rehak, *Imperium and Cosmos,* 112 with bibliography).

55 See Rehak, *Imperium and Cosmos,* 133 for a summary of the different possible interpretations for what these processions represent. Holliday argues that this procession alludes to a historical event, that of the *constitutio* of July 13 CE (P. J. Holliday, 'Time, History, and Ritual on the Ara Pacis Augustae', *The Art Bulletin* 72 (1990, pp. 542–57), 545), whereas Billows argues that it depicts an idealized version of history (R. Billows, 'The Religious Procession of the Ara Pacis Augustae: Augustus' *Supplicatio* in 13 B.C.', *JRA* 6 (1993, pp. 80–92), 91). See Rehak, *Imperium and Cosmos,* 121–31 for his identifications and for bibliography of other scholars' attempts to identify the figures of the North and South Processions.

56 Elsner, *Art and the Roman Viewer,* 197.

57 For a thorough discussion of the importance of the viewer in discussions of artistic representations and interpretations of monuments, see Elsner, 'Cult and Sculpture'.

58 Elsner, 'Cult and Sculpture', 53.

59 Favro argues that the viewer could 're-live' the experience of the commemorations and sacrificial rites that took place at the altar. In addition, the act of viewing becomes a dynamic experience, which moves the viewer through an expertly choreographed, Augustan experience (D. Favro, *The Urban Image of Augustan Rome* (Cambridge: Cambridge University Press, 1996), 235).

60 F. Baratte, 'L'image impériale sur les reliefs de l'Afrique Romaine', in *La Transmission de l'idéologie impériale dans l'occident romain. Colloque CTHS – Bastia 2003,* ed. M. Navarro Caballero and J.-M. Roddaz (Bordeaux-Paris: Actes des congrès nationaux des sociétés historiques et scientifiques, 2006), 274; F. Rakob, 'The Making of Augustan Carthage', in *Romanization and the city: Creation, transformations, and failures,* ed. E. Fentress (Portsmouth: Journal of Roman Archaeology Supplementary Series 38, 2000), 77–82. Hurlet argues that the monumental building program in this colony should be seen to represent imperial power and that Carthage then serves as a model to help diffuse these images of power throughout the province (F. Hurlet, 'Pouvoir des images, images du pouvoir imperial. La province d'Afrique aux deux premiers siècles de notre ère', *Mélanges de l'Ecole française de Rome. Antiquité* 112 (2000, pp. 297–364), 299).

61 Virg. *A.* 1.418–49. An excellent example of the connection between Augustus and his legendary ancestry within the city of Carthage is the Altar of the Gens Augusta, which includes a statue group in relief of Aeneas, Anchises and Ascanius. (See Galinsky, *Aeneas, Sicily, and Rome,* 9; Figure 7.)

62 Rakob, 'The Making of Augustan Carthage', 75.
63 Barrate, 'L'image impériale', 293. Rives also argues that in addition to embodying the major themes of Augustan ideology (the blessings of the gods and the prosperity of the empire) and evoking prototypes in Rome, this monument could have been something like the *Ara Pacis* in that it appears to have been erected on a major road near the limits of the city (J.B. Rives, *Religion and authority in Roman Carthage from Augustus to Constantine* (Oxford: Blackwell Publishing, 1995), 53). See Baratte, 'L'image impériale' and Spaeth, 'The Goddess Ceres', 95 for a thorough discussion of the problem of the circulation of images, especially relating to the Carthaginian panel and that on the *Ara Pacis*, and how these images came to be set up in both Rome and Carthage. Castriota discusses the Hellenistic influences on both altars (Castriota, *The Ara Pacis Augustae,* 54–5). Galinsky also attempts to determine the relationship between these two monuments and suggests that the Carthaginian altar was part of a series of altars erected throughout the empire after Augustus's death (Galinsky, 'Venus in a Relief', 240). Berczelly also suggests that the Carthage Altar is post-Augustan but from first half of first century CE (Berczelly, 'Ilia and the Divine Twins', 137).
64 Spaeth, 'The Goddess Ceres', 95–6 presents the different identities proposed in scholarship with bibliography and so will not be reproduced here.
65 The identification of this figure as a triton has most recently been argued by Baratte, 'L'image impériale', 277–8. Spaeth argues that he is in fact that god Poseidon (Spaeth, 'The Goddess Ceres', 97). For bibliography on the different interpretations, see Spaeth, 'The Goddess Ceres', 96–7. For his identification as Sol, see de Grummond, 'Pax Augusta and the Horae', 675; Galinsky, *Aeneas, Sicily, and Rome*, 232.
66 Galinsky, 'Sol and the 'Carmen Saeculare', 626–7. If we interpret this individual to be the personification of the ocean, this figure could represent her journey from her home in Carthage to the shores of Italy, but this is just speculation, since it is not possible to know how the audience would have viewed and interpreted this monument.
67 Baratte, 'L'image impériale', 277–8; Spaeth, 'The Goddess Ceres', 94–100 (with bibliography).
68 *Sunt quibus haec Luna est, quia mensibus impleat annum* (Some think that this goddess is the Moon, because it completes the year by the months, Ov. *Fast.* 3.657).
69 Strong has argued that the central figure, representing fertility on earth is flanked by representations of the sun and the moon (Strong, 'Terra Mater or Italia', 124). This interpretation does not provide any further insight into her identity as any of the fertility goddesses could fill this role.
70 The other panel associated with this altar has figures identified as Mars Ultor, Venus Genetrix, and a Julio–Claudian Prince (or even possibly Divus Julius), most recently discussed in Baratte, 'L'image impériale', 274–7.

4 Anna, Water, and Her Imminent Deification in *Aeneid* 4

* I would like to thank Timothy Joseph, David Christenson, and Leah Kronenberg for their comments on earlier drafts of this paper. Furthermore, I would like to thank The New York Public Library for their generous fellowship that provided me with the space and research materials to work on this project.

1 Notably F. Bömer, *P. Ovidius Naso: Die Fasten* (Heidelberg: C. Winter, 1958), 79–92; J.C. McKeown, 'Fabula Proposito Nulla Tegenda Meo' in *Poetry and Politics of the Age of Augustus*, ed. T. Woodman and D. West (Cambridge: Cambridge University Press, 1982), 169–74.

2 G. McIntyre (Chapter 3 in this volume) suggests that Anna Perenna (of Punic Origin) may be depicted on the Ara Pacis, a monument that predates the *Fasti*.

3 For all ancient etymologies of *lympha* and *nympha*, see R. Maltby, *A Lexicon of Ancient Latin Etymologies* (Leeds: Arca 25, 1991), 155 and 418, respectively.

4 See Var. *L*. 7.87 (who also quotes these lines of Pacuvius while treating *lymphata*) and Fest. s.v. *lympha* for the connection of *lymphatus* and νυμφόληπτος. For the phenomenon of possession by nymphs as insanity, see J. Larson, *Greek Nymphs* (Oxford: Oxford University Press, 2001), 62–3. The adjective related *lymphaticus* seems to have a similar meaning of 'rendered insane by the nymphs' in Pl. *Poen.* 345–6.

5 For the association of the nymphs and Dionysus/Bacchus, see J. Larson, *Greek Nymphs*, 91–6.

6 F. Cairns, 'Catullus 27', *Mnemosyne* 28.1 (1975), 26–7; M.C.J. Putnam, 'On Catullus 27', *Latomus* 28 (1968), 858.

7 See n.5 above for Dionysus/Bacchus and his association with the nymphs.

8 As we will see below, Virgil uses this same word and adapts the passage for his description of Amata, who also has Bacchic associations (Virg. A. 7.377).

9 R.G.M. Nisbet and M. Hubbard, *A Commentary on Horace: Odes Book 2* (Oxford Clarendon Press, 1978), ad loc.

10 For more on the anthropomorphic nature of these lines, see Nisbet and Hubbard, *Horace*, (ad loc.) and V. Pöschl, 'Die Horazode *Aequam memento* (c. 2, 3)', *Rheinisches Museum* 137 (1994), 123–4.

11 Other examples of the punning of *lympha* and nympha: Tib. 1.7.12, Hor. *S*. 15.97; *Epod*. 16.48; *Carm*. 3.13.16. For more commentary on the punning of *lympha* and *nympha* in these passages, see F.G. Ballentine, 'Some Phases of the Cult of the Nymphs', *HSCPh* 15 (1904), 90–4; J.R. Wilson, 'O Fons Bandusiae', *CJ* 63.7 (1968), 291.

12 1.701, 4.635, 4.638, 7.377, 9.23, 10.834, 12.420.

13 After Aeneas has a vision of the god of the Tiber river, he makes a prayer to the local nymphs: 'Laurentine nymphs from whom comes the race of **rivers**' (*Laurentes Nymphae, genus **amnibus** unde est, A.* 8.71). Turnus's sister, Juturna, was a nymph of

the Numicius River whose springs were supposed to have had healing properties (Serv. ad *A.* 12.139). At the end of the epic, she dives into a river (12.885-6). Later in Book 9, Aeneas's ships, transformed into nymphs, will dive into the river (118-25). See also discussion below of Anna as a 'river nymph' (*fluviali . . . lympha* at 4.635).

14 Serv. (ad *A.* 8.31) distinguishes between the three names used for the Tiber: '**For he is called in rites: 'Tiberinus'**, in common speech: 'Tiber', and in poetry: 'Thybris' (***nam in sacris Tiberinus****, in coenolexia Tiberis, in poemate Thybris vocatur*).

15 Aeneas associates the god of the Tiber with the nymphs in a prayer to them at 8.71-2. Perhaps the vertical juxtaposition of *lymphis* and *Tiberini* further adds to the polyvalence of the words.

16 Varro calls Juturna a *lympha* (*L* 5.71). Her spring was associated with healing. According to Pliny (*Nat.* 31.6-8), after the death of Cicero, several springs sprouted forth in one of his villas. He records an epigram of Tullius Laurea, one of Cicero's freedmen. The poem calls the springs *lymphae*, and credits the water with salubrious properties.

17 R. Tarrant, *Virgil: Aeneid XII* (Cambridge: Cambridge University Press, 2012), ad loc.

18 O'Hara argues that this vertical juxtaposition is common in etymological wordplay (J. O'Hara, *True Names: Vergil and the Alexandrian Tradition of Etymological Wordplay* (Ann Arbor: University of Michigan Press, 2017), 86-9).

19 I give credit to Leah Kronenberg for finding this acrostic. The use of acrostics is well-attested in Virgil: E.L. Brown, *Numeri Vergiliani: Studies in 'Eclogues' and 'Georgics'* (Bruxelles-Berchem, 1963), 96-114; D. Fowler, '*Mea Tempora*: Patterning of Time in the *Metamorphoses*' in *Ovidian Transformations: Essays on the Metamorphoses and its Reception*, ed. A. Barchiesi and S. Hinds (Cambridge: Cambridge Philological Society, 1983), 13-30; J.J. Clauss, 'An Acrostic in Vergil (*Eclogues* I 5-8): The Chance that Mimics Choice?', *Aevum Antiquum* 10 (1997, pp. 267-87); D. Feeney and D. Nelis, 'Two Vergilian Acrostics: *Certissima Signa*', *CQ* 50.2 (2005, pp. 644-6); A. Grishin, '*Ludus in Undis*: An Acrostic in *Eclogue 9*', *HSPh* 104 (2008, pp. 237-40); N. Adkin, 'Read the Edge', *ACD* 50 (2014, pp. 45-73); Excitingly, Julia Hejduk has recently argued, in presentation at the 2015 Symposium Cumanum, that the 'Isaiah speaks' acrostic at *G.* 4.458-65 is intentional.

20 Tib. 7.149, 2,1,35; [Tib.] 3.10.1-2; Virg. *Ecl.* 2.45 (with W. Clausen, *Virgil: Eclogues* (Oxford: Clarendon Press, 1994), ad loc.); Ov. *Met.* 8.598.

21 L. Kronenberg, 'Tibullus the Elegiac *Vates*: Acrostics in Tibullus 2.5', *Mnemosyne* 71 (2018, pp. 508-14). Adkin reads similar hortative acrostics in Virg. *Ecl.* 7.6-13 and *G.* 2.44-7 (Adkin, 'Edge').

22 For water and funerary ritual, see P.J. Jones, *Reading Rivers in Roman Literature and Culture* (Lantham, MD: Lexington Books, 2005), 22-3.

23 Larson, *Greek Nymphs*, 108-15.

24 For other examples, see Ov. *Met.* 2.324, 14.601; V. Fl. 9.208; Tac. *Ger.* 40.

25 See note where he cites Pease's on 4.635, which connects this passage to the passage discussed above (2.217–20). N. Horsfall, *Virgil, Aeneid 2* (Leiden: Brill), ad loc. See also A.S. Pease, *Publi Vergil Maronis Aeneidos Liber Quartus* (Cambridge, MA: Harvard University Press, 1935), ad loc.

26 Hardie notes the connotations of ritual purification that these lines evoke. He also connects it to Pease's note on 4.635, as well as the words of Aeneas from Book 2 quoted above (217–20) (P. Hardie, *Virgil: Aeneid, Book IX* (Cambridge: Cambridge University Press, 1995), ad loc,).

27 Pease and Williams make the suggestion that these lines may refer to that tradition (Pease, *Liber Quartus*, ad loc.; R.D. Williams, *The Aeneid of Vergil* (London: Bristol Classical Press), ad loc.). Barrett gives full treatment of this theory (A.A. Barrett, 'Anna's Conduct in *Aeneid* 4', *Vergilius* 16 (1970, pp. 21–5). See McCallum (Chapter 1) in this volume.

28 E. Swallow, 'Anna Soror', *CW* 44.10 (1951, pp. 145–50), 148.

29 See J. O'Hara, *Inconsistencies in Roman Epic: Studies in Catullus, Lucretius, Vergil, Ovid, and Lucan* (Cambridge: Cambridge University Press, 2007).

30 E. Norden, *Agnostos Theos: Untersuchungen zur Formengeshichte religiöser Rede* (Leipzig: Teubner, 1923), 143–63.

31 This description of Anna's skills corresponds well to Anna Perenna's areas of expertise.

32 For a paradigmatic example of a hymn earlier in Latin literature with many of these elements, see Lucretius's invocation of Venus at proem of the *De Rerum Natura* (1.1–61). Just as Dido's words at 4.421–3, Lucretius's invocation also suggests that the deity has no parallel in certain aspects of her power and similarly contains the word *solus*: *quae quoniam rerum naturam* **sola** *gubernas* (Since it is you **alone** who guides the nature of the universe ..., 1.21). This same notion occurs later in the proem: *nam tu* **sola** *potes tranquilla pace iuvare/ mortalis* (For you **alone** are able to help mortals with untroubled peace ..., 1.30–1). ad (1923: 245 n.1) gives an extensive list of the μόνος/*solus* topos in hymn. One could read all of Ovid's presentation of Anna Perenna as this aspect of hymnic formula through listing of the numerous *aitia*, names, and identifications that Anna Perenna bears (*Fast*. 3.443–696). Miller notes this tendency in the *Fasti* (J. Miller, 'The *Fasti* and Hellenistic Didactic: Ovid's Variant Aetiologies', *Arethousa* 25.1 (1992, pp. 11–31), 27).

33 For the sexual connotation of *aditus* and *noscere*, see J.N. Adams, *The Latin Sexual Vocabulary* (Baltimore: Johns Hopkins University Press, 1982), 176, 32–3 respectively.

34 B. Fortson, *Language and Rhythm in Plautus: Synchronic and Diachronic Studies* (Berlin: Walter de Gruyter, 2008), 100.

35 For vertical juxtapositions in consecutive lines that suggest wordplay, see O'Hara, *True Names*, 86–91. This type of wordplay that spans multiple words is not uncommon in Virgil's epic predecessor, Lucretius. In the following passage, Lucretius

discusses the nature of the soul, and coincidentally, pays homage to his own predecessors:

> ignoratur enim quae sit natura animai,
> nata sit an contra nascentibus insinuetur
> et simul intereat nobiscum morte dirempta
> an tenebras Orci visat vastasque lacunas 115
> an pecudes alias divinitus insinuet se,
> Ennius ut noster cecinit, qui primus amoeno
> detulit ex Helicone **perenni** fronde coronam,
> per gentis Italas hominum quae **clara clueret**.

For they are ignorant of what nature the soul is: whether it is born or whether, in turn, it enters us after we are born and it perishes at the same time along with us, destroyed by death, or whether it goes to the darkness and expansive void of Orcus or whether it divinely inhabits other animals as our man Ennius sang who first brought from lovely Helicon a garland of **everlasting** leaves which **became famous** throughout the Italian races of men.

Lucr. 1.112–19

Several scholars have already noted Lucretius's wordplay with Ennius's name and the adjective *perenni* (118). Gale has suggested that the last two lines of this passage allude to another one of Lucretius's predecessors: Empedocles. She maintains that the *perenni* indicates the first half of his name since ἔμπεδος can mean 'lasting' or 'continual'. The *clara clueret* (119) corresponds to the second half of his name: κλέος. Thus, the learned close-reader may have picked up on this pun and subtle allusion that spans two lines in Lucretius (M. Gale, 'Etymological Wordplay and Poetic Succession in Lucretius', *CP* 96 (2001, pp. 168–72)). In light of the precedent of Lucretius's wordplay, I posit that the second line of Anna's speech may make a similar allusion.

36 O'Hara, *True Names*, 79–85.

37 *Apud Medos nascitur quaedam arbor, ferens mala, quae medica vocantur quam per periphrasin ostendit, eius supprimmens nomen.* (Among the Medes grows a certain tree that bears apples which are called 'medical' which he, suppressing the name, shows through periphrasis).

38 I might also add, given the sexually charged nature of Anna Perenna and her festival, perhaps we can see allusions to this aspect of her at 4.18–19 and 4.31–54. Clausen sees sexual connotations at 4.18–19 (W. Clausen, *Virgil's Aeneid: Decorum, Allusion, and Ideology* (Leipzig: K.G. Saur, 2002), 77–88). Thomas posits similar valences at 4.54 (R.F. Thomas, *Virgil and the Augustan Reception* (Cambridge: Cambridge University Press, 2001), 117). One of Anna's main functions in the book is to encourage Dido to have sex with Aeneas. This is essentially the spirit of Anna

Perenna's festival: indulgence in unrestrained sex and bawdy verses (*Fast.* 3.523–41, 675–6).

39 G.S. West, 'Vergil's Helpful Sisters: Anna and Juturna in the 'Aeneid', *Vergilius* 25 (1979, pp. 10–19); V. Castellani, 'Anna and Juturna in the *Aeneid*', *Vergilius* 33 (1987, pp. 49–57).

40 West, 'Helpful Sisters', 16; Castellani, 'Anna and Juturna', 52.

41 Castellani, 'Anna and Juturna', 52 notes the sameness of these lines as well.
A somewhat similar, but not identical, line describes the aged squire of Pallas at the funeral of the youth: *pectora nunc foedans pugnis, nunc unguibus ora* (11.86).

42 Interestingly, Castellani attempts to determine who is more to blame for their siblings' death. He finds Juturna more culpable. He reads her as a mere henchman of Juno who abandons her brother in his time of most need (54–6). Castellani ('Anna and Juturna', 56–7) takes his reading a step further to posit that a parallelism between Anna and Juturna suggests a parallel between their siblings, Dido and Turnus. He reads Dido as a less sympathetic because she deliberately deceives her sister to bring about her own death. In his reading, Turnus, however, most deserves our sympathy because of his abandonment by his sister.

43 See Virg. *A.* 12.140–1, 878.

44 cf. Beek (Chapter 5) in this volume for a discussion on how her deification is not a direct result of rape.

45 Most likely not coincidentally, this is the river in which Aeneas is said to have drowned. For the primary sources on this tradition, see [Aur. Vict.] *Orig.* 14.2–3; D.H. 1.64.4–5; Ov. *Met.* 14.581–608; Tib. 2.5.43–4; Serv. *ad* 4.620, 7.150, 7.797; Serv. Auct. *ad* 1.259, 7.797, 12.794.

46 *Iuturna fons est in Italia saluberrimus iuxta Numicum fluvium* (The most healthful fountain of Juturna in Italy is next to the river Numicius, Serv. *ad A.* 12.139).

47 For the Numicius, see Serv. ad *A.* 7.150. For Juturna's spring in Lavinium, see ad *A.* 12.139.

48 For Dido as perverted sacrifice, see V. Panoussi, *Greek Tragedy in Vergil's Aeneid: Ritual and Intertext* (Cambridge: Cambridge University Press, 2009), 46, 52, 55.

49 A painting shows Agamemnon with a veiled head at the sacrifice of his daughter Iphigeneia (*LIMC* s.v. Agamemnon 41). Cicero mentions this painting as well as Agamemnon's veiled head (*Orat.* 74).

50 For Turnus as sacrifice, see Tarrant, *Aeneid XII*, 21–2; Panoussi, *Greek Tragedy*, 56–7, 70; J. T. Dyson, *King of the Wood: The Sacrificial Victor in Vergil's Aeneid* (Norman: University of Oklahoma Press, 2001), passim; J. O'Hara, *Death and Optimistic Prophecy in Vergil's Aeneid* (Princeton: Princeton University Press, 1990), 82–4, 103–4.

51 Var. *L.* 5.71; Prop. 3.22.26; Fron. *Aq.* 4; Serv. ad 12.139.

52 They reputedly appeared there after the battle of Regillus Lake in 496 (D.H. 6.13, Ov. *Fast.* 1.706) and the battle of Pydna in 168 (Val. Max. 1.8.1).

53 Nymphs, especially water nymphs, are often associated with fertility (Larson, *Greek Nymphs*, 100) and Anna's festival also contains aeschrological elements (the 'bawdy verses', *Fast.* 3.675–6) which has common components in fertility rituals. Dedications found at Anna Perenna's spring include pinecones and eggshells, both associated with deities of fertility. For fertility votives at Anna Perenna's cult site see M. Piranomonte, 'Religion and Magic at Rome: The Fountain of Anna Perenna' in *Magical Practices in the Latin West*, ed. R.L. Gordan and F.M. Simón (Leiden: Brill, 2010), 203. G. McIntyre's (Chapter 3 in this volume) suggestion that the central figure on the so-called fertility panel of the Ara Pacis is Anna Perenna makes the nymph's association with fertility even more salient.

54 1.712, 1.749, 4.68, 4.450, 4.596, 6.456.

55 Pease, *Liber Quartus*, ad 4.68.

56 O'Hara has written extensively on Virgil's propensity to allude to multiple, often contradictory, versions of the myth (*Inconsistencies*, 77–103).

57 For parallelisms between Turnus and Dido, see R.O.A.M. Lyne, *Further Voices in Vergil's Aeneid* (Oxford: Oxford University Press, 1987), 136; R.O.A.M. Lyne, *Words of the Poet: Characteristics Techniques of Style Vergil's Aeneid* (Oxford: Oxford University Press, 1989), 163; M.C.J. Putnam, *The Poetry of the Aeneid* (Cambridge, MA: Cambridge University Press 1965), 155–6.

5 How to Become a Hero: Gendering the Apotheosis of Ovid's Anna Perenna

1 I have presented this argument in detail in the first chapter of A.E. Beek, 'Always Look on the Bright Side of Death: Violence, Death, and Supernatural Transformation in Ovid's *Fasti*', (PhD diss., University of Minnesota, Minneapolis, 2015).

2 See Chapter 3 of Beek, 'Always Look on the Bright Side of Death'.

3 Given Ovid's multiple and diverse origin stories for Anna Perenna (she is not consistently represented as originating as Dido's sister; in *Fast.* 3.657–60 Ovid presents a variety of mutually exclusive explanations for Anna Perenna's origin), it is extremely difficult to synthesize everything Ovid says about Anna Perenna into one consistent portrait. While Anna Perenna's origin seems to be a question that Ovid is unwilling to answer definitively, Ovid devotes more lines of poetry to the adventures of Dido's sister than he does to any other possibility. For further elaboration on multiple aetiologies within the *Fasti* and the synthesis of contradictory stories, see A. Barchiesi, 'Discordant Muses', *PCPhS* 37 (1991, pp. 1–21); J.F. Miller, 'The *Fasti* and Hellenistic Didactic: Ovid's Variant Aetiologies', *Arethusa* 25, no. 1 (1992, pp. 11–31);

M. Beard, 'A Complex of Times: No More Sheep on Romulus' Birthday', *PCPhS* 33 (1987, pp. 1–15); J.F. Miller, 'Ovid's Divine Interlocutors in the *Fasti*' in *Studies in Latin Literature and Roman History III*, ed. C. Deroux (Brussels: Revue d'Études Latines, 1983), 156–92; B. Harries, 'Causation and the Authority of the Poet in Ovid's *Fasti*', *CQ* 39, no. 1 (1989, pp. 164–85); R.J. Littlewood, 'Ovid and the Ides of March (*Fasti* 3.523–710): a Further Study in the Artistry of the Fasti' in *Studies in Latin Literature and Roman History II*, ed. C. Deroux (Brussels: Revue d'Études Latines, 1980), 320–1; E. Fantham, ed., *Ovid* Fasti *Book IV* (Cambridge: Cambridge University Press, 1998), 289; H. Parker, *Greek Gods in Italy in Ovid's* Fasti: *A Greater Greece* (Lewiston: The Edwin Mellen Press, 1997), 10; A. Barchiesi, *The Poet and the Prince: Ovid and Augustan Discourse* (Berkeley: University of California Press, 1997), 129.

   Ultimately, I find Beard's reading of the origin of the Parilia ('A Complex of Times', 6–7) most useful in interpreting Ovid's aetiological inconsistencies: 'The wide variety of different explanations offered by our ancient sources is an indication of the strongly evocative power of the festival itself: it had no single meaning; it constantly generated new and changing stories and interpretations'. The relevance of a festival, according to Beard, depended on its 'capacity to be constantly reinterpreted and re-understood'. Ovid freely engages in this process of reinterpreting aspects of religion in ways that are relevant to his own literary aims, even if this makes his myths idiosyncratic and distances them from the consensus of others.

4 Although Ovid is the first surviving source to conflate Dido's sister Anna to the Italian goddess Anna Perenna (see F. Bömer, *P. Ovidius Naso: Die Fasten* (Heidelberg: Carl Winter, 1958), 182), Littlewood ('Ovid and the Ides of March', 305) assumes that there is a pre-Ovidian source for Anna's adventures but admits that this source 'has yet to be discovered'. T.P. Wiseman, *The Myths of Rome* (Exeter: University of Exeter Press, 2004), 84 also assumes that Ovid's stories of Anna Perenna are drawn from earlier dramas. For an overview of Anna Perenna in the *Fasti*, see G. Brugnoli, 'Anna Perenna' in *Cultura, Poesia, Ideologia nell'Opera di Ovidio,* ed. I. Gallo and L. Nicastri (Salerno: Edizioni Scientifiche Italiane, 1991), 147–68; J. G. Frazer, *Publii Ovidii Nasonis Fastorum Libri Sex* (London: Macmillan and Co., 1929), s.v. 3.523–689; M. Kötzle, *Weibliche Gottheiten in Ovids 'Fasten'* (Frankfurt: Peter Lang, 1991), 65–72.

5 On constructions of gender within the *Fasti*, see P.M. Keegan, 'Seen, not Heard: *Feminea Lingua* in Ovid's *Fasti* and the Critical Gaze' in *Ovid's* Fasti: *Historical Readings at its Bimillennium*, ed. G. Herbert-Brown (Oxford: Oxford University Press, 2002), 129–53; Kötzle, *Weibliche Gottheiten in Ovids 'Fasten'*; M. Gamel, 'Reading as a Man: Performance and Gender in Roman Elegy', *Helios* 25, no. 1 (1998, pp. 79–95); R. King, *Desiring Rome: Male Subjectivity and Reading Ovid's* Fasti (Columbus: Ohio State University Press, 2006) (particularly Chapter 6, which discusses 'transvestism', that is, characters who do not conform to their given

gender). The construction of Anna's gender within the *Fasti* has been heavily influenced by contemporary epics that feature Aeneas, namely the *Aeneid* and the *Metamorphoses*. For more background on the construction of gender in Ovid's *Met.*, see A. Keith, 'Versions of Epic Masculinity in Ovid's *Metamorphoses*' in *Ovidian Transformations: Essays on the* Metamorphoses *and its Reception*, ed. P. Hardie, A. Barchiesi, and S. Hinds (Cambridge: Cambridge Philological Society, 1999), 214-39; P.B. Salzman-Mitchell, *A Web of Fantasies: Gaze, Image, and Gender in Ovid's* Metamorphoses (Columbus: Ohio State University Press, 2005); A. Sharrock, 'Gender and Sexuality' in *The Cambridge Companion to Ovid*, ed. P. Hardie (Cambridge: Cambridge University Press, 2002), 95-107. For more background on the construction of gender in Vergil's *Aen.*, see H. Lovatt, 'The Eloquence of Dido: Exploring Speech and Gender in Virgil's *Aeneid*', *Dictynna* 10 (2013); E. Oliensis, 'Sons and Lovers: Sexuality and Gender in Virgil's Poetry' in *The Cambridge Companion to Virgil*, ed. C. Martindale (Cambridge: Cambridge University Press, 1997), 294-311; C.G. Perkell, 'On Creusa, Dido, and the Quality of Victory in Virgil's *Aeneid*' in *Reflections of Women in Antiquity*, ed. H. P. Foley (New York: Gordon and Breach Science Publishers, 1981), 355-78; A. Keith, *Engendering Rome: Women in Latin Epic* (Cambridge: Cambridge University Press, 2000); and S.G. Nugent, 'The Women of the *Aeneid*: Vanishing Bodies, Lingering Voices' in *Reading Vergil's* Aeneid: *An Interpretive Guide*, ed. C. Perkell, (Norman: University of Oklahoma Press, 1999), 251-70. Keith, 'Versions of Epic Masculinity', and Lovatt, 'The Eloquence of Dido', are particularly relevant to the present paper, since they contain detailed analysis of what traits are associated with which characters and how that data affects the construction of a character's gender.

6   See Chapter 3 of Beek, 'Always Look on the Bright Side of Death'.
7   Likewise, when Anna meets Aeneas in the *Fasti*, her role will take on the potential for sexual drama, although Anna will stand clear of romantic attachment to Aeneas.
8   Nugent, 'The Women of the *Aeneid*', 260-1, and M. Desmond, *Reading Dido: Gender, Textuality, and the Medieval* Aeneid (Minneapolis: University of Minnesota Press, 1994), 30.
9   On Ovid's *Metamorphoses* as an unconventional epic, see E. Fantham, *Ovid's Metamorphoses* (Oxford: Oxford University Press, 2004), 3-20 and A. Keith, 'Sources and genres in Ovid's Metamorphoses 1-5' in *Companion to Ovid*, ed. B. Weiden Boyd (Leiden: Brill, 2002), 235-69. B. Otis, *Ovid as an Epic Poet*, 2nd ed (Cambridge: Cambridge University Press, 1970), effectively outlines the qualities that constitute epic and the place of Ovid's *Metamorphoses* within the genre, though Otis focuses more on what qualities define an epic narrative, rather than an epic hero. Some of the paramount characteristics he uses to separate epic from elegy are 'epic decorum' and 'narrative continuity', as opposed to the 'elegiac levity' and 'ellipsis' of elegy

(Otis, *Ovid as an Epic Poet*, 58). Otis characterizes the *Metamorphoses* as more exaggerated and grandiose than the *Aeneid*, which is used as a yardstick for the qualities of good epic.

10 M. McAuley, 'Matermorphoses: Motherhood and the Ovidian Epic Subject', *EuGeStA: Journal on Gender Studies* 2 (2012, pp. 123–68); C.E. Newlands, 'Ovid' in *A Companion to Ancient Epic*, ed. J.M. Foley (Oxford: Blackwell, 2005), 483–4.

11 Newlands, 'Ovid', 483.

12 For a detailed discussion of the generic classification of the *Fasti*, see R.W. Brewer, 'Epic vs. Elegiac Identity: A New Model for Roman Leadership in Ovid's *Fasti*' (PhD diss., University of Florida, Gainesville, 2012); S. Harrison, 'Ovid and Genre: Evolutions of an Elegist' in *The Cambridge Companion to Ovid*, ed. P. Hardie (Cambridge: Cambridge University Press, 2002), 79–94.

13 This is affirmed by Barchiesi, *The Poet and the Prince*, 21: '[The *Fasti*] gives some room to narrative themes suitable for epic poetry, and an excellent example of this is the long story of Anna (3.545–656), which has epic aspects both in its lengthy narration and, more important, because at first sight it appears to be a continuation, completion, and replica of the *Aeneid*'.

14 D. Porte, *L'Étiologie Religieuse dans les Fastes d'Ovide* (Paris: Société d'Édition 'Les Belles Lettres', 1985), 144–50. Anna's similarities to Aeneas are discussed by A. Chiu, *Ovid's Women of the Year: Narratives of Roman Identity in the* Fasti (Ann Arbor: University of Michigan Press, 2016), 72–9; Littlewood, 'Ovid and the Ides of March'; J.C. McKeown, 'Fabula Proposito Nulla Tegenda Meo: Ovid's *Fasti* and Augustan Politics' in *Poetry and Politics in the Age of Augustus*, ed. J. Woodman and D.A. West (Cambridge: Cambridge University Press, 1984), 169–87; Barchiesi, *The Poet and the Prince*, 21–3. For further discussion of the influence of the *Aeneid* on the *Fasti*, see P. Murgatroyd, *Mythical and Legendary Narrative in Ovid's* Fasti (Leiden: Brill, 2005), 97–140.

15 Chiu, *Ovid's Women of the Year*, 75 compiles a useful table of the similarities between Aeneas's and Anna's travels. Porte, *L'Étiologie Religieuse dans les Fastes d'Ovide,* 145 speaks of 'une *assimilation* complète entre Énée et Anna'.

16 Additionally, these events stem from a conflict well known from a previous epic: in the *Aeneid*, the destruction of Troy recalls the *Iliad*; in the *Fasti*, the destruction of Carthage leans on the *Aeneid*. Although Anna's adventures in the *Fasti* are generally presented as the journey of a single individual (for example, her arrivals and departures are usually communicated with singular verbs ('*linquit*' 3.559, '*petit*' 3.569, '*fugit*' 3.579), and she is the only person addressed by characters such as Battus, Achates, and Aeneas), Anna is certainly not alone in her travels: she departs accompanied by '*comites*' (3.565), and during the storm an unnamed '*navita*' gives an order in the plural (3.586). Some Tyrians may have dispersed after Iarbas's attack '*ut olim amisso dubiae rege vagantur apes*' (3.555–6), but, like Aeneas, Anna still has refugees to lead in forming a new city.

17 There is a strong similarity between Anna Perenna's wanderings at sea and those of Aeneas, as noted by Littlewood, 'Ovid and the Ides of March', 306.
18 Ov. *Met.* 14.598–608. Despite the variant names, Numicus and Numicius are the same river, generally agreed to be the Rio Torto near Lavinium (modern Pratica di Mare), on which see Frazer, *Publii Ovidii Nasonis Fastorum Libri Sex,* s.v. 3.647. Interestingly, Dionysius of Halicarnassus (1.64.4–5) provides two alternative traditions of Aeneas's fate: either he fell in battle near Lavinium, or he drowned in the Numicius. Ovid presents only a single version. The mystic double tradition resembles the double tradition of Romulus's fate, well known from Livy (1.16.3–5) although its double nature is denied by Ovid in the *Fasti* (2.497–8). Near the site of ancient Lavinium and the ancient course of the Numicius is a *heroon* dedicated to Aeneas, adjacent to the archaic Altars of the Latin League, dated to the seventh century by T.J. Cornell, *The Beginnings of Rome: Italy and Rome from the Bronze Age to the Punic Wars (c. 1000–264 BC)* (London: Routledge, 1995), 68. A. Alföldi, *Early Rome and the Latins* (Ann Arbor: University of Michigan Press, 1965), 250–4 discusses this site's importance in the cult of Aeneas and Aeneas's unique nature among divinities.
19 As I have discussed in Beek, 'Always Look on the Bright Side of Death', 13–20, Ovid narrates so many and so varied apotheoses in the *Metamorphoses* and the *Fasti* that it is difficult to make generalizations about them. For example, the apotheoses of minor characters such as Glaucus or Acis are frequently overlooked alongside those of Aeneas and Romulus. All the same, there are unquestionably more male than female characters apotheosed in the *Metamorphoses*, and those males are more often a hero famous for heroic exploits, such as Hercules, rather than a forgettable erotic hero, such as Acis.
20 All quotations from Virgil come from Mynors's OCT edition.
21 McKeown, 'Ovid's *Fasti* and Augustan Politics', 170–1; cf. Chiu, *Ovid's Women of the Year*, 72: '[Anna] becomes an analogue of both Dido and Aeneas'.
22 The analogy of Dido as Cleopatra is well established; see e.g. J.M. Benario, 'Dido and Cleopatra', *Vergilius*, 16 (1970, pp. 2–6); Desmond, *Reading Dido*, 31–3; A. Parry, 'The Two Voices of Virgil's *Aeneid*', *Arion,* 2, no. 4 (1963, pp. 66–80), 73–4.
23 In the *Aeneid*, Anna foresees this disaster when Dido commits suicide (*A.* 4.682–3).
24 Chiu, *Ovid's Women of the Year*, 74.
25 For a discussion of Aeneas's epic masculinity, particularly how it contrasts with the precedent established by Odysseus, see e.g. B. Otis, *Virgil: A Study in Civilized Poetry* (Oxford: Oxford University Press, 1964), 306–7, 312–13; G. K. Galinsky, 'The Anger of Aeneas', *AJP* 109 (1988, pp. 321–48); T. van Nortwick, 'Woman Warrior? Aeneas' Encounters with the Feminine' in *Roman Literature, Gender and Reception: Domina Illustris*, ed. D. Lateiner, B.K. Gold, and J. Perkins (New York: Routledge, 2013), 136–52.

26 Virg. *A.* 2.594–620, 776–84.
27 Littlewood, 'Ovid and the Ides of March', 306 and 314 briefly remarks on this connection. There is also a connection to Aeneas's nocturnal departure from Carthage, and Mercury's warning (Virg. *A.* 4.554–70); note the mirroring of Aeneas's flight from Anna's home versus Anna's flight from Aeneas's home. At Virg. *A.* 1.353–9, Dido receives a similar warning from the ghost of Sychaeus to flee from Tyre, which once again highlights Dido's role as a doublet of Aeneas and narrative model for Anna.
28 All quotations of the *Fasti* are from the Teubner edition by Alton, Wormell, and Courtney.
29 On the potential rape of Anna Perenna, see below.
30 The similarity to Caesar's story is marked since the narrative of Caesar's apotheosis immediately follows Ovid's discussion of Anna Perenna: *Fast.* 3.697–710.
31 All quotations from the *Met.* are from Tarrant's OCT edition.
32 Ov. *Fast.* 3.619: 'ne refer'.
33 E.g. Brugnoli, 'Anna Perenna', 148.
34 See Chapter 3 of Beek, 'Always Look on the Bright Side of Death'.
35 J. Heath, 'Diana's Understanding of Ovid's *Metamorphoses*', *CJ* 86, no. 3 (1991, pp. 233–43).

6 Instability and Permanence in Ceremonial Epigraphy: the Example of Anna Perenna

1 For the excavations and the site, see for example M. Piranomonte (ed.), *Il santuario della musica e il bosco sacro di Anna Perenna* (Roma: Electa, 2002). The inscriptions have been published by R. Friggeri, 'Le iscrizioni' in *Il Santuario della musica e il bosco sacro di Anna Perenna*, ed. M. Piranomonte (Roma: Electa, 2002), 26–33; *AE* 2003: 215–53; with English translation, by T.P. Wiseman, 'The cult site of Anna Perenna: documentation, visualization, imagination' in *Imaging Ancient Rome: Documentation, Visualization, Imagination*, ed. L. Haselberger and J. Humphrey, *Journal of Roman Archaeology* Suppl. 61 (2006), 51–62.
2 Apart from Rome, there are some further epigraphic evidence: a short inscription on a limestone altar mentioning Anna Perenna was found in Feltre in 1922, and an inscription in Greek found in Buscemi, Sicily may refer to Anna. M. Piranomonte, 'Religion and Magic at Rome: The Fountain of Anna Perenna' in *Magical Practice in the Latin West: Papers from the international conference held at the University of Zaragoza*, ed. R.L. Gordon and F.M. Simón, (Leiden: Brill 2010), 195.
3 Friggeri, 'Le iscrizioni'.

4 Friggeri, 'Le iscrizioni', 26; Piranomonte, 'Religion and Magic at Rome', 199; J. Blänsdorf, 'The Texts from the Fons Annae Perennae' in *Magical Practice in the Latin West: Papers from the international conference held at the University of Zaragoza* (2005), ed. R.L. Gordon & F.M. Simón (Leiden: Brill, 2010), 215–44; J. Blänsdorf, 'Gods and Demons in Texts: Figures and Symbols of the Defixion Inscriptions in the Nymphaeum of Anna Perenna at Rome' in *Ancient Magic and the Supernatural in the Modern Visual and Performing Arts*, ed. F. Carlá and I. Berti (London and New York: Bloomsbury Academic 2015), 20.

5 Friggeri, 'Le iscrizioni'; Wiseman, 'The Cult Site of Anna Perenna', 51. Rosanna Friggeri has observed that the inscription refers to the monument as an altar, when it in fact is a votive base. Friggeri, 'Le iscrizioni', 28.

6 Friggeri, 'Le iscrizioni'; Wiseman, 'The Cult Site of Anna Perenna', 53.

7 Friggeri, 'Le iscrizioni'; Wiseman, 'The Cult Site of Anna Perenna', 51.

8 Anna's connection with nymphs as highlighted in these inscriptions is discussed by G. McIntyre (Chapter 3) in this volume.

9 Friggeri, 'Le iscrizioni', 31, has discussed whether the two Germanus inscriptions concern the same votive offering, or if they describe one votive offering and one offering of an altar once the victory was granted. However, as shown in my overview of votive inscriptions, epigraphic monuments like these must have been produced only when the vow had been granted.

10 Ton Derks has performed a thorough study of the votive process and votive inscriptions, both in general and as an in-depth study of Northern Roman Gaul. T. Derks, *Gods, Temples and Ritual Practices. The transformation of religious ideas and values in Roman Gaul* (Amsterdam: Amsterdam University Press, 1998), 234–8; R. Haensch, 'Inscriptions as Sources of Knowledge for Religions and Cults in the Roman World of Imperial Times' in *A Companion to Roman Religion*, ed. J. Rüpke (Chichester: Wiley-Blackwell, 2011), 183–5.

11 N. Belayche, 'Religious Actors in Daily Life: Practices and Related Beliefs' in *A Companion to Roman Religion*, ed. J. Rüpke (Chichester: Wiley-Blackwell, 2011), 281–4; Haensch, 'Inscriptions as Sources', 180–3; A.E. Cooley, *The Cambridge Manual of Latin Epigraphy* (Cambridge: Cambridge University Press, 2012), 67–8.

12 M. Beard, 'Ancient Literacy and the Function of the Written Word in Roman Religion' in *Literacy in the Roman World*, ed. J.H. Humphrey (Ann Arbor: University of Michigan, 1991), 35–58; Derks, *Gods, Temples and Ritual Practices*, 215–39; Haensch, 'Inscriptions as Sources', 183; Belayche, 'Religious Actors in Daily Life', 283; Cooley, *The Cambridge Manual of Latin Epigraphy*, 67–8, 182–3.

13 Haensch, 'Inscriptions as Sources', 176.

14 *CIL* I² 1, 242: *Feriae Annae Perennae (in) via Flam(inia) ad lapidem prim(um)*. The festival of Anna Perenna on via Flaminia at the first milestone. The *Fasti Vaticani* date to the early first century CE. See for example U. Egelhaaf-Gaiser, 'Jahresfest am

Tiberufer: Anna Perenna und die "Topographie der Zeit" in Ovids *Fasten*' in *Kommunikationsräume im kaiserzeitlichen Rom*, ed. F. Mundt (Berlin and Boston: de Gruyter, 2012), 205.
15 Ov. *Fast*. 3.523–4: Mart. 4.64.16–17.
16 Friggeri observed that the date of one of the inscriptions, April 5, does not align with the date of the festival of Anna Perenna on March 15, but concluded that the continuous references to victories still indicate a connection with the cult of Anna Perenna. Friggeri, 'Le iscrizioni', 31. Ov. *Fast*. 3.525–42.
17 Piranomonte, 'Religion and Magic at Rome', 199; Wiseman, 'The Cult Site of Anna Perenna'.
18 Wiseman, 'The Cult Site of Anna Perenna', 55–9.
19 F. Buecheler, *Carmina Latina Epigraphica* I (Leipzig: B.G. Teubner, 1895); Christer Bruun and Jonathan Edmondson, *The Oxford Handbook of Roman Epigraphy* (Oxford: Oxford University Press, 2014), 167; 770.
20 Friggeri, 'Le iscrizioni'.
21 U. Egelhaaf-Gaiser states this as a fact in her chapter 'Roman cult sites – a pragmatic approach' in *A Companion to Roman Religion*, ed. J. Rüpke (Chichester: Wiley-Blackwell, 2011), 212–15, and Blänsdorf reports that the inscriptions 'tell that in the early Empire competitions of an unknown genre took place during the festival,' Blänsdorf, 'Gods and Demons', 19–20.
22 R. MacMullen, 'The Epigraphic Habit in the Roman Empire', *AJP* 103, No. 3 (1982, pp. 233–6); E. Meyer, 'Explaining the Epigraphic Habit in the Roman Empire: the Evidence of Epitaphs', *JRS* 80 (1990, pp. 74–96); G. Woolf, 'Monumental Writing and the Expansion of Roman Society in the Early Empire', *JRS* 86 (1996, pp. 22–39).
23 See for example Cooley, *The Cambridge Manual of Latin Epigraphy*, 117.
24 *CIL* VI.1033. The phrase *et Publio Septimio Lucii filio Getae nobilissimo Caesari* (and to Publius Septimius Geta, son of Lucius, the most noble emperor) was erased and substituted with *patri patriae optimis fortissimisque prinicipibus* (to the father of the fatherland, to the best and strongest princes). Traces of the old text remain visible on the stone.
25 For an overview of medieval Latin epigraphy, see for example R. Favreau, *Épigraphie Médiévale* (*L'Atelier du Médiéviste* 5) (Turnhout: Brepols, 1997).
26 Blänsdorf, 'The Texts from the Fons Annae Perennae', inv. nos. 475722 and 475567, 219–27.
27 Derks, *Gods, Temples and Ritual Practices*, 155–6.
28 Friggeri, 'Le iscrizioni'; Wiseman, 'The Cult Site of Anna Perenna', 55–9.
29 The Arval inscriptions has been edited and studied in detail above all by Scheid: J. Scheid, ed., *Commentarii Fratrum Arvalium qui supersunt* (Rome: École Française de Rome and Soprintendenza Archeologica di Roma, 1998); J. Scheid, 'Hierarchy and Structure in Roman Polytheism: Roman Methods of Conceiving Action' in *Roman*

Religion, ed. C. Ando (Edinburgh: Edinburgh University Press, 2003), 164–89. The inscriptions are arranged on display in the *Museo delle Terme* in Rome: C. Caruso, 'I rendiconti degli arvali: le iscrizioni e l'allestimento' in *Terme di Diocleziano. Il chiostro piccolo della Certosa di Santa Maria degli Angeli*, eds. R. Friggeri, M. Magnani Cianetti, C. Caruso (Milano: Electa/Mondadori, 2014), 61–5; J. Scheid, 'Gli Arvali e il sito ad Deam Diam' in *Terme di Diocleziano. Il chiostro piccolo della Certosa di Santa Maria degli Angeli*, eds. R. Friggeri, M. Magnani Cianetti, C. Caruso (Milano: Electa/Mondadori, 2014), 49–59.

30 Egelhaaf-Gaiser, 'Roman cult sites', 212–14. The detailed descriptions of the vows in the inscriptions has enabled the thorough reconstruction of the entire vow process performed by Derks, *Gods, Temples and Ritual Practices*, 217–20.
31 Scheid, 'Gli Arvali'.
32 M. Beard, 'Writing and Ritual: a Study of Diversity and Expansion in the *Arval Acta*', PBSR 53 (1985, pp. 114–62).
33 The *tabellae defixionum* in the sanctuary of Anna Perenna has previously been studied by J. Blänsdorf, see Blänsdorf, 'The Texts from the Fons Annae Perennae', and Blänsdorf, 'Gods and Demons'.
34 Cooley, *The Cambridge Manual of Latin Epigraphy*, 179; Blänsdorf, 'The Texts from the Fons Annae Perennae', 221–7; Blänsdorf, 'Gods and Demons', 20–2.

7 Ovid's Anna Perenna and the Coin of Gaius Annius

* I wish to thank many for their help and encouragement in writing this piece, while pointing out that any errors or deficiencies are my own. Gilles Bransbourg, Curator of Roman Coins at the American Numismatic Society, was very helpful in offering his expertise and answering my many questions. I also wish to thank Christine Kondoleon, Curator of Roman Art at the Massachusetts Fine Arts Museum, and her colleagues for answering my questions about the coin of Gaius Annius in the MFA collection. The editors of this volume provided much aid and advice, and Sarah McCallum's excellent and substantive suggestions shaped the final version of this paper. Peter Wiseman's expertise aided this paper greatly as well. I am grateful also to colleagues whose suggestions aided the production of this paper: Sinclair Bell, John Berneche, Laetitia La Follette, Eleanor Leach, Geoff Sumi and Ted Zarrow. Caitlin Eddings provided helpful aid as a research assistant. I am solely responsible for any remaining deficiencies in the paper. The text quoted from the *Fasti* comes from E. Alton, D. Wormell and E. Courtney, eds. *P. Ovidi Nasonis Fastorum Libri Sex* (Munich: Saur, 1997). My translations of Ovid are my own, though occasionally owe some aspects to J. Frazer and G. Goold, eds. *Ovid*: Fasti, 2nd edn (Cambridge, MA: Harvard University Press, 1996).

1 See notably M. Crawford, *Roman Republican Coinage, vols 1–2* (London: Cambridge University Press, 1974), vol. 1, 386.
2 See Wiseman's introduction in this volume for a summary of the literary representations of Anna Perenna.
3 Ov. *Fast.* 3.663–74. Livy (2.32–3) narrates the events of the secession, but with no mention of an old woman bringing food. See A. Chiu, *Ovid's Women of the Year: Narratives of Roman Identity in the* Fasti (Ann Arbor: University of Michigan Press, 2016), 23–8, on the counterpoint between Ovid's story and Livy's narrative where the hero of the secession is the plebeian Menenius Agrippa. Chiu, 26, notes also the appearance of cakes (*liba*) in association with old women and Bacchus, *Fast.* 3.761–70.
4 See M. Maas, *John Lydus and the Roman Past: Antiquarianism and Politics in the Age of Justinian* (London and New York: Routledge Press, 1992), 62–4, on these documents and their value to Lydus's research. Lydus is our only source for other recognized events as well, as noted in D. Fishwick, 'The *Cannophori* and the March Festival of Magna Mater', *TAPA* 97 (1966, pp. 193–202): 194, regarding the March *dendrophoria*. Macrobius, only a century closer to Ovid's story, provides the phrase that many scholars have used to explain the function and name of Anna Perenna: one prays to her, *ut annare perannareque commode liceat* (Macr. 1.12.6). G. Wissowa, *Religion und Kultus der Römer* (Munich: Beck, [1902] 1971), 240, refers to Macrobius in his work, but see D. Porte, 'Anna Perenna, Bonne et heureuse année!', *RPh* 45 (1971, pp. 282–91) for a fuller development of this etymology.
5 By contrast, see Newlands (Chapter 8) in this volume for the suggestion that Ovid made Anna mortal to 'insert Anna Perenna into the new ideology of deification'. Wiseman (Introduction) considers the story of Anna Bovillae in keeping with the legacy of the secession and its import to a majority of Rome's population, and may have been a source of theatrical treatment for decades, as Laberius's mime tantalizingly suggests.
6 Ovid, similarly in the case of Pales, offers a number of sources for the ritual to honour the god and validates the last one he mentions: one situated in the legend of Rome's early history (Ov. *Fast.* 4.801–6). Chiu, *Ovid's Women of the Year*, 28, proposes that the many explanations for Anna suggest 'the numerous perspectives that are always in play and that any kind of group identity is flexible to some degree'.
7 So far as we know, there are no extant busts, statues, mosaics, or wall paintings depicting Anna Perenna, despite Ovid's claim that the plebs built a statue to honour her. See G. McIntyre's piece in this collection regarding the possibility that depictions of Anna Perenna do in fact exist, but are mistakenly identified due to a lack of precisely identifiable iconography.
8 See G. McIntyre (Chapter 3) in this volume on the possible representation of Anna Perenna as the central seated figure on the Ara Pacis often associated with Tellus or Pax, thus suggesting a familiarity with her sculpted representation at Rome.

9   On the mime and its fragments, see C. Panayotakis, *Decimus Laberius: The Fragments* (Cambridge: Cambridge University Press, 2010), 115–19; see also T.P. Wiseman, *Roman Drama and Roman History* (Exeter: University of Exeter Press, 1998), 72–3. See the chapters in this volume by McIntyre (Chapter 3) and Wright (Chapter 4) on the associations between Anna Perenna and water as established by the Augustan-period fountain discovered in 1999. I could find no watery associations with Anna Perenna on the coin in question, and could find little evidence of depictions of nymphs on any Roman republican coin, though nymphs on Greek coins abound.

10 E. Alton, 'Anna Perenna and Mamurius Veturius', *Hermathena* 19 (1920, pp. 100–4): 101: 'Ovid is describing her *festa*: when, therefore he mentions a pompa, he means not **a** *pompa*, but **the** *pompa*, the procession of Anna Perenna'. We know of an event called the Mamuralia in March, but only from John Lydus, who speaks of Mamurius dressed in a goatskin being beaten with rods (*De mens.* 4.49). Alton also sees correspondence between this act of driving out Mamurius and the Salian ritual on the Kalends of March during which Mamurius was celebrated in song (102): 'the flouting of the Old Man is one of those mimetic actions which are not uncommon in Roman rites'. G. Dumézil, *Déesses latines et mythes védiques* (1956; repr., New York: Arno Press, 1978), 30–1, was the first to tie the Salian ritual to the ushering out of the old year. We know from Ovid (*Fast.* 3.259–392) and Livy (1.20) that the Salii celebrated a new year ritual on the Kalends of March, and that they included the shield-maker Mamurius Veturius in their song. To complicate things further, Varro (*L.* 6.49) depicts the name Mamurius as tied to the word for *memory* in Latin, making the calling of his name by the Salii an invocation to ancient memory.

11 Ov. *Fast.* 3.525–6: *plebs venit ac virides passim disiecta per herbas / potat, et accumbit cum pare quisque sua* ('the plebeians gather and drink, scattered here and there on the green grass, and each lies beside his companion'). See Wiseman, *Roman Drama*, 68–71, on the intriguing implications that arise from a festival where couples lie together under tents made from togas and theatrical songs are sung. On such a setting having a philosophical character, see Cic. *de Orat.* 1.7.28.

12 See C. Newlands, 'Transgressive Acts: Ovid's Treatment of the Ides of March', *CP* 91 (1996, pp. 320–38): 332, for an interpretation of the treatment of Anna Perenna and the Ides of March as carnivalesque, working in counterpoint to Augustan authority over the day and its meaning.

13 See Newlands (Chapter 8) in this volume for more on the 'collision of social and cultural values on the Ides of March' intrinsic to Anna's festival.

14 G. Herbert-Brown, '*Fasti*: the poet, the prince, and the plebs', in *A Companion to Ovid*, ed. P. Knox (Chichester and Malden: Wiley-Blackwell, 2013), 133–4, demonstrates the significant role of plebeian goddesses in Ovid's *Fasti*, with Flora, Anna Perenna and Vesta receiving emphasis in the six months of narrative we possess: 'Anna Perenna

and Flora are defenders of the plebs against the senate. Their festivals are occasions of institutionalized license for the common people. Both share a date with Vesta and her new Julian gods'. On Flora's festival see also T.P. Wiseman, *The Myths of Rome* (Exeter: University of Exeter, 2004), 6–9. Our ancient sources on Flora are Ovid (*Fast.* 4.945–6 and 5.312–30), Valerius Maximus (2.10.8), and Martial (*Spect.* 1. pref. 8).

15 Chiu, *Women of the Year*, 28.

16 The coin's variations, and all coins referred to later in this paper, are available for viewing online at the website of the Roman Republican Coinage at the British Museum: www.britishmuseum.org/research/publications/online_research_catalogues/rrc/roman_republican_coins/roman_republican_coinage.aspx. The reference numbers provided, '*RRC* . . .' will render them all. To see all the variants of the Annian coin at the British Museum, search for *RRC* 366/1, *RRC* 366/1a, *RRC* 366/1b and *RRC* 366/1c. Keywords, like Annius, will also yield helpful results.

17 C. Cavedoni, *Ragguaglio storico archeologico de'precipui ripostigli antichi di medaglie consolari* (Modena: Eredi Soliani, 1854), 51. The following also identify the woman as Anna Perenna: A. Hands, 'Chats on Roman Coins with Young Collectors', *Numismatic Circular* 4 (1896, pp. 1808–94): 1808–9; H. Grueber, *Coins of the Roman Republic in the British Museum* (London: British Museum, 1910), 353; E.A. Sydenham, *The Coinage of the Roman Republic* (London: Spink, 1952), 121–2; E. Babelon, *Description historique et chronologique des Monnaies de la Republique romaine* (Paris: Rollin et Feuardent, 1963), 138–9; and H. Zehnacker, *Moneta: recherches sur l'organisation et l'art des émissions monétaires de la République romaine (289–31 av. J.-C.)* (Rome: École française de Rome, 1973), 491.

18 S. Stevenson, *Dictionary of Roman Coins, Republican and Imperial* (London: Seaby, 1964), 48–9, states that she is Juno Moneta or Aequitas; Crawford, *Roman Republican Coinage*, vol. 1, 386, states that 'the identity of the deity who forms the obverse type is entirely uncertain'.

19 See, for example, the obverse of the denarius of L. Rubrius Dossenus, *RRC* 348/2, from 87 BCE.

20 For the sceptre consisting of dots, see reverse of the 135 BCE coin by C. Curiatius, *RRC* 240/1b, and for Juno holding a spear, see *RRC* 379/1, by L. Procilius dating to 80 BCE.

21 See, for example the coin of L. Plaetorius (Cestianus), *RRC* 396/1a, from 74 BCE.

22 See Hands, 'Chats on Roman Coins with Young Collectors', 1891–4, for a lengthy discussion on the appearance of personified virtues on Roman coins.

23 See, for example, the goddess Concordia on *RRC* 415/1, 417/1a and 417/1b, all dating to 62 BCE; and Fides on *RRC* 454/1 and 454/2, dating to 47 BCE.

24 J. Williams, 'Religion and Roman Coins' in *A Companion to Roman Religion*, ed. J. Rüpke (Chichester: Wiley-Blackwell, 2011), 144, interprets this 'an aspect of a wider

trend toward the monumentalization of various aspects of Roman public life ... in reaction to a changing social and political environment'. See also A. Kuttner, 'Roman Art During the Republic' in *The Cambridge Companion to the Roman Republic*, ed. H. Flower (Cambridge and New York: Cambridge University Press, 2004), 316: 'much studied are the ways in which moneyers used coin images to look after others' *monumenta* as well as their own achievements, trying to make people remember their own famous ancestors ...'. Note also the paronomasia in Silius Italicus that, according to J. McIntyre (Chapter 2), 'embeds Anna within the very battle of CANNAe itself'.

25 Appian (*BC* 4.42) relates the event; on the coin of Pius, see also Grueber, *Coins of the Roman Republic in the British Museum*, v.1, 155 & v. 2, 357 and C. Konrad, *Plutarch's* Sertorius: *A Historical Commentary* (Chapel Hill: University of North Carolina, 1994), 133. The reverse of Metellus's coin features an elephant, a symbol adopted by the *gens* Caecilia after the victory of L. Caecilius Metellus over the Carthaginians at Panormus in Sicily around 250 BCE. According to Polybius (1.40) Caecilius captured many of Hasdrubal's war elephants, and hence the symbol on the coinage.

26 See the 129 BCE the coin of Sextus Julius (*RRC* 258/1) who depicts Venus *in biga* on the reverse of an image of Roma. Lucius Julius Caesar in 103 BCE (*RRC* 320/1) depicts the helmeted head of Mars on the obverse and Venus in *biga* with Cupids in harness on reverse. The association comes to full bloom in the age of Caesar's dictatorship with coin *RRC* 458/1 depicting Venus on the obverse and Aeneas carrying Anchises on the reverse in 47 BCE. Interestingly, in the Republican period there are no known coins minted by the Caesarian clan that depict Iulus or, as he is also known, Ascanius.

27 *RRC* 290/1; Sydenham, *The Coinage of the Roman Republic*, 74, identifies the duo as Fons or Fontus; see also G. Heath, 'The Coins of Republican Rome', *The Numismatist* 12 (1899, pp. 159–63, 234–9): 234. Arnobius (*Adv. Nat.* 3.29) tells us that Janus was the father of Fons. Crawford, *RRC,* v.1, 305, identifies the duo as the Dioscuri, corresponding to the jugate heads of the Dioscuri on the coins of Mn. Fonteius that appeared six years later (*RRC* 307/1a): 'both moneyers came from the *gens* Fonteia and therefore from Tusculum, the chief cult-centre of the Dioscuri in Latium'. Despite being only six years apart, however, the portraits are very different, one being janiform, the other showing a jugate portrait of the twins with a star over each of their heads. The janiform Dioscuri had been used on prior coins, but not for nearly 100 years: see *RRC* 30/1 and 42/1.

28 *RRC* 363/1; Wiseman, *The Myths of Rome*, 68–9, points out that the Marcii, a plebeian clan, regarded themselves famous for their seers, citing Serv. Dan. *ad Aen.* 3.359.

29 Wiseman, *The Myths of Rome*, 68, offers a brief discussion on the *libertas* that Marsyas represented after the *plebiscita* of the fourth century BCE that gave one of

the annual consulships to the plebs and outlawed the enslavement of free citizens for debt. Marcius's coin may therefore suggest an affinity for the plebeian cause, which would make sense given the fact that he was the brother of Gaius Censorinus who died in battle against Sulla at the battle of the Colline gate. Crawford, *Roman Republican Coinage,* v.1, 378, denies that there would be any association of the Marcian coin with populist causes. Though Crawford does not go into detail on this statement, to make a claim that no one would dare declare plebeian associations in the atmosphere of a Sullan victory over-simplifies the nature of plebeian partisanship at Rome throughout its history.

30 *RRC* 455/2a; see Apollod. 2.7.8 for this story. There are other families who might have exploited onomastic similarities to divinities, but did not, such as the Plautius Silvani who never depict the god Silvanus on their coinage; I thank Prof. Bransbourg of the ANS for pointing this out to me.

31 The possibility that Annius is associating his name with the goddess of the grain-dole Annona rather than Anna Perenna is highly unlikely since her first certain appearance on a coin dates to the Neronian age, 64–68 CE, when, according to C. Sutherland and R. Carson, *The Roman Imperial Coinage from 31 BC to AD 69, vol. 1* (London: Spink, 1984), 139, Nero had an interest 'to ensure the loyalty of the praetorians and the adequacy of the corn-supply'. On that coin Annona's name clearly appears to identify her as she appears along with Ceres. Visit the site of the ANS, Online Coins of the Roman Empire (http://numismatics.org/ocre/), and enter into the search engine 'ric.1(2).ner.98' to view this coin.

32 *RRC* 258/1 and *RRC* 320/1.

33 See H. Flower, 'Were Women Ever "Ancestors" in Republican Rome?', in *Images of Ancestors*, ed. J. Højte (Aarhus: Aarhus University Press, 2002), 167ff., on the rise of female ancestries in the first century BCE.

34 *RRC* 419/3b; see Sydenham, *The Coinage of the Roman Republic*, 137, for the identification of this veiled woman as the vestal, Aemilia.

35 *RRC* 494/1.

36 Flower, 'Were Women Ever "Ancestors" in Republican Rome?', 169, notes that the triumviral period marks the appearance of the first living Roman woman on a coin, Fulvia, wife of Antony.

37 See these coins for other examples of the carnyx used to denote Roman victory: *RRC* 281/1, 282/1, 326/2, 332/1 and 333/1.

38 I thank Sarah McCallum for her aid in this interpretation.

39 On the caduceus as symbol of peace, see Plin. *Nat.* 29.12, and Gel. 10.27.3; I am grateful to Peter Wiseman for these references.

40 See the coin of Sulla and his quaestor Manlius Torquatus, *RRC* 367/3.

41 *E.g. RIC* 1(2).Galba.121 with Aequitas on reverse holding scales; note that her name is inscribed to identify her.

42 The statue may have carried a caduceus, a scepter often associated with Asclepius the god of good health, a significant factor in any new beginning. N. Belayche, 'Religious Actors in Daily Life: Practices and Related Beliefs' in *A Companion to Roman Religion*, ed. J. Rüpke (Chichester: Wiley-Blackwell, 2011), 281, points out that 'on every January *calends*, *Salus publica* received a vow in terms of caution and anticipation for the year', demonstrating the association Romans made between physical wellbeing and the new year. The caduceus may also be evidence of another possible conflation of the powers of Isis and Asclepius with Anna Perenna (whom Ovid also associates with Io /Isis in *Fast.* 3.658: *Inachiam pars putat esse bovem*, 'some believe she is the bovine Io'), based on the observation by John Lydus (*De mens.* 4.45) that on the fourth day of March, Anna's feast-month, the Romans celebrated the sailing of Isis, an event called the 'Ploiaphesia' or 'ship-launching'. Lydus adds that Isis refers to the waning moon, and that she receives honours from those embarking out to sea, and that she grants good health, as Asclepius does.

43 On the statue of Marsyas, see L. Richardson, *A New Topographical Dictionary of Ancient Rome* (Baltimore: Johns Hopkins University Press, 1992), 371, and M. Torelli, *Typology and Structure of Roman Historical Reliefs* (Ann Arbor: University of Michigan Press, 1982), 98–106.

44 Plu. *TG.* 14.4–6; that Annius Luscus was an enemy of Tiberius Gracchus, a *tribunus plebis*, may raise questions as to Annian loyalty to the plebs, but it should be noted that Luscus disliked Gracchus in part for the disdainful way he treated Marcus Octavius, his colleague in the tribunate; see also Liv. *Epit.* 58.

45 Livy reports (8.3–6) that in response to Annius's demands, the Roman consul Titus Manlius turned to the statue of Jupiter within the temple and expressed his dismay at the disrespect being offered to Rome. Annius then reportedly muttered a rejection of Jupiter's godhead. Shortly afterward, as Annius stormed out of the meeting, he tripped and fell down the Capitol steps, striking his head so hard on the bottom step that he passed out or died – Livy isn't sure which.

46 Sal. *Jug.* 77; I thank Geoff Sumi for this reference.

47 See P. Spann, *Quintus Sertorius and the Legacy of Sulla* (Fayetteville: University of Arkansas Press, 1987), 38–9, on the political snub Carbo, Scipio and Marius delivered to Sertorius, due likely to his low birth. Plutarch mentions this fact (*Sert.* 25.2) within the context of the events of 72 BCE that led to his assassination at the hands of Marcus Perpenna Vento who resented his subservience to a man well beneath him in birth and rank.

48 See Konrad, *Plutarch's* Sertorius, 74, on the likelihood that he had served as praetor before 83 BCE, and had prorogued his proconsular position for the purposes of remaining in Italy to engage in the skirmishes between the Sullan and Marian factions.

49 According to Plutarch, *Sert.* 6.3, even as Sertorius made his way into Spain over the mountains, he paid a rather exorbitant sum to the Cerratani, who demanded

payment for passage, against the advisement of his Roman lieutenants who preferred to engage in battle.

50 Konrad, *Plutarch's* Sertorius, 99, asserts that Sertorius would have heard of that fact by early 81.

51 This decision is predictive of his later legislation on *maiestas* that ensured orderly succession in the provinces, a cornerstone of his policies to shore up the new political order he was establishing. See H. Flower, *Roman Republics* (Princeton: Princeton University Press, 2010), 128–9, on Sulla's policy.

52 Konrad, *Plutarch's* Sertorius, 101, offers this reasonable conjecture on the number of legions.

53 See Konrad, *Plutarch's* Sertorius, 100, on the identity of Calpurnius, and note a possible reference to him in Cicero, *Off.* 3.66, regarding a real estate purchase.

54 Konrad, *Plutarch's* Sertorius, 101, discusses the greater likelihood that Calpurnius was a turncoat soldier of Salinator than that he was Annius's man who strategically drew Salinator and his troops into some sort of fatal ambush.

55 See App. *Mith.* 59–60.

56 Sal. *Hist.* 3.48M; Geoff Sumi made me aware of this. On the unmistakability of Macer's authentic voice in Sallust's history, see T.P. Wiseman, *Remembering the Roman People: Essays on Late-Republican Politics and Literature* (Oxford: Oxford University Press, 2009), 20–1.

57 See S. Chrissanthos, 'Freedom of Speech and the Roman Republican Army', in *Free Speech in Classical Antiquity*, eds. I. Sluiter and R. Rosen (Leiden: Brill, 2004), 349–67, for many examples of the ways the *contio* contributed to communication in military affairs.

58 See Liv. *Epit.* 75, and Plutarch, *Sull.* 6; Chrissanthos, 'Freedom of Speech and the Roman Republican Army', 349–50, explains the circumstances.

59 See G. Watson, 'The Pay of the Roman Army: The Republic', *Historia: Zeitschrift für Alte Geschichte* 7 (1958: pp. 113–20), and R. Alston, 'Roman Military Pay from Caesar to Diocletian', *JRS* 84 (1994: pp. 113–23), on the significance of the denarius in Roman pay and the dispersal of the *stipendium*.

60 See Wiseman (Introduction) in this volume for the possibility that Julius Caesar as *pontifex maximus* made *Anna ac Peranna* an anthropomorphic divinity; if so, it may have been the coin of Annius minted two decades earlier that prompted Caesar's idea of using Anna as a deity to serve his own *popularis* purposes.

61 Of Gaius Annius's governorship in Hispania we know only what Plutarch tells us. He drove Sertorius initially out of Spain to Africa, though Sertorius returned to the Pityussian islands in the summer of 81 and, with the help of Cilician pirates, drove out a garrison placed there by Annius. It was likely this rout that prompted Sulla to

send another governor, Lucius Fufidius, to straighten things out. It is presumable that Annius engaged in some of the unfair practices of prior Roman governors, for in late 81 BCE when Sulla ordered Fufidius to Spain, the Lusitanians, with the support of other Spanish tribes, invited Sertorius to return to Spain and, as head of their army, ward off the new Roman successor. Plutarch (*Sert.* 10.1) states that they did so on account of their fear of the Romans. What the Lusitani feared exactly is not stated explicitly, but see Konrad, *Plutarch's* Sertorius, 116–17, on the possibility that Fufidius was planning a punitive expedition for the harbouring of Sertorian and Marian supporters in Further Spain. This of course launched the Sertorian rebellion that lasted nearly a decade until Pompey finally put an end to it. In any case, the end of 81 marks the end of our knowledge of Gaius Annius.

8 Infiltrating Julian History: Anna Perenna at Lavinium and Bovillae (Ovid, *Fast.* 3.523–710)

1   See M. Piranamonte, 'Anna Perenna a dieci anni della scoperta', *MHNH* 9 (2009, pp. 251–64); 'Religion and Magic at Rome: the Fountain of Anna Perenna' in *Magical Practices in the Latin West*, ed. R.L. Gordon and F.M. Simón (Leiden: Brill, 2010).
2   J. Fabre-Serris, *Mythologie et littérature à Rome* (Lausanne: Editions Payot, 1998), 71.
3   S. Weinstock, *Divus Iulius* (Oxford: Clarendon Press, 1971), 83–90; O. Hekster, *Emperors and Ancestors* (Oxford: Oxford University Press, 2015).
4   C. Newlands, 'Transgressive Acts: Ovid's Treatment of the Ides of March', *CP* 91 (1996, pp. 320–38); M. Bakhtin, *Rabelais and his World*, trans. H. Iswolsky (Cambridge, MA: M.I.T. Press, 1968).
5   See the critique of the carnivalesque in N. Zemon Davis, 'Women on top: symbolic sexual inversion and political disorder in early modern Europe' in *The Reversible World: Symbolic Inversion in Art and Society*, ed. B.A. Babcock (Ithaca, NY: Cornell University Press, 1978).
6   See E. Fantham, 'Ovid, Germanicus, and the Composition of the *Fasti*', *Papers of the Liverpool Latin Seminar* 5 (1985, pp. 243–81); E. Fantham (ed.), *Ovid Fasti Book IV* (Cambridge: Cambridge University Press, 1998), 1–4; P.E. Knox, 'The Poet and the Second Prince: Ovid in the Age of Tiberius', *Memoirs of the American Academy in Rome* 49 (2004, pp. 1–20).
7   For a discussion of Anna's deification as a more masculine than feminine transformative experience, see Beek (Chapter 5) in this volume.
8   M. Beard, 'A Complex of Times: No More Sheep on Romulus's Birthday', *PCPhS* 33 (1987, pp. 1–15).

9   D. Feeney, *Literature and Religion at Rome* (Cambridge: Cambridge University Press, 1998), 123–5; D. Feeney, *Caesar's Calendar* (Berkeley and Los Angeles: University of California Press, 2007), 167–211.
10 Feeney, *Caesar's Calendar*, 185.
11 As I. Ziogas argues, 'The Poet as Prince: Author and Authority Under Augustus' in *The Art of Veiled Speech*, ed. H. Baltussen and P. J. Davis (Philadelphia: University of Pennsylvania Press, 2015), both emperor and poets, moreover, strive to shape literary creation, the former, for instance, often through control of publication; there is also ample evidence of Augustus's own literary efforts.
12 See T.P. Wiseman, 'The cult site of Anna Perenna: documentation, visualization, imagination'. in *Imaging Ancient Rome,* ed. L. Haselberger and J. Humphreys (Portsmouth, RI: *JRA* Supplement 61, 2006). Wiseman discusses votive inscriptions built into the wall of the fountain basin and dedicated to Anna Perenna and the 'consecrated nymphs'; they suggest the presence of artistic competitions in the post–Ovidian period when the cult had moved from near the centre of Rome, at the first milestone on the Via Flaminia, to the area of the present-day Piazza Euclide four miles north.
13 T.P. Wiseman, *Roman Drama and History* (Exeter: Exeter University Press, 1998), 68–9, suggests that prostitutes took part in the festival since couples camped out under togas for shelter, and only elite males and prostitutes wore the toga.
14 E. Gowers, 'Talking Trees: Baucis and Philemon Revisited', *Arethusa* 38 (2005, pp. 331–65), 353–7.
15 *OLD calamus* 2 and 3.
16 Cf. *Fast.* 4.948–54; G. Herbert-Brown, *Ovid and the Fasti, an Historical Study* (Oxford: Oxford University Press, 1994), 71; A. Barchiesi, *The Poet and the Prince* (Berkeley and Los Angeles: University of California Press, 1997), 137–40.
17 F. Bömer (ed.), *P. Ovidius Naso: Die Fasten* (Heidelberg: Carl Winter, 1958), 192.
18 See N. B. Pandey, 'Caesar's Comet, the Julian Star, and the Invention of Augustus', *TAPA* 143 (2013, pp. 405–49).
19 Feeney, *Literature and Religion*, 127–31.
20 See Macr. 1.12.6; Mart. 4.64.16–17.
21 Ovid also briefly offers four other possibilities at 3.657–60: she is a moon goddess, the goddess Themis, the goddess Io, or a nymph who gave the infant Jupiter his first food.
22 See Wright (Chapter 4) in this volume for how Virgil hints at Anna's imminent transformation into a nymph/water deity.
23 K.S. Myers (ed.), *Ovid, Metamorphoses Book XIV* (Cambridge: Cambridge University Press, 2009), 11; on 'Ovid's *Aeneid*' in the *Metamorphoses* see 10–19. See also B. Gladhill, 'Gods, Caesars and Fate in *Aeneid* 1 and *Metamorphoses* 15', *Dictynna* 9 (2012, pp. 2–17).

24 L. Hutcheon and M. Woodman, 'Parody' in *The Princeton Encyclopedia of Poetry and Poetics*, ed. R. Greene and S. Cushman (Princeton: Princeton University Press, 2012).

25 M.A. Rose, *Parody: Ancient, Modern, and Post-Modern* (Cambridge: Cambridge University Press), 22–5.

26 Rose, *Parody*, 41.

27 McCallum (Chapter 1) in this volume.

28 See the detailed comparison in A. Chiu, *Ovid's Women of the Year: Narratives of Roman Identity in the Fasti* (Ann Arbor: University of Michigan Press, 2016), 72–9; also McCallum (Chapter 1) in this volume.

29 See S. Hinds, *Allusion and Intertext* (Cambridge: Cambridge University Press, 1998) 119; also 116–22.

30 On Silius's more peaceable rendition of Anna's deification, as told by Anna herself, see J. McIntyre (Chapter 2) in this volume.

31 Even so, it is understandable that when, a century later, the Flavian poet Silius Italicus (8.29–192) in his *Punica* reclaims Anna Perenna for epic, her loyalties go with the Carthaginians. See J. McIntyre (Chapter 2) in this volume.

32 A. Barchiesi, 'Voci e istanze narrative nelle Metamorfosi di Ovidio', *MD* 23 (1989, pp. 55–97), 62–3.

33 See J. O'Hara, *Vergil and the Alexandrian Tradition of Etymological Wordplay* (Ann Arbor: University of Michigan Press, 1996), 207, on Virg. *A*. 8.322–3, *Latiumque vocari/maluit, his quoniam latuisset tutus in oris*.

34 D. Feeney, 'Patterns of Time in the Metamorphoses', in *Ovidian Transformations*, ed. P. Hardie, A. Barchiesi, and S. Hinds (Cambridge: Cambridge Philological Society, 1999), 16–17.

35 Cf. *Am*. 1.15.7, *fama perennis*; *Met*. 15.875. *perennis* was strongly associated with closural statements of literary immortality; cf. Catul. 1.10; Hor. *Carm*. 3.30.1.

36 S.L. James, 'Rape and Repetition in Ovid's *Metamorphoses*: Myth, History, Structure' in *Repeat Performances: Ovidian Repetition and the Metamorphoses*, ed. L. Fulkerson and T. Stover (Madison, WI: University of Wisconsin Press, 2016). James builds on the foundational work of Sandra Joshel and others, who trace a pattern in Roman history whereby Roman institutions are established from sexual violence against women. See S.R. Joshel, 'The Body Female and the Body Politic: Livy's Lucretia and Verginia' in *Sexuality and Gender in the Classical World*, ed. L.K. McClure (Oxford: Blackwell, 2002).

37 On Aeneas's deification in the Numicius see Myers, *Metamorphoses Book* XIV, 154–5; on his cult see S. Weinstock, 'Two Archaic Inscriptions from Latium', *JRS* 50 (1960, pp. 112–18): 114–18. In both the *Fasti* and the *Metamorphoses* the river is called *corniger* in initial line position (*Fast*. 3.647; *Met*. 14.602), but the Numicius in

Book 14 of the *Metamorphoses* is a slow-moving river (*serpit*, 598), lacking the sexually charged waters of the *Fasti* (*tumidis . . . undis*, 647).

38 Gladhill, 'Gods, Caesars and Fate', 2, notes that Ovid includes what Virgil excludes, the politically sensitive topics of assassination and apotheosis.

39 See C. Newlands, *Playing with Time: Ovid and the Fasti* (Ithaca, NY: Cornell University Press, 1995), 43–4; 61–2; 88–9.

40 Barchiesi, *The Poet and the Prince,* 124–6; Gladhill, 'Gods, Caesars, and Fate'.

41 It occurs as such in the plural (OLD 1b); cf. Ov. *Am.* 3.7.65.

42 J.N. Adams, *Latin Sexual Vocabulary* (Baltimore: Johns Hopkins University Press, 1990), 90–1; he cites, for instance, Ov. *Fast.* 5.256, *tangitur et tacto concipit illa sinu.*

43 Barchiesi, *The Poet and the Prince,* 33.

44 Fabre-Serris, *Mythologie et littérature à Rome*, 94–8.

45 Hinds, *Allusion and Intertext*, 95.

46 Bömer, *Die Fasten*, 188.

47 Ovid probably plays off an alternative tradition according to which Anna, not Dido, was in love with Aeneas in Carthage. See Servius on *Aeneid* 4.682, citing Varro as an authority, who also says that Anna killed herself on the Carthaginian pyre. F. Ahl, *Metaformations* (Ithaca, NY: Cornell University Press, 1985), 309–15, comments on the irony, therefore, that through their shared site of deification, the river Numicius, Dido's sister and Aeneas are at least joined in death.

48 Translation by G. P. Goold (Loeb edition, 1986).

49 Bömer, *Die Fasten,* 190–1.

50 G. Hutchinson, *Propertius Elegies Book IV* (Cambridge: Cambridge University Press, 2006), 67, notes that Bovillae is approximately 17 km (around 10 miles) from Rome.

51 Plin. *Nat.* 34.28–9. Plin. *Nat.* 34.31 reports that there was deep political unease during the Republic about statues to women, but that there was a statue (of Republican date) of Cornelia, mother of the Gracchi brothers, in the Augustan Porticus of Octavia.

52 L.M. Mignone, 'Remembering a Geography of Resistance' in *Memoria Romana: Memory in Rome and Rome in Memory*, ed. K. Galinsky (University of Michigan Press: Ann Arbor, 2014).

53 Bömer, *Die Fasten*, 190.

54 Chiu, *Ovid's Women of the Year,* 26.

55 On the influence of the *Hecale* and of Callimachean hymnic and devotional elements on the *Fasti* see Fantham, *Fasti Book IV*, 11–9; on the influence of the *Hecale* on the *Metamorphoses* see A.S. Hollis (ed.), *Callimachus, Hecale* (Oxford: Oxford University Press, 2009), 33–4.

56 Hollis, *Hecale*, 268–9.

57 *Neue-Pauly* II, 759.

58 J.F. Miller, 'Ovid's Liberalia' in *Ovid's Fasti: Historical Readings at its Bimillenium*, ed. G. Herbert-Brown (Oxford: Oxford University Press, 2002), 205–12, esp. 208.
59 R. Maltby, *A Lexicon of Ancient Latin Etymologies* (Leeds: Francis Cairns, 1991), 84. See also Weinstock, *Divus Iulius*, 6; D. Petrain, *Homer in Stone: the Tabulae Iliacae in their Roman Context* (Cambridge: Cambridge University Press, 2014), 143.
60 See Weinstock, *Divus Iulius*, 5–7; W. Smith, *Dictionary of Greek and Roman Geography* (London: Murray, 1872), 426–7, an old but valuable source for Bovillae (which does not merit an entry in the *Princeton Encyclopedia of Classical Sites*). D. Porte, *L'etiologie religieuse dans les Fastes d'Ovide* (Paris: Les Belles Lettres, 1985), 381–5, suggests a connection with Augustus and a possible maternal grandfather who was a baker (cf. Suet. *Aug*. 4).
61 Petrain, *Homer in Stone*, 140; 143; cf. N. Horsfall, 'Stesichorus at Bovillae?' *JHS* 99 (1979, pp. 26–48).
62 Weinstock, 'Two Archaic Inscriptions'.
63 Smith, *Dictionary*, 426; Petrain, *Homer in Stone*, 143.
64 See Petrain, *Homer in Stone*, 140, 142–3.
65 Fabre-Serris, *Mythologie et littérature à Rome*, 94–8.
66 On Anna's apparent associations with the plebeian class see Wiseman (Introduction) and Ramsby (Chapter 7) in this volume.
67 For the fragments of the mime see C. Panayotakis (ed.), *Decimus Laberius: The Fragments* (Cambridge: Cambridge University Press, 2010), 115–19.
68 T.P. Wiseman, 'Politics and the People: What Counts as Evidence?', *BICS* 60-1 (2017, pp. 16–33), 19. A story circulated in late Antiquity claiming that Laberius fell afoul of Julius Caesar probably has no basis. See Wiseman, 'Politics and the People', 24–9; Panayotakis, *Laberius*, 43–9.
69 Eg. Barchiesi, *The Poet and the Prince*, 124, assumes she is a separate character.
70 Barchiesi, *The Poet and the Prince*, 124.
71 *OLD* 6 *verba dare*.
72 Fabre-Serris, *Mythologie et littérature à Rome*, 76.
73 See D. Feeney, '*Si licet et fas est*: Ovid's *Fasti* and the problem of free speech under the principate' in *Poetry and Propaganda in the Age of Augustus*, ed. A. Powell (London: Bristol Classical Press, 1992).
74 R.F. Thomas (ed.), *Virgil Georgics* (Cambridge: Cambridge University Press, 1988), 167.
75 See Newlands, 'Transgressive Acts', 333–7 for the ambiguities of this passage. Although editors grant this speech to Ovid, it is possible that the entire speech is spoken by Vesta, not simply lines 699–702.
76 Barchiesi, *The Poet and the Prince*, 130.
77 Wiseman, 'The cult site of Anna Perenna'; T.P. Wiseman, *Unwritten Rome* (Exeter: Exeter University Press, 2008), 18–22; S. Heyworth, 'Roman topography and Latin

diction', *PBSR* 79 (2011, pp. 43–69). Piranamonte, 'Religion and Magic at Rome' argues against any change of location for the cult.

78 See the discussion of the Liberalia by Miller, 'Ovid's Liberalia'.
79 Cf. *B. Hisp.* 31, *ipsis Liberalibus fusi fugatique* (they (sc. Caesar's opponents, the army of Gn. Pompey) were routed and put to flight on the very day of the Liberalia); Miller, 'Ovid's Liberalia', 199.
80 Fabre-Serris, *Mythologie et littérature à Rome*, 73–4, points out that the Battle of Munda also underlies Ovid's rewriting of Ennius's famous dream of Ilia. Her prophetic vision of two palm trees, one of which overshadows the other, seems to draw on an omen at Munda recorded by Suetonius (*Aug.* 94). When Caesar was cutting down a wood to make his camp, he saved an unusual palm tree. It sprouted a shoot that within a few days had grown to overshadow its parent. Caesar took this as an omen that he should appoint Octavian, his nephew, as his heir. As Fabre-Serris comments, Ovid thus subtly links Rome's founder Mars with the *princeps*, at the same time as he exposes the fabrications employed to elevate Augustus.
81 V. Turner, 'Comments and Conclusions' in *The Reversible World*, ed. B.A. Babcock (Ithaca, NY: Cornell University Press, 1978), 294–5.
82 See for instance P. Hardie, 'Questions of Authority: The Invention of Tradition in Ovid *Metamorphoses* 15' in *The Roman Cultural Revolution*, ed. T. Habinek and A. Schiesaro (Cambridge: Cambridge University Press, 1997); Pandey, 'Caesar's Comet', 440–5.
83 See for instance S. Cole, 'Cicero, Ennius, and the Concept of Apotheosis in Rome', *Arethusa* 39, no. 3 (2006, pp. 531–48); S. Cole, 'Elite Scepticism in the *Apocolocyntosis*: Some Qualifications' in *Seeing Seneca Whole*, ed. K. Volk and G. D. Williams (Leiden: Brill, 2006); Feeney, *Literature and Religion*, 109–10; Gladhill, 'Gods, Caesars, and Fate'. On imperial cult in general see the foundational work of D. Fishwick, *The Imperial Cult in the Latin West: Studies in the Ruler Cult of the Western Provinces of the Roman Empire* (Leiden: Brill, 1987–2005).
84 C. Newlands, 'Becoming a "Diva" in Imperial Rome: Ovid and the Problem of "the First Lady"', *Humanities Australia* 7 (2016, pp. 80–93) focuses on Ovid's representation of Augustus's spouse Livia. On female deification in the context of worship of the imperial family, see G. McIntyre, *A Family of Gods: The Worship of the Imperial Family in the Latin West* (Ann Arbor: University of Michigan Press, 2016).
85 Hekster, *Emperors and Ancestors*, 247.
86 J. Assmann, *Religion and Cultural Memory*, trans. R. Livingstone (Stanford: Stanford University Press, 2006).
87 Feeney, *Caesar's Calendar*, 182.
88 Ziogas, 'The Poet as Prince', 115.

9 Riverrun: Channelling Anna Perenna in *Finnegans Wake*

1. 'Finnegans' may be analysed thus: 'fin' < *finis*, end + 'negans' < *negare*, deny.
2. Throughout this chapter I employ the standard abbreviations for Joyce's major works: *P* for *A Portrait of the Artist as a Young Man* (1916), *U* for *Ulysses* (1922), and *FW* for *Finnegans Wake* (1939).
3. Sentence-final 'the' occurs five times in the *Wake* (*FW* 020.18, 257.27, 334.30, 343.36 and 628.16). No less 'antediluvian' than the final occurrence, which reissues the tremendous flood of words that is the work itself, is the penultimate one: 'Of manifest 'tis obedience and the. Flute!' The tides of English literature have turned, and the 'fruit' of Milton's *Paradise Lost* has ripened here – via the exchange of one liquid consonant (*r*) for another (*l*) – into Joyce's pun on German *Flut* (flood).
4. H. Bloom, *The Anatomy of Influence: Literature as a Way of Life* (New Haven: Yale University Press, 2011), 8.
5. H. Bloom, *The Anxiety of Influence: A Theory of Poetry*, 2nd edn (Oxford: Oxford University Press, [1973] 1997).
6. R. Ellmann, *The Consciousness of Joyce* (Oxford: Oxford University Press, 1977), 47–8.
7. T. Ziolkowski, *Ovid and the Moderns* (Ithaca: Cornell University Press, 2005), 36.
8. Bloom, *The Anxiety of Influence* ([1973] 1997), 14.
9. Bloom, *The Anatomy of Influence* (2011), 218–34 plucks the term 'tally' from Whitman's poetry, where it contains a multitude of meanings. I, in turn, borrow the term from Bloom to denote the process whereby a text – sometimes quite independent of its author's will – signals its indebtedness to the literary past.
10. W.K. Wimsatt and M. Beardsley, 'The Intentional Fallacy', *The Sewanee Review* 54, no. 3 (1946, pp. 468–88).
11. R. Barthes, 'The Death of the Author', *Aspen* 5–6 (1967).
12. For an excellent discussion of these terms in the context of Roman poetry, see S. Hinds, *Allusion and Intertext: Dynamics of Appropriation in Roman Poetry* (Cambridge: Cambridge University Press, 1998).
13. On Joyce's 'extravagance', see Bloom, *The Anatomy of Influence*, 11. For his 'provection' (carried-away-ness) see F. Senn, *Inductive Scrutinies: Focus on Joyce* (Dublin: The Lilliput Press, 1995), 41.
14. Joyce's early exposure to Ovid is well documented. In 1894, when he was still just a twelve-year-old student at Belvedere College, he sat for an examination on Caesar, Ovid and Roman history. His score (700/1200) was considered extraordinarily high, and he earned similarly high marks on a later exam whose syllabus included the eighth book of Ovid's epic, in which is related the tale of Daedalus and Icarus. For more on Joyce's educational background, see R.J. Schork, *Latin and Roman Culture in Joyce* (Gainesville: University Press of Florida, 1997), 275.

15 See in the bibliography the works by Senn, Schork, Brown, Ziolkowski, Freedman and Fallon.
16 But note the following: 'did not I *fest*fix with mortarboard my *unniversiries* wholly rational and gottalike' (*FW* 551.28–9, my emphasis). 'At the core of this boast', writes Schork, *Latin and Roman Culture in Joyce*, 158–9, 'I see and hear the presence of Ovid's *Fasti*. That work is an elaborate, day-by-day explanation of the origin, purpose and ritual for the many feasts of the Roman religious calendar. All of these annual celebrations were fixed to a certain date, and Ovid supplies a legendary theological and anthropological context for their exotic details'. An even stronger ripple can perhaps be felt in the words 'Clap hands postilium! Fastintide is by' (*FW* 453.36). As R. McHugh, *Annotations to Finnegans Wake*, 4th edn. (Baltimore: Johns Hopkins University Press, 2016) notes, 'Fastintide' refers to the season of Lent. It is, however, difficult to disregard the presence of the Ovidian title within this word.
17 D. Barnes, *Vagaries Malicieux: Two Stories* (New York: Frank Hallman, 1974), 253.
18 For a more detailed discussion of Joyce's month-men, see J.S. Atherton, 'A Man of Four Watches: Macrobius in *FW*', *A Wake Newslitter*, no. 9 (1972, pp. 39–40) and Schork, *Latin and Roman Culture in Joyce*, 249–51.
19 I detect allusions to the Fugalia ('*regifugium persecutorum*', *FW* 51.31) and the Lupercalia ('Luperca Latouche', *FW* 67.36) of February, the Liberalia of March ('It is not a hear or say of some anomorous letter, signed Toga Girilis, (teasy dear). We have a copy of her fist right against our nosibos', *FW* 112.29–31), and the Parilia of April ('ancient flash and crash habits of old Pales', *FW* 289.08–09).
20 Sometime between 1936, when Joyce added this phrase to his 'Work in Progress', and 1939, when *Finnegans Wake* was finally published, editors mistakenly changed Joyce's 'commodious' to 'commodius'.
21 R. Graves, *The White Goddess: A Historical Grammar of Poetic Myth* (New York: Farrar, Straus and Giroux, 1948), 372.
22 J. Kroll, *Chapters in a Mythology: The Poetry of Sylvia Plath* (Stroud: The History Press, 2007), 52.
23 Ellmann, *James Joyce*, 574.
24 I rely throughout on the Latin text printed in Frazer's Loeb edition.
25 S. Gilbert, *Letters of James Joyce* Vol. 1. (New York: Viking Press, 1957), 213.
26 For an analysis of Ovid's own river catalogues, see P.J. Jones, *Reading Rivers in Roman Literature and Culture* (Lanham, MD: Lexington Books, 2005).
27 Readers of this volume are perhaps more likely to be familiar with the relegated Roman's *Tristia* and *Epistulae ex Ponto* than with Joyce's play *Exiles*.
28 For ALP's various associations with the peoples, lands and languages of Africa, see S. Brivic, *Joyce's Waking Women: An Introduction to Finnegans Wake* (Madison: University of Wisconsin Press, 1995), 54–67.

29 Thus does the *Wake* playfully refer to itself: 'So you need hardly spell me how every word will be bound over to carry three score and ten toptypsical readings throughout the book of Doublends Jined . . . till *Daleth*, mahomahouma, who oped it closeth thereof the. *Dor!*' (*FW* 20.13–18, my emphasis).

30 Schork, *Latin and Roman Culture in Joyce*, 250.

31 References to Themis occur at *FW* 138.10, 167.10 and 167.25. It is worth noting that the latter two occur within the Burrus and Caseous episode, and in close proximity to the words 'nefand' (*FW* 167.19) and '*fas*' (*FW* 167.34). Io rears her head at *FW* 583.10. As E. Rosenbloom, *A Word in Your Ear: How & Why to Read James Joyce's Finnegans Wake* (East Hardwick, VT: BookSurge Publishing, 2006), 117 notes, 'ALP is the Hebrew spelling of the first letter, *aleph*, a glottal stop, the point from which all the letters and numbers flow: from *beth* to *tav* (the vaudeville team Butt and Taff in *Finnegans Wake*) and around again. The symbol whence aleph derives is the head of a cow, Io, the ∀-shaped head of Taurus whose red star once marked the new year at the spring equinox'.

32 See McHugh, *Annotations to Finnegans Wake*, 206.

33 H.G. Wells, 'James Joyce', *Nation*, no. 20 (1917, pp. 710, 712).

34 C. Martindale, 'Reception – a new humanism? Receptivity, pedagogy, the transhistorical', *Classical Receptions Journal* 5, no. 2 (2013, pp. 169–83): 171.

35 Bloom, *The Anxiety of Influence*, 16, likewise conceives of influence as a potentially two-way stream. The effect of the revisionary ratio which he calls *apophrades*, or 'the return of the dead', is that 'the new poem's achievement makes it seem to us, not as though the precursor were writing it, but as though the later poet himself had written the precursor's characteristic work'. A self-professed Longinian critic, Bloom appears here to be echoing his own precursor, who claims that when faced with the true sublime the soul is lifted up, 'as if it had produced that which it has heard' ([Longinus], *Subl.* 7.2).

36 For Ovid's engagement with Virgil's Anna see McCallum (Chapter 1) in this volume.

37 Other scholars mine Ovid's account of Anna for its political meaning. See, e.g., J.C. McKeown, '*Fabula proposito nulla tegenda meo*: Ovid's *Fasti* and Augustan Politics', in *Poetry and Politics in the Age of Augustus*, ed. T. Woodman and D. West (Cambridge: Cambridge University Press, 1984), 169–87. Though I do not seek to deny the episode a political significance, I do maintain that the stakes in Ovid's struggle against his precursor are primarily literary.

38 According to Varro (*L.* 7.87), *lymphata dicta a lympha; lympha a nympha*.

39 See Wright (Chapter 4) in this volume, which argues that Virgil was aware of Anna's nymph identity.

40 These include 'lymph' (*FW* 309.05, 577.11), 'lymphing' (*FW* 367.13), 'lymphyamphyre' (*FW* 137.24), 'nymphant' (*FW* 202.33), 'nympholept' (*FW* 115.30), 'nymphosis' (*FW* 107.13), and 'nymphs' (*FW* 399.03 and 415.02).

41 Bloom, *The Anatomy of Influence*, 125 arrives at a similar conclusion regarding Joyce and two of his other precursors: 'The binding agency that holds together Shakespeare, Milton and Joyce, is their sense of how meaning gets started, which always is overflow. Falstaff, Adam, Satan and [Leopold] Bloom are all troubling because they do not declare their own fictiveness. Effluence, not influence, is their true function in literary history'.

42 A. Burgess, *A Shorter Finnegans Wake* (New York: Viking Press, 1967), 13.

43 Joyce's use of the word has been variously analysed. According to C. Hart, *Structure and Motif in Finnegans Wake* (Evanston: Northwestern University Press, 1962), 153–4, anastomosis represents a 'duality of being' at the heart of the *Wake*. For M. Norris, 'The Last Chapter of *Finnegans Wake*', *James Joyce Quarterly* 25, no.1 (1987, pp. 11–30), 11, it is the device whereby Joyce attempts 'to bridge all the great ontological chasms: between time and space, between life and death, between male and female'. For J. Bishop, *Joyce's Book of the Dark: Finnegans Wake* (Madison: University of Wisconsin Press, 1993), 371, it is a symbol for how the *Wake* 'makes us all ... the freshly reinvested "flesh and flood" of one body'. For J.H. Miller, *Ariadne's Thread: Story Lines* (New Haven: Yale University Press, 1992), 157, it has a double reference: 'one to the invagination of the male member in sexual intercourse ... the other to the twining back from navelcord to navelcord which relates us all to mankind and ultimately to the great mother of all, Eve'.

44 N. Krevans, 'Ilia's Dream: Ennius, Virgil and the Mythology of Seduction', *HSPh* 95 (1993, pp. 257–71).

45 Two modern scholars do, however, gesture toward this verbal resemblance: see J.P. Hallett, *Fathers and Daughters in Roman Society: Women and the Elite Family* (Princeton: Princeton University Press, 1984), 181; J. Fisher, *The Annals of Quintus Ennius and the Italic Tradition* (Baltimore: Johns Hopkins University Press, 2014), 147. Even more suggestive is the following note on Ennius's '*germana soror*' by a sixteenth-century commentator: *affectus a generis propinquitate, Vergilius, Anna soror*. What is more, Dido's '*Anna soror*' also echoes her poet's '*sic unanimam adloquitur male **sana soror**em*' in the previous verse.

Bibliography

Adams, J.N. *The Latin Sexual Vocabulary*, Baltimore: Johns Hopkins University Press, 1990.
Adkin, N. 'Read the Edge'. *ACD* 50 (2014): 45–72.
Ahl, F. *Metaformations: Soundplay and Wordplay in Ovid and Other Classical Poets*, Ithaca and London: Cornell University Press, 1985.
Ahl, F. trans. *Virgil: Aeneid*, Oxford: Oxford University Press, 2007.
Ahl, F., Davies, M.A. and Pomeroy, A. 'Silius Italicus'. *Aufstieg und Niedergang der Römischen Welt*. 32, no. 4 (1986): 2492–561.
Alföldi, A. *Early Rome and the Latins,* Ann Arbor: University of Michigan Press, 1965.
Alston, R. 'Roman Military Pay from Caesar to Diocletian'. *JRS* 84 (1994): 113–23.
Alton, E.H. 'Anna Perenna and Mamurius Veturius'. *Hermathena* 19 (1920): 100–4.
Alton, E.H., Wormell, D.E.W., and Courtney, E. *P. Ovidi Nasonis Fastorum Libri Sex*, 4th edn, Leipzig: Teubner Verlagsgesellschaft, 1997.
Assmann, E. 'Zu Martialis 4,64'. *Rheinisches Museum für Philologie* 60 (1905): 637–9.
Assman, J. *Religion and Cultural Memory*, trans. R. Livingstone, Stanford: Stanford University Press, 2006.
Atherton, J.S. 'A Man of Four Watches: Macrobius in *FW*'. *A Wake Newslitter* 9 (1972): 39–40.
Augoustakis, A. *Motherhood and the Other: Fashioning Female Power in Flavian Epic*, Oxford and New York: Oxford University Press, 2010.
Austin, R.G. *P. Vergili Maronis Aeneidos Liber Quartus*, Oxford: Clarendon Press, 1955.
Babelon, E. *Description Historique et Chronologique des Monnaies de la Republique Romaine*, Paris: Rollin et Feuardent, 1886.
Bakhtin, M. *Rabelais and his World*, trans. H. Iswolsky, Cambridge, MA: M.I.T. Press, 1968.
Ballentine, F.G. 'Some Phases of the Cult of the Nymphs'. *HSCPh* 15 (1904): 77–119.
Baratte, F. 'L'image impériale sur les reliefs de l'Afrique Romaine', in *La Transmission de l'idéologie impériale dans l'occident romain. Colloque CTHS – Bastia 2003*, edited by M. Navarro Caballero and J.-M. Roddaz, 273–96. Bordeaux–Paris: Actes des congrès nationaux des sociétés historiques et scientifiques, 2006.
Barchiesi, A. 'Voci e istanze narrative nelle Metamorfosi di Ovidio'. *MD* 23 (1989): 55–97.
Barchiesi, A. 'Discordant Muses'. *PCPhS* 37 (1991): 1–21.
Barchiesi, A. *The Poet and the Prince: Ovid and Augustan Discourse*, Berkeley and Los Angeles, Ca.: University of California Press, 1997.
Barnes, D. *Vagaries Malicieux: Two Stories*, New York: Frank Hallman, 1974.
Barrett, A.A. 'Anna's Conduct in *Aeneid* 4'. *Vergilius* 16 (1970): 21–5.
Barthes, R. 'The Death of the Author'. *Aspen* 5–6, 1967.

Beard, M. 'Writing and Ritual: a Study of Diversity and Expansion in the *Arval Acta*'. *PBSR* 53 (1985): 114–62.

Beard, M. 'A Complex of Times: No More Sheep on Romulus' Birthday'. *PCPhS* 33 (1987): 1–15.

Beard, M. 'Ancient Literacy and the Function of the Written Word in Roman Religion', in *Literacy in the Roman World*, edited by J.H. Humphrey, 35–58. Ann Arbor: University of Michigan, 1991.

Bednarowski, K.P. 'Dido and the Motif of Deception in *Aeneid* 2 and 3'. *TAPA* 145, no. 1 (2015): 135–72.

Beek, A.E. 'Always Look on the Bright Side of Death: Violence, Death, and Supernatural Transformation in Ovid's *Fasti*'. PhD diss., University of Minnesota, Minneapolis, 2015.

Belayche, N. 'Religious Actors in Daily Life: Practices and Related Beliefs', in *A Companion to Roman Religion*, edited by J. Rüpke, 275–91. Chichester: Wiley-Blackwell, 2011.

Benario, J.M. 'Dido and Cleopatra'. *Vergilius* 16 (1970): 2–6.

Berczelly, L. 'Ilia and the Divine Twins: A Reconstruction of two Relief Panels from the Ara Pacis Augustae'. *Acta ad archaeologiam et artium historiam pertinentia* 5 (1985): 89–149.

Billows, R. 'The Religious Procession of the Ara Pacis Augustae: Augustus' *Supplicatio* in 13 B.C.'. *JRA* 6 (1993): 80–92.

Bishop, J. *Joyce's Book of the Dark: Finnegans Wake*, Madison: University of Wisconsin Press, 1993.

Blänsdorf, J. 'The Texts from the Fons Annae Perennae', in *Magical Practice in the Latin West: Papers from the International Conference Held at the University of Zaragoza (2005)*, edited by R.L. Gordon and F.M. Simón, 215–44. Leiden: Brill, 2010.

Blänsdorf, J. 'Gods and Demons in Texts: Figures and Symbols of the Defixion Inscriptions in the Nymphaeum of Anna Perenna at Rome', in *Ancient Magic and the Supernatural in the Modern Visual and Performing Arts*, edited by F. Carlá and I. Berti, 19–37. London and New York: Bloomsbury Academic, 2015.

Bloom, H. *The Anxiety of Influence: A Theory of Poetry*, 2nd edn, Oxford: Oxford University Press, 1997.

Bloom, H. *The Anatomy of Influence: Literature as a Way of Life*, New Haven: Yale University Press, 2011.

Bömer, F. *P. Ovidius Naso: Die Fasten*, Heidelberg: Carl Winter, 1958.

Booth, A. 'Venus on the Ara Pacis'. *Latomus* 25 (1966): 873–9.

Boyd, B.W. *Ovid's Literary Loves: Influence and Innovation in the Amores*, Ann Arbor: University of Michigan Press, 1997.

Brewer, R.W. 'Epic vs. Elegiac Identity: A New Model for Roman Leadership in Ovid's *Fasti*'. PhD diss., University of Florida, Gainesville, 2012.

Brivic, S. *Joyce's Waking Women: An Introduction to Finnegans Wake*, Madison: University of Wisconsin Press, 1995.

Brown, E.L. *Numeri Vergiliani: Studies in 'Eclogues' and 'Georgics'*, Bruxelles-Berchem: Latomus, 1963.
Brugnoli, G. 'Anna Perenna', in *Cultura, Poesia, Ideologia nell'Opera di Ovidio*, edited by I. Gallo and L. Nicastri, 147–68. Salerno: Edizioni Scientifiche Italiane, 1991.
Brugnoli, G. and Santini, C. *L'Additamentum Aldinum di Silio Italico*, Roma: Accademia Nazionale dei Lincei, 1995.
Bruun, C. and Edmondson, J. *The Oxford Handbook of Roman Epigraphy*, Oxford: Oxford University Press, 2014.
Buecheler, F. *Carmina Latina Epigraphica I*, Leipzig: B.G. Teubner, 1895.
Burgess, A. *A Shorter Finnegans Wake*, New York: Viking Press, 1967.
Cairns, F. 'Catullus 27'. *Mnemosyne* 28.1 (1975): 24–9.
Cairns, F. *Virgil's Augustan Epic*, Cambridge: Cambridge University Press, 1989.
Caruso, C. 'I rendiconti degli arvali: le iscrizioni e l'allestimento', in *Terme di Diocleziano. Il chiostro piccolo della Certosa di Santa Maria degli Angeli*, edited by R. Friggeri, M. Magnani Cianetti, and C. Caruso, 61–5. Milano: Electa/Mondadori, 2014.
Casali, S. '*Ecce* ἀμφιβολικῶς *dixit*': allusioni 'irrazionali' alle varianti scartate della storia di Didone e Anna secondo Servio', in *Servio: stratificazioni esegetiche e modelli culturali*, edited by S. Casali and F. Stok, 24–37. Bruxelles: Éditions Latomus, 2008.
Castellani, V. 'Anna and Juturna in the *Aeneid*'. *Vergilius* 33 (1987): 49–57.
Castriota, D. *The Ara Pacis Augustae and the Imagery of Abundance in Later Greek and Early Roman Imperial Art*, Princeton: Princeton University Press, 1995.
Cavedoni, C. *Ragguaglio storico archeologico de'precipui ripostigli antichi di medaglie consolari e di famiglie Romane d'argento pel riscontro de' quali viensi a definire o limitare l'età d'altronde incerta di molte di quelle, e che può service anche di repertorio delle medaglie medesime*, Modena: Eredi Soliani, 1854.
de la Cerda, J.L. (=Ioannes Ludovicus de la). *P. Virgilii Maronis Aeneidos Libri Sex Priores: Argumentis, Explicationibus et Notis Illustrati*, Lyon: Horace Cardon, 1612.
Chiu, A. *Ovid's Women of the Year: Narratives of Roman Identity in the* Fasti, Ann Arbor: University of Michigan Press, 2016.
Chrissanthos, S. 'Freedom of Speech and the Roman Republican Army', in *Free Speech in Classical Antiquity*, edited by I. Sluiter and R. Rosen, 341–67. Leiden: Brill, 2004.
Clausen, W. *Virgil: Eclogues*, Oxford: Clarendon Press, 1994.
Clausen, W. *Virgil's Aeneid: Decorum, Allusion, and Ideology*, Leipzig: K.G. Saur, 2002.
Clauss, J.J. 'An Acrostic in Vergil (Eclogues I 5–8): The Chance that Mimics Choice?' *Aevum Antiquum* 10 (1997): 267–87.
Cole, S. 'Cicero, Ennius, and the Concept of Apotheosis in Rome'. *Arethusa* 39, no.3 (2006): 531–48.
Cole, S. 'Elite Scepticism in the *Apocolocyntosis*: Some Qualifications', in *Seeing Seneca Whole*, edited by K. Volk and G. D. Williams, 175–82. Leiden: Brill, 2006.
Conte, G.B. *Memoria dei poeti e sistema letterario: Catullo, Virgilio, Ovidio, Lucano*, Turin: Giulio Einaudi Editore, 1974.

Conte, G.B. *The Rhetoric of Imitation: Genre and Poetic Memory in Virgil and Other Latin Poets.* edited by C. Segal. Ithaca: Cornell University Press, 1986.

Conte, G.B. 'Proems in the Middle'. *YCIS* 29 (1992): 147–59.

Conte, G.B. *Latin Literature: A History*, translated by J. B. Solodow. Revised by D. Fowler and G.W. Most. Baltimore and London: The John Hopkins University Press, 1994.

Cooley, A.E. *The Cambridge Manual of Latin Epigraphy*, Cambridge: Cambridge University Press, 2012.

Cornell, T.J. *The Beginnings of Rome: Italy and Rome from the Bronze Age to the Punic Wars (c. 1000–264 BC)*, London: Routledge, 1995.

Crawford, M. *Roman Republican Coinage, vols 1 and 2*, London: Cambridge University, 1974.

Delvigo, M.L. '*Per transitum tangit historiam*: Intersecting developments of Roman identity in Virgil', in *Augustan Poetry and the Roman Republic*, edited by J. Farrell and D. Nelis, 19–39. Oxford: Oxford University Press, 2013.

Delz, J. *Silius Italicus:* Punica, Stuttgart: Teubner, 1987.

Derks, T. *Gods, Temples and Ritual Practices. The Transformation of Religious Ideas and Values in Roman Gaul*, Amsterdam: Amsterdam University Press, 1998.

Desmond, M. *Reading Dido: Gender, Textuality, and the Medieval* Aeneid, Minneapolis: University of Minnesota Press, 1994.

Dominik, W.J. 'Hannibal at the Gates: Programmatising Rome and *Romanitas* in Silius Italicus' *Punica* 1 and 2', in *Flavian Rome: Culture, Image, Text*, edited by A.J. Boyle and W.J. Dominik, 469–97. Leiden and Boston: Brill, 2003.

Dominik, W.J. 'Rome Then and Now: Linking the Saguntum and Cannae Episodes in Silius Italicus' Punica', in *Flavian Poetry*, edited by R.R. Nauta, H–J van Dam and J.J.L. Smolenaars, 113–27. Leiden: Brill, 2006.

Dumézil, G. *Déesses latines et mythes védiques*, Brussels: *Collection Latomus* 25 (1956); Reprinted with notes and introduction, New York: Arno Press, 1978.

Dyson, J.T. *King of the Wood: The Sacrificial Victor in Virgil's Aeneid*, Norman: University of Oklahoma Press, 2001.

Edlund-Berry, I. 'Hot, Cold, or Smelly: the Power of Sacred Water in Roman Religion, 400–100 BCE', in *Religion in Republican Italy*, edited by C.E. Schultz and P.B. Harvey Jr., 162–80. Cambridge: Cambridge University Press, 2006.

Egelhaaf-Gaiser, U. 'Roman Cult Sites: A Pragmatic Approach', in *A Companion to Roman Religion*, edited by J. Rüpke, 205–21. Chichester: Wiley-Blackwell, 2011.

Egelhaaf-Gaiser, U. 'Jahresfest am Tiberufer: Anna Perenna und die "Topographie der Zeit" in Ovids *Fasten*', in *Kommunikationsräume im kaiserzeitlichen Rom*, edited by F. Mundt, 197–226. Berlin and Boston: de Gruyter, 2012.

Ellmann, R. *The Consciousness of Joyce*, Oxford: Oxford University Press, 1977.

Ellmann, R. *James Joyce*, Oxford: Oxford University Press, 1982.

Elsner, J. 'Cult and Sculpture: Sacrifice in the Ara Pacis Augustae'. *JRS* 81 (1991): 50–61.

Elsner, J. *Art and the Roman Viewer: The Transformation of Art from the Pagan World to Christianity*, Cambridge: Cambridge University Press, 1995.

Erasmus, 'De ratione studii ac legendi interpretandique auctores, Paris 1511', in *Opera omnia Desiderii Erasmi Roterodami*, edited by J.H. Waszink, Amsterdam: Brill, 1971.
Fabre-Serris, J. *Mythologie et littérature à Rome*, Lausanne: Editions Payot, 1998.
Fantham, E. 'Ovid, Germanicus and the composition of the *Fasti*'. *Papers of the Liverpool Latin Seminar* 5 (1985): 243–81.
Fantham, E. ed. *Ovid* Fasti *Book IV*, Cambridge: Cambridge University Press, 1998.
Fantham, E. *Ovid's Metamorphoses*, Oxford: Oxford University Press, 2004.
Favreau, R. *Épigraphie Médiévale (L'Atelier du Médiéviste* 5), Turnhout: Brepols, 1997.
Favro, D. *The Urban Image of Augustan Rome*, Cambridge: Cambridge University Press, 1996.
Feeney, D. '*Si licet et fas est*: Ovid's *Fasti* and the Problem of Free Speech Under the Principate', in *Poetry and Propaganda in the Age of Augustus*, edited by A. Powell, 1–25. London: Bristol Classical Press, 1992.
Feeney, D. *Literature and Religion at Rome*, Cambridge: Cambridge University Press, 1998.
Feeney, D. 'Patterns of Time in the *Metamorphoses*', in *Ovidian Transformations*, edited by P. Hardie, A. Barchiesi, and S. Hinds, 13–30. Cambridge: Cambridge Philological Society, 1999.
Feeney, D. *Caesar's Calendar*, Berkeley and Los Angeles: University of California Press, 2007.
Feeney, D. and Nelis. D. 'Two Vergilian Acrostics: *Certissima Signa*'. *CQ* 50.2 (2005): 644–6.
Feeney, D.C. 'A Commentary on Silius Italicus Book 1'. PhD diss., University of Oxford, Oxford, 1982.
Feeney, D.C. *The Gods in Epic: Poets and Critics of the Classical Tradition*, Oxford and New York: Oxford University Press, 1991.
Fisher, J. *The Annals of Quintus Ennius and the Italic Tradition*, Baltimore: Johns Hopkins University Press, 2014.
Fishwick, D. 'The *Cannophori* and the March Festival of Magna Mater'. *TAPA* 97 (1966): 193–202.
Fishwick, D. *The Imperial Cult in the Latin West: Studies in the Ruler Cult of the Western Provinces of the Roman Empire*, 3 vols. Leiden: Brill, 1987–2005.
Fitzgerald, R. trans. *Virgil: The Aeneid*, New York: Vintage Classics, 1990.
Flower, H. 'Were Women Ever 'Ancestors' in Republican Rome?' in *Images of Ancestors*, edited by J. Højte, 157–84. Aarhus: Aarhus University Press, 2002.
Flower, H. *Roman Republics*, Princeton: Princeton University Press, 2010.
Forston, B. *Language and Rhythm in Plautus: Synchronic and Diachronic Studies*, Berlin: Walter de Gruyter, 2008.
Fowler, D. '*Mea Tempora*: Patterning of Time in the *Metamorphoses*', in *Ovidian Transformations: Essays on the Metamorphoses and its Reception*, edited by A. Barchiesi and S. Hinds, 13–30. Cambridge: Cambridge Philological Society, 1983.
Fowler, D.P. 'An Acrostic in Vergil (*Aeneid* 7.601–4)?' *CQ* 33 (1983): 298.
Frazer, J.G. *Publii Ovidii Nasonis Fastorum Libri Sex*, London: Macmillan and Co., 1929.

Frazer, J. and Goold, G. eds. *Ovid*: Fasti, 2nd edn, 1989; reprinted with corrections Cambridge, MA: Harvard University Press, 1996.
Friedländer, P. 'Patterns of Sound and Atomic Theory in Lucretius'. *AJP* 62 (1941): 16–34.
Friggeri, R. 'Le iscrizioni', in *Il Santuario della musica e il bosco sacro di Anna Perenna*, edited by M. Piranomonte, 26–33. Roma: Electa, 2002.
Fucecchi, M. 'With (a) God on Our Side: Ancient Ritual Practices and Imagery in Flavian Epic', in *Ritual and Religion in Flavian Epic*, edited by A. Augoustakis, 17–32. Oxford and New York: Oxford University Press, 2013.
Gale, M. 'Etymological Wordplay and Poetic Succession in Lucretius'. *CP* 96 (2001): 168–72.
Galinsky, G.K. 'The Anger of Aeneas'. *AJP* 109 (1988): 321–48.
Galinsky, K. 'Venus in a Relief on the Ara Pacis Augustae'. *AJA* 70 (1966): 223–43.
Galinsky, K. 'Sol and the 'Carmen Saeculare'. *Latomus* 26 (1967): 619–33.
Galinsky, K. *Aeneas, Sicily, and Rome*, Princeton: Princeton University Press, 1969.
Galinsky, K. 'Venus, Polysemy, and the Ara Pacis Augustae'. *AJA* 96 (1992): 457–75.
Gamel, M. 'Reading as a Man: Performance and Gender in Roman Elegy'. *Helios* 25, no. 1 (1998): 79–95.
Ganiban, R.T. 'Virgil's Dido and the Heroism of Hannibal in Silius' *Punica*', in *Brill's Companion to Silius Italicus*, edited by A. Augoustakis, 73–98. Leiden and Boston: Brill. 2010.
Gilbert, S, ed. *Letters of James Joyce*, Vol. 1. Rev. edn, New York: Viking Press, 1957.
Gladhill, B. 'Gods, Caesars and Fate in *Aeneid* 1 and *Metamorphoses* 15'. *Dictynna* 9 (2012): 2–17.
Goold, G.P. 'Observationes in Codicem Matritensem M. 31'. *RhM* 99 (1956): 9–17.
Gowers, E. 'Talking Trees: Baucis and Philemon Revisited'. *Arethusa* 38 (2005): 331–65.
Graves, R. *The White Goddess: A Historical Grammar of Poetic Myth*, New York: Farrar, Straus and Giroux, 1948.
Green, S.J. *Ovid*, Fasti *1: A Commentary*, Leiden and Boston: Brill, 2004.
Griffith, M. 'What Does Aeneas Look like?' *CP* 80 (1985): 309–19.
Grishin, A. '*Ludus in Undis*: An Acrostic in *Eclogue* 9'. *HSPh* 104 (2008): 237–40.
Grueber, H. *Coins of the Roman Republic in the British Museum*, London: British Museum, 1910.
de Grummond, N. 'Pax Augusta and the Horae on the Ara Pacis Augustae'. *AJA* 94 (1990): 663–77.
Guarducci, M. 'Il culto di Anna e delle Paides nelle iscrizioni sicule di Buscemi e il culto latino di Anna Perenna'. *Studi e materiali di storia delle Religioni* 12 (1936): 25–50.
Haensch, R. 'Inscriptions as Sources of Knowledge for Religions and Cults in the Roman World of Imperial Times', in *A Companion to Roman Religion*, edited by J. Rüpke, 176–87. Chichester: Wiley-Blackwell, 2011.
Hallett, J.P. *Fathers and Daughters in Roman Society: Women and the Elite Family*, Princeton: Princeton University Press, 1984.

Hands, A. 'Chats on Roman Coins with Young Collectors'. *Numismatic Circular* 4 (1986): 1808–1894.
Hardie, P. *The Epic Successors of Virgil: A Study in the Dynamics of a Tradition*, Cambridge and New York: Cambridge University Press, 1993.
Hardie, P. *Vergil: Aeneid, Book IX*, Cambridge: Cambridge University Press, 1995.
Hardie, P. 'Questions of Authority: The Invention of Tradition in Ovid *Metamorphoses* 15', in *The Roman Cultural Revolution*, edited by T. Habinek and A. Schiesaro, 182–98. Cambridge: Cambridge University Press, 1997.
Harries, B. 'Causation and the Authority of the Poet in Ovid's *Fasti*'. *CQ* 39, no. 1 (1989): 164–85.
Harrison, S. 'Ovid and Genre: Evolutions of an Elegist', in *The Cambridge Companion to Ovid*, edited by P. Hardie, 79–94. Cambridge: Cambridge University Press, 2002.
Harrison, S.J. 'Some Views of the *Aeneid* in the Twentieth Century', in *Oxford Readings in Vergil's* Aeneid, edited by S.J. Harrison, 1–20. Oxford and New York: Oxford University Press, 1990.
Hart, C. *Structure and Motif in Finnegans Wake*, Evanston: Northwestern University Press, 1962.
Heath, G. 'The Coins of Republican Rome'. *The Numismatist* 12 (1899): 159–63, 234–9.
Heath, J. 'Diana's Understanding of Ovid's *Metamorphoses*'. *CJ* 86, no. 3 (1991): 233–43.
Heinze, R. *Virgil's Epic Technique*, translated by H. and D. Harvey and F. Robertson, Berkeley: University of California Press, 1993.
Heitland, W.E. 'The "Great Lacuna" in the Eighth Book of Silius Italicus'. *The Journal of Philology* 24, no. 48 (1896): 188–211.
Hejduk, J. 'If Isaiah Speaks: Original Sin and an Astonishing Acrostic in Virgil's *Orpheus and Eurydice*'. Paper presented at the summer Symposium Cumanum in Cuma, Italy, 2015.
Herbert-Brown, G. *Ovid and the Fasti, an Historical Study*, Oxford: Oxford University Press, 1994.
Herbert-Brown, G. '*Fasti*: the Poet, the Prince, and the Plebs', in *A Companion to Ovid*, edited by P. Knox, 120–39. Chichester and Malden, MA: Wiley-Blackwell, 2013.
Heyworth, S.J. 'Roman topography and Latin diction'. *PBSR* 79 (2011): 43–69.
Hinds, S. *The Metamorphosis of Persephone: Ovid and the Self-conscious Muse*, Cambridge and New York: Cambridge University Press, 1987.
Hinds, S. 'Generalizing about Ovid'. *Ramus* 16 (1987): 4–31.
Hinds, S. '*Arma* in Ovid's *Fasti* Part 1: Genre and Mannerism'. *Arethusa* 25.1 (1992): 81–112.
Hinds, S. '*Arma* in Ovid's *Fasti* Part 2: Genre, Romulean Rome and Augustan Ideology'. *Arethusa* 25.1 (1992): 113–53.
Hinds, S. *Allusion and Intertext*, Cambridge: Cambridge University Press, 1998.
Holliday, P.J. 'Time, History, and Ritual on the Ara Pacis Augustae'. *The Art Bulletin* 72 (1990): 542–57.
Hollis, A.S. (ed.). *Callimachus, Hecale*, Oxford: Oxford University Press, 2009.

Horsfall, N. 'Stesichorus at Bovillae?' *JHS* 99 (1979): 26–48.
Horsfall, N. *Virgil, Aeneid 7: A Commentary*, Leiden: Brill, 2000.
Horsfall, N. *Virgil, Aeneid 2*, Leiden: Brill, 2008.
Horsfall, N. *Virgil: Aeneid 6*, Berlin and Boston: De Gruyter, 2013.
Hurlet, F. 'Pouvoir des images, images du pouvoir imperial. La province d'Afrique aux deux premiers siècles de notre ère'. *Mélanges de l'Ecole française de Rome. Antiquité* 112 (2000): 297–364.
Hutcheon, L. and Woodman, M. 'Parody', in *The Princeton Encyclopedia of Poetry and Poetics*, edited by R. Greene and S. Cushman, 1001–3. Princeton: Princeton University Press, 2012.
Hutchinson, G. (ed.). *Propertius Elegies Book IV*, Cambridge: Cambridge University Press, 2006.
James, S.L. *Learned Girls and Male Persuasion: Gender and Reading in Roman Love Elegy*, Berkeley: University of California Press, 2003.
James, S.L. 'Rape and Repetition in Ovid's *Metamorphoses*: Myth, History, Structure', in *Repeat Performances: Ovidian Repetition and the Metamorphoses*, edited by L. Fulkerson and T. Stover, 154–75. Madison, WI: University of Wisconsin Press, 2016.
Jones, P.J. *Reading Rivers in Roman Literature and Culture*, Lanham, MD: Lexington Books, 2005.
Joshel, S. 'The Body Female and the Body Politic', in *Sexuality and Gender in the Classical World*, edited by L.K. McClure, 112–30. Oxford: Blackwell, 2002.
Joyce, J. *Finnegans Wake*, 1939. New York: Viking Press, 1958.
Keegan, P.M. 'Seen, not Heard: *Feminea Lingua* in Ovid's *Fasti* and the Critical Gaze', in *Ovid's* Fasti: *Historical Readings at its Bimillennium*, edited by G. Herbert-Brown, 129–53. Oxford: Oxford University Press, 2002.
Keith, A. 'Versions of Epic Masculinity in Ovid's *Metamorphoses*', in *Ovidian Transformations: Essays on the* Metamorphoses *and its Reception*, edited by P. Hardie, A. Barchiesi, and S. Hinds, 214–39. Cambridge: Cambridge Philological Society, 1999.
Keith, A. *Engendering Rome: Women in Latin Epic*, Cambridge: Cambridge University Press, 2000.
Keith, A. 'Sources and genres in Ovid's Metamorphoses 1–5', in *Companion to Ovid*, edited by B. Weiden Boyd, 235–69. Leiden: Brill, 2002.
Keith, A. 'Sisters and Their Secrets in Flavian Epic', in *Family in Flavian Epic*, edited by N. Manioti, 248–75. Leiden: Brill 2016.
Kennedy, D.F. *The Arts of Love: Five Studies in the Discourse of Latin Love Elegy*, Cambridge: Cambridge University Press, 1993.
King, R. *Desiring Rome: Male Subjectivity and Reading Ovid's* Fasti, Columbus: Ohio State University Press, 2006.
Kleiner, D.E.E. 'Semblance and Storytelling in Augustan Rome', in *The Cambridge Companion to Augustus*, edited by K. Galinsky, 197–233. Cambridge: Cambridge University Press, 2005.

Knox, P. 'The Poet and the Second Prince: Ovid in the Age of Tiberius'. *Memoirs of the American Academy in Rome* 49 (2004): 1–20.
Knox, P.E. *Ovid: Heroides. Select Epistles*, Cambridge: Cambridge University Press, 1995.
Konrad, C. *Plutarch's* Sertorius*: A Historical Commentary*, Chapel Hill: University of North Carolina Press, 1994.
Kötzle, M. *Weibliche Gottheiten in Ovids 'Fasten'*, Frankfurt: Peter Lang, 1991.
Krevans, N. 'Ilia's Dream: Ennius, Virgil, and the Mythology of Seduction'. *HSPh* 95 (1993): 257–71.
Kroll, J. *Chapters in a Mythology: The Poetry of Sylvia Plath*, Stroud: The History Press, 2007.
Kronenberg, L. 'Tibullus the Elegiac *Vates*: Acrostics in Tibullus 2.5'. *Mnemosyne* 71 (2018): 508–14.
Kuttner, A. 'Roman Art During the Republic', in *The Cambridge Companion to the Roman Republic*, edited by H. Flower, 294–321. Cambridge and New York: Cambridge University Press, 2004.
Larson, J. *Greek Nymphs. Myth, Cult, Lore*, Oxford: Oxford University Press, 2001.
Latte, K. *Römische Religionsgeschichte.* München: C.H. Beck, 1960.
Lhote-Birot, M.-C. 'Les nymphs en Gaule Narbonnaise et dans les Trois Gaules'. *Latomus* 63 (2004): 58–69.
Littlewood, R.J. 'Ovid and the Ides of March (*Fasti* 3.523–710): a Further Study in the Artistry of the Fasti', in *Studies in Latin Literature and Roman History II*, edited by C. Deroux, 301–21. Brussels: Revue d'Études Latines, 1980.
Lovatt, H. 'The Eloquence of Dido: Exploring Speech and Gender in Virgil's *Aeneid*'. *Dictynna* 10 (2013).
Lyne, R.O.A.M. *Further Voices in Vergil's Aeneid*, Oxford: Oxford University Press, 1987.
Lyne, R.O.A.M. *Words of the Poet: Characteristic Techniques of Style in Vergil's Aeneid*, Oxford: Clarendon Press, 1989.
Maas, M. *John Lydus and the Roman Past: Antiquarianism and Politics in the Age of Justinian*, London and New York: Routledge, 1992.
MacMullen, R. 'The Epigraphic Habit in the Roman Empire', in *AJP* 103, No. 3 (1982): 233–46.
Magini, L. *Astronomy and Calendar in Ancient Rome: The Eclipse Festivals*, Rome: <<L'Erma>> di Bretschneider, 2001.
Maltby, R. *A Lexicon of Ancient Latin Etymologies*, Leeds: Francis Cairns, 1991.
Marks, R. 'Silius Italicus', in *A Companion to Ancient Epic*, edited by J.M. Foley, 528–37. Oxford: Blackwell Publishing, 2005.
Marks, R. 'Reconcilable Differences: Anna Perenna and the Battle of Cannae in the *Punica*', in *Ritual and Religion in Flavian Epic*, edited by A. Augoustakis, 287–301. Oxford and New York: Oxford University Press, 2013.
Martindale, C. 'Reception – a new humanism? Receptivity, pedagogy, the transhistorical'. *Classical Receptions Journal* 5.2 (2013): 169–83.

Mastrocinque, A. *Bona Dea and the Cults of Roman Women*. Stuttgart: Franz Steiner Verlag, 2014.
McAuley, M. 'Matermorphoses: Motherhood and the Ovidian Epic Subject'. *EuGeSta: Journal on Gender Studies* 2 (2012): 123–68.
McGuire, D.T. *Acts of Silence: Civil War, Tyranny, and Suicide in the Flavian Epics*, Hildesheim: Olms-Weidmann, 1997.
McGushin, P. *The Transmission of the Punica of Silius Italicus*, Amsterdam: Adolf M. Hakkert, 1985.
McHugh, R. *Annotations to Finnegans Wake*, 4th edn, Baltimore: Johns Hopkins University Press, 2016.
McIntyre, G. *A Family of Gods: The Worship of the Imperial Family in the Latin West*. Ann Arbor: University of Michigan Press, 2016.
McKeown, J.C. '*Fabula Proposito Nulla Tegenda Meo*: Ovid's *Fasti* and Augustan Politics', in *Poetry and Politics in the Age of Augustus*, edited by T. Woodman and D. West, 169–87. Cambridge and New York: Cambridge University Press, 1984.
Meyer, E. 'Explaining the Epigraphic Habit in the Roman Empire: the Evidence of Epitaphs'. *JRS* 80 (1990): 74–96.
Mignone, L.M. 'Remembering a Geography of Resistance', in *Memoria Romana: Memory in Rome and Rome in Memory*, edited by K. Galinsky, 137–50. University of Michigan Press: Ann Arbor, 2014.
Miller, J.F. 'Ovid's Divine Interlocutors in the *Fasti*', in *Studies in Latin Literature and Roman History III*, edited by C. Deroux, 156–92. Bruxelles: Revue d'Études Latines, 1983.
Miller, J.F. *Ariadne's Thread: Story Lines*, New Haven: Yale University Press, 1992.
Miller, J.F. 'The *Fasti* and Hellenistic Didactic: Ovid's Variant Aetiologies'. *Arethusa* 25, no. 1 (1992): 11–31.
Miller, J.F. 'Ovidian Allusion and the Vocabulary of Memory'. *MD* 30 (1993): 153–64.
Miller, J.F. 'Ovid's Liberalia', in *Ovid's Fasti: Historical Readings at its Bimillenium*, edited by G. Herbert-Brown, 199–224. Oxford: Oxford University Press, 2002.
Moreno Soldevila, R. (ed). *Martial, Book IV. A Commentary*. Leiden: Brill, 2006.
Moret, J.-M. 'Le feste dei nani', in *Nani in Festa. Iconografia, religione e politica a Ostia durante il secondo triumvirato*, edited by C. Bocherens, 49–108. Bari: Edipuglia, 2012.
Murgatroyd, P. *Mythical and Legendary Narrative in Ovid's* Fasti. Leiden: Brill, 2005.
Myers, K.S. (ed.). *Ovid, Metamorphoses Book XIV*, Cambridge: Cambridge University Press. 2009.
Mynors, R.A.B. *P. Vergili Maronis Opera*, Oxford: Clarendon Press, 1969.
Nelis, D. *Vergil's Aeneid and the Argonautica of Apollonius Rhodius*, Leeds: Francis Cairns, 2001.
Newlands, C. 'Becoming a "Diva" in Imperial Rome: Ovid and the Problem of "the First Lady"'. *Humanities Australia* 7 (2016): 80–93.
Newlands, C.E. *Playing with Time: Ovid and the Fasti*, Ithaca and London: Cornell University Press, 1995.

Newlands, C.E. 'Transgressive Acts: Ovid's Treatment of the Ides of March'. *CP* 91, no. 4 (1996): 320–38.
Newlands, C.E. 'Ovid', in *A Companion to Ancient Epic*, edited by J.M. Foley, 476–91, Oxford: Blackwell, 2005.
Nisbet, R.G.M. and Hubbard, M. *A Commentary on Horace: Odes Book 2*, Oxford: Clarendon Press, 1978.
Norden, E. *Agnostos Theos: Untersuchungen zur Formengeschichte religiöser Rede*, Leipzig: Teubner, 1923.
Norris, M. 'The Last Chapter of *Finnegans Wake*'. *James Joyce Quarterly* 25.1 (1987): 11–30.
Nugent, S.G. 'The Women of the *Aeneid*: Vanishing Bodies, Lingering Voices', in *Reading Vergil's* Aeneid: *An Interpretive Guide*, edited by C. Perkell, 251–70. Norman: University of Oklahoma Press, 1999.
Odgers, M.M. 'Some Appearances of the Dido Story'. *The Classical Weekly* 18.19 (1925): 145–8.
O'Hara, J. *Death and Optimistic Prophecy in Vergil's* Aeneid, Princeton: Princeton University Press, 1990.
O'Hara, J. *Vergil and the Alexandrian Tradition of Etymological Wordplay*, Ann Arbor: University of Michigan Press, 1996.
O'Hara, J. *Inconsistencies in Roman Epic: Studies in Catullus, Lucretius, Vergil, Ovid, and Lucan*, Cambridge: Cambridge University Press, 2007.
O'Hara, J. *True Names: Vergil and the Alexandrian Tradition of Etymological Wordplay* (New and Expanded Edition), Ann Arbor: University of Michigan Press, 2017.
O'Hara, J.J. 'Vergil's Best Reader?: Ovidian Commentary on Vergilian Etymological Wordplay'. *CJ* 91.3 (1996): 255–76.
Oliensis, E. 'Sons and Lovers: Sexuality and Gender in Virgil's Poetry', in *The Cambridge Companion to Virgil*, edited by C. Martindale, 294–311. Cambridge: Cambridge University Press, 1997.
Otis, B. *Virgil: A Study in Civilized Poetry*, Oxford: Oxford University Press, 1964.
Otis, B. *Ovid as an Epic Poet*, 2nd edn, Cambridge: Cambridge University Press, 1970.
Pace, B. *Arte e civilita della sicilia antica. III. Cultura e vita religiosa*, Roma: Societa anonima editrice dante Alighieri, 1945.
Panayotakis, C. (ed.) *Decimus Laberius: The Fragments*, Cambridge: Cambridge University Press, 2010.
Pandey, N.B. 'Caesar's Comet, the Julian Star, and the Invention of Augustus'. *TAPA* 143 (2013): 405–49.
Panoussi, V. *Greek Tragedy in Vergil's* Aeneid: *Ritual, Empire, and Intertext*, Cambridge: Cambridge University Press, 1998.
Parker, H. *Greek Gods in Italy in Ovid's* Fasti: *A Greater Greece*, Lewiston: The Edwin Mellen Press, 1997.
Parry, A. 'The Two Voices of Virgil's *Aeneid*'. *Arion* 2, no. 4 (1963): 66–80.
Parry, H. 'Ovid's *Metamorphoses*: Violence in a Pastoral Landscape'. *TAPA* 95 (1964): 268–82.

Pasco-Pranger, M. *Founding the Year. Ovid's* Fasti *and the Poetics of the Roman Calendar* (*Mnemosyne* Supplementum 276), Leiden and Boston: Brill, 2006.

Pease, A.S. *Publi Vergili Maronis Aeneidos Liber Quartus*, Cambridge, MA: Harvard University Press, 1935.

Perea, S. 'Anna Perenna: Religión y ejemplaridad mitica'. *Espacio, Tiempo y Forma. Serie II, Historia Antigua*, 11 (1998): 185–219.

Perkell, C.G. 'On Creusa, Dido, and the Quality of Victory in Virgil's *Aeneid*', in *Reflections of Women in Antiquity*, edited by H. P. Foley, 355–78. New York: Gordon and Breach Science Publishers, 1981.

Petrain, D. *Homer in Stone: the Tabulae Iliacae in their Roman Context*, Cambridge: Cambridge University Press, 2014.

Pichon, R. *Index Verborum Amatorium*, Hildesheim, 1966.

Piranomonte, M. (ed). *Il santuario della musica e il bosco sacro di Anna Perenna*, Roma: Mondadori Electa, 2002.

Piranomonte, M. 'Anna Perenna a dieci anni della scoperta'. *MHNH* 9 (2009): 251–64.

Piranomonte, M. 'Religion and Magic at Rome: The Fountain of Anna Perenna', in *Magical Practice in the Latin West: Papers from the international conference held at the University of Zaragoza (2005)*, edited by R.L. Gordon and F.M. Simón, 191–214. Leiden: Brill, 2010.

Piranomonte, M. 'The discovery of the fountain of Anna Perenna and its influence on the study of ancient magic', in *The Wisdom of Thoth: Magical Texts in Ancient Mediterranean Civilisations*, edited by G. Bąkowska-Czerner, A. Roccati, and A. Świerzowska, 71–86. Oxford: Archaeopress Publishing Ltd, 2015.

Pomeroy, A.J. 'Silius Italicus as "Doctus Poeta"', in *The Imperial Muse: Ramus Essays on Roman Literature of the Empire*, edited by A.J. Boyle, 119–39. Bendigo, Victoria: Aureal Publications, 1990.

Porte, D. 'Anna Perenna, Bonne et heureuse année!' *RPh* 45 (1971): 282–91.

Porte, D. *L'Étiologie Religieuse dans les Fastes d'Ovide*, Paris: Société d'Édition 'Les Belles Lettres'. 1985.

Pöscl, V. 'Die Horazode *Aequam memento* (c. 2, 3)'. *RhM* 137 (1994): 118–27.

Price, T.H. *Kourotrophos: Cults and Representations of the Greek Nursing Deities*, Leiden: Brill, 1978.

Pugliese Carratelli, G. 'Sul culto delle paides e di anna in acre'. *La parola del passato: Rivista di studi antichi* 6 (1951): 68–75.

Putnam, M.C.J. *The Poetry of the Aeneid*, Cambridge, MA: Harvard University Press, 1965.

Putnam, M.C.J. 'On Catullus 27'. *Latomus* 28 (1969): 850–7.

Rakob, F. 'The Making of Augustan Carthage', in *Romanization and the city: Creation, transformations, and failures*, edited by E. Fentress, 73–82. Portsmouth: Journal of Roman Archaeology Supplementary Series 38, 2000.

Rehak, P. 'Aeneas or Numa? Rethinking the Meaning of the Ara Pacis Augustae'. *The Art Bulletin*, 83 (2001): 190–208.

Rehak, P. *Imperium and Cosmos: Augustus and the Northern Campus Martius*, Madison: The University of Wisconsin Press, 2006.
Richardson, L. *A New Topographical Dictionary of Ancient Rome*, Baltimore: Johns Hopkins University Press, 1992.
Rives, J.B. *Religion and Authority in Roman Carthage from Augustus to Constantine*, Oxford: Blackwell Publishing, 1995.
Rose, H.J. 'A Misunderstood Passage in Martial'. *CR* 38 (1924): 64–5.
Rose, M.A. *Parody: Ancient, Modern, and Post-Modern*, Cambridge: Cambridge University Press, 1993.
Rosenbloom, E. *A Word in Your Ear: How & Why to Read James Joyce's Finnegans Wake*, East Hardwick, VT: BookSurge Publishing, 2006.
Salzman-Mitchell, P.B. *A Web of Fantasies: Gaze, Image, and Gender in Ovid's* Metamorphoses, Columbus: Ohio State University Press, 2005.
Santini, C. *Silius Italicus and his view of the Past*, Amsterdam: J. C. Gieben, 1991.
Schäfer, M. 'Zum Tellusbild auf der Ara Pacis Augustae'. *Gymnasium* 66 (1959): 288–301.
Scheid, J. ed., *Commentarii Fratrum Arvalium qui supersunt*, Rome: École Française de Rome and Soprintendenza Archeologica di Roma, 1998.
Scheid, J. 'Hierarchy and Structure in Roman Polytheism: Roman Methods of Conceiving Action', in *Roman Religion*, edited by C. Ando, 164–89. Edinburgh: Edinburgh University Press, 2003.
Scheid, J. 'Gli Arvali e il sito ad Deam Diam', in *Terme di Diocleziano. Il chiostro piccolo della Certosa di Santa Maria degli Angeli*, edited by R. Friggeri, M. Magnani Cianetti, C. Caruso, 49–59. Milano: Electa/Mondadori, 2014.
Schork, R.J. *Latin and Roman Culture in Joyce*, Gainesville: University Press of Florida, 1997.
Segal, C. *Landscape in Ovid's* Metamorphoses*: A Study in the Transformation of a Literary Symbol*, Wiesbaden: Franz Steiner Verlag, 1969.
Senn, F. *Joyce's Dislocutions: Essays on Reading as Translation*, Baltimore: Johns Hopkins University Press, 1984.
Senn, F. 'Ovidian Roots of Gigantism in Joyce's "Ulysses"'. *Journal of Modern Literature* 15.4 (1989): 561–77.
Senn, F. 'Ovid's Not-Yet-Icity'. *James Joyce Quarterly* 29.2 (1992): 401–3.
Senn, F. 'Met Whom What?' *James Joyce Quarterly* 30.1 (1992): 109–13.
Senn, F. *Inductive Scrutinies: Focus on Joyce*, Dublin: The Lilliput Press, 1995.
Sharrock, A. 'Gender and Sexuality', in *The Cambridge Companion to Ovid*, edited by P. Hardie, 95–107. Cambridge: Cambridge University Press, 2002.
Sherk, R.K. 'The Eponymous Officials of Greek Cities V: The Register: Part VI: Sicily'. *ZPE* 96 (1993): 267–95.
Smith, R.A. *Poetic Allusion and Poetic Embrace in Ovid and Virgil*, Ann Arbor: University of Michigan Press, 1997.
Smith, W. *Dictionary of Greek and Roman Geography*, vol. 1, London: Murray 1872.
Snyder, J.M. *Puns and Poetry in Lucretius' De Rerum Natura*, Amsterdam: B.R. Grüner, 1980.

Solodow, J.B. *The World of Ovid's Metamorphoses*, Chapel Hill: University of North Carolina Press, 1988.
Spaeth, B. 'The Goddess Ceres in the Ara Pacis Augustae and the Carthage Relief'. *AJA* 98 (1994): 65–100.
Spaltenstein, F. *Commentaire des* Punica *de Silius Italicus (livres 1 à 8)*, Genève: Droz, 1986.
Spaltenstein, F. *Commentaire des* Punica *de Silius Italicus (livres 9 á 17)*, Genève: Droz, 1990.
Spann, P. *Quintus Sertorius and the Legacy of Sulla*, Fayetteville: University of Arkansas Press, 1987.
Stevenson, S. *Dictionary of Roman Coins, Republican and Imperial*, London: Seaby, 1964.
Stocks, C. *The Roman Hannibal: Remembering the Enemy in Silius Italicus*, Punica, Liverpool: Liverpool University Press, 2014.
Strong, E. 'Terra Mater or Italia'. *JRS* 27 (1937): 114–26.
Sutherland, C. and Carson, R. *The Roman Imperial Coinage from 31 BC to AD 69, vol. 1*. London: Spink, 1984.
Swallow, E. 'Anna Soror'. *CW* 44.10 (1951): 145–50.
Sydenham, E.A. *The Coinage of the Roman Republic*, London: Spink, 1952.
Tarrant, R. 'Poetry and Power: Virgil's poetry in contemporary context', in *The Cambridge Companion to Virgil*, edited by C. Martindale, 169–87. Cambridge and New York: Cambridge University Press, 1997.
Tarrant, R. *Virgil: Aeneid XII*, Cambridge: Cambridge University Press, 2012.
Tarrant, R.J., ed. *P. Ovidi Nasonis: Metamorphoses*, Oxford: Oxford University Press, 2004.
Thilo, G. and Hagen, H. eds. *Servii Grammatici qui feruntur in Vergilii carmina commentarii*, 3 vols. Hildesheim, Zurich, New York: Georg Olms Verlag, 1986.
Thomas, R. (ed.). *Vergil Georgics*, Cambridge: Cambridge University Press, 1988.
Thomas, R. F. *Virgil and the Augustan Reception*, Cambridge: Cambridge University Press, 2001.
Tipping, B. *Exemplary Epic: Silius Italicus* Punica, Oxford and New York: Oxford University Press, 2010.
Torelli, M. *Typology and Structure of Roman Historical Reliefs*, Ann Arbor: University of Michigan Press, 1982.
Turner, V. 'Comments and Conclusions', in *The Reversible World*, edited by B.A, Babcock, 276–96. Ithaca, NY: Cornell University Press, 1978.
Van Nortwick, T. 'Woman Warrior? Aeneas' Encounters with the Feminine', in *Roman Literature, Gender and Reception: Domina Illustris*, edited by D. Lateiner, B.K. Gold, and J. Perkins, 136–52. New York: Routledge, 2013.
Vessey, D.W.T.C. 'Silius Italicus and the Fall of Saguntum'. *CP* 69, no. 1 (1974): 28–36.
Vessey, D.W.T.C. 'Silius Italicus: The Shield of Hannibal'. *AJP* 96 (1975): 391–405.
Vessey, D.W.T.C. 'Flavian Epic', in *The Cambridge History of Classical Literature Vol. 2.4: The Early Principate*, edited by E.J. Kenney, 62–100. Cambridge and New York: Cambridge University Press, 1982.
Volpilhac, J., Miniconi, P. and Devallet, G. *Silius Italicus – Tome II: Livres V–VIII*, Paris: Belles lettres, 1981.

Watson, G. 'The Pay of the Roman Army: The Republic'. *Historia: Zeitschrift für Alte Geschichte* 7 (1958): 113–20.
Weinstock, S. 'Pax and the Ara Pacis'. *JRS* 50 (1960): 44–58.
Weinstock, S. 'Two Archaic Inscriptions from Latium'. *JRS* 50 (1960): 112–18.
Weinstock, S. *Divus Iulius*, Oxford: Clarendon Press, 1971.
Wells, H.G. 'James Joyce'. *Nation* 20 (1917): 710, 712.
West, G.S. 'Vergil's Helpful Sisters: Anna and Juturna in the "Aeneid"'. *Vergilius* 25 (1979): 10–19.
Williams, J. 'Religion and Roman Coins', in *A Companion to Roman Religion*, edited by J. Rüpke, 143–63. Chichester: Wiley-Blackwell, 2011.
Williams, R.D. *The Aeneid of Vergil*, 2 vols. London: Bristol Classical Press, 1972.
Wilson, J.R. 'O Fons Bandusiae'. *CJ* 63.7 (1968): 289–96.
Wilson, M. 'Ovidian Silius'. *Arethusa* 37, no. 2 (2004): 225–49.
Wilson, R.J.A. *Sicily under the Roman Empire: The archaeology of a Roman province, 36 BC – AD 535*, Warminster: Aris & Phillips, 1990.
Wimsatt, W.K. and Beardsley, M. 'The Intentional Fallacy'. *The Sewanee Review* 54.3 (1946): 468–88.
Wiseman, T.P. *Roman Drama and Roman History*, Exeter: University of Exeter Press, 1998.
Wiseman, T.P. *The Myths of Rome*, Exeter: University of Exeter Press, 2004.
Wiseman, T.P. 'The Cult Site of Anna Perenna: Documentation, Visualization, Imagination', in *Imaging Ancient Rome: Documentation – Visualization – Imagination*, edited by L. Haselberger and J. Humphrey, 51–62. Portsmouth: Journal of Roman Archaeology Supplementary Series 61, 2006.
Wiseman, T.P. *Unwritten Rome*, Exeter: Exeter University Press, 2008.
Wiseman, T.P. *Remembering the Roman People: Essays on Late-Republican Politics and Literature*, Oxford: Oxford University Press, 2009.
Wiseman, T.P. 'Politics and the People: What Counts as Evidence?' *BICS* 60–1 (2017): 16–33.
Wissowa, G. *Religion und Kultus der Römer,* Munich: Beck, 1971.
Woolf, G. 'Monumental Writing and the Expansion of Roman Society in the Early Empire'. *The Journal of Roman Studies* 86 (1996): 22–39.
Zanker, P. *The Power of Images in the Age of Augustus*, translated by A. Shapiro, Ann Arbor: The University of Michigan Press, 1990.
Zehnacker, H. *Moneta: recherches sur l'organisation et l'art des émissions monétaires de la République romaine (289–31 av. J.-C.)*, Rome: École française de Rome, 1966.
Zemon Davis, N. 'Women on Top: Symbolic Sexual Inversion and Political Disorder in Early Modern Europe', in *The Reversible World: Symbolic Inversion in Art and Society*, edited by B.A. Babcock, 147–90. Ithaca, NY: Cornell University Press, 1978.
Ziogas, I. 'The Poet as Prince: Author and Authority Under Augustus', in *The Art of Veiled Speech*, edited by H. Baltussen and P.J. Davis, 115–36. Philadelphia: University of Pennsylvania Press, 2008.
Ziolkowski, T. *Ovid and the Moderns*, Ithaca: Cornell University Press, 2005.

Index Locorum

LITERARY SOURCES

Augustine
  C.D.
    4.11.3: 163 n.11
    4.22.1: 3
    6.1.7: 163 n.11
    6.3.4: 3
    6.6.3: 165 n.47
    6.7.1: 165 n.47
    7.2.1: 163 n.11
    7.3.7: 4

Caesar
  B. Hisp.
    31: 211 n.79
  Civ.
    1.22.5: 11, 164 n.21

Callimachus
  Hec. (Hollis)
    fr. 35: 138

Catullus
  27.1-7: 72
  64.254: 72
  66.51: 171-2 n.32

Cicero
  Catil.
    4.9: 164 n.24
  Div.
    1.80: 72
  N.D.
    2.55: 79
  Rep.
    1.31: 164 n.17

Dio Cassius
  37.37.1: 6
  37.37.2: 164 n.24

Ennius
  Ann. (Skutsch)
    40: 162

Festus
  142L: 167 n.89

Horace
  Carm.
    2.3.11-2: 73
  Sat.
    1.8.10: 168 n.104

Livy
  1.20.5-6: 5
  2.13.11: 137

Lucretius
  1.21: 187 n.32
  1.30-1: 187 n.32
  1.112-19: 187-8 n.35
  1.117-18: 133

Macrobius
  1.12.6: 2, 199 n.4

Martial
  1. pref.: 166 n.61
  3.68.5-10: 13
  4.64.11-24: 12-13
  4.64.18: 179 n.20
  8.49.3-4: 166 n.67

Ovid
  Ep.
    7.17-18: 136
    7.195-6: 30, 131
  Fast.
    1.396: 166 n.62

2.304: 166 n.62
2.586: 8, 166 n.57
2.613-5: 91
3.524: 167 n.85
3.525-6: 200 n.11
3.525-38: 127-8
3.535-6: 115
3.539: 125
3.539-42: 86-7, 128
3.541-2: 115
3.543-4: 28, 41, 54, 154, 160
3.544: 29, 54, 160
3.545-6: 30
3.545-50: 29
3.549-50: 30, 131
3.553: 31
3.555-6: 193 n.16
3.559-64: 31
3.562: 171 n.32
3.563: 32, 154, 160
3.564: 32
3.571: 36
3.595: 154
3.599: 45
3.603: 33, 136
3.605-12: 33
3.607: 33, 174 n.26
3.609: 34
3.610: 34, 46
3.619: 195 n.32
3.619-20: 48
3.623-4: 35
3.626: 45
3.629-30: 46
3.632: 36
3.633-54: 88-9
3.637: 132
3.637-8: 46-7
3.639-41: 47
3.639-42: 86-7
3.642-8: 49
3.643: 50
3.645: 49
3.647-8: 46, 81, 132
3.649: 50
3.652-4: 51, 132-3
3.653: 71
3.653-4: 81, 132, 160, 179 n.21
3.654: 77, 133

3.657: 66, 184 n.68
3.657-60: 6
3.658: 204 n.42
3.659-60: 71
3.661-2: 41, 114
3.663: 166 n.72
3.670: 138
3.673: 166 n.71
3.673-4: 114, 138
3.675: 154
3.675-6: 140
3.677: 141
3.683-4: 141
3.690: 156
3.693: 156
3.693-4: 141
3.695: 166 n.65
3.696: 142
3.697: 129, 157
3.699: 145
3.701-2: 134
3.707-10: 142
3.735: 166 n.62
4.326: 166 n.58
4.946: 166 n.61
5.18-20: 166 n.66
5.183: 166 n.61
5.202-5: 91
5.331-2: 166 n.61
5.349: 166 n.61
5.352: 166 n.61
6.223-4: 167 n.91
6.320: 166 n.62
6.659: 166 n.64
6.667: 166 n.64
6.692: 166 n.64
6.697: 167 n.83

Ib.
81-2: 9

Met.
1.173: 10, 166 n.69
1.192-95: 10
8.188: 150
14.598-608: 90
15.61-2: 155
15.760-1: 140
15.844-5: 135
15.847-8: 135
15.865: 129

Index Locorum

Pont.
    4.8.55-6: 146
Rem.
    651-2: 79-80

Petronius
    133.3: 167 n.93

Plautus
  Pers.
    329-31: 79

Pliny the Elder
  Nat.
    36.26: 56

Pliny the Younger
  Ep.
    3.7.5: 38

Plutarch
  Num.
    9.4: 5
  Sert.
    6.2-4: 121-2

Propertius
    1.2.9-12: 73
    4.9.32: 8, 166 n.57

Quintilian
  Inst.
    10.1.88: 151

Schol. Pers.
    6, 55: 139

Seneca
  Ep.
    97.8: 166 n.61

Servius
  ad Virg. *A.*
    4.366: 170 n.21
    4.676: 20, 25
    4.682: 7, 20, 25
    5.4: 7, 20
    8.31: 186 n.14
    12.139: 189 n.46

ad Virg. *G.*
    1.21: 3
    1.126: 80, 188 n.37

Silius Italicus
    1.13-14: 42
    1.17: 43
    1.38-9: 43
    1.81-4: 43-4
    1.94: 44
    1.95-6: 44
    8.27-8: 40
    8.39: 62
    8.39-43: 44
    8.43: 42
    8.44-9: 41
    8.68: 45
    8.77-8: 48
    8.79-80: 46
    8.145-7: 48
    8.176-7: 47
    8.179-81: 50
    8.183: 46
    8.184-91: 49-50
    8.190-1: 46, 168 n.96, 179 n.21
    8.194: 50
    8.196-7: 51
    8.197-9: 51, 58
    8.198: 51, 168 n.96
    8.239: 52
    10.657-8: 175 n.36

Suetonius
  Jul.
    88: 11

Tacitus
  Ann.
    1.8.6: 15, 168 n.98

Valerius Maximus
    2.10.8: 9, 166 n.61

Varro
  Antiquitates divinae
    fr. 3: 3
    fr. 7: 7, 165 n.48
    fr. 10: 7
    fr. 151: 13

234 Index Locorum

L.
   7.87: 214 n.38
Men.
   fr. 506: 2
   fr. 513: 8

Velleius Paterculus
   2.3.2-3: 4, 164 n.18

Virgil
   A.
      1.312: 33
      1.353-4: 87-8
      1.357: 88
      1.441: 43
      1.628-9: 85
      1.701: 73-4
      2.270-3: 87
      2.277-80: 87
      2.287-9: 87
      2.717-20: 77
      4.9: 162
      4.31-3: 78-9
      4.283-4: 34
      4.305: 170 n.20
      4.366: 170 n.20
      4.413: 26
      4.413-15: 25-6
      4.420-3: 77-8
      4.420-4: 22
      4.423: 24
      4.424: 26
      4.460: 171 n.32
      4.476: 80
      4.494-7: 26
      4.503: 26
      4.504-8: 27
      4.509-11: 32
      4.634-6: 75
      4.635: 159
      4.659-60: 27, 34
      4.673: 80
      4.675-83: 24, 29-30
      4.676: 20, 25
      4.678-9: 25
      4.682: 25
      4.683-4: 159
      4.683-5: 76
      4.690-1: 32, 160
      7.312: 44
      8.71: 185-6 n.13
      9.23-4: 74
      9.816-8: 77
      10.833-5: 74
      11.86: 189
      12.416-21: 75
      12.682: 80
      12.841: 44
      12.885: 81-2

INSCRIPTIONS

AE
   2003, 251: 15, **96**-97
   2003, 252: 15, 60, 97, **98**, 181 n.37
   2003, 253: 60, 97-98, **99**, 181 n.36

CIL
   1² 1.242: 196-7 n.14
   6.896: 104
   6.1033: 197 n.24
   6.10114: 16
   14.2408: 168 n.100
   14.3565.13-22: 14

ILLRP (Fasti Antiates Maiores)
   9: 1

General Index

Page numbers in **bold** refer to figures.

Achates, 33
Acilius Eutyches, Gaius, 15–16, **96**–7, 101
Actaeon, 8, 92
Aemilia the Vestal virgin, 119
Aeneas, 132
    Anna as doublet of, 86
    Anna's encounter with, 33–4, 45–6, 132
    apotheosis, 62, 85, 90, 91
    Ara Pacis Augustae panel, 181–2 n.44
    betrayal of Dido, 43
    connection to Anna, 85–8, 90
    death of, 194 n.18
    deification, 66, 134
    depiction as a hero, 93
    and Dido, 19–20, 22, 86
    at Dido's temple, 43–4
    encounter with Dido in the Underworld, 47–8
    escape from Troy, 77, 86–7
    in the *Fasti*, 136
    first meets Dido, 85
    importance of, 63
    leaves Carthage, 22, 25–6, 77–8
    murder of Turnus, 39
    relationship with Anna, 19, 22–4, 78
    reunion with Anna, 34–5
    travels, 84
    wounding, 74–5
Aeneid (Virgil), 37, 145
    Aeneas's decision to leave Carthage, 77–8
    Aeneas's depiction as a hero, 93
    allusions to goddess's name, 78–80
    allusive references, 25
    Anna and Juturna, 80–2
    Anna–Aeneas Tradition, 19–27
    Anna's final speech, 20–1
    Anna's role in, 21–5, 38
    Book 1, 35, 73–4, 85, 158
    Book 2, 39, 77, 86
    Book 4, 21–7, 28, 29, 31, 34, 35, 40–1, 43, 71–82, 130, 132, 136, 159, 171 n.32
    Book 5, 20
    Book 7, 43
    Book 8, 129, 185–6 n.13
    Book 9, 74, 77
    Book 12, 74–5, 80
    death of Dido, 24–5, 26–7, 31–2, 44, 45, 48, 76–7, 80–1
    depiction of Dido, 20
    Dido and Aeneas first meet, 85
    Dido's epithet, 82
    Dido's hair, 171 n.32
    Dido's role, 84, 86
    dying words of Dido, 20
    mytho-cosmic framework, 43
    narrative of Carthage, 65
    occurrences of *lympha*, 73–5
    political readings, 172 n.1
    wordplay, 40–2, 72–3, 80, 160
Aequitas, 116–17, 120, 201 n.18, 203 n.41
Alba Longa, 7, 139
altars, 15–16, 30, 32, 100, 101
ambiguity, 38–42, 47, 55, 63, 65, 67, 131
anastomosis, 161–2
Anna
    address to the Trojans, 51
    apotheosis, 85, 88–93
    arrival in Italy, 33–5, 41, 46, 47, 89, 91, 132
    arrival in Latium, 33–4
    of Bovillae, 6, 7–10, 41, 137–41, 156, 199 n.5
    Carthaginian, 6–7, 14–15, 19, 54, 58
    connection with the moon, 66
    and Dido, 21–5
    as doublet of Aeneas, 86
    encounter with Aeneas, 45–6

escape from Lavinia, 86–8, 91, 92–3, 132
farewell to Dido, 32
flight from Carthage, 45–6, 49–50, 131
as Io, 156
and Juturna, 80–2
metamorphosis into Nymph, 50–1, 58, 61, 132–3
naval journey, 33, 59
otherness, 38
Ovid's treatment of, 28–36
role, 84
of Sicily, 59–61
Silius's treatment of, 37
sister of Dido, 21–5
status as a Nymph, 71, 75–6, 82
transformation, 92
travels, 84–8, 131–2, 177 n.2, 193 n.16
Virgil's treatment of, 19, 19–27
Anna Perenna (Laberius), 6
Anna soror, 7, 21, 76, 162
Anna–Aeneas Tradition
Ovid's treatment, 28–36
Virgil's treatment, 19–27, 29
Annius, Gaius, 113, 116, 116–23, 203 n.31, 204 n.45
career, 122–3, 205–6 n.61
coins, 56, 113, **114**, 116–20, 123–4
family background, 121, 204 n.44
name, 117
strategy, 123–4
apotheosis, 54, 58
Aeneas, 62–4, 85, 90, 91
Anna, 85, 88, 88–93
Fasti narratives, 83
Ovid, 85, 88, 88–93
Ara Pacis Augustae, 62, 182 n.53
Aeneas panel, 181–2 n.44
ambiguity, 63
bull, 57
central figure, 56, 57–8, 67, 178 n.11, 178 n.12, 184 n.69, 184 n.70
children, 58
comparison with Carthaginan Altar, 65
consecration, 55
context, 62–4
ewe, 57
flanking figures, 56
nymphs, 56–7, 58

panels, 62
South-Eastern Panel, 55–8, **55**
artistic depictions, 54–67
Ara Pacis Augustae, 55–64, **55**, 67
the Carthage Altar, 64–7, **64**
inscriptions, 59–60, 61
Nereids, 56, **57**
nymphs, 58
Arval Brethren, inscriptions, 94, 107–8, 109
Augustine, *City of God*, 3, 8
Augustus, 11, 15, 62, 126, 127, 129
calendar reform, 143, 144, 145
deification, 135, 139–40, 140
deification under, 144
ideology, 63–4, 65, 66, 67, 184 n.63
Azan, 6, 54

Battus, 36, 45
Bovillae, 6–7, 10, 41, 54, 113–15, 125–6, 139–41
brides, pre-marriage initiation, 13
Buscemi, 60, 61

caduceus, 113, 120, 204 n.42
calendar, 126–7
Augustan reform, 143, 144, 145
Julian reform, 127
Calendar of Modern Letters, The, 154
Callimachus, 137–8
Cannae, battle of, 37, 39, 40–5, 52, 63
carnival, 126
Carthage, 65, 183 n.60
Carthage Altar, the, 64–7, **64**
Catullus, 72
Censorinus, Lucius Marcius, 118
change and change theory, 94, 103–5, 106–9
characteristics, 54, 63, 103, 120, 135, 151
Chloris, 91
Cicero, 4, 8, 72, 79, 81
City of God (Augustine), 3, 8
Clodius Vestalis, C., 119, **119**
coins, 12, **56**, 61, **117**, 132
ancestral references, 117–19
Annius, Gaius, 113, **114**, 116–20, 123–4
Censorinus, 118
Clodius Vestalis, 119, **119**
divine references, 117–19

Metellus Pius, 117–18, **118**, 202 n.25
  representation of Victory, 119–20, **119**
  Sextus Julius, 202 n.26
  Silanus, 119, **119**, 120
  Thorius Balbus, **117**
contests, 102, 107, 110
contio, 123
Cornelius Aquila, Lucius, 61
Cornificius, 4
cult, 14, 15, 107
  centre, 12–13, 14, 15, 59–60
  images, lack of, 67
  statue, 10
cultural integration, 52
cultural memory, 137
curse-tablets, 16, 108–9, 110
  see tabellae defixionum

De indigitamentis (Granius Flaccus), 4
deification, 45, 46, 50–2, 75–6, 81, 114, 126, 129–30, 130, 132–6, 137–41, 145
  Aeneas, 66, 134
  Augustus, 135, 139–40
  under Augustus, 144
  diva, use of, 62–3
  Julius Caesar, 126, 129–30, 134–5, 140
  by ruler, 134–5
  through merit, 140
  of women, 144
  see also apotheosis
deities, 1–4, 6, 9, 58–60,, 74, 108–9, 141
  hierarchy, 3–4
  naming, 2–3
  specialist, 3
Demeter/Ceres, 58, 60
Diana, 92
Diana Lucifera, 66
Dido, 19, 42
  and Aeneas, 19–20, 22, 86
  Aeneas's betrayal of, 43
  and Aeneas's departure, 25–6, 77–8
  and Anna, 21–5
  death of, 24–5, 26–7, 31–2, 44, 45, 48, 76–7, 80–1, 85, 131, 159–60, 169 n.9
  dream of Sychaeus, 87–8
  dying words, 20, 27
  epithet, 82
  first meets Aeneas, 85
  funeral pyre, 26–7

ghost, 46, 47, 86–7, 132
hair, 171 n.32
kinship with Anna, 31–2
letter to Aeneas, 130
Ovid's treatment, 28–31, 31–2, 34–5
precedent, 86
role in *Aeneid*, 84
story, 85–6
in the Underworld, 47–8
Dionysius Filocalus, Furius, 114
diva, use of, 62–3
Divine Antiquities (Varro), 3–4, 7–8, 13
drinking rituals, 101–2

Encyclopædia Britannica (1910–1911), 153, 157, 160, 161
Ennius, 133, 162, 187–8 n.35
epigraphic habit, 100, 102–3, 105, 108
epigraphic monuments, 104–5
epigraphy, 94–110
  categories, 104
  and change, 94, 103–5, 106–9
  functions, 104
  tabellae defixionum, 95, 108–9, 110
  votive context, 101
  votive inscriptions, 94–102, **96**, **98**, **99**
  see also inscriptions
erotic entertainment, 6–9
Eutychides libertus inscription, 96–7, **96**, 99, 101–2, 106

Fasti (Ovid), 6, 19, 101, 124
  account of Caesar's deification, 129–30
  Aeneas in, 136
  Aeneas's encounter with Dido in the Underworld, 47–8
  aim, 145–6
  Anna, the Phoenician princess, 6–7
  Anna of Bovillae, 7–10, 113–15, 137–41
  Anna–Mars episode, 114–15
  Anna's address to the Trojans, 51
  Anna's apotheosis, 85, 88, 88–93
  Anna's arrival in Italy, 33–5, 41, 46, 47, 89, 91, 132
  Anna's escape from Lavinia, 86–8, 91, 92–3, 132
  Anna's farewell to Dido, 32
  Anna's flight from Carthage, 45–6, 49–50, 131

Anna's metamorphosis, 50–1, 58, 132–3
Anna's naval journey, 33, 59
Anna's role in, 84
Anna's transformation, 92
Anna's travels, 84–8, 131–2, 177 n.2, 193 n.16
apotheosis narratives, 83
association with plebeian class, 113–16
Book 2, 91
Book 3, 28–36, 45, 54, 71, 80, 91, 113–15, 125, 127, 130, 131–3, 134–5, 136, 141, 142, 145, 155
Book 5, 9
Callimachean models, 137–8
commemoration of Dido, 29–31
composition, 126
death of Dido, 31–2, 85, 131
Dido role in, 84
framework, 126–7
gender perspective, 83–93
influence on Joyce, 152, 160–2, 213 n.16
iocus, 9
Jupiter, 10
lexical choice, 32
origin narratives, 38, 41–2, 54, 71, 81, 130–4, 137–41, 142, 190–1 n.3
role reversals, 132
Silius and, 37–8, 47–8
thematic focus, 30
treatment of the Ides of March, 125, 126–9, 136–7, 142–6, 154
Vesta in, 129–30
wordplay, 40–1
Fasti Antiates Maiores, 1–2
Fasti Filocaliani, 143
Faunus, 9
Feltre altar, 195 n.2
fertility, 61
  Anna's association with, 82
  nymphs association with, 190 n.53
fertility goddesses, 65, 66, 178 n.18
  attributes, 55–6, 58
fertility symbols, 58
festival of Anna Perenna, 12–14, 38, 54, 58–9, 82, 101–3, 125–9, 142–4, 152–4, 188–9 n.38, 207 n.12–13
festivals, 1–2, 115
festivities, 28, 101–2, 107

Fighting Shadows: On Nonsense (Varro), 2
Finnegans Wake (Joyce), 149–62
  ALP's laughter, 156–7
  anastomosis, 161–2
  Anna Livia Plurabelle, 150, 153–4, 155–6, 158, 159–60, 162
  Anna's presence, 153
  anxiety, 149–50
  defensive stance, 159–60
  ending, 149, 162
  final chapter, 154
  Julius Caesar reference, 157
  month-men, 155–6
  nana karlikeevna, 153
  nymph-onyms, 159
  Ovidianism, 149–52, 154–7, 160–2, 213 n.16
  protagonist, 152
  references to Themis, 214 n.31
  reverse osmosis, 160–1
  structure, 157
fountain of Anna Perenna, 95, 106–7

gender, 83–93, 126, 138, 142
  roles, 84, 86, 92
gens Iulia, 7, 65
Granius Flaccus, 4
grotto, 59
grove, 12–13, 14, 54, 58, 61, 101, 179 n.20

Hannibal, 39, 42, 42–3, 45, 52, 182 n.51
Hercules, 8, 85, 90, 107, 118, 134, 194 n.19
Horace, 63, 73

Iapyx, 74–5
identity
  Anna's, 33, 39, 44
  crisis, 42, 53
  multiplicity of, 54, 142
  plebeian, 115–16
  poetic, 29
Ides of March, 1–2, 9, 11, 39, 59
  beginning, 127
  ending, 129
  Ovid's treatment, 125, 126–9, 136–7, 142–6, 154
Ides of June, 9
immortality, 57
Indiges, 45, 62, 63, 66, 90

inscriptions, 59–60, 61
   Arval Brethren, 94, 107–8, 109
   durability, 102
   Eutychides libertus, 96–7, **96**, 99, 101–2, 106
   functions, 108
   funerary, 104
   honorary, 104–5
   location, 94, 105, 107
   message, 104
   Suetonius Germanus, 97–8, **99**, 106, 181 n.36
   Suetonius Germanus and Licinia, 97, **98**, 99, 106, 107, 181 n.37
   tabellae defixionum, 95, 108–9, 110
   votive, 94–102, **96**, **98**, **99**
   votive context, 100–1
   see also epigraphy
Io, 156
iocus, 9

Joyce, James
   anastomosis, 161–2
   cloacal obsession, 157
   defensive stance, 159–60
   Finnegans Wake, 149–62
   influence of Ovid, 149–52, 154–7, 160–2, 212 n.14, 213 n.16
   notebooks, 155–6
   A Portrait of the Artist as a Young Man, 150, 154
   reverse osmosis, 160–1
   Ulysses, 152, 154–5, 161
Julian calendar, 127
Julius Caesar, 4, 15, 89
   advance into Italy, 10–1
   assassination of, 11, 39, 62, 125, 129, 142, 145
   calendar reform, 127
   connection with Bovillae, 139
   deification, 126, 129–30, 134–5, 140
   divinity, 11
   Joyce's reference to, 157
   pontificate, 5–6, 9, 10
   as *princeps*, 129
   rise of, 42
Juno, 37, 39, 40, 42–5, 116–17, **117**
Jupiter, 8, 9, 10, 42
Juturna, 80–2, 186 n.16, 189 n.42

Laberius, Decimus, 6, 124, 140
Lacus Iuturnae, Rome, 82
Lara, 91
Late Republican identity, 113–24
Lavinia, 36, 46, 86–8, 92–3, 132
Lepidus, Aemilius, 119
Liberalia, festival of the, 139, 143
Livy, 39, 121, 137, 204 n.45
locus amoenus, 50
Lucan, 37, 39, 45
Lucretius, 133, 187–8 n.35
ludi Florales, the, 9
ludi scaenici, the, 8
Lydus, John, 114, 200 n.10
lympha
   anthropomorphic traits, 72–3
   association with, 71–4, 75–8, 159
   and healing, 74–5
   meanings, 72
   occurrences in *Aeneid*, 73–5

Macrobius, 2
magic, 16, 61, 109
Magna Mater, 60
Mamuralia, the, 200 n.10
Mars, 7, 8, 92, 114, 141, 141–2, 142, 156
Marsyas, 118
Martial, 12–13, 38, 101
masculine virtues, 84, 86, 134
memory, 103
Mena, 3
merit, deification through, 140
Metamorphoses (Ovid), 47, 62, 83, 84, 85, 90, 91–2, 93, 130, 132, 134, 135, 140, 152, 155, 158–9, 192–3 n.9
Metellus Pius, Quintus Caecilius, 5, 117–18, **118**, 202 n.25
Minerva, 7, 141–2, 156–7
moon, the, connection with, 66, 153, 155
multiplicity, 54, 66–7
Munda, battle of, 143, 211 n.80
Mutunus Tutunus, 13

Naevius, 6–7, 14
Numa, 5
Numicius and the Numicius River, 45, 46, 50–1, 58, 61, 62, 71, 81, 85, 90, 92, 132, 194 n.18

nymphs, 14, 46, 58–61, 67, 99–100
    Anna's metamorphosis, 50–1, 61
    Anna's status as, 71, 75–6, 82
    Ara Pacis Augustae, 56, 58
    artistic depictions, 58
    association with fertility, 190 n.53
    Carthage Altar, 65
    connection with healing, 61
    identification with, 54
    Naiads, **56**
    Nereids, 56–7, **57**, 178 n.10
    ritualistic baths, 76–7
    worship, 61

Odysseus, 84, 93
origin narratives
    Ovid, 28–9, 38, 41–2, 54, 58, 71, 81,
        130–4, 137–41, 142, 190–1 n.3
    Silius, 37–53, 58
Ovid
    allusion to Ennius, 133
    allusive techniques, 28–31
    and Caesar's assassination, 11
    Carthaginian Anna, 28–36
    commemoration of Dido, 29–31
    defence against Virgil, 158–60
    engagement with Virgil, 19, 28–31,
        34–5, 35–6
    female characters, 83–4
    influence on Joyce, 149–52, 154–7,
        160–2, 212 n.14, 213 n.16
    Metamorphoses, 47, 62, 83, 84, 85, 90,
        91–2, 93, 130, 132, 134, 135, 140,
        152, 155, 158–9, 192–3 n.9
    origin narratives, 28–9, 54, 58
    reading of *Aeneid* 4, 28
    Remedia Amoris, 79–80
    reputation, 28
    Silius and, 39
    technique of narrative gemination,
        33–4, 35
    treatment of the Ides of March, 59, 125,
        126–9, 136–7, 142–6, 154
    see also Fasti (Ovid)

Paides, 59–60, 61
palindromic personage, 157–8
pantomimus dance-drama, 8
parody, 130–1

paronomasia, 113, 117
Perennial Anna, 41, 66
perennis, 79–80
perpetua, 78–80
Piazza Euclide, Rome, 12, 16, 59, 94, 101–2,
    125, 133, 143
Plautus, 79
plebeian class
    association with, 113–16, 121–4, 141
    secession, 4, 7, 114, 141, 199 n.3
    tribunate, 10
plebeian gods, 3–4
Pliny the Elder, 56
Pliny the Younger, 38, 100
Polyhymnia, 9
pomegranates, 58
pompa, 115
pontifex maximus, 5–6
pontifices, 2–3
popularity, 71
praeteritio, 142
Priapus, 9, 13–14
Prima Porta Augustus statue, 57–8
princeps, Julius Caesar as, 129
Propertius, 8, 72–3
Punica (Silius Italicus), 14, 37
    Aeneas's encounter with Dido in the
        Underworld, 48
    Anna narrative, 173 n.7
    Anna's address to the Trojans, 51
    Anna's arrival in Italy, 39, 46–7
    Anna's encounter with Aeneas,
        45–6
    Anna's flight from Carthage, 45–6,
        49–50
    Anna's metamorphosis, 50–1
    Anna's mission, 42–3
    Anna's role in, 39–40
    assessments of, 38–9
    battle of Cannae, 40–5, 52, 63
    characterization of Anna, 63
    death of Dido, 48
    Dido's ghost, 46, 47
    Dido's temple, 43–4
    Juno, 37, 39, 40, 42–5
    mytho-cosmic framework, 43
    origin narratives, 58
    origins, 42–3
    tone of violence, 49–50

treatment of the Anna, 37–53
wordplay, 40–1
Pygmalion, 45

Quintilian, 151

rape, 49–51, 81, 88–92, 132–4
Regulus, L. Livineius, 119
reverse osmosis, 160–1
Rhinthon, 8
ritual purification, 76–7
roles, 34, 54, 84, 88
Roman Republic
   civil war, 4, 10–1, 42
   corruption, 4
   death of, 39, 42
   plebeian secession, 4, 7, 114, 141,
     199 n.3
Romanization, 103
Rome
   Ara Pacis, 55–64, **55**, 67
   foundation and foundation narratives,
     38, 40, 126, 133–4, 140
   Lacus Iuturnae, 82
   Piazza Euclide, 12, 16, 59, 94, 101–2,
     125, 133, 143
   Via Flaminia, 12, 101, 153
Romulus, 62, 83, 85, 90, 114, 127, 133,
   134
ruler deification, 134–5

sacrifice, 2, 5, 13, 60, 62, 63, 81, 82, 139
Sallust, 4–5
sanctuary, 95, 102, 106–7, 108–9
Second Punic War, 37, 39, 42, 45, 52
Servius, 2–3, 7, 20–1, 62, 74
Sextus Julius, 202 n.26
sexual identity, 84
Sicilian cave cult, 59–60
Silanus, Decimus Iunius, 119, **119**,
   120
Silius Italicus
   Anna narrative, 173 n.7
   engagement with Ovid, 39
   engagement with the Fasti, 47–8
   use of *diva*, 62–3
   see also Punica
Silvius, Polemius, 114
Sol, 66

stage, the, association with, 16
Suetonius Germanus and Licinia
   inscription, 97, **98**, 99, 106, 107,
   181 n.37
Suetonius Germanus, Gaius, 11, 60
Suetonius Germanus inscription, 97–8, **99**,
   106, 181 n.36
Sulla, 4, 5, 120, 122
Syracuse, 59

tabellae defixionum, 95, 108–9, 110
Tacitus, 139
Tellus, 57–8
Terra Mater, 57–8
Themis, 6, 117, 156, 165 n.35, 207 n.21,
   214 n.31
Thorius Balbus, Lucius, **117**
Tiber, the, 186 n.14, 186 n.15
Tiberinus, 74
Tiberius, 139, 143
Tiberius Gracchus, murder of, 4
triumphal arches, 104, 105
Triumvirs, the, 11
Trojans
   settlement in Italy, 39
   voyage to Italy, 7
Troy, Aeneas escapes from, 77, 86–7
Turnus, 74, 77, 80, 81–2

underworld, the, 44, 47–8

Varro, Marcus Terentius, 20, 21, 25,
   27, 62, 72, 78, 169 n.2,
   186 n.16
   Divine Antiquities, 3–4, 7–8, 13
   Fighting Shadows: On Nonsense, 2
   Menippean satires, 8, 14
Venus, 74–5, 86, 134, 135, 141
Vesta, 129–30, 135, 142, 143, 145
Victory/Victoria, 116, 117, 119, 120
Virgil, 14
   Aeneid, 37, 145
   allusion to Varro, 20, 21
   allusive references, 25
   Anna soror, first reference to, 7
   Carthaginian Anna, 19, 19–27
   Ovid's defence against, 158–60
   Ovid's engagement with, 19, 28–31,
     34–5, 35–6

Servius's commentary on, 2–3
technique of narrative gemination, 30, 34, 35
see also Aeneid
virgineo cruore, 167 n.88 (*virginius cruor*), 179 n.20
Vitruvius, 128
votive altars, 100
votive inscriptions *see* inscriptions
votive offerings, 60, 98
vows, 101, 106, 110

water
association with, 59, 71, 75–8, 82, 133, 159, 200 n.9
sentient, 73
women, deification of, 144
wordplay, 38–42, 47, 55, 64, 65, 67, 131